ROBERT GRAVES

Praise for *Robert Graves: From Great War Poet to Good-bye to All That (1895-1929)*

'Commanding ... To encounter [Graves] in these pages is to feel
something of the relentlessly explosive energy with which he lived
the first half of his life. Wilson lands him like a Zeppelin bomb.'

Observer

'Jean Moorcroft Wilson has built an unassailable reputation as our leading
authority on the poets of the Great War ... Combining intelligent and perceptive
criticism of his work, with revealing insights into the man, this study of the
devastating impact of the conflict on Graves makes for compelling reading.
I cannot recommend it too highly.'

Nigel Jones, author of *Rupert Brooke: Life, Death & Myth*

'Diligent and insightful ... Jean Moorcroft Wilson teases the truth
from Graves's exaggerations, mis-rememberings and downright
gibs ... She is by turns compassionate and caustic and is clear
sighted ... [Her] close reading of the war poems is illuminating.'

The Times

'Wilson unveils the poet behind the man struggling to make, not write,
poetry [and] clarifies our understanding of what Graves was about.'

Literary Review

'Consistently illuminating.'

Andrew Motion, *Spectator*

'A sensitive rendering of the poet's formative years ... finely nuanced.'

Kirkus Reviews

'A fine attempt to give Graves his due in the context of the Great War.'

Evening Standard

'This is an exemplary biography and a terrific entertainment ...
Wilson brings this difficult, unlovable but strangely impressive
man yelpingly to life.'

Sunday Times

'Readable and absorbing.'

TLS

'Deft and commanding ... On a par with her other outstanding
biographies.'

BBC History Magazine

'25 years after the last biography, a fresh approach ...
Measured and dispassionate ... This is biography at its best.'

Country Life

'A well-researched, readable biography.'

Library Journal

'Anyone reading this book will come away with a fresh, and deeper,
understanding of Graves and his writing – even if they have read previous
biographies [...] There is no doubt that in many ways Jean Moorcroft Wilson
has outdone her predecessors.'

PN Review

ROBERT GRAVES

From Great War Poet to *Good-bye to All That* (1895–1929)

Jean Moorcroft Wilson

BLOOMSBURY CONTINUUM
LONDON · NEW YORK · OXFORD · NEW DELHI · SYDNEY

BLOOMSBURY CONTINUUM
Bloomsbury Publishing Plc
Bloomsbury Publishing Ireland Limited
29 Earlsfort Terrace, Dublin 2, D02 AY28, Ireland

BLOOMSBURY, BLOOMSBURY CONTINUUM and the Diana logo are
trademarks of Bloomsbury Publishing Plc

First published in Great Britain 2018
Paperback 2026

A catalogue record for this book is available from the British Library

Library of Congress Cataloguing-in-Publication data has been applied for

ISBN: PB: 978-1-3994-2630-5; ePDF: 978-1-4729-2916-7;
ePub: 978-1-4729-2915-0

2 4 6 8 10 9 7 5 3 1

Typeset by Newgen KnowledgeWorks Pvt. Ltd., Chennai, India
Printed and bound in Great Britain by Clays Ltd, Elcograf S.p.A

To find out more about our authors and books
visit www.bloomsbury.com and sign up for our newsletters
For product safety related questions contact productsafety@bloomsbury.com

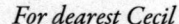
For dearest Cecil

Drawing of Robert Graves by Eric Kennington (Courtesy of Alasdair Kennington)

Graves Family Tree (condensed)

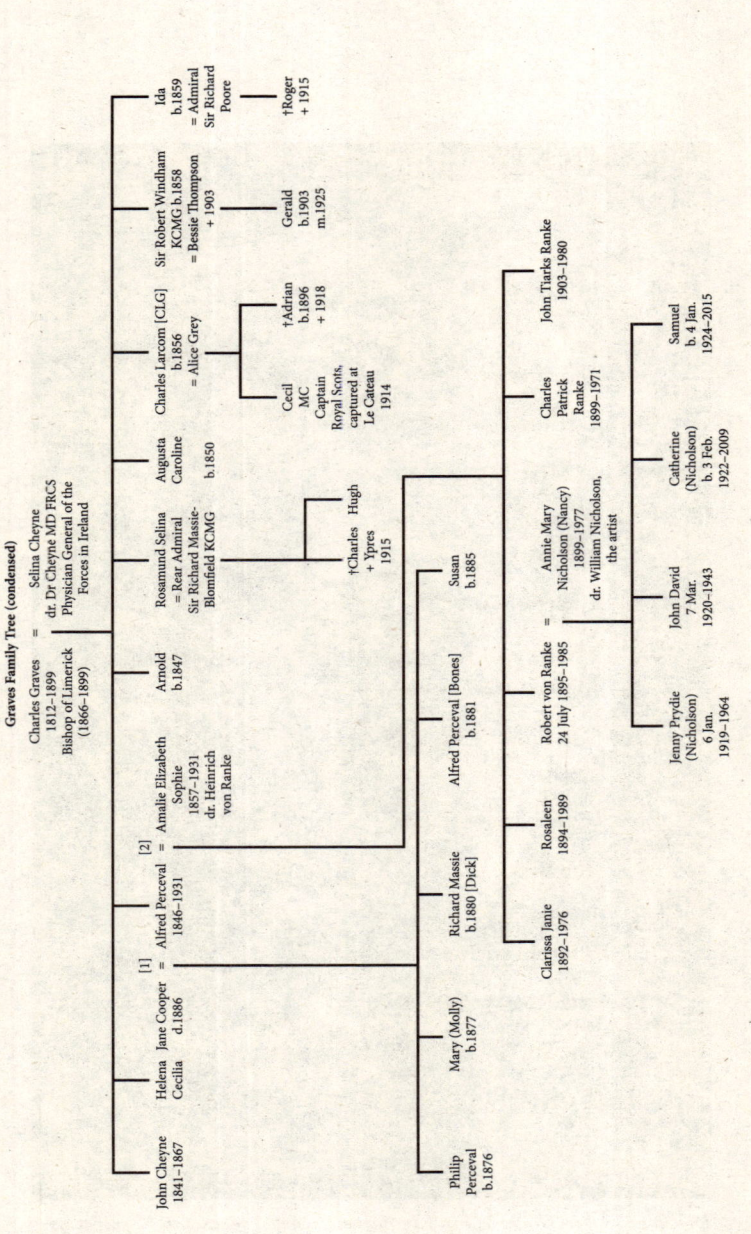

Charles Graves = Selina Cheyne
1812–1899   dr. Dr Cheyne MD FRCS
Bishop of Limerick   Physician General of the
(1866–1899)   Forces in Ireland

John Cheyne
1841–1867

Helena
Cecilia

Jane Cooper [1] = Alfred Perceval = [2] Amalie Elizabeth
d.1886   1846–1931   Sophie
                                 1857–1931
                                 dr. Heinrich
                                 von Ranke

Arnold
b.1847

Rosamund Selina
= Rear Admiral
Sir Richard Massie-
Blomfield KCMG

Augusta
Caroline
b.1850

Charles Larcom [CLG]
b.1856
= Alice Grey

Sir Robert Windham
KCMG b.1858
= Bessie Thompson
+ 1903

Ida
b.1859
= Admiral
Sir Richard
Poore

†Roger
+ 1915

Gerald
b.1903
m.1925

†Adrian
b.1896
+ 1918

Cecil
MC
Captain
Royal Scots,
captured at
Le Cateau
1914

†Charles   Hugh
+ Ypres
1915

Philip
Perceval
b.1876

Mary (Molly)
b.1877

Clarissa Janie
1892–1976

Richard Massie
b.1880 [Dick]

Rosaleen
1894–1989

Alfred Perceval [Bones]
b.1881

Robert von Ranke
24 July 1895–1985

Susan
b.1885

Annie Mary Nicholson (Nancy)
1899–1977
dr. William Nicholson,
the artist

Charles
Patrick
Ranke
1899–1971

John Tiarks Ranke
1903–1980

Jenny Prydie
(Nicholson)
6 Jan.
1919–1964

John David
7 Mar.
1920–1943

Catherine
(Nicholson)
b. 3 Feb.
1922–2009

Samuel
b. 4 Jan.
1924–2015

CONTENTS

LIST OF ILLUSTRATIONS

All unattributed images are reproduced courtesy of the
Robert Graves Estate, with the exception of illustrations
16, 21, 23, 24, 26, 33, 34, 35.

Section One

INTRODUCTION

When peace time comes and horror's over,
Despair and darkness like a dream,
When fields are ripe with corn and clover,
The cool white dairy full of cream,
Shall we work happily in the sun,
And think 'It's over now and done',
Or suddenly shall we seem
To watch a second bristling shadow
Of armed men move across the meadow?

Will it be over once for all…?[1]

On 11 November 1985 when the poet laureate, Ted Hughes, unveiled a memorial stone in Westminster Abbey to sixteen of the First World War poets, Robert Graves's name was among them, the only poet on the list still alive, though he would die less than four weeks later, aged ninety. It had been over seventy years since that war had produced its unprecedented outpouring of verse and critical opinion had had time to settle down, so the choice had been far from hasty or random. And if you ask any group of reasonably well-read adults who the Great War poets are, you will usually be given six to eight names, one of whom will almost certainly be Robert Graves. He is also represented in most anthologies of First World War verse.

If you ask the same group of people to list some war poems by Graves, however, they would probably struggle to name two or three, if that. Yet he wrote well over a hundred war poems, nearly twice as many as Wilfred Owen, for example, who is far better represented in the anthologies. As late as 1980 Graves's sister Rosaleen noted that in a BBC film about Graves, Owen and Sassoon she 'didn't hear one line of Robert's poetry'.[2]

The explanation for this absence lies partly in Graves's own changing attitude towards his war poetry. Initially proud to be seen as a war poet, his first three publications, *Over the Brazier* (1916), *Goliath and David* (1917) and *Fairies and Fusiliers* (1917), focused almost solely on the conflict. A fourth collection *The Patchwork Flag,* did so too, but never appeared in Graves's lifetime,[3] since he allowed himself to be dissuaded from publication by Siegfried Sassoon and Robbie Ross. Although Graves was pleased by his inclusion in Marsh's *Georgian Poetry 1916–1917*, devoted largely to the war poets, by the time *The Patchwork Flag* failed to appear in 1919, he himself was having doubts about his war poetry. He would turn, in his next publication, *Country Sentiment* (1920), to other matters, though some poems from *The Patchwork Flag* would find their way into it. *The Pier-Glass* (1921), *Whipperginny* (1923), *Mock Beggar Hall* (1924) and *Welchman's Hose* (1925) would also contain some war poems. But by the time of *Poems (1914–1927)* Graves had 'suppressed' (his word) virtually all the verse written during and just after the war and only seventeen of his many poems of that period survived to be included in his 'War: 1915–19' section. When, in 1938, Graves published his first *Collected Poems*, he 'found [he] could not conscientiously reprint any of [his] war poems', which seemed to him 'too obviously written in the war-poetry boom'.[4] It was his first publisher, Harold Monro, he claimed, who had 'fastened the war-poet label on me in 1916'.[5] *Collected Poems* (1938), therefore, contained only a single poem related to the subject, 'Recalling War', hitherto unpublished. And the same is true of *Poems (1914–1947)*, which featured 'Last Day of Leave'.

Both 'Recalling War' and 'Last Day of Leave' suggest another reason for Graves's relatively poor showing in war poetry anthologies: their length. This is true of a significant number of his most successful war poems, notably 'Goliath and David' and three of his four verse-letters to Sassoon. It may also explain why a poem like 'Night March' was not published in Graves's lifetime; its twenty-three quatrains, reflecting the number of miles covered on the march, would take up a lot of space in the usually slim poetry collections of the day and in subsequent anthologies.

It seems ironic that Sassoon, whose poems make ideal anthology pieces, was first awoken to the possibilities of the short, sharp, realistic poem after reading Graves's 'A Dead Boche'. Yet this punchy, gruesome description of a dead German soldier, who:

> ... scowled and stunk
>> With clothes and face a sodden green,
> Big-bellied, spectacled, crop-haired,
> Dribbling black blood from nose and beard[6]

is by no means characteristic of Graves's war poetry, which depends mainly on a more indirect approach through myth, legend and ancient history. Although no less powerful in its impact than a satire like Sassoon's 'The General', this makes some of his poems less immediately accessible. 'Dead Cow Farm', for instance, one of Graves's most outspoken comments on the war, puzzles many readers initially, even though Graves spells out in its opening lines its link to the Old Norse creation myth in which the cow Audhumla licks salty stones, out of which Man emerges. It also helps to know that Dead Cow Farm was a strategic point on the Western Front:

> An ancient saga tells us how
> In the beginning the First Cow
> (For nothing living yet had birth
> But elemental Cow on Earth)
> Began to lick cold stones and mud:
> Under her warm tongue flesh and blood
> Blossomed, a miracle to believe;
> And so was Adam born, and Eve.
> Here now is chaos once again,
> Primeval mud, cold stones and rain.
> Here flesh decays and blood drips red
> And the Cow's dead, the old Cow's dead.[7]

This is a poem about a general loss of faith on the Western Front, expressed forcefully in that last line: 'And the Cow's dead, the old Cow's dead.' The use of a phrase of extreme disrespect in everyday life in reference here to God adds to the shock.

Another of Graves's initially puzzling techniques is to approach his subject from a child's point of view. In looking for a way to convey his experiences on the Western Front, his imagination reverts to his childhood, when his life had been lived with a similar intensity and full of fear and exhilaration. The shock for the reader when she realizes that a poem such as 'The First Funeral', ostensibly about a child's discovery of a dead dog (autobiographical in this case), is also about decaying corpses on the Western Front, is intended and highly effective:

The whole field was so smelly;
    We smelt the poor dog first:
His horrid swollen belly
    Looked just like going burst.[8]

Similarly, dreams about a 'gigantic, formless' figure that haunted his sleep as a young boy is linked in 'A Child's Nightmare' with his terror as he lay badly wounded on the Somme:

He was there with straddling legs,
Staring eyes as big as eggs,
Purring as he lapped my blood,
His black bulk darkening the day...[9]

Part of the power of Graves's poetry springs from what D. N. G. Carter has called the 'irrational', by which he means 'simply those forms and types of experience before which reason halts perplexed, such as hauntings, nightmares, psychoses, grief, inspiration, time, death, the void itself'.[10]

For, as another First World War poet, Edmund Blunden, pointed out, unlike many of his contemporaries, notably Sassoon, Graves was not concerned with making 'a Protest'. He wanted to convey the 'reality' of war and for him this reality lay more in dreams, myths and nightmares than in realistic details of the carnage. This failure to conform to the archetype of what the public came increasingly to expect from war poetry – beside making it difficult to 'place' him among the war poets – may also help to explain his relative obscurity as a war poet. It was in his prose account, *Good-bye to All That*, that a 'protest' of sorts could be found, overshadowing his more subtle picture of war in his verse. In addition, as Patrick Quinn has observed, after the publication of *The White Goddess* in 1948, the public 'saw in Graves only a mythic interpreter of the White Goddess's demands' and 'the war poetry [became] largely ... forgotten'.[11]

Graves's status as a war *poet* seems, therefore, to have depended largely on his *prose* memoir. And despite William Graves's efforts to restore his father's work to the canon of First World War poetry with his edition of *Poems About War* (1988), Dunstan Ward and Beryl Graves's *Complete Poems* (2000), Sebastian Barfield's BBC documentary *War of Words: Soldier-Poets of the Somme* (2014) and Charles Mundye's *War Poems* (2016), that remains largely the position today. Although leading Graves scholars, including Fran Brearton, Paul O'Prey and Charles Mundye, have done their best to redress this, the originally suppressed poems are still mainly unknown to the general public and absent from the popular imagination.

But as Michael Longley, an eminent poet in his own right and shrewd critic of the genre, claims: 'the story of Great War Poetry is incomplete without the war poems of Robert Graves'.[12] Graves was ideally equipped to tell that story. Already a poet when war broke out, he enlisted only a week later, aged just nineteen, fought in two of its bloodiest battles, Loos in 1915 and the Somme in 1916 (where he was left for dead), and remained in the Army until two months after the end of the war. At the most basic level he can be seen as a linchpin in the development of First World War poetry, passing on his admiration for Charles Hamilton Sorley, together with the influence of his own early, realistic poetry to Sassoon, who in turn influenced Wilfred Owen.

More importantly, Graves's poetry itself is among the best to come out of that war. It was Blunden again who begged Graves, some fifty years after the event, not to 'finally condemn your war poems ... they are most original'.[13] They are also unsurpassed in their variety, ranging from the brutally realistic and harrowing to the allegorical, and drawing on a wide range of backgrounds. Some of his most successful poems adopt the epistolary form, unusual in war poetry; there are at least four to Sassoon, for example. In addition, early though these poems are, Graves shows the technical brilliance that marks most of his work. Even if they are, as Fran Brearton argues, 'occasionally uneven (compared with his flawless lyrics of the middle years)', she is also right to claim that 'their power and poignancy', 'their inventive rhythmical syntax', is 'undiminished by the passage of time'.[14] And though never a full-blown Modernist like David Jones or Isaac Rosenberg, the technical innovation Graves introduced into his war poetry, including that written after the event, makes him a relatively rare phenomenon among First World War poets.

Of equal importance, since that war was a defining experience in his life, the poetry which emerged from it is crucial to a full understanding both of that life and the work which followed. As Brearton reminds us, 'his poetic aesthetic was forged in the battlefields where he "died" and was resurrected in 1916', and his experience there 'determined the kind of poet and writer he was to be, even the extraordinary life he lived', quoting as evidence one of Graves's verse-letters to Sassoon, his fellow officer in the Royal Welch Fusiliers:

... By wire and wood and stake we're bound,
By Fricourt and by Festubert,
By whipping rain, by the sun's glare,
By all the misery and loud sound,
By a Spring day,
By Picard clay...[15]

Graves related his 'poetic style' to his experience of drafting terse messages on the Western Front, 'a style of still further elimination of what is not pertinent'.[16] In addition, his neurasthenia (or 'shell-shock' as he sometimes referred to it) had a palpable effect on his poetry in the early 1920s, leading him to experiment in both psychological and philosophical approaches. He himself accepted that the war permanently changed his outlook on life,[17] and could never understand the contention that a poet's life is irrelevant to his work. War poems such as '1915' and 'The Fusilier' can even illuminate a pre-war experience such as his passionate feelings for a younger boy at Charterhouse, a phase regarded by him as quasi-homosexual. He suspected that verse written during the war 'was very frequently due to an insupportable conflict between suppressed instincts of love and fear; the officer's actual love which he could never openly show for the boys he commanded, and the fear, also hidden under a forced gaiety, of the horrible death that threatened them all'.[18] Peter Parker goes so far as to argue that Graves 'associated the

Great War with homosexuality, producing a homosexual melodrama [*But It Still Goes On* (1930)] when asked for a play about the War, and excising his War poetry from later sections of his work'.[19] Whilst acknowledging the possible association, however, Graves denied its relevance in his case: when asked in the *Paris Review* in 1969 why he did *not* write 'war poems – of his trench experience in World War I', like Sassoon and Owen, he replied:

> I did. But I destroyed them. They were journalistic. Sassoon and Wilfred Owen were homosexuals; though Sassoon tried to think he wasn't. To them seeing *men* killed was as horrible as if you or I had to see fields of corpses of women.[20]

Graves may have been able to 'destroy' (as he describes it) most of his war poetry during his lifetime, but he was unable to suppress completely the influence that war had on both his life and his subsequent writing. Memories of it would come back to torment him in old age. And though he had resolved to become a poet at the age of fifteen, it was the war that broke out less than a month after his nineteenth birthday which turned him into a serious one, giving him a subject that he could handle with an authenticity and intensity lacking in his juvenile work. A poem like 'Goliath and David', for instance, inspired by the death of a close friend, David Thomas, is one of the first of his successful poems.

The influence of the war on Graves's life is particularly clear in the decade that followed it. His early marriage during the war and fathering of four children in quick succession, though undertaken partly to 'prove' his heterosexuality, also stemmed from an increased need for stability and a sense of new life, after the chaos and destruction he had witnessed. The war had affected his nerves badly and he was diagnosed officially with neurasthenia. But marriage to eighteen-year-old Nancy Nicholson in 1918 was not the cure for his 'shell-shock' that he had hoped for and he turned instead in 1926 to a far more authoritarian figure, the American poet Laura Riding. Her enormous self-belief, according to her first biographer, Deborah Baker, was 'as gripping and addictive as the sustaining shock of the war itself, and thus, in the richest resources of his imagination, Riding became Graves's war. As the enemy, she sharpened his sense and kept him alert.'[21] Although Riding could not herself cure Graves fully, she did indirectly bring about a release of sorts. For it was her long and expensive stay in hospital after her suicidal leap from a fourth-storey window which led Graves to write *Good-bye to All That* in order to pay the bill. His reliving of his wartime experience in *Good-bye*, however, also had a cathartic effect, leading him to leave England for Spain a few months later.

Looking back over the first half of Graves's life, it is clear that his sheltered upbringing in middle-class comfort by loving parents and a later start than usual at boarding school made him rather naïve for his age. It was not an ideal preparation for the rigours of army life in the First World War. At the same time the sense of confidence, even arrogance, with which his privileges endowed him, together with an innate humour and appreciation of the absurd, helped him survive in appalling conditions. (Graves maintained that he had 'no sense of humour' in a 1965 interview with Malcolm Muggeridge but accepted Muggeridge's reply: 'You haven't got a sense of humour, I quite agree ... but you've got quite a lot of humour ... a sense of the ridiculous, a sense of the inappropriateness of things, the absurdity of life.')[22]

Graves's mixed heritage of an Irish father and a German mother may account for the fact that his character seems more contradictory than most, his absolute certainty in areas like literature contrasting strongly with his lack of confidence in others, such as his relations with women. He himself admitted that he had an 'inferiority complex' caused by his mother's 'shortcomings'.[23] He was called 'super-generous' by his sister Rosaleen[24] and went to endless trouble to encourage writers like Frank Richards, whose book *Old Soldiers Never Die* he helped make publishable. Yet he could be ruthless towards others, such as Ezra Pound, when he chose. He had been something of a bully at school on occasion, as well as a prude, a victim, Martin Seymour-Smith argued, of the puritanical overkill of his upbringing.[25] Although the bullying and prudery did not survive more than four years of army life, he would retain a genuine craving for purity and remain an idealist of sorts all his life.

He also remained aggressive, even 'pugnacious' as he saw it, particularly on the football pitch.[26] Some people viewed this side of him as a form of daring, yet others as recklessness. His son Tomás noted his 'tremendous temper'.[27] Yet he could be gentle and caring with children, while at the same time capable of abandoning his own first four without apparent hesitation when he left England in 1929. His rigorously intellectual approach to life was balanced by a pronounced superstitiousness and credulity in certain areas, especially where Laura Riding was concerned. He remained highly suggestible into the 1920s, falling first under the influence of the psychiatrist Dr W. H. R. Rivers, then of the Indian philosopher Basanta Mallik, before succumbing to Riding in 1926. His arrogance, which he believed a 'necessity' for the poet,[28] was in strong contrast to his humility in the presence of people he admired greatly, such as George Mallory and T. E. Lawrence. Monumentally tactless at times and perverse – he described himself as 'Flying Crooked' in one of his poems[29] – he was also stubborn and determined in pursuit of his art. (Lawrence claimed that he was built 'without a reverse gear'.)[30] Of a 'naturally sanguine temperament',[31] he enjoyed life and had no difficulty making friends, who talked of 'his kindness, his loyalty, and his love of gossip'.[32] At the same time, he was ready to abandon them all in the 1920s in the service of the woman who had become his muse. He considered himself to be an outsider to society, as he believed all true poets were.

The most revealing comment on Graves's character comes also from himself, in response to the accusation of having quoted a private letter without the owner's permission:

> I plead in extenuation that I have very little of what is called 'ordinary imagination'; it often does not occur to me that people can possibly have strong feelings about things which appear to me perfectly trivial. For instance, I cannot imagine myself getting angry at any moral failure in the past of any member of my family in a very personal way...
>
> It is wrong to suppose that I enjoy trouble, and getting my publishers into trouble; as I say, it is an imaginative defect in me that leads me into these uncomfortable situations.[33]

This is a remarkable admission from one of the greatest imaginations of the twentieth century, suggesting that what Sassoon among others regarded as Graves's tactlessness, insensitivity and apparent callousness stemmed from a limited imagination in certain areas.

As far as his work was concerned, however, Graves's imagination seems to have known no bounds. Over a period of nearly sixty years, he produced 55 collections of poetry (56 if we include the unpublished *The Patchwork*

Flag), a successful autobiography written less than halfway through his life, a biography of his great friend T. E. Lawrence, at least 40 works of non-fiction including the controversial best-seller *The White Goddess*, 15 novels (not counting the one he drafted for Laura Riding), ten translations from various languages, several screenplays and at least one play featuring a barely disguised Sassoon. As Frances Wilson points out in her highly entertaining *Literary Seductions*, the range of subjects covered in his non-fiction 'stretched with easy confidence from Freudian dream theory to ancient Welsh ballads'.[34]

It is clearly impossible to do full justice to all these works in one volume, but, by focusing on the first half of his life, it has been possible to give the necessary emphasis to the profound effect the First World War had on Graves's life and his work. Some of his best poetry was written between 1916 and 1929, as were two of his most successful prose books, *Lawrence and the Arabs* (1927) and *Good-bye to All That* (1929). In addition the seeds of four of his equally successful books, *I, Claudius*, *Claudius the God*, *The White Goddess* and his retelling of the *Greek Myths*, would be sown in this early period.

Not surprisingly, a life as eventful and full of achievements as Graves's has been told a number of times, most notably by Martin Seymour-Smith, Miranda Seymour and Richard Perceval Graves to mark the centenary of his birth in 1995. They are all excellent in their own way and have been extremely helpful to me. But nearly a quarter of a century has elapsed since their publication and new material has emerged. Graves's working-library, together with countless letters between him and his friends, was donated to St John's College, Oxford, and has proved an invaluable resource, as has William Graves's online collection of his father's letters from the First World War.

As a result of the publication of the three biographies, for instance, Graves's letters to a fellow soldier and patient at Somerville College Hospital, Oxford, in 1917 were published by the soldier's daughter; written during and after the war, they are particularly frank, revealing Graves's feelings about his sexuality at a turbulent period of his life. Another eight letters to his sister Rosaleen, covering a similar period and hitherto unseen, add to our knowledge of him at that time. I was also able to study a new cache of letters from George Mallory to Lytton Strachey revealing Mallory's willingness to explore not just mountains but his own sexuality, many of them covering the period of his friendship with Graves at Charterhouse. Unpublished letters from Dr W. H. R. Rivers to Graves in the early 1920s help to fill out the picture. And the publication of two volumes of Laura Riding's autobiographical writings, *Who I Am*, in 2011, has added details to his life in the second half of the 1920s, together with another full-length biography of her, containing more new material. A recent biography of the filmmaker and sculptor Len Lye quotes from hitherto unseen letters to and about Graves. Other fascinating material has surfaced, such as the details of a sexual scandal surrounding the headmaster of Hillbrow, Rupert Brooke's prep school in Rugby subsequently attended by Graves.

The most dramatic new material in this biography has been my discovery of a second annotated published copy of *Good-bye to All That*, Sassoon's personal copy, which he worked on alone after helping Blunden and Dr Dunn to pour scorn on Graves's efforts in the copy now at the Berg. Buried first in Sassoon's private library until long after his death in 1967, then in the hands of private collectors, his personal copy emerged only recently at the Beinecke Library at Yale University, together with the heavily revised proofs of *Good-bye to All That*. It reveals the full extent of Sassoon's feelings about Graves after their break-up, as well as Sassoon's humour, some of it extremely sardonic.

New material of this calibre has made it well worthwhile to revisit the first half of Graves's life and helped greatly in this attempt to shift the emphasis back to what was the defining experience of his life, the First World War.

1

'A Mixed Litter'[1]

> ... a poet is born not made ... a poet is not a poet unless there is
> some peculiar event in his family history to account for him. The
> poet, like poetry itself, is the fusion of incongruous forces.[2]

Robert Graves celebrated the eve of his twenty-first birthday, which fell on 24 July 1916, with an excruciating train journey from the Somme battlefield to No. 8 Hospital, Rouen. He recalled it later 'only as a nightmare'.[3]

The nightmare had started four days earlier in Bazentin churchyard as his battalion, 2nd Royal Welch Fusiliers, waited in reserve for a planned attack on High Wood. In retreating from a German artillery barrage put down along the ridge where he and his company were positioned, Graves had been hit by shrapnel from an eight-inch shell, which penetrated his left thigh and passed through his right lung and shoulder. In a poem reconstructing the event a year later, he described lying, morphia-drowsed, in a crater by High Wood when an old 'hideous nightmare thing' from childhood had returned to him, a 'gigantic, formless' vampire figure which 'lapped [his] blood' and repeated endlessly in a 'cruel and flat' voice the words 'Cat! ... Cat! ... Cat!'[4] It was this same grotesque creature which, after his further nightmarish experience of being left for dead in a Field Dressing Station overnight, leapt on him again as the hospital train clanked its way from Heilly to Rouen a few days later.

The poem describing this near-death experience, 'A Child's Nightmare', appears to be based wholly on fact. Yet there is little in either Graves's or his family's accounts of his early years to suggest that he had been unhappy or traumatized as a child. His earliest biographer, Martin Seymour-Smith, held Graves's strict-minded, devout mother responsible for his childhood nightmares by 'inculcating in her imaginative son terrible fears ... of eternal damnation, of burning fiery furnaces and of fearful prophecies'.[5] Deeply religious though Amy Graves was, however, and fearful though her son, like most children, was of hell, it is impossible to reconcile this with Robert's own statement that he was 'lucky' to be her son and his 'astonishment' at the idea 'that any mother could possibly behave unkindly to her own child'.[6] His own explanation for the nightmares is more convincing – that his highly active imagination as a child had created for him 'a private nightmare life' consisting of such diverse elements as Max Beerbohm's 'fantastic' caricatures of 'politicians and big-wigs' in *John Bull*, Jack the Ripper, Old Kruger, Og King of Bashan and the Great Agrippa of *Struwwelpeter*.[7] While his mother, who was German, was probably responsible for introducing Robert to the last item on this list – Heinrich Hoffmann's book of German children's stories – Robert's overactive imagination seems to have supplied the rest without her help.

In any case, while accepting that mothers might influence their children, Robert did not believe that they should be held responsible for their characters: as the eighth of a family of ten, he noted how 'wholly dissimilar all the Graves children were'.[8] The first five of these offspring were from the first marriage of Robert's father, Alfred Perceval Graves, to Jane Cooper, who died in 1886, five years before Alfred met and married Robert's mother, Amalie ('Amy') Elizabeth Sophie von Ranke. Robert was the third child of this second marriage.

It was Amy's most pronounced characteristic, her strong sense of moral duty, that had led her to accept marriage to a widower with five young children. It was also her powerful sense of duty that had propelled her to live in England in the first place. Her mother, Luise Tiarks, daughter of the Greenwich astronomer Johann Ludwig Tiarks, a German-speaking Schleswig Dane, had been orphaned at an early age.[9] Johann's childless brother had adopted her and her sister, and Luise grew up regarding his wife, Sarah, as her mother. It was in London that Luise had met and married Robert's grandfather, a young doctor based at the German Hospital, Heinrich Israel Ranke (the 'von' would come later).

Unlike Luise, whom Robert remembered as 'tiny, saintly, frightened', Heinrich was a robust atheist of outspoken opinions. Robert claimed to have inherited his 'clumsy largeness, [his] endurance, energy, seriousness and [his] thick hair' from Heinrich, his maternal grandfather who had died in 1909 when Robert was fourteen.[10] As a medical student at Berlin and other German universities, Heinrich had taken part in the political disturbances of 1848 that had swept through Europe. Whether or not this was his reason for leaving for England, by 1853 he was working at the German Hospital in London, mainly among the poor of the East End. Two years later he travelled out to the Crimea as a civilian physician to the British government to help with the terrible war casualties there. Robert remembered Heinrich telling him as a child: 'It is not always the big bodies that are the strongest. When I was at Sevastopol in the trenches I saw the great British Guards crack up and die by the score, while the little sappers took no harm.'[11] It was on his return to London in 1855 that Heinrich had met and married Luise Tiarks.

After their first child, Amy, was born there in 1857, Heinrich took his family back to Germany, settling in Bavaria, his birthplace. He eventually became Professor of Medicine at the University of Munich. As a physiologist and paediatrician he was particularly concerned with the introduction of pure water and milk to Munich, to prevent further outbreaks of cholera and other diseases, as well as the welfare of children, campaigning energetically for both causes. In recognition of his services and like his uncle, the distinguished historian Leopold von Ranke, to whom Robert believed he owed his 'historical method',[12] Heinrich was ennobled to 'von Ranke'. With such a father and a deeply religious mother, it is not difficult to see where Amy's main characteristics originated.

Amy had been taken back to London twice as a child and had grown to love the great-aunt she called 'Granny', so that when in 1876, aged 18, she received an invitation to go and live with 'dear Granny' in her large house in Gloucester Terrace, Bayswater, she was 'glad to accept'.[13] Although her great-aunt tended to the tyrannical, working Amy hard as her housekeeper and secretary as well as companion, she recognized her musical talent and paid for Amy to have piano lessons and training for her promising contralto voice. Amy continued to educate herself with books from Smith's lending library, which included works on physiology and first aid as well as literature. She was soon reading as well as speaking English fluently, tackling the whole of Spenser's *Faerie Queene* and Milton's *Paradise Lost* on her own. And in accordance with the strict Protestant principles inculcated in her by her mother, she also taught Sunday school. Educated by an English nanny, she was already fluent in English but now lost all traces of a German accent.

Amy attracted several offers of marriage during her fifteen years with her great-aunt but none was considered suitable. Mrs Tiarks herself was not anxious to lose her great-niece to a husband. Convinced that she was on the verge of bankruptcy, she found the conscientious Amy an ideal housekeeper in the circumstances. It was only shortly before Mrs Tiarks died in 1891 that she discovered herself to be, in fact, a wealthy woman. She wanted to leave the bulk of her fortune to Amy, but at Amy's insistence she divided it up equally among Amy and her siblings. Amy was also left the use of the large house and the money to run it for a year. She was bequeathed a further £10,000 in bearer bonds, which she divided up conscientiously among the ten unmarried Tiarks cousins who had been left out of Mrs Tiarks's will despite Amy's best efforts.

Freed from her obligations to her great-aunt, Amy was determined to go to India as a medical missionary until her family showed their disapproval. Consequently, when her sister Selma (known as 'Lily') started matchmaking, Amy was more open to the idea of marriage. Lily's husband, Frieduhelm, was the son of Leopold von Ranke, which made him her father's cousin. But Frieduhelm's mother had been Clarissa Graves and it was Clarissa's cousin, the widowed Alfred Perceval Graves, who seemed to the family the most suitable candidate for Amy's hand. After some initial resistance on her part, some clever manoeuvring by her family and persistence from Alfred, Amy accepted him when he proposed in November 1891, less than a month after their first meeting. The wedding, in Munich, followed equally quickly on 30 December.

Amy made it clear in her autobiography that she had not married for love. She had accepted Alfred's proposal, she wrote, because his five motherless children would provide her with the 'vocation' she longed for, as well as the marriage her family wanted for her and the knowledge of 'pleasing [her] father'. But she 'became so fond of' Alfred and 'believed in his affection so much' that 'at the last', she confessed, she would have married him even without any children at all.[14]

Robert grew up secure in the knowledge of this happy and stable marriage. He had heard the story of the courtship many times, as well as details of Amy's years with Mrs Tiarks, and in his early seventies wrote what he called 'her story', 'Miss Briton's Lady-Companion'.[15] Although a number of facts in it are wrong – Amy was eighteen, not twenty, when she came to live in London, for instance – this is an invaluable source, since it gives a first-hand account of his mother as he knew and reacted to her. Despite including the story in *The Crane Bag* and in his *Collected Short Stories*, 'Miss Briton's Lady-Companion' is *not* fictional: 'pure fiction', Graves wrote in the introduction to his *Collected Short Stories*, was 'beyond my imaginative range', adding that most of his 'stories' were true to life, with only 'occasional names and references altered'.

What emerges clearly from 'Miss Briton's Lady-Companion' is how much he loved and admired his mother, despite their misunderstandings at times. Amy's devotion to him was never in doubt and he seems to have regarded himself as her favourite. He certainly saw her as 'a very loving woman' who 'loved [him] very dearly', as he told Malcolm Muggeridge in 1965, adding 'that has been a great help to me all my life'.[16] Although her third child, Robert was her first son and, as her eldest daughter Clarissa wrote to him much later, with perhaps a little understandable resentment, 'She is so primitive that sons mean far more to her than daughters.'[17] According to Robert, Amy made no secret of her preferences and appeared to believe that 'girl babies [were] quite useful to practise on' but that 'boys were all that really counted in God's eyes'.[18] As the eldest child of a family of six daughters and three surviving sons, she had seen how eagerly awaited the first son had been and accepted unquestioningly the superior rights accorded him. Her own first son, Robert, was made much of in a similar way, which may help to explain his strong sense of entitlement as he grew up. With two loving older sisters – Rosaleen had been born two years after Clarissa, in 1894, a year before Robert's birth on 24 July 1895 – and two younger brothers to lord it over, Charles, born in 1899, and John, in 1903 – he was literally the centre of the family.

Amy may have favoured Robert, but she adored all five of her children. She was a strict as well as loving mother; her younger sisters and brothers had christened her 'the scrubbing-brush' for her rigorous approach to keeping them clean and under control, as her father had instructed her. Once married, she supported her husband's insistence on family prayers every morning and two visits to church on Sundays, the day on which the children were also forbidden to play cards or other games of chance. Amy's strict moral standards left Robert with a 'superstitious conscience' and 'sexual embarrassment', he claimed, which it took him some time to lose in adulthood. Amy's eldest child certainly believed her to be the 'true head' of the Graves family, although Robert did not.[19] She was perhaps the earliest of Robert's models for the demanding and powerful figure of the White Goddess.

It is tempting to exaggerate Amy's strictness and controlling ways. However, she was far from inflexible. Robert remembered persuading her to let them play charades on a Sunday, for example, provided that the scenes were all Biblical. And as they grew older she allowed them a great deal of freedom among the Welsh mountains of their holiday home. As teenagers, none of them drank, or smoked, or had friends of the opposite sex, yet 'somehow', Robert recalled, 'we never felt deprived'.[20] In later life he gave his mother 'full marks for nobility of heart'.[21] Although she would often disapprove deeply of his actions, and while he could see that his protected upbringing had given him 'no hint of the world's dirtiness and intrigue and lustfulness',[22] he claimed 'never' to have 'resented her attitude in the least'.[23]

In fact, as Robert grew older, he could see how much he owed to his mother. He believed that she was responsible for one of his most distinctive characteristics, his sometimes brutal honesty, by teaching him 'to speak the truth and shame the devil'.[24] And his enormous output as a writer almost certainly owed something to his mother's favourite Biblical exhortation: 'My son, whatever thy hand findeth to do, do it with all thy might.'[25]

Amy's own determination was legendary in the family, from seizing the reins in a runaway carriage in Bavaria, to carrying out a flaming kerosene lamp that threatened to set fire to their house in England; perhaps her most impressive achievement was helping her second son, Charles, to walk again despite the doctors' fears after he had contracted polio as a child. Her resourcefulness and practical business sense, too, became family legend;

the youngest son, John, tells in his own autobiography of an occasion when Amy arrived home from Wales penniless, having managed to buy a large table she thought a bargain on the way. Her years of saving money for Mrs Tiarks had given her valuable experience in frugality. At the same time, the stringent economy they had both mistakenly thought necessary had left Amy unwilling to throw anything away, including cupboards full of out-of-date medicines, all carefully labelled by her. Robert recalled one occasion when visitors had left half a sandwich behind, which his mother conscientiously forwarded to them, an incident he found simultaneously absurd and endearing.

It would be wrong to think of Amy as mean, however: her 'generosity', together with her 'seriousness and strength', were the three things Robert admired most in his mother. His own generosity may have been inspired partly by her example. She took her children's upbringing and education very seriously and led by example. And though he would afterwards claim that neither she nor their father spent much time with them as children, it is clear from his father's and also her autobiography that she was involved with his education from his earliest years.

Amy also conveyed her love of music to her children. Her youngest, John, remembered her singing to them in her rich contralto voice and Rosaleen, the next to eldest, would train as a professional musician before turning to medicine: she had fond memories of Amy introducing them to folk songs in French, German and Italian, as well as English, Irish, Welsh and Scots.[26] Robert, who remembered his mother's powerful voice, had a lifelong love of folk song.

His picture of his mother is almost wholly positive. Her few possible shortcomings are described affectionately, with 'no criticism' intended.[27] But even he, famously indifferent to clothes, noted that Amy 'did not know how to dress, having been warned as a girl never to indulge female vanity'.[28] She and her whole family were 'entirely without style', according to Graves.[29] And in contrast to her eldest son, Amy also 'lacked any sense of humour except the simplest and most innocuous kind'.[30] (Though Amy's daughter Rosaleen remembered that when she gave the money [sent out to France by her mother to buy a hat] to the troops [to buy cigarettes], her mother next sent her a pair of pink knickers: 'At least you can't give these to the troops.'[31]) Again Graves saw this as no criticism of her, convinced that it stemmed simply from one of her virtues, her scrupulous honesty: 'To her white was white, black was black and every word except parables and metaphors must be taken literally. She did not understand irony, sarcasm or jokes about other people's misfortunes.'[32] Amy's failure in this respect may help to explain Robert's own interest in humour, which he attempted to analyse in *Mrs Fisher, or the Future of Humour* (1927).

The 'deep affection' Robert felt for his mother emerges in every line of 'Miss Briton's Lady-Companion', his one serious attempt to describe her.[33] He owed much to her, he believed, not only in physique – he inherited her height and her mouth – but also more generally:

> She taught me to despise fame and riches, not to be deceived by appearances, to tell the truth on all possible occasions – I regret having taken her too literally at times – and to keep my head in time of danger. I have inherited her conscience, her disinterest in sartorial fashions, her joy in making marmalades and jams, and her frugality (I hate throwing away crusts) though it often conflicts with a spendthrift extravagance learned from my father.[34]

Robert ended his account by claiming that he learnt his 'spendthrift extravagance' from his father, but it is far less easy to establish what exactly he did inherit from Alfred Perceval Graves or how he felt about him, since his feelings towards his father changed far more than towards his mother and were more complex. His attitude to his father's family was similarly mixed. On the one hand he presented the Graveses as 'thin-nosed and inclined to petulance',[35] noting a 'coldness' about them entirely absent in his warm-hearted, outgoing German relatives, whom he freely admitted preferring in his autobiography. Yet he also seemed proud of a family which boasted a pedigree, he claimed, 'that date[d] back to [William] the Conqueror'.[36]

One thing not in doubt was the usefulness of connections for Alfred Perceval Graves (known to family and friends as 'APG') and, by extension, his son Robert in such a family. Born in Dublin on 22 July 1846, Alfred was the third of the eight children, and second son, of the Reverend Charles Graves, one in a long line of Protestant clerics and a gifted mathematician and authority on the Ogham script. Alfred's social advantages included a father who, from being Dean of the Chapel Royal in Dublin, would become Bishop of Limerick from 1866 until his death in 1899, and a mother, Selina (née Cheyne), who was the daughter of the Physician-General of the forces in Ireland and from a line that claimed to stretch back to the mediaeval Scottish kings. Robert thought it a better pedigree even than the Graves's and was proud of his Scottish blood. (When he took Homer's *Odyssey* to the trenches in 1915, for instance, he said it was his 'Scots blood coming out', because 'only a Scotsman would take his classics out to the front'.)[37] Alfred's paternal grandfather, John Crosbie Graves, was first cousin to one of Ireland's most celebrated surgeons, Robert James Graves (famous for his first description of the eponymous Graves' Disease), while his paternal grandmother, Helena, was from the illustrious Perceval family and granddaughter of the Earl of Egmont. Alfred's sister, Rosamund Selina, was married to Rear-Admiral Sir Richard Massie Blomfield, and another sister, Ida, to Admiral Sir Richard Poore.

There were also some useful literary connections within the family. Before matriculating at Trinity College Dublin, for instance, Alfred had been sent to Windermere College, Westmorland, near his uncle, Robert Perceval Graves, who was the curate of Undermillbeck and a good friend of William Wordsworth and his sister Dorothy, whose encomium he wrote. Although Wordsworth himself was dead by the time Alfred arrived, Robert Perceval, himself a writer, became a mentor to the young man, who had his first poem published in 1863 in the Dublin University magazine.

Before completing his Master of Arts degree at Trinity College Dublin, Alfred returned to England in 1869 to work as a clerk in the British Home Office. Five years later, like another much better-known poet, Matthew Arnold, he became one of Her Majesty's Inspectors of Schools. He and Arnold would overlap by twelve years, knowing each other but never becoming close friends. Alfred, like Arnold, may have found his job 'drudgery' at times,[38] but he wanted to marry and was unable to support a wife and family on poetry alone. And, also like Arnold, he believed passionately in the value of education; he would introduce his own reforms into the system, still in its infancy just four years after the passage of the Education Act of 1870. He won government permission for laying out school playgrounds where, according to Robert, 'children could learn football and other organized games instead of fighting and throwing stones at one another in the street'.[39]

Alfred had managed to continue with his own writing, despite his demanding job, publishing his first collection of poems, *Songs of Killarney*, in 1873, and getting both his prose and verse published in *The Spectator*, *Punch*, *John Bull* and *The Athenaeum*. Once his younger brother, Charles Larcom Graves, arrived in London to work for *The Spectator* and *Punch*, Alfred found an even more reliable outlet in those two magazines. By the time he was introduced to Amy in 1891 he was well known for his light-hearted verses as well as his interest in folk song and folklore. The title poem of *Father O'Flynn & Other Lyrics*, published two years before they met, had made him famous when he set it to a traditional jig tune he remembered from childhood, 'The Top of the Cork Road'. Amy had told him at their first meeting that she was particularly fond of the song, which could easily have brought him in a reasonable income. Alfred, unlike Amy, however, had a poor head for business and sold his rights for very little, whereas his friend (Sir) Charles Stanford, who was responsible only for the harmonization of the original air, continued to draw a royalty and the publisher, according to Robert, 'made thousands'.[40] The most revealing aspect of this well-known story is that Alfred was not particularly bitter about this, confirming a general impression of an easy-going, sunny character.

Alfred himself explained in the 'Preface' to his *Irish Poems*[41] that his verse owed its 'prime impulse' to the music of the old Irish airs to which he had danced and sung as a boy, and which haunted him through life with its 'inexhaustible freshness'.[42] His upbringing partly in the Irish countryside had given him, he believed, the advantage of having constantly in his ears 'that translation into English of Irish idioms which renders the speech of the Kerry peasant so peculiarly poignant and picturesque'.[43] He worked hard from an early age to promote interest in Irish folklore and literature, helping to found the Folk-Song Society in 1898 and editing *Every Irishman's Library* magazine from 1914 to 1918, as well as being a member – and twice President – of the *Irish Literary Society*. In collaboration with Charles Stanford he also published *Songs of Old Ireland* (1882) and *Irish Songs and Ballads* (1893); with Charles Wood *Irish Folk-Songs* (1897) and *Songs of Erin* (1901). When he and Amy built a holiday home near Harlech, he became interested in Welsh folklore too, translating their folk songs into English, and was in 1902 made a 'bard'.

Unsurprisingly, Robert saw relatively little of his busy father as he was growing up, though when Alfred was at home he would tell his children stories that began not 'Once upon a time' but, more originally, 'And so the old gardener blew his nose on a red pocket handkerchief.'[44] Although Robert described him as 'very sweet and playful' on such occasions, there is a hint of resentment in his comment, which ends 'when he was not doing educational work he was doing literary work or being president'. Born less than a decade after the popularity of 'Father O'Flynn', Robert could not have been unaware of his father's success with it. He maintained that Alfred's 'light-hearted early work is the best', quoting the opening of his 'Invention of Wine' as evidence:

> Ere Bacchus could talk
> Or dacently walk,
> Down Olympus he jumped
> From the arms of his nurse,
> And though ten years in all
> Were consumed by the fall,
> He might have fallen farther
> And fared a dale worse...[45]

Robert also fails to give his father credit for his work to promote folk song and folk literature. His tone in discussing his father's poetry is altogether condescending and disingenuous:

> ... his work was never an oppression to me. I am even very pleased when I meet people who know his work and not mine. Some of his songs I sing without prejudice; when washing up after meals or shelling peas or on similar occasions.[46]

Particularly striking in Robert's account of his father is his denial that Alfred influenced his own determination to become a poet, even claiming that he owed 'much more as a writer' to his mother than to his father.[47] The characteristics he believed he had inherited from Alfred were by and large eccentricities:

> Such as finding it difficult to walk straight down a street, getting tired of sentences when half-way through and leaving them in the air, walking with the hands folded in a particular way behind the back, and being subject to sudden and most disconcerting spells of complete amnesia.

These fits, so far as I can discover, serve no useful purpose, and the worst about them is that they tend to produce in the subject the same sort of dishonesty that deaf people have when they miss the thread of conversation. They dare not be left behind and rely on their intuition and bluff to get them through. This disability is most marked in very cold weather. I do not now talk too much except when I have been drinking or when I meet someone who was with me in France. The Graves' have good minds for purposes like examinations, writing graceful Latin verse, filling in forms, and solving puzzles (when we children were invited to parties where guessing games and brain-tests were played we never failed to win). They have a good eye for ball games, and a graceful style. I inherited the eye, but not the style...[48]

Robert claimed that the 'most useful' trait he inherited from his father's family was the ability to 'masquerade as a gentleman', a remark which reveals not only how class-conscious he still was at the age of thirty-four, but also implies that he could only ever *pretend* to be a 'gentleman'.

The most significant aspect of Robert's account, however, remains how pointedly it omits the one characteristic a reader might expect he inherited from his father, a poetic talent. In fact he suggests the opposite:

I am glad in a way that my father was a poet. This at least saved me from any false reverence of poets ... He never once tried to teach me how to write, or showed any understanding of my serious work; he was always more ready to ask advice about his own work than to offer it for mine.[49]

Robert even told a friend in later life that his father 'tried to stop [him] being a writer' and 'wanted [him] to become a schoolmaster'.[50] It is a grotesque claim; Alfred helped and encouraged his son at every turn, as will become clear.

To a detached observer, it is clear that Alfred's influence on his son's poetic development started at an early age. Robert himself implies as much in 'The Poet in the Nursery', in which he gives a glimpse of himself growing up with a father who sat composing verse in a room full of poetry books, one of which excites in the child narrator a similar love of words and rhythms:

The book was full of funny muddling mazes,
> Each rounded off into a lovely song,
And most extraordinary and monstrous phrases
> Knotted with rhymes like a slave-driver's thong,
And metre twisting like a chain of daisies
> With great big splendid words a sentence long.[51]

Robert has added a note to this poem, first published in *Over the Brazier* (1916), that the incident 'happened at Wimbledon [his childhood home] in the library'.[52] Growing up in such circumstances with his father as a model undoubtedly convinced Robert that literature was a serious and attractive occupation. Like his father, who believed that poetry should provide its own meaning, he would for the most part refuse to explain his work with footnotes or a glossary, and, also like his father in this at least, write melodious poetry of lyric intensity. As he grew older he also became interested, like his father, in 'folk' poetry, both ballads and songs, and his early war poetry would show some of the characteristics of his father's patriotic verses of the First World War.

Robert himself, in his more objective moments, could see that his attempt to attribute his vocation as a writer to his mother's influence rather than his father's was unconvincing: he came to realize that it was by 'some unusual complication of early environment or mixed parentage'.[53] Both Alfred and Amy had contributed much to the making of the future poet Robert Graves.

2

VICTORIAN BEGINNINGS AND AN EDWARDIAN EDUCATION (1895–1909)

'Don't forget that I began in the Victorian Era; I had a lot to throw off.'[1]

Robert Graves's first memory was of being held up by his mother 'to watch, through a well-glazed English nursery window, the decorated carriages and red-coated soldiers of Queen Victoria's Diamond Jubilee procession.'[2] It was early summer 1897 and he was less than two years old. Victoria had only four more years to reign but there were as yet few signs of the changes to come. Lord Salisbury's Conservative Party, for which Alfred Perceval Graves voted, had increased its majority in the 1895 election and was to remain in power until 1906. And in poetry, of most concern to Robert throughout his long life, the influence of the Victorian giants, Tennyson, Browning and Arnold, still prevailed, though all three were dead by 1892. The innovations of Yeats and the Georgians had yet to bring about a change in which Graves himself would be involved.

Born early on the morning of Wednesday, 24 July 1895, Robert von Ranke Graves arrived two days after Alfred's 49th birthday and was welcomed by his sister Clarissa, two and a half at the time, as 'a late birthday present for her father'.[3] He was named after his great-uncle, the friend of Wordsworth and mentor to Alfred, Robert Perceval Graves, who had died only two years earlier. None of Alfred's three sons by his first marriage, to Jane Cooper, had shown any sign of becoming a poet and by naming this fourth son after his most prestigious literary ancestor, Alfred may have been hoping to influence events. Robert's middle name, 'von Ranke', in honour of Amy's family, was chosen, Alfred emphasized, 'at a time when the relations between England and Germany were far more cordial than those between England and France'.[4] The name was to cause trouble for Robert both at public school and in the Army, as that 'cordial' relationship deteriorated. But as a small child his happiest holidays were spent in Germany at his maternal grandfather's country house.

Although not quite recognizable as a 'Poet in the Nursery', Robert gave hints of his future calling in the fascination with words he describes in the poem of that name, which ends:

> While round the nursery for long months there floated
> Wonderful words no one could understand.[5]

It was not so much the intelligibility of Robert's words as a small child, however, as his precocious use of them that stood out for his family. His sister Rosaleen, a year older than he, remembered Robert announcing from his sickbed at a very early age, for instance: 'I am amusing myself with books and papers.'[6] And Clarissa reminded him, over half a century after the event, of what had happened when their mother had banished him from her room for misbehaving during the lesson in religious instruction she gave her children on Sunday:

> Even so, she could not get on with Rosaleen and me, for you refused to stay outside but opened the door and continued to look in. When she remonstrated with you, you replied: 'I had rather be a doorkeeper in the house of my God, than to dwell in the tents of ungodliness.'[7]

Beside giving a foretaste of Robert's quick-wittedness, this anecdote also destroys any idea that Amy repressed her children and turned them into little plaster saints, though she did make them into strong moralists for a time. Robert remembered, for instance, a printed notice by Rosaleen in the corner of their nursery, which 'might just as well have been put up by me: "I must not say bang, bust or pig bucket, for it is rude."'[8] And Amy did instil in them a love of the Bible and its stories, which remained with Robert long after he had lost his Christian faith, inspiring works such as *My Head! My Head!* (1925), his retelling of the Biblical story of Elisha and the Shunamite woman. But from all first-hand accounts of this period, Amy's strict beliefs did not appear to weigh heavily upon her children: Robert himself believed that he had had a 'happy' childhood (the word is his).[9] He would write longingly in a poem, as an adult: 'Oh, to be a child once more.'[10]

Robert's first four and a half years, before the birth of his brother Charles, were spent in a self-contained world with his two older sisters. Charles, with what sounds like a sense of exclusion, wrote that even as he was growing up the three eldest children 'always went round together'.[11] Their parents' busy lives beyond the nursery did them no harm, according to Robert, for 'we had each other'.[12] Their sense of being a separate little unit was almost certainly increased by the existence of Alfred's five older children by his first marriage. Two of the three boys were away at school and university during term time, though they joined the family for holidays in Wales. The eldest son, Philip ('Eli'), born in 1876, had left school by the time Robert was born. A scholar of Oriel College, Oxford, he was intended for the Indian Civil Service, but became a journalist instead, working in the Middle East as *The Times* correspondent. His friendship with T. E. Lawrence in Cairo during the First World War would ease the way for Robert's own friendship with Lawrence in the 1920s and Philip would help Robert get a job in Cairo in 1926. He was Robert's favourite stepbrother.

Richard ('Dick'), four years Philip's junior, was 'tall, dark, proconsular', according to Charles Graves, and would have 'the rare experience of going to Magdalen College, Oxford, as well as King's College, Cambridge'.[13] He too spent most of his adult life in the Middle East, in the Levant Civil Service, where he served with distinction. The youngest son, Perceval ('Bones'), was 'the playboy of the family', Charles claimed, practising as a lawyer in various exotic locations, and something of a worry to his father in his youth.[14] Their two sisters, Mary ('Molly'), who was almost a second mother to Robert, and Susan, only eight years his senior, were living mainly at Red Branch House in Robert's early years. Molly, after qualifying as a horticulturalist, would, like her brothers, spend most of her life in the Middle East. Accordingly, when Robert took up his job in Cairo in 1926, there would be a number of familiar figures around him.

Charles had no doubt that 'the education provided by a large family is the perfect one',[15] but Robert believed that 'a family of ten means a dilution of parental affection' and that 'the members tend to become indistinct'.[16] Nevertheless he grew up cocooned by his two older sisters, Clarissa and Rosaleen.

Clarissa ('Claree' to his 'Robbie'), the eldest of Amy and Alfred's children, was widely gifted in an unusually talented family. In addition to the short stories, poems and songs she wrote with both Robert and Rosaleen, she became a sufficiently skilled artist to be accepted into the Slade School of Art in 1911, alongside such outstanding figures as Stanley Spencer, David Bomberg, Christopher Nevinson, Dora Carrington and Isaac Rosenberg, also a poet, whom Robert would come to admire. Clarissa would go on to study English at Manchester University and Speech Training in London, complete at least one novel and have a book of her poems published.[17] Charles remembered her as an imposing figure, 'tall' and 'hawk-eyed',[18] but Clarissa was emotionally frail. Amy feared this was a result of her own failure to show sufficient maternal affection towards Clarissa as a baby for fear of her stepchildren's jealousy. And at least one biographer has suggested that Clarissa suffered from not having been born a boy. Whatever the roots of her problems, they clearly affected Clarissa's life and she would suffer periodic bouts of deep depression. She experienced several nervous breakdowns, moved constantly between jobs as a young woman, and never married. She would eventually find some consolation in Christian Science and in moving to Jerusalem, where she had a small house until the late 1940s. Clarissa and Robert would be close as children, but also at several other periods in later life. In 1915, for instance, he would call her his 'best critic'.[19] She would also consult him about her own poetry and help out with childcare.

There was never any doubt, however, that Robert's closest ally was his more robust, confident, and also highly talented sister Rosaleen ('Ros'), his 'best friend' according to him.[20] Rosaleen felt the same affinity. A photograph of the three children taken in April 1901 reflects the dynamics of the three-sided relationship well: Clarissa, aged eight, and Robert, five, look tentatively, rather shyly, at the camera, whereas Rosaleen, only just seven, looks confidently at it, even boldly, holding Robert's hand reassuringly as she does so. She was known to her siblings, apparently, as 'our Amazon'.[21]

Named almost certainly after James Mangan's 'Dark Rosaleen', Rosaleen Graves, like Clarissa, was multi-talented, achieving success as a musician as well as an author both of poetry and of prose. After gaining a diploma from the Royal College of Music, when the First World War broke out she volunteered for the Voluntary Aid Detachment (V.A.D.), serving as a nurse in the 4th London Hospital, Denmark Hill, and the 54th General Hospital at Wimereux in France. When, in 1919, she returned to civilian life it seemed to her 'rather useless ... just teaching little girls to play the piano after what [she] had been through',[22] and she applied to study medicine at Merton College, Oxford. But she would continue to write poetry and prose during her long life as a busy GP in the West Country, publishing two verse collections, *Night Sounds* (1933) and *Snapdragons* (1983), and one prose work, *Games from an Edwardian Childhood* (1982), a revealing glimpse into the Graves children's own upbringing.

Besides collaborating with Clarissa on a number of songs and poems as a child, Rosaleen also wrote stories and nonsense verse with Robert. His third publication, apart from verse in his school magazine, was a short story written jointly with Rosaleen, and published in the 1912 Christmas edition of *The Westminster Gazette*.[23] Their father, who had no doubt engineered its publication, was also proud of Robert and Rosaleen's collection of nonsense verses, *Alpha Beta Pie*, having introduced them to Edward Lear's *Nonsense Rhymes* early on. He almost succeeded in getting their collection published as a book, but had to be content with Arthur Mee's purchase of twelve of the verses for his monthly *Children's New Encyclopaedia*, together with two songs each by Clarissa and Rosaleen.

Miranda Seymour has suggested that Robert viewed Rosaleen not only as a collaborator but also as a rival, citing his use of a scheming older sister in *Antigua, Penny, Puce* (1936) and another clever sister, Dorothy, in his play *But It Still Goes On* (1930). It is quite possible that an element of rivalry existed between them as they grew up, but they would be on very good terms for almost the whole of their adult lives and Robert would try to help Rosaleen with generous gifts of money as she struggled to bring up her three sons on her own after her divorce from Jim Cooper. Writing to Robert in 1973, just before his descent into Alzheimer's, she told him that 'all through my childhood and youth you were the person I loved best in the world'. When, at the age of four and a half, and with his brother Charles newly born, Robert was rushed to hospital with scarlet fever, she had hidden his most precious Christmas present, a toy soldier's helmet, to keep it from being destroyed as potentially infectious. She remembered climbing up on a chair to reach the day-nursery mantelpiece and take it down: 'I held it and thought of you'.[24] And as Graves neared his death in 1985 and she was forced to accept that he was 'hardly a real person' any more, she repeated to his wife Beryl, 'he was my first friend and I loved him dearly'.[25]

Since their father Alfred could rarely spend much time with his children, except in the holidays, his influence was largely one of encouragement and example, the latter crucial to Robert's development: when questioning himself about becoming a poet his answer was:

> Poetry is ... my father's trade,
> Familiar since my childhood...[26]

Amy, for all her reputed religious narrowness, was more actively involved in nurturing any talents their children might have. Her method was fairly straightforward and, judging by the results, highly effective: she told them stories from an early age. Apart from the usual fairy tales of Jack the Giant-Killer, Mother Goose, Bluebeard, Robin Hood, Little Red Riding Hood, Sir Galahad, Captain Kidd, Puck, Lob and many others, Robert remembered his mother's own, decidedly moral stories 'about inventors and doctors who gave their lives for the suffering, and the poor boys who struggled to the top of the tree, and saintly men who made examples of themselves'.[27]

Before Robert was four, Amy had started what she called *The Red Branch Song Book*, initially to entertain Clarissa, Rosaleen and Robert, who had all caught whooping cough. In it she wrote down some of the poems she had invented for their diversion, also (being Amy) to make a moral point. In addition she included any of their own sayings she thought poetic. Robert's first recorded verse of August 1898 ('Two little flowers / In the towers') may not have been a conscious attempt at poetry, likewise his next recorded 'verse' ('My fingers are very tall / And I put my soapy fingers on the wall'). But both suggest she believed that poetry is defined by rhyme. Like Siegfried Sassoon's mother, who presented her three-year-old son with Coleridge's lectures on Shakespeare, Amy may have been hoping to steer her son towards poetry. Another undated entry in the *Red Branch Song Book* shows Robert making a conscious attempt to compose a 'poem', almost certainly before the age of four. And however much it owes to 'Who Killed Cock Robin?', it demonstrates the same precociousness his sisters noted in him:

> Who did that?
> Said the grown-up cat.
> I not
> Said the dot [.]
> I did, said the spider
> With my glass of cider...

The last line of the poem ('Under the silver moon') is taken from one by Amy, which had clearly impressed her son, who found a new rhyme for 'moon' in 'Wimbledon'. By 1902, when Robert was six, Amy had also started a family magazine, to which he and his two sisters contributed.

Although Amy did not attempt to give her children their formal education, she did try to expand their horizons. It was from his mother, for example, that Robert learnt the names of the stars.[28] She also took her children to Kew Gardens, Hampton Court Park, London Zoo, the British Museum and the Natural History Museum, though never to plays or pantomimes, which Amy considered frivolous. As her efforts to continue her own education after leaving school showed, she valued education greatly.

Amy's enthusiasm for culture probably had some negative effects, however. Robert's provocative dismissal of Milton in later life, for instance, may have been a reaction to his mother's early enthusiasm for the poet. But she was more successful in passing on her love of music. Robert grew up to the sound of his mother playing the piano and singing to him, and his taste for music, especially singing, started at an early age. Alfred's songs and a wide range of other folk songs were also familiar to the children. They knew many airs from F. M. Keel's collection of Elizabethan love songs, which they 'loved a lot', Rosaleen remembered.[29] Since they sang many of these songs in parts, Charles recalled, they were clearly quite sophisticated in musical terms. Robert, Rosaleen and Clarissa would all go on to compose songs of their own. Robert and Rosaleen were particularly proud of a joint effort that opened: 'To the Tintinnabulations of the Tuneful Tambourine / Stalked Morella King of Cakeland and his daughter Margerine'.[30] Again, like his father, Robert was attracted to humorous songs and was often called on at the family's frequent musical evenings to sing 'The Whiskey Skin' and his variations on 'Widdicombe Fair', with Rosaleen accompanying him. He would later infuriate Siegfried Sassoon by arguing that northern folk songs were better than classical music, despite his own love of Mozart as a child. He would join the choir at school and like his father, consciously or not, would try to find a suitable composer to set some of his more ballad-type poems to music when he grew older.

It was a very different world from television and smartphones, as Rosaleen emphasized in her account of her 'long-ago childhood before cars, planes, phones or electric fires and in the days of "servants"'.[31] Robert was 22 before wireless broadcasting began in earnest in England, and at the age of 18 he had been the first member of his family to own a gramophone. His own memories of early childhood were more graphic, almost Dickensian: apart from the absence of cars, he remembered 'the streets cobbled, and so filthy with horse-droppings and mud that everyone wore boots. Ragged boys with dirty faces used to sweep the crossings with brooms and beg for halfpennies. Sometimes they turned cartwheels to attract attention.'[32] Robert's awareness of social differences evidently started early. His younger brother John, born in 1903, had more romantic memories than Robert's, but it was the same world – the afternoon visit of the muffin-man 'ringing a hand bell to draw attention to his wares stacked on a tray with a green baize cloth carried on his head', at dusk the lamp-lighter with his ladder, 'which he propped against each lamp-post in turn while he lit the lamp by hand'.[33]

The setting for all these memories is Wimbledon, chosen by Alfred and Amy as their new home when he was transferred from his School-Inspectorate in Somerset to the London district of Southwark, Bermondsey and Rotherhithe. With six children already and the possibility of more to come, they wanted a healthier and less deprived environment in which to raise their family than London's East End. Wimbledon, with its spacious Common, seemed ideal, especially since Alfred already had two Irish friends living there. Wimbledon at the turn of the century consisted of two distinct social and geographical levels. Alfred and Amy had, predictably, chosen to

live in the more privileged residential area, but their children were familiar
with a rougher side to the town that frightened them. Robert remembered
his terror at 'one blind beggar at Wimbledon who used to sit on the
pavement reading the Bible aloud in Braille; he was not really blind but
able to turn his eyes up'.[34] And his sister Rosaleen reminded him many years
later of the 'unemployed marching about – a terrifying band'.[35] Another
daily reminder of that other world was the presence of a public house in
The Ridgway opposite the Graves residence, with its 'soused' customers,
'foul stable yard', and its 'adjoining network of howling, stinking, typhoidal
slums'.[36] This public house is nowadays a highly respectable establishment.

Whatever criticisms Robert later levelled at Wimbledon, he had
positive memories of his early years there, spent in the house that Alfred and
Amy had built for their family shortly before his birth. Settling temporarily
in a comfortable rented house with an attractive garden in Arterberry
Road in 1893, they had started to look for something suitable to buy. But
all the houses large enough to accommodate their growing family had
stables, billiard rooms and other luxuries that made them too expensive for
their means; so that when an enterprising young architect came to them
unsolicited, offering to design a large house for them, Amy decided to invest
in it. It would have rooms for all the children from Alfred's two marriages and
also servants' quarters. The result, in Robert's memory, was a 'yellow-brick,
slate-roofed, creeper-clad late-Victorian mansion of twenty-four rooms and
the usual offices ... The proportions ... were good, the construction sound,
the decorations unpretentious'.[37]

What Robert left out of his description, and probably took for granted
as a child, was how well situated the house was. The first to be built in
Lauriston Road, it was a few minutes' walk from the south side of Wimbledon
Common, within minutes of shops in The Ridgway, but also not far from
the High Street and the railway station. Alfred was keener to emphasize
the 'special features' that he and Amy had included in the plans for their
house at extra cost, 'the large over-hanging eaves and green Cumberland
slate' of the roof in particular.[38] He was even prouder of the name, chosen
in honour of his antecedents, 'Red Branch House, after the knights of the
red branch, celebrated in Irish chivalry for their poetry and hospitality'.[39]
Robert later judged the name inappropriate, almost certainly in reaction
to his father, finding the main attraction of Red Branch 'its well-stocked

book shelves and the staircases (one for the family, one for the staff) that allowed the children to run races round the house in opposite directions simultaneously'[40] – yet another indication that the Graves offspring were hardly suppressed as children. His final memory, of a house 'with no electric light or lift, or vacuum cleaner, or refrigerator, or radio, or telly', only 'rather dim gas-lamps, and coal-fires, and a grand piano', reminds the reader once more that Robert was born into the Victorian age.[41] It was a more formal, class-conscious age, which left its mark on him, and also on Rosaleen:

> The house-parlour-maid lit the drawing-room fire at four o'clock in the afternoon and then changed from her print-dress into her black dress and frilly apron. When we were little we wore pinafores and came down in these to the drawing-room on Mother's Wednesday 'At Homes'. I hated being kissed by the old ladies through their veils. Sometimes they wiped their noses through their veils, which I thought 'Ga-ga'.[42]

Robert afterwards claimed that he had been oppressed even as a child by the Victorian décor: 'the shabby, solid, characterless furniture; the *art nouveau* ugliness of the fireplaces; the dismally utilitarian iron bedsteads; the dull-brown paintwork on doors, windows, banisters; the triviality of the wallpaper patterns', a style he would resolutely shun in adult life.[43] His response as a child, he claimed, was to stay 'out of doors as much as possible',[44] though it is more likely that it was Amy who prescribed that. The house had a garden large enough to have accommodated a tennis court, had she and Alfred not been reluctant to cut down an ancient chestnut tree. But the children could play on the putting green which they installed instead, still leaving room for the many other games they played outside. In her *Games from an Edwardian Childhood* Rosaleen's list of those specifically for the garden is undoubtedly based on her own experience growing up with Robert and includes intriguing titles such as 'French and English' and 'Kicking the Can', as well as more familiar games along the lines of 'Hide and Seek'. Robert's later love of children and their world suggests that his own childhood had been an exciting one that he was unwilling to relinquish entirely.

Robert's brother Charles described another outside activity for the children: their parents gave each of them 'a section of garden for our very own to dig and plant as we pleased', which reminded him later of the allotments of the two World Wars.[45] One of Robert's early poems would be about his favourite flowers, 'Double Red Daisies', which gives the flavour of his life in a house full of young and highly competitive children:

> Double red daisies, they're my flowers,
>   Which nobody else may grow.
> In a big quarrelsome house like ours
>   They try it sometimes – but no,
> I root them up because they're my flowers,
>   Which nobody else may grow.[46]

He became an enthusiastic gardener, even attempting a little landscaping. On at least one occasion before his tenth birthday, his mother caught him making a pond, moat and bridge on the adults' lawn, causing a mess that she tried not to mind.[47]

Offering even more freedom was Wimbledon Common, which became almost as familiar to Robert as his own garden. He was first wheeled there in a pram by the elderly Nurse Sutterley, who had cared for the children of Alfred's first marriage. Then, when she retired a year after Robert's birth, by Amy's house parlourmaid, Emily Dykes, who 'in a practical way', Robert claimed, 'came to be more to us than our mother'.[48] Although she called them 'Miss' and 'Master', 'she spoke it in no servant tone', according to him, and established her identity firmly when she announced upon her arrival to take charge of them: 'Emily Dykes is my name; England is my nation; Netheravon is my dwelling place and Christ is my salvation.'[49] Rosaleen confirmed Emily's central role in their childhood and also remembered a Welsh 'under-nurse' and their daily walks on the common 'with Nurse Emily pushing the pram'.[50] Wimbledon Common and adjoining Putney Heath, well over 1,000 acres between them, constitute the largest expanse of heathland in the London area. There, at the turn of the century, Robert and his siblings 'could walk for miles across real country by way of Robin Hood Church and Richmond Park as far as the Thames, keeping clear of streets and houses until the very end'.[51] (Another South London poet, Edward Thomas, born eighteen years before Robert, had enjoyed a similar sense of freedom and contact with nature as he walked across London's commons as a boy.)

Wimbledon Common itself was full of interest for children of any age: eighty years later Rosaleen would remember their childhood expeditions to Cannizaro Park, not far from their house and the scene of yearly fêtes, as well as trips to Pen Pond in nearby Richmond Park. Less organized, more independent outings later on would include 'pelt[ing]' the horse-chestnut trees with 'sticks and stones long before the chestnuts were ripe and in defiance of an energetic common keeper', or meeting in the ancient, disused windmill, an ideal den for local children. Ice-skating on one of the several ponds or tobogganing in winter were other favourite pastimes. By all accounts Robert was relatively free to enjoy the opportunities that a large, open, fairly wild space offered, and led a less oppressive existence than a 'Victorian' upbringing leads one to imagine. One of Charles Graves's most vivid memories of the Common, for instance, was of birds-nesting with Robert and 'conniving at Robert's abstraction of an egg from a sparrow-hawk's nest'.[52] On Sundays, if fine, the whole family would walk together to church, up Lauriston Road, past the pond, across the Common, skirting Caesar's Camp on the left, to the little church of St John the Baptist, a Church of England establishment near Beverley Brook in Robin Hood Lane, more than an hour's walk each way.

Robert experienced an even greater sense of freedom and closer contact with nature at his grandparents' holiday home in Germany. In 1860 Heinrich von Ranke had bought a sixteenth-century hunting lodge, 'Laufzorn',[53] as a retreat from his busy professional life in Munich only ten miles away to the north. His daughter Amy, and her children in turn, loved the big old manor house. Robert, who visited it six times between his birth and Heinrich's death in 1909, devotes more space to describing it in his autobiography than to any of his childhood haunts. He was particularly struck by its enormous banqueting hall, which seemed to him as big as a cathedral and carried with it a powerful sense of the past.

Robert's first visit at ten months old unsurprisingly goes undocumented, but the subsequent ones he remembered as 'easily the best things of my early childhood':

> Pine forests and hot sun, red deer and black and red squirrels, acres of blueberries and wild strawberries; nine or ten kinds of edible mushrooms that we went into the forests to pick ... the rye bread, the black honey ...

the huge ice-cream puddings made with fresh raspberry juice, and the
venison and honey cakes ... And the bretzels, and carrots cooked with
sugar, and summer puddings of cranberries and blueberries.[54]

Robert would later describe himself as 'greedy',[55] but the list is that of
someone with a relish for life and genuinely interested in cooking. As an
adult, he would often cook for his family and, like his mother, would relax
by making jam.

At Laufzorn everything seemed so much freer and more brightly
coloured than his life in London. Instead of exploring an increasingly
familiar Wimbledon Common, he and his siblings were allowed to bathe
and play in the nearby river Iser, 'under a waterfall'; he remembered the Iser
as 'bright green and said to be the fastest river in Europe'.[56] Other highly
coloured memories included trips to Amy's brothers on their peacock farm,
or to Heinrich's brother on the lakeshore of Tegernsee, where everyone
seemed to Robert to have 'buttercup-blonde hair'.[57]

The most exciting visit, undoubtedly, was to Amy's sister Agnes, who
had married Baron von Aufsess and lived in Aufsess Castle, high up in
the Bavarian Alps some hours away from Laufzorn by train. (The Baron
would be killed in 1917 as an officer of the Imperial German staff in the
First World War.) The ninth-century castle with its mediaeval additions was
too remote to have been plundered through the ages and was a storehouse
of treasures, the most remarkable of which for Robert was an iron chest
in a small, thick-walled, white-washed, windowless room at the top of
the keep. Since the chest was twice the size of the door, it could only have
been constructed inside the room and, tradition demanded, must never be
opened unless the castle were in extreme danger. Although it was forbidden
to speculate what might lie inside, the Graves children speculated endlessly.
They were also thrilled by the castle ghost, that of a former Baron known as
the Red Knight. Robert's own openness to the supernatural received a huge
boost at Aufsess Castle and, though Laufzorn 'had nothing to compare'
with it, its own two resident ghosts further stimulated his imagination as
they reputedly roamed the lodge. One of them was particularly frightening,
'a carriage which drove furiously along without any horses, and before the
days of motor-cars'.[58] All this is described with evident relish by Robert in
Good-bye to All That. The Graves side of his family had already alerted him

to the possibility of another, more magical world with their Irish legends and observation of various rituals, such as bowing nine times to the new moon, which they feared seeing through glass. Bavaria would intensify that awareness, as would the legends and myths of Wales. His childhood, he claimed, was 'ghost-ridden',[59] and Rosaleen believed he was 'psychic'.[60]

Graves's sense of class differences was also intensified at Laufzorn. He had become aware of his own privileged middle-class status at the age of four and a half, during his stay in hospital with scarlet fever. But at Laufzorn, because the farm servants spoke a harsh dialect he could not understand and because they were Catholics 'and poor and sweaty and savage-looking', they frightened him, heightening his sense of class distinctions: 'they were lower even than the servants at home'.[61] The Italians who worked in the tile-making factory that Heinrich had revived seemed to him 'even lower', a sense of difference reinforced by the exaggerated respect shown to his grandfather in the surrounding villages on their outings with him.

These trips in Heinrich's carriage through the lovely countryside were marred for Robert by the many wayside crucifixes they passed, 'with the realistic blood and wounds, and the ex-voto pictures, little sign-boards, of naked souls in purgatory, grinning with anguish in the middle of high red and yellow flames'.[62] These graphic reminders of Hell were more likely to be responsible for Robert's childhood nightmares than Amy's gentle religious teachings. Stories of the morgue in Munich added to his terror; the corpses of 'notable' citizens were placed in a chair there, to sit in state for a day or two, a 'nightmare' thought as far as Robert was concerned.[63]

Yet on all his visits to Bavaria, taken with his German mother, Robert 'felt a sense of home in [his] blood in a natural human way'.[64] Although he and his siblings did not speak German well – 'our genders and minor parts of speech were shaky' – and never learnt to read Gothic script, they had 'the feel of German so strongly' that all his life Robert would believe he knew German far better than French, even after a much more rigorous training in the latter language. He refers to having a German nanny, who showed him German picture-books before he was five, and Amy encouraged the children to speak German, as well as French and Italian, at mealtimes to keep them fluent. Robert's identification with Germany would overshadow his life for at least a decade from 1909 onwards, when hostility towards that country was building up. It would complicate his own attitude towards the

First World War, in which at least ten of his own relatives were fighting on the enemy side. His personal history of that period, he recalled, was 'a forced rejection of the German in me'.[65]

Charles Graves believed that it was the 'mixed blood' in their family which made Robert and two of his other siblings 'unsettled mentally and psychologically'.[66] Robert seemed to him 'almost fifty-fifty Graves-von Ranke', with the result that 'his left hand seldom kn[e]w what his right hand [was] going to do'.[67]

It is an appealing theory that nonetheless fails to take into account Robert's own lack of identification with his Irish side, at least in his early life. He even claimed to be grateful to his father for breaking the 'geographical connection' with Ireland.[68] If he had visited Ireland regularly as a child, as he did Laufzorn, he would almost certainly have felt differently, but Alfred and Amy's first family holiday there when Robert was a year old was not a success and was not repeated. Instead, in 1897, they took Clarissa, Rosaleen and the two-year-old Robert to the small seaside village (as it was then) of Harlech, in North Wales. Retrospectively, Robert was 'glad' that it was Wales rather than Ireland which became their regular Easter and summer retreat: 'if it had been Ireland,' he believed, 'we would have self-consciously learned Irish and the local legends'.[69] Instead they came to know the country 'more purely', in his opinion, as a place whose history was 'too old for local legends, allowing them to make up their own'.[70] His love of Harlech would outlast his love of Bavaria and would be a particular consolation to him during the First World War, when it had become, in his words, 'the country of my choice'.[71]

His parents had chosen Harlech initially through the advice of a Wimbledon neighbour, Sir William Preece, a Welsh electrical engineer and inventor involved in the development of the telegraph, the telephone and radio. They all enjoyed the sea-bathing so much and Alfred the promise of a golf course to come, that he and Amy decided to return the following year. But Amy saw no sense in living in rented accommodation, especially as they needed two of the available houses for their large family, and she decided in her practical way that they should build another house for themselves, 'take the summer holidays as the interest and let [it] at other times'.[72] She found the site for it by chance one day, as she followed her children up a rocky slope beyond Harlech, where they were picking blackberries. After some difficulty buying the land, Amy was able to instruct a Mr Bowen Jones of Caernarvon to draw up plans, using the front of Red Branch House as a model. And with Amy supervising from rented accommodation in Harlech, building began in 1898, with three-year-old Robert going regularly with her and his sisters to 'see the ruins' as they called their future holiday home. His first summer in the completed house coincided with his fourth birthday.

The name chosen for their new house was 'Erinfa', the Welsh for 'towards Ireland'. Like Red Branch House this was partly in deference to Alfred, but it was also in recognition of its magnificent views, one of which looked west across Cardigan Bay and the Irish Sea towards Alfred's birthplace. Rosaleen, who was five when the family spent the first summer at Erinfa, could still remember over 74 years later the children's almost uncontainable excitement as the visit approached, reminding Robert of the white tiles below their nursery mantelpiece 'on which we daubed "30, 29, 28 (etc) days till we go to Harlech", wiping one figure off each day'.[73] This was the time of year they loved best, she remembered, starting with the journey in an 'enormous private bus' drawn by two horses. As in most large families, perhaps even more than most, there was a great deal of competition between the children, who 'all fought to sit on the box', while the adults and current babies sat inside. Amy enjoyed the rare chance to read on the long train journey and Alfred retired to the dining car for a good lunch. Robert, Clarissa and Rosaleen, far too excited to settle, 'tore up and down the corridors' and 'waltzed in the luggage-van'.[74]

Life at Erinfa was equally free from discipline and must have been blissful for the children. Rosaleen remembered learning to swim at Harlech, collecting ammonites and shells on the shore and playing games in the sandhills. Robert found visits to nearby Harlech Castle, where they went climbing among its ruined turrets and towers, particularly memorable. Its 'immense, scary moated pile' was one of many nightmare images in his otherwise happy childhood he would feel compelled to explore.

The view north from Erinfa, across an enormous plain to the Snowdonia range, was equally magnificent. Below the house was a wood – 'our wood', Rosaleen claimed,[75] – where the children built 'a little house called "Holly Mosset" on a rock, played Hide and Seek, and lay in hammocks reading books by Ernest Thom[p]son Seton, with pictures of little bears and other animals in the margins'.[76] They also spoke their secret language to each other, with words like 'Wingle' (their name for Amy's last child, John, born in 1903), 'balther' and 'slig'.[77] The mountain stream that supplied the family's drinking water 'poured down from the mountain behind the house in a glorious rush',[78] according to Rosaleen, who shared most of Robert's tastes in childhood. They both enjoyed the sandy beach, also the blackberries, raspberries, blueberries, flowers and mushrooms they found growing wild, but Robert's favourite area was the one he called 'Rocky Acres', which lay behind their house and which he would later celebrate in verse.

Before the days of motor traffic, Harlech was a quiet place and little known, even as a golf course. It fell into three parts; the village itself, approximately five hundred feet up in the foothills of Snowdonia, dominated by its mediaeval castle built by Edward I against the rebellious Welsh; the Morfa, below the castle, a flat plain from which the sea had receded and where the Royal St David's Golf Club was opened shortly after the Graves's first visit; and the desolate hill country behind Harlech village. As Robert grew older he spent more and more time among these 'Rocky Acres', often with Rosaleen, sometimes with Clarissa, and it informed the landscape of his mind.

A stile at the back of their 'large, wild, boulder-strewn, steeply-sloped garden'[79] and a 20-minute walk eastward over rough hills would take them to an area where they could walk for 15 or 20 miles without crossing a road or passing close to the very occasional farms there. Originally, they had gone with a practical purpose in mind – to pick blueberries on the hills near Maesygarnedd, cranberries at Gwlawllyn, raspberries near Cwmbychan Lake, globe-flowers in the upper Artro, or to find fragments of Roman hypocaust tiling in the ruined Roman villas near Castell Tomen y Mur, or look for white heather on a hill to the north of the Roman steps:

> But after a time, we walked about those hills simply because they were good to walk about on. They had a penny plain quality about them that was even better than the twopence coloured quality of the Bavarian Alps ... On the hills behind Harlech I found a personal harmony independent of history or geography.[80]

It was this bare, bleak country that would figure in one of Robert's first poems to appear in print, 'The Mountain Side at Evening'. The same area would inspire the first poem Robert claimed to have written 'as himself', 'Rocky Acres', in which he struggles to capture the harmony he found there. From the choice of a deliberately irregular metre onwards, the emphasis is on absence, on the lack of any obviously 'Romantic' features, though it is reminiscent in parts of Keats's 'La Belle Dame Sans Merci':

> This is a wild land, country of my choice,
> With harsh craggy mountains, moor ample and bare.
> Seldom in these acres is heard any voice
> But voice of cold water that runs here and there
> Through rock and lank heather growing without care.
> No mice in the heath run, no song-birds fly
> For fear of the buzzards that float in the sky.[81]

Robert's poetry about Wales lay in the future, but his love of it started in early childhood and he would visit it regularly until he left for the Army in 1914. (Erinfa would become his parents' main residence in 1919.) It was always an anticlimax to return to Wimbledon, which seemed to him as he grew up 'a wrong place, neither town nor country'.[82] But since the Common was the nearest that he could get to real countryside, Robert continued to explore it with his siblings. 'And in bad weather,' he wrote, 'I always had a retreat into story books.'[83] There was a large stock of these, brought into the house by his five stepbrothers and stepsisters. The magazine for boys, *Chums*, was also a great favourite.[84]

It was not just story-books that Robert read. When Charles Graves came to sit his finals at Oxford after insufficient preparation, at least he knew that he 'could metaphorically walk all the straightforward English Literature papers, having been weaned on Wordsworth, suckled on Sir John Suckling and almost surfeited by a home diet of Chaucer, Pope, Malory and Milton'.[85] By Robert's own reckoning there were between four and five thousand books in the house, consisting of an 'old-fashioned scholar's library' bequeathed to Alfred by his uncle Robert, which included all the standard authors mentioned by Charles and many more: Alfred's own collection, largely of poetry, devotional books contributed by Amy, and educational books sent by publishers hopeful of Alfred's endorsement for government schools. This was quite apart from a cupboard in the children's nursery stacked to the ceiling with octavo volumes of Shakespeare, which filled Robert with 'a sort of despondent terror' as a small child.[86] His father's running of a Shakespeare Reading Circle in Wimbledon brought distinguished writers such as Sir Sidney Lee to the house. Alfred's involvement with Irish literature led on to friendships, first with William Allingham ('Up the Airy Mountain'), and later with the pre-Raphaelites Dante Gabriel Rossetti, William Morris, John Ruskin and Ford Madox Brown. Alfred also boasted of an evening spent with Tennyson in the late 1870s. But it was his close contact with editors and critics of many of the literary magazines of the day, such as Richard Holt Hutton of *The Spectator* or his brother, Charles, of *The Spectator* and *Punch*, which would be of most use to his son Robert in the future. Robert's own boast, of being patted on the head as a baby in his pram by Swinburne in Wimbledon, arose out of his father's friendship with the poet in Swinburne's earlier, less sober days.

When books did not appeal there were countless family games, as Rosaleen fondly recalled, such as 'Quaker's Wedding' or 'Turn the Trencher'.[87] And Robert himself reminisced about ' "Cheatings", "Ghosts in the Dark", "Up Jenkins", "Sardines" and all sorts of jolly good games you never find written down'.[88] As they grew older they played the usual board games and a German strategy game called 'Halma'; there was also the intriguingly named 'Squails', a form of table-bowls. Card games were allowed, but not for gambling. The children were called 'clever Graves' at children's parties because of their skill at paper games.

These parties took place mainly at Christmas, the only holiday the family spent in Wimbledon after Erinfa was built. And Amy made sure that it was memorable for the children. There was always a large tree in the drawing room, lit with candles and hung with the same coloured-glass decorations year after year, one of Robert's many happy memories of childhood. 'The children,' he remembered, 'always waited outside in the dark cold hall for an hour or so, telling ghost stories, while Mother and Father dressed the tree and sorted out the presents.'[89] The drawing room had been closed to them for days while grown-ups crept in and out with parcels. When they were finally allowed in, the tree seemed to the romantically inclined Robert to blaze out at them 'like the Jewelled Garden of Paradise'.[90] Amy, more conscious of the religious implications of the festival, made them first sing 'O Come All Ye Faithful', which she played loudly on the piano. Each child had its own presents laid out on a chair, sofa or small table covered with a white linen cloth. And they were exciting presents; Robert remembered his presents at the age of four in particular – a musical box, toy helmet and drum, a prayer book, a painting-book, a clockwork horse and two boxes of tin soldiers – not just because they were exactly what he wanted, but also because those were the presents the doctor ordered burnt after Robert caught scarlet fever, because of the new baby, Charles, and the fear of infection.

With the exception of his loss of toys, his stay in hospital with scarlet fever and a few incidents of mild punishment for misbehaviour, Robert's early childhood was carefree and largely happy. So much so, indeed, that when it came to writing about war almost two decades later in a collaboration with Sassoon, in which they decided to 'define [it] ... by making contrasted definitions' of peace, Graves chose childhood, explaining: 'When I was in France I used to spend much of my spare time playing with the French children of the village in which I was billeted. I put them into my poems and my own childhood at Harlech.'[91] His two sisters were his closest allies and he had no sense of sexual differences, and certainly none of the sexual embarrassment he experienced later. Also, according to him, he was never bullied until he began school at the age of six, when his cocoon was shattered.

***

Robert's feelings on beginning school were of bewilderment and fear, but they could have been far worse. For, unlike many contemporaries of his social class, he was not sent away to board, possibly for reasons of economy but also, almost certainly, to give him a less harsh introduction to the outside world. The local dame school chosen by his parents, however, was a far from gentle start and his father took him away after a few terms when he found him crying over having to learn the twenty-three times table. Even allowing for Robert's tendency to exaggerate, the school was clearly not suitable for a young child. Much worse was the practice of making the children do mental arithmetic to a metronome, which resulted in Robert wetting himself in terror. Alfred quickly moved his son to King's College School, Wimbledon, which had recently transferred its premises from central London and was now only one street away from the Graveses, in spacious grounds facing the Common. Robert was just seven years old in an institution which went up to nineteen-year-olds and again his main feelings were of confusion and fear. He did not understand the lessons, particularly Latin, and he was 'oppressed by the huge hall, the enormous boys, the frightening rowdiness of the corridors' and of rugby football, of which no one had explained the rules.[92] This time it may have been Amy's decision to take him away, when she heard Robert using what the family called 'naughty words', which he himself did not understand.

His parents' third choice, Rokeby, was a prep school of what Robert called 'the ordinary type'.[93] By 'ordinary type' he may simply have been referring to a school with the standard curriculum of Latin, Greek, English, Maths, French, History, Geography, Divinity, Art and Music, with extra-curricular activities such as cricket, rugby and possibly tennis, though he may have been contrasting Rokeby with the more prestigious King's College School. Whatever the explanation, Robert felt less of a failure at Rokeby and remained there, with a short break, from 1903 to 1906. It was situated not much further away from King's College School at 17 The Downs, just off the Ridgway.[94] Here he started to cope with life in an all-male school: he began 'playing games seriously, was quarrelsome, boastful and talkative ... and collected things'.[95] His character began to emerge: while the other boys collected stamps, he collected coins, his own explanation being that the value of coins seemed 'less fictitious' than that of stamps, but almost certainly from a need to be different. It also gave him a sense of history and an increased interest in the subject, as the *Claudius* novels and other writings would show.

Robert's intellectual ability also began to emerge at Rokeby and he started to win prizes, an early sign of the ease with which he would deal with academic work when he chose to do so. In addition, he claimed, it gave him his 'first training as a gentleman'.[96] Class assumptions start early and there is no doubt that his education in the private school system gave him great confidence in many areas later on. He may have been right to attribute his ability to pass as a 'gentleman' to his Graves ancestors, but his schooling was a strong contributory factor.

A third characteristic emerged when Robert received his only caning at Rokeby. Although a mild one – two strokes on the hand – he remembered almost a quarter of a century later being 'hot with fury', since his hands had a 'great importance' for him.[97] His explanation for this is curious and bears particularly on his poetry: 'my visual imagery is defective and I memorize largely by sense of touch'.[98]

Only two incidents frightened Robert during these years, both of them related to sex. His first sight of a naked body other than his own was at Penrallt, a boarding school in the Welsh countryside near Llanbedr, where he was sent for a term in 1904 to convalesce from measles and double pneumonia. (An unfortunate year for the family, it also witnessed Amy going to a Swiss hospital for a goitre operation, the death of her mother Luise, and the hospitalization of Clarissa with scarlet fever.) Although this was Robert's first extended stay away from the family, Penrallt was only three miles from Harlech in countryside he knew well. It was the sight of all the boys in the school bathing naked together in the open-air swimming pool that dismayed him. He was especially repulsed, but evidently also fascinated, by 'one boy there of nineteen with red hair, real bad, Irish red hair all over his body'.[99] He had not known until then that hair grew on bodies.

Even worse, in some respects, were the attempts by the headmaster's daughter and her friend, neither of whom had brothers, 'to find out about male anatomy' from him by exploring down his shirt-neck.[100]

Then when, aged about ten and back in London, he had to meet his sisters at their all-girls Wimbledon High School for a family visit to the photographer, he was acutely embarrassed by his wait for them, when what seemed like 'hundreds and hundreds' of girls passed him, all looking at him and giggling.[101] Even his sisters failed to comfort him when they eventually arrived, 'look[ing] ashamed of [him] and quite different from the girls [he] knew at home'.[102] For years afterwards the worst of his many nightmares were of this 'secret world' he had 'blundered into' and he claimed that it had set back his 'normal impulses' by years. Placed as this anecdote is in *Good-bye to All That* just before his account of his infatuation with 'Peter' Johnstone at Charterhouse, it seems like an attempt to explain what he afterwards regarded as an aberration:

> In English preparatory and public schools romance is necessarily homo-sexual. The opposite sex is despised and hated, treated as something obscene. Many boys never recover from this perversion. I only recovered by a shock at the age of twenty-one. For every one born homo-sexual there are at least ten permanent pseudo-homo-sexuals made by the public school system. And nine of these are as honourably chaste and sentimental as I was.[103]

There were also some positive experiences during the Rokeby years, if we include Penrallt in them. He made friends at the boarding school, for instance, one in particular called Ronny, whom he worshipped. A more lasting experience was his introduction to the poems 'Chevy Chace' and 'Sir Andrew Barton', which left him with an admiration for the ballad form. Beside composing ballads of his own, he would later write two books on the subject, the first with the help of his father, who also practised the form.[104]

Apart from this reference to poetry and an earlier one to his initial fear of Latin, Robert tells us little of what he learnt up to the age of ten; it seems not to have engaged him. Certainly his father was not satisfied by Rokeby's teaching. Since the birth of his sixth son, John, in 1903, it had become more important to him than ever that Robert should win a scholarship to a public school. So Robert was again moved, this time to a boarding school in the Midlands.

Alfred had chosen Hillbrow School at Rugby 'because the headmaster's wife was the sister of an old literary friend of his', an unwise choice as it turned out.[105] The friend in question was Charles Tindall Gatty, son of the children's writer Margaret Gatty and brother of another children's writer, Juliana Horatia Ewing (famous for *Jackanapes*), and of Horatia Eden (née Gatty), who had married the headmaster concerned, Thomas Bainbridge Eden. Horatia Gatty was 43 when she married, her husband ten years younger, and the balance of power was on her side. James Strachey, who had boarded at Hillbrow in the 1890s, remembered Mrs Eden as 'an embittered martinet who intimidated her husband and the form assistant masters quite as much as the boys',[106] though she did read Dickens to the pupils on Sunday evenings.

The school appeared on the surface to be an excellent choice. Hillbrow was a 'feeder' school for Rugby, which lay only a few hundred yards away. It was far more ambitious than Rokeby with much higher academic standards, and Robert would be put in for a scholarship to Winchester in his second year there. It was by no means the 'ordinary type' of prep school, as Robert labelled Rokeby, for this and other reasons. Although the other reasons never became entirely clear to him during his two years there, it was not just hindsight or word-play that made him describe Hillbrow as 'a queer place' which he 'did not like'.[107] Even in 1908 he realized that there was 'a secret about the headmaster which a few of the older boys shared', something 'sinister': 'All I knew was that he came weeping into the classroom one day beating his head with his fists and groaning: "Would to God I hadn't done it! Would to God I hadn't done it!"'[108]

At the time Mr Eden was said to be ill; later it emerged that he had been ordered to leave, some said by the police, some said by the headmaster of Rugby. The painter Duncan Grant, who had been at Hillbrow in the 1890s with James Strachey and Rupert Brooke, remembered 'Tommy' Eden, not unsympathetically, as a 'funny little man who was too fond of his boys' and how he enjoyed 'birching' the boys, humming with anticipation before doing so.[109] Grant recalled Eden birching him several times 'with pleasure' – whose, he does not say. But he also remembered that Eden liked to visit the little boys while they were having their baths: 'And ... he did do ... improper gestures towards those ... he was fond of.' One of these boys, a contemporary of Robert's, had reported this to his father, who happened to be a master at Rugby School. A 'frightful scandal' ensued and Eden fled, but Grant's intriguing footnote to the story suggests that some of the boys were fond of their headmaster: Rupert Brooke, who had left Hillbrow in 1901, discovering where Eden had gone, followed him to Liverpool and persuaded him to contact his wife and make a more dignified exit.

Fortunately for Robert, who had already suffered enough disruption to his schooling, the scandal broke at the end rather than in the middle of the summer term of 1908. He had already sat, and failed, the Winchester Scholarship examinations at Hillbrow and his parents were desperate to find him another school that could help him to win a scholarship. Amy, who had accompanied her son to Winchester for the exams, had the very practical idea of asking the headmaster, Montague Rendall, for advice. He recommended the prep school Copthorne, run by his brother Bernard and founded six years earlier as a 'feeder' school for Winchester. Although Bernard Rendall was reluctant to take a boy of thirteen, especially one coming from Hillbrow after Eden's disgrace, he eventually accepted Robert, almost certainly because of Alfred's position in the literary world.

If Robert is to be believed, he left Hillbrow with no regrets but with gratitude towards at least one teacher there, the assistant headmaster Mr J. A. Lush. It was Lush, he claimed (ironically, in view of his name), who taught him:

... how to write English by eliminating all phrases that could be done without, and using verbs and nouns instead of adjectives and adverbs wherever possible. And where to start new paragraphs, and the difference between O and Oh.[110]

Robert's spare prose suggests that he benefited from Lush's teaching. He also learnt a quite different skill at Hillbrow – namely rugby football, at which he would later excel.

Copthorne, Robert wrote, was a 'typically good school'. Although this was not written entirely without irony, since he came to believe that all schools were bad, he did respect Copthorne's outstanding academic achievements: it averaged four scholarships a year to top schools such as Eton, Winchester and Charterhouse. Just as importantly for him, he found it a happy place. Bernard Rendall and his wife were kind and caring, a couple he remembered with affection. The premises were less Spartan than Hillbrow and the surrounding countryside on the borders of Surrey and Sussex between Crawley and East Grinstead was attractive. The daily routine was also relatively relaxed in comparison. Although the boys were woken at 6.30 a.m., had to take a cold bath and attend chapel and early school before breakfast, there were breaks for games of all kinds, including backgammon, bezique and golf, played occasionally with the headmaster according to Charles Graves, who followed Robert there in 1909. Singing was also encouraged, Charles remembered; there was a school choir as well as school theatricals. Altogether he found Copthorne 'the greatest fun', though what he called Robert's 'perhaps unconscious personal aversion from popularity' made it difficult initially for him to get on well with the other boys.[111] Robert did make friends, however, and the 'depressed state' he had been in at Hillbrow 'ended the moment [he] arrived' at Copthorne.[112] His father, with his probable awareness of the unsettling aspect of six changes of school in as many years, was able to describe it as Robert's 'happiest school year' with great relief.[113] 'At this school,' Robert claimed, 'I learned to keep a straight bat at cricket and to have a high moral sense, and my fifth different pronunciation of Latin, and my fifth or sixth different way of doing simple arithmetic.'[114]

Despite Robert's disrupted education, he qualified for the highest form on arrival and in due course he won a top scholarship in classics, not to

Winchester but to Charterhouse. For when Alfred asked Rendall if he could 'guarantee' a scholarship to Winchester, Rendall replied, quite rightly, that no one could guarantee that. Afraid to take the risk, Robert's parents put him in for Charterhouse instead.[115] Although he took first place, Robert was left with a slight sense of inferiority and a need to explain:

> And why Charterhouse? Because of ἵστημι and ἵημι. Charterhouse was the only public school whose scholarship examinations did not contain a Greek grammar paper, and though I was good enough at Greek Unseen and Greek Composition, I could not conjugate ἵστημι and ἵημι conventionally. If it had not been for these two verbs I would almost certainly have gone to the very different atmosphere of Winchester.[116]

Robert's use of the word 'conventionally' rather than 'correctly' is curious, even defensive in this context, and seems to underline his sensitivity about this academic weakness. The most significant point to emerge from this saga, however, is Robert's intellectual ability, the fact that even after such irregular schooling he was able not only to catch up on his education but to excel at it. Alfred believed that Robert 'would have succeeded at Winchester', in spite of his shaky knowledge of Greek verbs.[117] Regretting that he was not at Winchester was an unfortunate beginning to Robert's life at Charterhouse.

3

CHARTERHOUSE: 'THE PUBLIC SCHOOL SPIRIT'[1] (1909–12)

'My history from the age of fourteen, when I went to Charterhouse, to just before the end of the war ... was a forced rejection of the German in me.'[2]

Graves devotes only six of the 448 pages of *Good-bye to All That* to his first seven years at six different schools, yet almost five times that amount to his five years at Charterhouse. His time there evidently appealed more to his imagination, or seemed worthier of recording. At one point he claimed that 'from the moment I arrived at the school I suffered from an oppression of spirit that I hesitate now to recall in its full intensity', comparing it to being in the chilly cellar of his grandfather's Bavarian house, 'among the potatoes, but being a potato out of a different bag from the rest'.[3] Yet there are other passages in *Good-bye* that record entirely positive experiences, such as having his poetry published in the school magazine, making his first close friend, falling in love, triumphing against all the odds at boxing, or being mentored by one of the greatest climbers of his time, George Mallory, who introduced him to the influential literary figure, the classical scholar and translator Edward Marsh.

It is conceivable that Robert remained deeply unhappy throughout all these experiences. But it is more likely that, in his desire to make a compelling story out of his life at school, he heightened some aspects of his time at Charterhouse and played down others, unhappiness being easier to dramatize than contentment. When planning to write a 'novel of public-school' life in 1916, he feared 'distorting my material with a plot'.[4]

In fact, a closer look at the Charterhouse years, as described not just in his autobiography but also in his letters and his father's diary, makes it clear that his feelings fluctuated a great deal during those five years. And in one sense his happiness or unhappiness at Charterhouse is less important than the formative effect it had on him, more than any other period of his pre-war life.

As Graves himself noted in his review of a book written by pupils at Charterhouse in the early 1960s, there were both advantages and disadvantages to the school selected for him by Bernard Rendall and his parents.[5] Founded in 1611 on the site of an old Carthusian Monastery in Charterhouse Square, London, it was moved to its present 68-acre site on a hill overlooking Godalming near Guildford in Surrey in 1872. While the young authors of the book Graves reviewed call this 'a touch of genius' because of the beauty of the surrounding Surrey countryside, Graves argued that 'the new Charterhouse would have been more happily built into some small market-town where, as at Eton or Oundle, the boys could walk from dormitory house to classroom along with pubs and bustle, inhabited by ordinary people of all classes and both sexes'.[6] For 'the less attractive aspects of school life', he claimed, were 'due to its monastic isolation from the lay world: the boys have to depend too much on one another's company and resources.'[7] Graves's use of the word 'monastic' here suggests that he was thinking of the aspect of school life that depressed him most, a topic of 'major importance', its sexual mores.[8] He counted himself particularly unlucky to have been placed in one of the school's oldest houses, Gownboys, though it was for scholars only and considered itself superior to the other ten houses in 1909. He was for once in agreement with his brother Charles, who described it four years later as the 'reigning cess-pit of Charterhouse'.[9] Although unlike Charles he did not describe attempts to assault him sexually, he did detail, with some disgust, what was known as 'tarting', in which 'boys of the same age, who were not in love' nevertheless used each other coldly as 'convenient sex-instruments'.[10] For someone who described himself as still 'prudishly innocent of sex' by the age of fourteen, this aspect of school life came as a great shock. Later, when he fell in love with a younger boy at the school, he would distinguish between 'amorousness ... a sentimental falling in love with younger boys' and 'eroticism, which was adolescent lust'.[11] Another, related, problem for Robert on his arrival at Charterhouse in September 1909 was a weak headmaster, Dr Gerald Rendall. Frank Fletcher, who was brought in to replace Rendall as headmaster in September 1911 at the beginning of Robert's third year, was told that the 'tone and discipline' of the school needed urgent attention, by which its *moral* tone was clearly implied.[12] While describing Rendall as an 'able' scholar with 'a kindly attitude to life', he leaves his reader in no doubt that a firmer hand was needed to control 600 or so adolescent boys.[13] So while Rendall reigned for the first two years of Robert's time at Charterhouse, the 'tarting' as well as bullying continued unchecked.

One of Robert's greatest problems in 1909, however, was that he was arriving as the top scholar of the year at a school where, according to him, 'school-work was despised'.[14] Unless scholars were also outstanding at games and ready to declare that they hated school work, they were ostracized. Since Robert actually enjoyed Latin – as did a previous pupil he got to know, Max Beerbohm – and was not yet good at games, he was made to suffer. For the school was ruled by the leading sportsmen, the 'bloods'. When Fletcher arrived,[15] he could see that the reign of the 'bloods' was 'bad for the intellectual boys, who either accepted their position of inferiority or asserted themselves by eccentricities and ill-timed violations of recognized conventions'.[16] He saw this tendency coming to a head in Robert's generation at the school, that is 'the generation before the war'.[17] Scholars were also largely despised because some of them came from less wealthy families than the rest of the school. Although Robert's parents were not poor, they continued as they had always done to give him very little pocket money, partly on principle, partly because Alfred now had ten children to think of. As a result, Robert was unable to join in the custom of 'treating' fellow pupils at the school tuck shop. And his clothes, though conforming to the uniform of narrow dark-grey trousers, black jacket, Eton collar and, for the first two years, small house cap, were the most economical his thrifty mother could find, ready-made and of inferior quality. In any case, as Robert observed, neither of his parents had any regard for the 'niceties of modern dress'[18] All new boys ('new bugs') were treated to ritual humiliation with a rigged initiation exam, described by Robert in a maverick school magazine he would help to publish in his next to last year at Charterhouse.[19] But for his first term at least he was 'left alone more or less'.[20] It was in the second term of Spring 1910 that trouble began. He was still ignorant not only of sex, but also of what he called 'bawdy talk', and his shocked reaction to what another pupil remembered as 'foul' language added to the impression of priggishness.[21] In addition, he was ready to talk too much, according to him. Two of the topics that another fellow pupil, H. L. Gandell, remembered him 'rubbing in' were the aristocratic 'von' of his middle name and the fact that his father was the author of 'Father O'Flynn',[22] neither of which endeared him to his contemporaries apparently. Gandell also points out another crucial factor in Robert's treatment at Charterhouse, that he was 'an individualist and as such strongly suspect at a Public School, where his interests and pursuits tended to keep him rather apart'.[23]

Graves claimed that he was unaware of the 'von' in his name until it appeared on the Charterhouse School List, although this is hard to believe. Either way, the unfortunate fact was that 'von Ranke' appeared there quite clearly. Boys from what Graves called 'the business class' (about which he was snobbishly dismissive) were already aware of their fathers' strong sense of threat from Germany's astonishing industrial and commercial growth by 1909, a fear that was fostered by an increasing focus on it in the British press and elsewhere. There was also apprehension over Germany's territorial ambitions and her growing military strength, which the Franco-Russian Alliance of 1894, the Anglo-French Pact of 1904 and the Anglo-Russian Entente of 1907 had underlined. A best-selling novel by William Le Queux in 1906 – *The Invasion of 1910* – encouraged a growing paranoia, mass hysteria and Germanophobia among the British public. Fears of German naval supremacy came to a head in 1909, the year Robert entered Charterhouse, when Germany responded to Britain's production of the fearsome Dreadnought destroyers with seven of their own. German was beginning to mean 'dirty German' by this point, according to Graves; there was also 'considerable anti-Jewish feeling'.[24] So that to be labelled 'a German Jew', as he was, made life very unpleasant indeed. His attempt to hide behind his Irish ancestry was sabotaged by an older Irish boy in his house, and he claimed to have come close to a nervous breakdown in 1910.

By March 1911 Robert was so unhappy at school that he wrote to his parents, begging to be taken away, telling them that 'the house was making it plain that I did not belong and that it did not want me'.[25] Unaware of the full extent of his problems – their son had not dared to mention what he called 'the sexual irregularities in the house, so bad at one point that the top of each boy's cubicle was wired with an alarm to ward off predators'[26] – Alfred and Amy 'contented themselves with visiting [him] and giving [him] assurances of the power of prayer and faith'.[27] They were in any case coming to Charterhouse for Robert's confirmation on 28 March 1911. Their son, who was still very religious, had prepared devoutly for this event, but was unable to take any comfort from their advice. Worse still, his parents believed it was their 'religious duty' to report his complaints, made to them in confidence, to his housemaster 'Gosh' Parry, 'an excitable elderly man', Graves recalled, who had taken over Gownboys in September 1910 from J. E. Judson.[28] Parry merely made a speech to the house that night on the evils of bullying, at the same time making it clear how much he disliked 'informers' and outside interference. Since Mr and Mrs Graves's non-holiday visit and lunch with Parry had been duly noted, it was quite clear who the 'informer' was and Robert's situation became even more unbearable. By now in the Upper School – most scholars started halfway up the system in the Remove – he had a study of his own, but without a lock: 'It was always being wrecked.'[29] He could not even use the ordinary house changing room for games. Whether his 'heart went wrong' as a result, for physical or psychological reasons, is impossible to say, but he was forbidden to play football for a time. His most extreme measure was to 'sham insanity', which succeeded unexpectedly well, especially after his first poem appeared in the school magazine, *The Carthusian*: 'This was considered stronger proof of insanity than the formal straws I wore in my hair.'[30]

Robert's first poem, he believed, was the result of being thrown entirely on his own resources and was quite different from what he called 'the easy showing-off witty stuff' he had written with Rosaleen and Clarissa, 'the kind that all the Graves' write'. He was thinking of his father in particular and it may have been partly in reaction to his father, whom he felt had let him down, that he wrote 'The Mountain Side at Evening', which he described as 'poetry dissatisfied with itself'.[31] Yet his poem suggests that he had been influenced by his father, especially by Alfred's love of the Romantic poets, Wordsworth and Coleridge, whose *Prelude* and *Ancient Mariner* respectively lie behind its supernatural element. Its setting, too, is Romantic, though based firmly in Wales, where Robert had spent the previous Easter holiday of 1911:

The Mountain Side at Evening
      Now even falls
   And fresh, cold breezes blow
   Adown the grey-green mountain side
   Strewn with rough boulders. Soft and low
   Night speaks, her tongue untied
   Darkness to Darkness calls.

      'Tis now men say
   From rugged piles of stones
   Steal Shapes and Things that should be still;
   Green terror ripples through our bones,
   Our inmost heart-strings thrill
   And yearn for careless day.

Despite its archaisms and derivativeness, there are touches of originality in the poem ('... her tongue untied / Darkness to Darkness calls') and an ambitious stanza form of increasing and diminishing line lengths in this first attempt at serious poetry. There is also a hint here in 'Green terror ripples through our bones' of Robert's own fears and sense of persecution at this time. Although he was unable to prevent the bullying, he found relief from it in poetry, which became from now on his 'ruling passion'.[32]

So he was delighted to be invited to join the recently formed Poetry Society on the strength of 'The Mountain Side at Evening'. Run by Guy Kendall, who was still in his early thirties by 1911 and married with a young family, the Society, like Kendall, was a breath of fresh air in a school that had its fair share of what Graves called 'old fossils', some of whom had been at Charterhouse since its move to Surrey in 1872. Kendall was one of the few masters, Graves wrote, 'who insisted on treating the boys better than they were'.[33] A poet himself, he had gathered around him a small group of poetry enthusiasts, one of them only a few months older than Robert called Raymond Rodakowski.[34] Graves believed he owed 'a great debt of gratitude to Kendall', since the meetings of the Poetry Society were 'all that [he] had to look forward to when things were at their worst' for him.[35]

None of the other members was from Robert's house, a most unusual situation at a school where no friendship was allowed between boys from different houses or of different ages. So the close friendship that developed between Robert and Raymond Rodakowski was 'most unconventional', according to Graves, a situation which evidently appealed to his growing maverick tendencies.[36] George Mallory, who had started as an assistant master at Charterhouse in September 1910, thought Raymond 'a wonderfully innocent creature'; no boy had ever 'quite come up to him for unconscious natural enjoyment'.[37] He also found Raymond 'extraordinarily kind and thoughtful'.[38] The son of a Polish father and Scottish mother, both from the aristocracy, Raymond sympathized deeply with Robert over the bullying, having suffered himself due to his foreign name. And when Robert told him of a recent raid on his study and the theft of one of his 'more personal poems', Raymond advised him to take up boxing, as he had done, and defend himself: 'You know these cricketers and footballers are all afraid of boxers, almost superstitious,' he told Robert. 'They won't box themselves for fear of losing their good looks...'[39]

So although the Poetry Society was disbanded when two of its members were discovered sending coded love poems to younger boys, Robert's friendship with Raymond continued, stronger than ever. They were now able to meet in the boxing-room, over the school tuck shop, where Robert began training 'seriously and savagely and developed physically'.[40] As his father noted in his diary when his son came home on 21 June 1911, for the coronation of George V, 'Robby ... is much grown ... now'.[41] He was not far short of his eventual height of 6 feet 2 inches.

Another factor that helped Robert combat the bullying in the Summer term (or 'Cricket Quarter' as it was known) of 1911 was his improvement at cricket. When he was chosen to play for 'The Etceteras', a new league formed from third and fourth house-club games, his father noted his score of '44 not out' with some complacency, having been an excellent sportsman himself.

Robert was now at the end of his second of five years at Charterhouse when, as a scholar, he was obliged to sit for a renewal of his scholarship. The school was divided along the lines adopted by most public schools of the time into the 'Classic' and 'Modern' sides. Robert's work on the Classical side, which included English, History and Divinity, involved Greek and Latin translations, unseens and prose, and took up the greater part of his time. This work had continued to be satisfactory, his verse translations particularly so. But his mathematics, which occupied less than a quarter of his syllabus, worried his father, who organized extra tuition for him in the subject.

Since French and Science occupied only a few hours weekly, Alfred was less anxious about his son's progress in them, though he would arrange a stay in Belgium during Christmas 1912 to help improve his family's French.

In the event, Robert took fourth place in the Senior Scholarship exam, ensuring him £95 a year until he left school. It removed one more worry from him as well as from his father, who was relieved to report that 'Robby [is] reconciled to staying on at the school.'[42] It was a turning point in his fortunes. He had 'pulled [him]self together', as Raymond had advised, and would find his third year at Charterhouse 'very much easier'.[43] His claim to have 'no friends' among his own age group is contradicted by his relationship with Rodakowski, who by autumn 1911 had persuaded him to join the Debating Society. Although Graves wrote retrospectively that his feeling for Raymond was 'more comradely than amorous,'[44] he also described a boxing-match with him which suggests otherwise:

> There is a lot of sex-feeling in boxing – the dual play, the reciprocity, the pain not felt as pain. This exhibition match to me had something of quality that Dr Marie Stopes would call sacramental. We were out neither to hurt nor win though we hit each other hard.[45]

The boxing-match with Raymond had helped Robert's position in the house, as had his improvement in football once the doctor allowed him to play again in 1911. But the most dramatic change in his life at Charterhouse was the arrival of Frank Fletcher to replace Dr Rendall in September 1911. From the moment 'Fifi', as he was nicknamed, 'turned a cold approving eye on us', one of Robert's contemporaries recalled, the 'old order' changed.[46]

Fletcher, who had transformed Marlborough College during his eight-year headmastership, had left it at the age of 41 with great reluctance, and only after the Archbishop of Canterbury had told him it was a 'call of duty'.[47] Since he believed that Rendall's lack of discipline had had a particularly damaging effect on the 'pre-war generation', Fletcher could have been thinking specifically of Robert when he wrote:

> They were a warped generation, whose outlook on life was distorted by their experiences during their first two years at school. These had left some of the best of them morbid or cynical, and turned others into intellectual rebels, with an exaggerated idea of their own intelligence and a prejudice against a society which seemed to have given them inadequate recognition.[48]

Fletcher's understanding of this problem might explain why on a number of occasions he showed unusual tolerance towards Robert, who was not an easy pupil. ('Not humble' was Fletcher's restrained reaction on one occasion.)[49] Visiting Fletcher afterwards, Robert would apologize, for, as he told Charles in 1917, Fletcher was always 'very kind when it's an honest case'.[50] Strict disciplinarian though he was, Fletcher recognized 'that there is nothing about which boys are more sensitive than justice. Severity they will accept … injustice they will long remember and resent.'[51] This mixture of firmness and understanding convinced Robert from the start that Fletcher would 'keep the school in good order'.[52] With 'several undesirables "bunked"', or expelled, and the headmaster firmly in control, life became even more tolerable.[53] The news that some of his collaborative verses with Rosaleen and Clarissa in *The Bobbety Ballads* had been accepted for publication, and that his attempt at the difficult 'englyn' metre was to be published in his father's *Welsh Poetry Old and New* in the summer of 1912, added to Robert's confidence and to his growing belief in himself as a poet. His happiness showed itself in more 'affectionate' behaviour towards his parents, though his father feared that he was still 'too absorbed in himself'.[54] But his friendship with Raymond was beginning to open him up to a world beyond his own. And by the end of summer 1912 he was ready to make a new friendship with someone who would influence him even more than Raymond, George Mallory.

It was almost certainly Raymond who was responsible for the introduction. Mallory, a Cambridge History graduate, taught History, French, Maths and Latin on the Modern Side, not the Classical Side, at the start. But he went on to establish a Dramatic Society, give lectures on Renaissance art and take part in school debates (usually on the radical, unpopular side), all activities that appealed to Rodakowski. By 27 September 1911 Mallory was already including Rodakowski in a group of 'the more interesting ... young men' he was hoping 'to see more of', writing to his friend Lytton Strachey: 'I wish they were more beautiful – but my charming Pole [i.e. Rodakowski] wrote me a letter of 28 pages in the holidays, so I suppose I mustn't grumble.'[55]

Like Kendall, Mallory was younger and more innovative in his approach to teaching than the average teacher Robert encountered at Charterhouse, so young-looking at 26 that he was often mistaken for one of his pupils. His more informed, less punitive approach went with a more expansive view of the curriculum. He encouraged his students to read round the subject and to study the art as well as the literature of the period concerned, as well as the politics, for instance. Fletcher had worked slowly but surely to make changes and it took him a year to introduce a revised curriculum. When he did so, it was one to please Robert, since it laid greater influence on English literature and brought him into contact with Mallory as a teacher.

What Robert appreciated most about Mallory's teaching was that 'from the first', he treated him 'as an equal'.[56] He remembered spending his spare time reading books in his room, in the house Mallory shared with a few other unmarried masters. It was a room, in the words of one visitor, 'littered with books and papers – books in French and English, modern plays which were being examined with a view to readings with his brighter spirits, Fabian tracts. Reproductions of Greek sculpture or modern French paintings – all more or less drowned in a sea of essays from his form.'[57] Mallory's approach to knowledge was far wider, more stimulating than Robert had yet experienced, one that would help him to respond to modern movements in the arts with far less suspicion than his parents and that would influence his poetry. Mallory introduced him to modern authors he had never heard of – 'my father being two generations older than myself and my only link with books'[58] – Samuel Butler, George Bernard Shaw, H. G. Wells, James Elroy Flecker, John Masefield and Mallory's Cambridge friend, Rupert Brooke.

Butler's *The Way of All Flesh* and *Erewhon* were particularly appealing to Graves, who was beginning to share his disillusioned views on family relationships. To be taught in a classroom hung with paintings by another of Mallory's friends, Duncan Grant, at a time when the art Establishment was reacting violently against Roger Fry's 1912 Post-Impressionist Exhibition in which Grant's work appeared, was a challenging experience. Robert responded positively to what was a daring approach to education at the time, but not everyone appreciated it. According to John Graves, who followed his brother Robert to Charterhouse seven or eight years later: 'Like Guy Kendall, Mallory was considered an amiable ass, partly because he took no special interest in school sports, ... partly because he tried to humanise the Modern Side. Most of the boys resented his attempts at friendliness and only a few joined the Dramatic Society.'[59] Robert remembered the 'ragging' Mallory received but believed that he was 'always doomed to be ragged because he's too good for the set of greasy North-of-England and City-of-London profiteers' sons who swell the Modern Side ... who hate a gentleman and a man of enthusiasm because they can never understand him'.[60] Robert's snobbish dismissal of the Modern Side may have been a defensive reaction against his own family's lack of wealth, but it was also generated by a very real admiration for Mallory, 'the only friend to a succession of Carthusian Ugly Ducklings, who but for him, would have gone under altogether'.[61] Graves included himself in the 'Ugly Ducklings' rescued by Mallory whom he would still describe four years after leaving Charterhouse as 'next to my sister [Rosaleen] my oldest surviving friend'.[62]

John Graves had likened Mallory to Guy Kendall, but Mallory differed from him in one significant respect by 1912: he was unmarried and appeared ambivalent about his sexuality. He had known several members of the sexually liberated Bloomsbury Group at Cambridge, including Lytton Strachey, Maynard Keynes, Rupert Brooke, Duncan Grant – and James Strachey, with whom Mallory fell in love. Although James rejected his advances, his brother Lytton was strongly attracted to him, writing to Clive and Vanessa Bell in 1909, the year before Mallory arrived at Charterhouse:

> Mon dieu! – George Mallory! – When that's been written what more need be said? My hand trembles, my heart palpates, my whole being

swoons away at the words – oh heavens! heavens! ... he's six foot high, with the body of an athlete by Praxiteles, and a face – oh incredible – the mystery of Botticelli, the refinement and delicacy of a Chinese print, the youth and piquancy of an unimaginable English boy.[63]

Lytton visited Mallory several times at Charterhouse, though he failed to persuade him to become his lover. Duncan Grant, who also visited, might have been more successful but was already involved elsewhere. The painter in him, however, was deeply attracted to George's combination of physical beauty and strength, and he executed a number of nude portraits and took several photographs of what Lytton described passionately as Mallory's 'vast, pale, unbelievable body... a thing to melt into and die'.[64]

George Mallory's impressive physique came from years of mountaineering, which he had taken up at Winchester under the Alpinist, R. G. L. Irving. When he moved to Charterhouse, Mallory, like Irving, took some of his senior pupils to climb with him and Robert believed Mallory 'did something better than lend me books' when he invited him to climb with him in Snowdonia during the Easter holidays of 1913.[65] Robert had been practising overcoming his fear of heights on the rock face backing Erinfa and more precarious climbs in the ruins of Harlech Castle and was thrilled to be marked out by Mallory in this way. He was greatly attracted to the idea of being 'alone with a specially chosen band of people – people that one can trust completely'.[66] He was also beginning to enjoy taking risks, as several mad escapades on a family skiing holiday in 1914 would show. Mountaineering, he declared in his perverse way, was 'reasonably safe'.[67] It was an ironic statement in view of the fact that four of Mallory's closest friends had died in climbing accidents not long before Robert's first trip to Snowdonia and that Mallory himself would die in attempting – possibly succeeding in conquering – Everest in 1924. Robert himself would have an accident when climbing Snowdon in 1913, he claimed in his 1969 interview for the *Paris Review*, in which he 'broke [his] neck' when a rock fell on him. But as his poem 'Broken Neck' explained, this was a slightly less dramatic fracture of his sixth vertical vertebra that went unnoticed at the time though it resulted in rheumatism later on.[68] It did not prevent him from relishing his holiday with Mallory at the Snowdon Ranger Hotel, not all of which was spent climbing:

I never remember enjoying myself so much as at Quellyn [he wrote to Mallory in April 1913]. It was an experience to me in dozens of ways. I fear Hugh and I went rather too far in our festivity,[69] for which apologies. But you will have the whiphand of him next quarter, and I will be wonderfully humble and dutiful. The rafters of this house have been continually ringing to the strains of the enthusiastically adapted 'Green grow the rushes, O!' and the mournful history of the venerable and lamented episcopal personage who recollected that it was the Sabbath.[70]

A longer climbing trip of ten days with Mallory at Easter 1914 would bring Robert even closer to the master he now called 'George', and when he left school three months later the friendship would continue. Mallory made no secret of his attraction towards younger men when Robert first met him, yet there is no suggestion of any sexual advances toward them, or any proof that he had ever been a practising homosexual. His own analysis of his position to Lytton, after he had met and proposed to a young woman, Ruth Turner, in May 1914, was that he had been more of a 'fashionable homosexualist', though he did add: 'And I am still in part of that persuasion.'[71]

4

CHARTERHOUSE: OF CHERRY-WHISKY AND OTHER MATTERS (1912–14)

> O Holy Charterhouse, once alternately loved and loathed, and
> now only loved, and the whole tribe of Carthusians! Noble
> pagans these for the most part, whose heathen virtues on
> reconsideration seem always to have outweighed their more
> civilised vices. But there was and will always be a little rebellious
> section of classical scholars whose idealism is as laudable as their
> lack of prudence is regrettable.[1]

Robert's friendship with Mallory was only one factor that made his fourth year at Charterhouse a happy one. He had moved into the Classical Upper Sixth and his seniority now afforded him some protection from bullying. He was writing prolifically, prose as well as poetry, and had the satisfaction of seeing his short story, 'Why Jigsaws Went Out of Fashion', written jointly with Rosaleen, published in the Christmas number of the *Westminster Gazette*. Another prose piece, 'Ragtime', was accepted by *The Carthusian*'s sister magazine, *Greyfriars*.[2] While continuing to experiment with the difficult Welsh 'englyn' metre to which his father had introduced him, he was also producing numerous poems of his own. All of them reveal a similar metrical precision to the 'englyn', one result he believed of his intensive study of Greek and Latin metres, as well as his father's insistence on its importance. One of the most successful of these early poems, 'Jolly Yellow Moon', written in 1911 as a reminiscence of the Charterhouse Choir, records in swinging rhythms his continuing pleasure in song:

... And step we slowly, friend with friend,
    Let arm with arm entwine,
And voice with voice together blend,
    For the jolly yellow moon doth shine.

Whether we loudly sing or soft,
    The tune goes wondrous fine;
Our chorus sure will float aloft
    Where the jolly yellow moon doth shine.[3]

Singing in the choir made Robert particularly happy at Charterhouse in 1913, and especially with the arrival of a new member, George Harcourt Vanden-Bempde-Johnstone. A 'strikingly handsome' boy, according to John Graves, with dark hair and pale skin,[4] he was also academically brilliant and, like Robert, the top scholar of his year. Like Robert, too, he loved poetry, in particular Baudelaire, Verlaine and Mallarmé. He also wrote his own and would go on to win the Newdigate Prize for Poetry at Oxford.[5] Known as 'Peter' to his friends, Johnstone entered Saunders (Frank Fletcher's) house in January 1913, two terms before Charles Graves joined his brother in Gownboys. Like Charles, 'Peter' was more than four years younger than Robert, a significant age gap reduced in *Good-bye to All That* to three years by Graves, who conceals Johnstone's identity further by calling him 'Dick'. His ostensible reason – that Johnstone's first name, George, was the same as another character in *Good-bye*, George Mallory – is unconvincing, since the younger boy was known as 'Peter' and there was no one else called Peter in the story at this point. Graves's true motive is clearly to hide Johnstone's identity. He claims to have been 'unconscious of sexual feeling' for the boy, to have been attracted to him by his intelligence and 'fine spirits', and that the conversations he had with him were 'always impersonal'.[6]

    Yet their acquaintance was immediately 'commented on' and a warning issued to Robert by one of the masters to end it.[7] Despite his protest that 'this boy was interested in the same things as [him]self, particularly in books; that the disparity in age was unfortunate, but that a lack of intelligence among the boys of [his] own age made it necessary for [him] to find friends where [he] could', Robert was sent to the headmaster. Whether he then actually 'lectured' Fletcher on 'the advantage of friendship between elder and younger boys, citing Plato, the Greek poets, Shakespeare, Michael Angelo and others', as he claimed, cannot be verified, but Fletcher seems to have been convinced that the relationship was acceptable and took no action. He may also have been influenced by the fact that Johnstone was a member of his house, stayed with him and his wife in the holidays sometimes, and was second in line to become Baron Derwent when his uncle, the second Baron, died.[8] It is an early example of Graves in lecturing mode, of his firm belief in the rightness of his position and his fearlessness, at times recklessness, in the face of opposition. And he, too, was almost certainly influenced by Johnstone's aristocratic background, sharing as he did Johnstone's professed distaste 'for the sons of chemists and Indian Civil Servants, Trinidad sugar-merchants and country-doctors' with whom he was 'obliged to rub shoulders'.[9]

Charles Graves, who also joined the school choir, remembered Johnstone having 'the voice of an angel', a clear, pure treble frequently chosen for solos, though according to Charles, 'the combination of pretty boys and pretty voices was unconsciously effective' – 'most of the school-tarts ... were in the choir'.[10] Robert would have been horrified at any attempt to link pretty choirboys with angelic voices to 'school-tarts', but he was now in his eighteenth year and puberty was making itself felt, rather later than usual. He had developed late physically in some respects, but his father now regularly noted an increase in height and in February 1913 observed that Robert had started to shave. But he was still frightened of girls in a sexual context, as Charles remarked when 'a very pretty' 15-year-old girl had made advances to Robert during the family holiday in Brussels, two months earlier.[11] Boys seemed less threatening and he could allow himself to 'love' one without having to face what he called at 18 'the problems, doubts and suspicions' of sex.[12]

There is little doubt, however, that Robert was physically as well as intellectually attracted to Johnstone. In a letter written in May 1914 to the sexual pioneer of 'same-sex' relationships, Edward Carpenter, about his own homosexual feelings, Robert refers to a homosexual poet he has been reading, Richard Middleton, who 'died without understanding the matter, ashamed of it: when he wants to confess his love for a boy in a poem he puts the words into the mouth of a childless woman or a girl.'[13] Confessing that he too has often used these 'old evasions',[14] Graves then quotes a passage from Middleton's 'Hylas', almost certainly with 'Peter' in mind:

> Ah, dear boy with the lovely head
> And silver body of snow
> Laugh out again for the gods are dead
> And the dead gods homeward go.
> Ah dear boy with the red lips
> And the breast as soft as a girl
> Young love has brought a thousand ships
> And the stars are all a-whirl.[15]

While there is no suggestion in his letter to Carpenter that Robert felt apologetic about his attraction to another boy, he is more than ready to condemn any *physical* expression of this, feeling it a 'beastliness'. The only 'pure' expression of his love, he implies, is through poetry and in 1913 and 1914 poetry poured out of him. But the nine poems that have been preserved in the pages of *The Carthusian* in 1913 are not love poetry, evasive or otherwise.[16]

***

These verses read for the most part like literary exercises, including a competent handling of the ballad form in 'The Ballad of the White Monster', the rondeau in 'Rondeau: The Clouds', and the extended metaphor in 'The Cyclone', in which the 'baby' wind, tapping, shaking, rapping, 'drumming / With tiny white fingers' of the opening lines has become the 'pagan-hearted, wild unconscionable' boy of the full-blown storm by the end.

There are a few more personal touches, as well as a reminder of how steeped Graves was in classical metre in 'Alcaics addressed to my Study Fauna', which lists in slightly whimsical fashion the ornamental animals he keeps in his study. And 'Love and Black Magic' reveals a growing interest in legend and the supernatural, as a 'young maiden' sits alone in a wizard's grotto:

> ... 'Oh, here have I ever lain forlorn:
> My father died ere I was born,

Mother was by a wizard wed,
And oft I wish I had died instead –
Often I wish I were long time dead.
But, delving deep in my master's lore,
I have won of magic power such store
I can turn a skull – oh, fiddlededee
For all this curious craft!' quo'she.
'A soldier is the lad for me;
Hey and hither, my lad!'[17]

This was one of only two of the nine poems Graves chose to preserve in his later collections;[18] 'Jolly Yellow Moon' was the other.

Graves states plainly in the revised, 1957 edition of *Good-bye to All That* that he 'fell in love with Dick'.[19] But he was unable to express this clearly in his poetry at the time; he would have to wait until the war to do so in two poems in particular, '1915' and 'The Fusilier'.[20] In 1913 he was obliged to channel his feelings into less revealing poetry, which nevertheless became an invaluable part of his apprenticeship as a poet. But Johnstone still seemed to him the most important person in his life, which may help to explain his split with Rodakowski the same year.

The main reason for the break, according to Graves, however, was that Rodakowski was 'a complete and ruthless atheist', while he still put his 'religion and ... chances of salvation before human love'.[21] Robert had promised his anxious father to 'put more back into his work' in June 1913' and try to get a Leaving Exhibition from Charterhouse as well as a scholarship to Oxford: 'Rodakowski to be asked to Harlech to read with him' in the summer holidays, Alfred reported.[22] But Rodakowski never materialized; it may have been the thought of his parents' reaction to Rodakowski's unyieldingly atheistic views that caused their son to end the relationship. Although Robert quickly relented and sought a 'broad-church compromise', Rodakowski stood firm and Robert's one close friendship at the school ended.[23] It may be that Robert was repressing feelings of physical attraction towards his friend out of religious guilt, rather than being genuinely upset by his atheism.

Another part of Alfred's plan that summer also failed; he and Robert had agreed that 'Literature [should] be dropped awhile' to allow his son to focus on exams, though 'a literary career [was] to be ultimately adopted after

Oxford training'.[24] Alfred had good reason for his concerns. 'Literature' was occupying a good deal of Robert's time that summer as he helped Mallory to prepare a rival magazine to *The Carthusian*, to be called, in a witty acknowledgement of the school's monkish links but also a warning of its subversive intentions, *Green Chartreuse*. Its cover alone, designed by Mallory's irreverent Bloomsbury friend, Duncan Grant – a jolly monk raising a glass of the liqueur – emphasized its rather risqué nature. So too did its definition of 'Liberal Education' (unsigned, but identified by Graves as Mallory's work) as 'the principle of freedom violated by the enforced pursuit of learning and idea of education ridiculed by compulsory athletics'.[25] The whole tone of the magazine is jokey, but with the serious intention behind it of highlighting the absurdities of certain aspects of Charterhouse. Robert's annotated copy shows that he was responsible for six of its fifteen pages with contributions in prose and verse, only slightly outdone by Mallory's seven and a half pages. A poem by Rodakowski, a letter from Cyril Masson, and two pages by another friend of Robert's in the senior part of the school, Cyril Hartmann, made up the rest. Robert was sub-editor to Mallory's editor and the magazine is one more proof of Mallory's encouragement of Robert's latent rebellion by July 1913, when it was published.

Although *Green Chartreuse,* which sold out on publication, was never published as a second issue, Robert quickly found other outlets for his growing anti-Establishment views, all of them distracting him from his scholarship work despite his promise to his father. Most of these distractions came in the form of poetry. His commitment to it was encouraged in the autumn of 1913 by Edward Marsh, to whom he was introduced by Mallory at Charterhouse as 'a senior boy of literary promise'. Mallory also made sure that Marsh had copies of Robert's poems from *The Carthusian*. With the first number of his *Georgian Poetry* anthology '(1911–1912)' already published and the second, '(1913–1915)' in preparation, Marsh had established himself as a leading literary figure, as well as a distinguished civil servant and Private Secretary to Winston Churchill. A generous patron of the arts, he was keen to help young poets as well as painters and had responded positively to suggestions, Mallory's among them, of a Georgian poetry anthology. Accepting the arduous role of editor, he had arranged with Harold Monro to publish it. The first volume had proved enormously popular and four more would follow. What had started light-heartedly with

Marsh, Mallory, Duncan Grant, Rupert Brooke and others as the idea of a book of parodies on the small poetry books of the period was to become one of its defining publications. Graves would eventually be represented generously in three of the five collections. But he would have to accept some fairly severe criticism from Marsh about his old-fashioned technique that clashed with the Georgian ideals of a less elaborate, more down-to-earth language and subject matter than their Victorian and Edwardian predecessors. When Marsh revisited Charterhouse at the end of June 1914 to give a 'dramatic reading', he was more encouraging, telling Graves 'that his contributions to *The Carthusian* ... showed high promise of a future Georgian'.[26]

Graves would blame his father, fairly predictably, for any shortcomings in his poetry (while at the same time denying that his father influenced him at all as a poet). His father, in turn, would attribute his son's disappointing scholarship results to his obsession with poetry. By 10 December 1913 he knew that Robert had failed to win either a scholarship or an Exhibition to the highest group of Oxford colleges, in an unfortunate contrast with Alfred's brother Charles's son, Adrian, who was awarded a History Scholarship to Balliol. And when Robert heard eventually of an offer from St John's College, it was for a £40 to £60 Exhibition rather than a more prestigious and better-funded Scholarship. In a family of such high achievers, it felt like failure. It also had financial implications for Alfred, and Robert again promised to work hard for a leaving Exhibition from school.

Despite this 'satisfactory talk' with Robert about his work on 22 January 1914, however, by 28 February his father was forced to agree with Sir David Barbour, father of the then editor of *The Carthusian*, Nevill Barbour, who had persuaded Robert to be his assistant editor of the magazine:

> Sir [David] acknowledged N[evill] to be 'flighty' and will write to Fletcher about his jeopardising his chances of a [leaving] exhibition by too much 'Carthusian' and music, into the first of which he has drawn Robby...[27]

Robert had arrived at Copthorne School as Nevill left for Charterhouse and there is no mention of him in *Good-bye to All That* until their last year in the Senior School, when Barbour became Head of School, editor of *The*

Carthusian and President of the Debating Society. By autumn 1913 Robert was one of the few boys to support Barbour and Rodakowski in opposing the motion:

> That this House, profoundly convinced that the safety of the country and physical and moral well-being of the people demand the adoption of National Training, calls upon His Majesty's Government to complete the scheme of personal service in that force.

Robert's compulsory fortnight at the school's Officers' Training Corps (OTC) camp at Tidworth on Salisbury Plain in July 1913, where he had heard 'that war against Germany was inevitable within two or three years', had dismayed him.[28] It had not, however, changed his pacifist position, which he spelled out again in the debate and which Barbour, as editor, was able to report in *The Carthusian*:

> R. von R. Graves protested against wasting educated men on war, when they could be of far greater value in other lines. He deprecated the pseudo-patriotism of the National Service League, and questioned the advantages that would accrue if their programme were carried out. Finally he asked the House not to be biased in voting by politeness to Mr. Werner [the proposer of the motion] or admiration of Lord Roberts [President of the League and a Boer War hero].[29]

Although the motion had triumphed with 104 in favour to only 15 against, the debate had brought Nevill and Robert into contact and the invitation to become assistant editor of *The Carthusian* had followed. When Robert took up his position in January 1914, his influence (and behind him, Mallory's) was immediately felt. From defending the Public School system against the criticism of Dr Cecil Reddie, head of the progressive school Abbotsholme, in December 1913, *The Carthusian*, or rather its editors, now joined in the attack, accusing Charterhouse of being 'very much cut up into little separate compartments' that created artificial barriers between the boys.[30] With his experience on the *Green Chartreuse* not far behind him, it is more than likely that Robert was as firmly behind these remarks as Nevill, both of them in rebellious mood and wanting to shock, which they did. Another revolutionary suggestion from the editors, which no longer shocks today, but which created such an uproar at the time that it was reported in the *London Evening News*, was that lawn tennis (hardly recognized as a sport at the school) was a 'manlier and more vigorous' as well as a less selfish game (than rugby or cricket, presumably). The ensuing debate occupied *The Carthusian*'s March and April numbers, including a campaign for more tennis courts. Fortunately for Robert, his father managed to dissuade him from involving the *Morning Post* too, when he begged his son 'not to offend Kendall by publishing his attack on the 6th Form'.[31] But by then, and despite sales greatly increased by the controversy, Robert and Nevill were forced to resign and the June number was published under a new editor, who included an ironic 'obituary' on his predecessors.

The experience, rather than cowing Robert, increased his pugnaciousness, which was allowed a physical outlet when a fellow house monitor persuaded him to enter the inter-house boxing competition. Although his interest in boxing had waned since his break with Rodakowski, he felt that he had a 'reputation to keep up'. Out of training as he was, Robert decided that the only way to survive the ordeal was to make his fights as short as possible by straight knockouts. His novel solution was to fortify himself with a bottle of cherry-whisky, acquired from the house-butler, this despite his mother's gentle insistence that he 'sign the Pledge' at the age of seven. It was surprisingly effective and his description of the match among the most entertaining in *Good-bye to All That*. The outcome of the competition was so improbable that, taking into account Graves's love of embellishment and his generally cavalier attitude towards facts, one might be forgiven for dismissing his description of the whole affair as a gross exaggeration. But we have several eyewitness accounts to support his claim to have boxed five matches and won the welterweight and middleweight titles. 'Robby is the hero of the hour!' Charles wrote to their mother. 'In the boxing competitions he has not only won his own weight but also the weight above. So he has won two silver cups.' Not usually Robert's greatest admirer, Charles was deeply impressed that 'in doing so he knocked out (more or less) all the people against him to [the] number of 5!!!'[32]

Another spectator that day was 'Peter' Johnstone, and the consciousness of his presence helped Robert win against a particularly stubborn opponent, whose refusal to take the count despite being knocked down several times,

Robert believed, was because 'he loved [Johnstone] too'.[33] The 'stubborn opponent', G. D. Martineau, remembered fighting 'three wild, punishing rounds' with a 'strangely stimulated' Graves, who nonetheless denied having been in love with Johnstone.[34] Robert's boxing was unorthodox – a right swing not taught in the school boxing curriculum, probably because of the risks involved, as he discovered after the competition. He had broken both thumbs with his irregular methods and did poorly at the Public Schools Championship at Aldershot, where he himself was knocked out. But Robert's triumph at the Inter-House match stopped the bullying completely and, relieved of his editorial duties, he was now free, in theory at least, to concentrate on winning a leaving Exhibition. He was far too involved with his own work, however, to accept what he called in his last poem published in *The Carthusian* 'Books wed to books', which 'Bear bookish progeny that bids heed, / Denies my pen over the pages to speed.'[35] His father had reminded him that he would need a job to bring in money and educational publishing seemed an acceptable compromise to both. But, as Alfred pointed out, this must be '*after* [an] Oxford Training',[36] a firm answer to Robert's concluding question in 'The Tyranny of Books': 'Can I afford to find my books / Only in running brooks?'

The question came too late and Robert's schoolwork was not thought good enough for a leaving Exhibition. He had been unable to resist the opportunity of a guaranteed outlet for his poetry in the spring numbers of *The Carthusian* and he and Nevill had included 13 of them in the magazine before they were forced to resign in April 1914.[37] A similar mix as before of fantasy, nature poems and literary exercises, Robert thought only 'Ghost Music' worth preserving, in his first published collection, *Over the Brazier* (1916), perhaps for its concluding lines about the 'ghosts of long-dead melodies' in the chapel's organ loft, who 'huddled there in harmony / Like bats at noon-tide rafter hung'.[38]

When Robert and Nevill stopped editing *The Carthusian*, they did not abandon their criticism of the public school system that had subjected them to seemingly endless exams, and in April 1914, when Nevill went to stay with the headmaster, Dr Cecil Reddie (whose letter to *The Carthusian* had already caused a stir), he believed he had the right ideas about education. Robert followed suit in his short May break and returned full of enthusiasm for Reddie's alternative ideas. He was already tired of his conventional classical education and welcomed Reddie's determination to run a school along different lines, with the emphasis on modern languages, science, sports, crafts, and with pupils in closer contact with nature. (Bedales would be one result of his example, established by a former teacher at Abbotsholme.) Reddie's familiarity with Germany, where he had studied for his doctorate in chemistry, was another link between them, and later in the summer Reddie would visit the Graves family at Erinfa, although Robert was not there at the time.

Two of Reddie's greatest influences had been Walt Whitman and Edward Carpenter, both advocates of the nobility of love between men, a view Robert himself believed in passionately by 1914. Reddie encouraged romantic attachments among his pupils and Robert almost certainly discussed his own situation with him; his letter to Carpenter about it would follow shortly after his visit to Reddie. It may also have been Reddie who introduced him to the verse of the homosexual poet Richard Middleton, whose work had only recently become available in book form.[39]

Robert's rebelliousness was at its height in his last term at Charterhouse. Inflamed by Samuel Butler's attacks on the family and other sacred institutions in *The Way of All Flesh* and *Erewhon*, he was ready to question the Establishment at every point. Not only did he try to persuade his father to send his youngest son, John, to Abbotsholme – 'to save [him] from Charterhouse which though better than most Public Schools is one of the vilest places on God's earth',[40] – but he challenged authority recklessly: 'Poetry and Dick [i.e. Johnstone] were now the only two things that really mattered' to him.[41] With no guaranteed outlet for his poetry by the summer term of 1914 and the prospect of a separation from Johnstone ahead of him, it was the boy who now absorbed his attention. And combined with his quick temper, impetuousness, naïveté, stubbornness and self-righteousness, this would lead to what Graves later recalled as 'one of the worst quarters of an hour' of his life. For when a fellow chorister told Robert that he had seen the same master who warned him off Johnstone kissing the boy himself, he confessed to going 'quite mad'.[42] Without waiting for details or proof, he confronted the master and demanded his resignation, masking what he afterwards suspected was 'murderous jealousy' as moral outrage.[43] When Johnstone confirmed his story, the master agreed to resign at the end of term, which he did. He was killed the following year in France. The most disturbing aspect of the story is what it reveals of Robert, whose belief in his own rightness seems to have survived even Johnstone's later confession that he had been lying and that the master had never kissed him.

Then, four days before Robert turned 19, his father received 'a very trying letter' from his son.[44] Robert had caught a fellow monitor scratching up a pair of conjoined hearts in the bathroom with his and Johnstone's initials on them; furious, he had pushed him into the bath and turned the taps on. And when, in reprisal, the monitor and his friends annotated one of Robert's notebooks full of poetry and ideas for essays, he demanded an apology, failing which he would knock down the first monitor he saw. Although regretting that this turned out to be the head monitor, Thorpe, one of the few people at Charterhouse whom he respected, he carried out his threat. Even after two 'difficult' interviews, with his housemaster Parry and the headmaster himself, he was unrepentant and, to quote his father, 'far from wise in his behaviour' during his interview with Fletcher, 'quoting Abbotsholme and Reddie (called a quack by Fletcher) *v.* Charterhouse'.[45] As Alfred Graves observed, it was 'a very unfortunate finale for Robbie'.[46]

Graves chose not to end his account of Charterhouse with this incident but instead broke his largely chronological sequence by describing his ten-day (second) climbing trip with Mallory over three months earlier, thus concluding on a positive note. (His actual last memory, which may have been the most valuable lesson he learnt at school, was of his headmaster telling him to 'remember this, that your best friend is the waste-paper basket'.)[47] Meeting Mallory, he claimed, 'was the most important thing that happened to [him]' in his final year at school, apart from Johnstone. Mallory had not only introduced Robert to the joys of mountaineering but had also widened his literary and artistic horizons considerably. Above all he had taught Robert, as the Bloomsbury Group had taught him, to question conventions and defy them if necessary. Equally importantly for Robert's future career, Mallory had introduced him to Edward Marsh, who would make him known to a wide public by including him in his *Georgian Poetry* anthologies. Mallory was one of the reasons Graves found it so difficult to make up his mind about Charterhouse. Just as he had dismissed his five years there as a waste of time, he would remember that 'in the school at any given time there [were] always at least two really decent masters among the forty or fifty, and ten really decent fellows among the five or six hundred'.[48]

'I have some splendid friends here,' he wrote to his brother John in his last month at Charterhouse.[49]

Despite his fierce attack on the public school system in his final term and his provocative praise of Abbotsholme's focus on modern languages and science, Robert's subsequent writing would show how much he had benefited from his classical training and how much it had meant to him. *I, Claudius*, *Claudius the God*, *Count Belisarius*, *The Greek Myths* and many other of his books would reveal his familiarity and fascination with classical civilization.

The most important benefit of Charterhouse, however, may have been to teach him independence and how to get on with others. 'In that vanished Edwardian school,' Robert's boxing opponent G. D. Martineau wrote, 'a boy was expected to stand on his own feet, develop his own sense of values and make decisions with nothing but his own perceptions to guide him.'[50] Even Max Beerbohm, who had found it as difficult to fit in as Graves, believed he had learnt something positive there, 'a knack of understanding my fellow-creatures, of living in amity with them and not being rubbed the wrong way by their faults', and that he had 'not lost that good-humoured, give-and-take spirit which only the communal life of a public school could have given me'.[51]

Although Graves could not claim to have been made quite so tolerant by his time at Charterhouse and was far more critical of it than Beerbohm, only three months after leaving it he was already nostalgic: 'Yes, Ch[arterh]ouse is a grand place in spite of all its efforts to cut its own throat and pollute its own cistern!' he wrote to Cyril Hartmann.[52] By then the First World War had begun and a shocking number of his contemporaries were dead, the Charterhouse casualty list already 'awful'.[53]

5

'On Finding Myself a Soldier'[1]
(August 1914–May 1915)

My bud was backward to unclose,
    A pretty baby-queen,
Furled petal-tips of creamy rose
    Caught in a clasp of green.

Somehow, I never thought to doubt
    That when her heart should show
She would be coloured in as out,
    Like the flush of dawn on snow:

But yesterday aghast I found,
    Where last I'd left the bud,
Twelve flamy petals ringed around
    A heart more red than blood.[2]

On 4 August 1914, exactly one week after Graves had left Charterhouse, Britain declared war on Germany. And only eight days after that Graves enlisted in the British Army. He had been aware of the possibility of war for some time, but was still taken by surprise.

Events had moved rapidly since his father Alfred recorded a slightly inaccurate account in his diary on 29 June, the day after the event: 'Read the news of the Sarajevo murder of the heir presumptive to the Austrian throne and his wife, who heroically intervened between him and his murderers.' What began as a localized hostility reached international dimensions when Austria-Hungary issued an ultimatum to Serbia on 24 July. Germany, with its own barely concealed territorial ambitions, took sides with Austria, and France with Serbia. As the ultimatums flew and tensions mounted, the whole of Europe waited to hear whether Russia would side with Serbia against Austria and Germany. When, on 28 July, Austria declared war on Serbia, Russia, as Alfred noted, started 'mobilizing'.[3] By 1 August he had even more 'alarming' news to record: 'Stock Exchange closed, Bank rate up to 8%, martial law in Germany; Russia blown up bridge on Austrian frontier. Jaurès[4] assassinated.' Britain, which had an informal agreement with France and Russia to help protect them, felt more or less obliged to join in when, on 4 August, Germany invaded France's immediate neighbour, Belgium, a country whose neutrality Britain was pledged to preserve.

When Graves entered the Army as a second lieutenant on 12 August 1914, he was 19 years and 19 days old. It was an abrupt end to his boyhood, which he had expected to terminate more gradually with three years at Oxford. Instead of becoming a 'new boy' in yet another educational establishment, he suddenly found himself in a position of authority over others, a disturbing experience, as he told his parents:

> I am for fifty men, many of them old enough to be my father, a sort of combined schoolmaster, doctor, parson, foreman, general lawyer, official newsagent, and tyrant, with genuinely despotic powers ... and this is rather a strain on my youth...[5]

Graves was still 'under orders' to his superiors, however, and in some ways the Army, with its hierarchical set-up and rigid rules, was a continuation of the public school system he wanted to escape. As another war poet, Charles Hamilton Sorley, pointed out, the parallels were there: 'The house-master or platoon commander entrusts the discipline of his charge to the prefects or corporals, as the case may be.'[6] For many of Graves's schoolfellows on the 'Modern' side at Charterhouse, military training at Sandhurst or Dartmouth had been considered the equivalent of studying at Oxford or Cambridge.

In August 1914, however, the Army seemed to offer an immediate respite from Oxford to Graves, who had shared Barbour's dismay at the prospect of another three years of studying and exams. Discussing the problem together on their last day at school, Barbour had vowed 'to put something in between' himself and Oxford and to 'go abroad for the whole vacation'.[7] Graves, who could look forward only to a less exotic holiday in Wales, felt that three months was 'not long enough' and had had 'a vague intention of running away to sea'.[8] So that when war was declared, a war that he, like others, expected to last 'two or three months at the very outside', he jumped at the chance of delaying Oxford. He was 'only too glad to escape into the Army'.[9] He accepted unquestioningly newspaper claims that 'England and France had been drawn into a war they had never contemplated and for which they were entirely unprepared'.[10] And despite his wholly positive experiences of the Germans from his childhood years onwards, and his own half-German parentage, he was prepared to believe the worst of them, discounting only about a fifth of the atrocities they were reported to have carried out – 'not, of course, enough', he afterwards realized.[11] Like many other people in Britain, he was particularly outraged by what he, and they, viewed as a 'cynical violation of Belgian neutrality',[12] of 'plucky little Belgium', as she quickly became known.

So although realizing that he was violating all the 'cherished anti-war principles' he had expressed so recently and so eloquently at the Carthusian Debating Society, he believed he had no alternative but to join up. Barbour, who had taken the same side as Graves in that debate, also felt obliged to volunteer, introducing yet another aspect of the question when he declared that 'France is the only place for a gentleman now'.[13] For someone of Graves's education and background, there seemed very little choice in 1914. Even Sorley, a poet Graves came to admire greatly, despite serious misgivings about the war from the start, demonstrated that for a middle- or upper-class young man of public school education, there was no real alternative. For as Sorley would argue, in a reaction against the idealization of Rupert Brooke after his death in 1915: 'He is far too obsessed with his own sacrifice, regarding the going to war of himself (and others) as a highly intense, remarkable and sacrificial exploit, whereas it is merely the conduct demanded of him (and others) by the turn of circumstances, where the non-compliance with this demand would have made life intolerable.'[14]

Sorley and Graves had an unusual amount in common. Born in the same year only two months apart, they would both be critical of the public school education they received. They would both dread the continuation of it at Oxford, where both, sitting in the same examination hall, had won awards, Sorley a scholarship to University College. Both were beginning to reject their conventional Christian upbringing by the time they joined the Army. They would be sent out to France in the same month to the same Cuinchy-Cambrin sector and both participate in the Battle of Loos, where Sorley would be killed. One striking difference, however, would be their attitude to Germany. While Sorley, who had spent seven of the happiest months of his life there earlier in 1914, felt he must fight despite his love of the Germans, Graves felt obliged to show his loyalty to England, partly because of his German blood. With ten members of his mother's family fighting for Germany and nine of his father's for Britain, he needed to balance the numbers, he argued only half-jokingly.[15] Two of his uncles held senior positions in the German Army, including General Frieduhelm von Ranke, but it was his uncle, Admiral Sir Richard Poore, married to his father's sister Ida Graves, whom he chose to mention. Although he did not know exactly why he had volunteered, he told his old schoolfriend Cyril Hartmann that he was sure it was 'not for sentiment or patriotism certainly'.[16] In fact his loyalties were dangerously divided – several cousins and uncles he knew and liked were killed. Erinfa was filled with German relatives each summer, 1914 included. Robert had had a memorable holiday in Zurich with his cousin, Konrad, who was the same age as himself and son of the German consul in Zurich. He remembered him as 'a gentle, proud creature, whose chief interest was natural history'. A courageous soldier, Konrad had won the 'Pour La Mérite', a decoration more rarely awarded than the Victoria Cross, and although he survived the war, he was killed shortly afterwards by the Bolsheviks while making requisitions in Ukraine. It was a division of loyalties that may have contributed to Graves's breakdown after the war. In *Poetic Unreason*, written during the early 1920s, the possible reasons he gives for a soldier's serious breakdown include being 'of German blood on his mother's side so that the fear of being thought a traitor and the regard of his mother's family were continually interacting' – and in conflict, of course.[17] In *Good-bye to All That* he describes a conversation in the trenches among young officers who 'had either German mothers or naturalized

German fathers' and the 'extra pressure they felt to serve in the *British Army*'.[18]

Amy Graves's case was even worse; the loyal wife of an extremely patriotic Briton, with cousins, nephews and a brother-in-law fighting on the opposite side, her only explanation was that her 'race' had 'gone mad'.[19] And though Robert had overcome his anti-war principles in 1914 for what he saw as the greater good, they came back to torment him in old age, when he was haunted by the thought of having killed Germans.

Nevertheless, at the time when he enlisted, Graves experienced a sense of relief and adventure: relief at having put off Oxford and excitement at the thought of an entirely different way of life, probably abroad to boot. His first act was to write to the Oxford Board of Military Studies, applying for a commission through the Officers' Training Corps. When he learnt that they could not accept him until he had matriculated at the University, he next wrote to the Old Carthusian Corps. Meantime the Secretary of the Harlech Golf Club, Mr More, who had known the family well since he had helped found the Club in the mid-1890s, suggested that Robert try for a commission with the Royal Welch Fusiliers, whose regimental depot was at Wrexham, not far from Harlech. More then telephoned the adjutant, 'Tibbs' Crawshay, as Alfred noted, and 'commended Robbie on his own account and mine and the brothers and Dick Poore'.[20] More also mentioned that Robert was a public school boy who had been in the Officers' Training Corps at Charterhouse, though he was not to know that Robert had bartered with his father to have him excused O.T.C. training during his final year. The adjutant immediately offered Graves a Special Reserve Commission. (According to Sassoon, who was to follow Graves into the Royal Welch Fusiliers in mid-1915, the Special Reserve was a new name for the old Militia; a temporary commission would have come to much the same thing, he claimed, but the social cachet was greater.)

On 12 August 1914, a few days after More's phone call, Alfred was 'Up at 6 a.m. to see Robbie off to join the Welch Fusiliers at Wrexham. He started in good spirits and was waving to us as long as possible from the carriage window.'[21] The family's pride in Robert's decision was enormous and included his uncle, Charles Larcom Graves, who had been unhappy about his nephew's growing disaffection with the Establishment, but was now to write proudly of him in *Punch*:

My gifted nephew Eric
    Till just before the War
Was steeped in esoteric
    And antinomian lore,
Now verging on the mystic
Now darkly symbolistic
Now frankly futuristic
    And modern to the core...

In all its multiplicity
He worshipped eccentricity,
And found his chief felicity
    In aping the insane.

And yet this freak ink-slinger,
    When England called for men
Straight ceased to be a singer
    And threw away his pen...

Transformed by contact hourly
    With heroes simple-souled
He looks no longer sourly
    On men of normal mould,
But, purged of mental vanity
And erudite inanity,
The clay of his humanity
    Is turning fast to gold.[22]

Two days after arriving in Wrexham, Robert's family received 'a very nice letter' from him; he liked the regiment and seemed 'keen' on his work as a volunteer, hoping to be gazetted a second lieutenant in a few days, which he duly was. Amy, still very close to her eldest son, visited him less than a fortnight after he had left Harlech, staying overnight in Wrexham to do so. During the next four years, according to her husband, her hair would turn white with worry over him.

Graves congratulated himself 'on having chosen, quite blindly' the Royal Welch Fusiliers, whose record seemed to him 'beyond reproach'.[23] He 'caught the regimental tradition' very early on when he came across 'the Daily

Order-book of the 1st Battalion RWF in the trenches before Sebastopol' as they prepared an attack on the Redan Fort during the Crimean War.[24] It was certainly a regiment to appeal to his imagination. Raised originally in 1689 to help William III fight the deposed James II and his Irish and French Catholics in Ireland, it had a long and honourable history. From their first engagement at the Battle of the Boyne in 1690, the Royal Welch Fusiliers were at every one of the numerous wars Britain fought over the succeeding two centuries. Their battle honours included Namur, Blenheim, Ramillies, Corunna, Salamanca, the Peninsula, Waterloo, Inkerman, Sebastopol, Lucknow and the Relief of Ladysmith. And, as Graves pointed out, not only did the RWF have 29 battle honours by 1914 but 'they were all good bloody battle honours'.[25] According to him, they considered themselves second to none, even where the Guards were concerned. When offered the choice of becoming the Welsh Guards after the Boer War, they had indignantly turned down a change that would have made them junior in the Brigade even to the recently formed Irish Guards.

Graves never lost his pride in the RWF, later turning their role in the American War of Independence of the late eighteenth century into the Sergeant Lamb novels, written during the Second World War.[26] And when his eldest son, David, was planning to apply for a commission with the RWF in 1939, he was delighted, writing that 'it is and always was a corps d'élite'.[27]

Like Sassoon, who joined the regiment in a similarly chance fashion, Graves was particularly proud of the RWF's traditions, however absurd they might seem to outsiders – the St David's Day eating of a raw leek to the roll of a drum with one foot on a chair, for instance, or the singular spelling of 'Welch', which they had been allowed to keep and which seemed to Graves to refer 'us somehow to the antique Wales of Henry Tudor and Owen Glendower and Lord Herbert of Cherbury', their first colonel.[28] Both he and Sassoon saw fit to mention the most distinctive of these traditions, the wearing of a 'flash', five black ribbons attacked to the tunic collars of all ranks, in recognition of the fact that in 1805, when the Army had abolished the wearing of the pigtail (protected in a black leather bag), the Royal Welch Fusiliers had been at sea and thus the last regiment to carry out the order.

The most significant ritual in terms of Graves's poetry was one shared with several other Welsh regiments, the custom of being led on parade by a white goat with gilded and ornamental horns, a tradition which would form part of his inspiration for one of his earliest army poems, 'In the Wilderness'. The poem opens with a recognizable, though anonymous, reference to Christ and his forty days and forty nights wandering in the desert:

> He, of his gentleness,
> Thirsting and hungering
> Walked in the wilderness;
> Soft words of grace he spoke
> Unto lost desert-folk
> That listened wondering.
> He heard the bittern call
> From ruined palace-wall,
> Answered him brotherly;
> He held communion
> With the she-pelican
> Of lonely piety.[29]

After listing the other monstrous creatures who accompany Christ on his 'wanderings' – the basilisk and cockatrice, with 'Great bats on leathern wings / And old, blind, broken things' – the poem ends with the most significant of them, the 'scapegoat':

> Comrade, with ragged coat,
> Gaunt ribs – poor innocent –
> Bleeding foot, burning throat,
> The guileless young scapegoat:
> For forty nights and days
> Followed in Jesus' ways,
> Sure guard behind him kept,
> Tears like a lover wept.[30]

Although Graves viewed 'In the Wilderness' as a 'silly, quaint' poem by 1929, it would be one of only 28 of his many early verses to be included in his final volume of *Collected Poems* in 1975, and the first in the collection.[31] He had included it originally in *Fairies and Fusiliers* (1917), he told Charles Scott Moncrieff, only 'because you like it'.[32] But he had almost certainly been influenced by Alec Waugh's glowing review of it in February 1916, where Waugh detected 'the cadences of a very intricate metre' which 'rise and fall with a faultless rhythm'. Moncrieff argued that it was 'simple and impassioned with something of that playfulness' that he found in even Graves's 'most serious poetry'.[33]

Graves never doubted the existence of Jesus Christ and kept his vision of him as the perfect man 'sentimentally' for years,[34] but by August 1915 his early religious certainties were crumbling and 'In the Wilderness' is not conventionally religious, unlike many of the earliest poems written at the start of the conflict. His father, for instance, composed early on a 'Salute to the Belgian Flag', which he presented to the Duchess of Vendôme, the sister of the Belgian king.[35] A ripening non-conformist, Robert may even have rejected the patriotic or conventionally religious approach precisely *because* his father had taken it. He would write many poems during the next four years, but the majority of them would deal with the war obliquely.

The 'guileless young scapegoat' of the piece, Graves insisted, was inspired in the first instance by his regimental mascot, not the goat of Jewish ritual. But he was familiar with the latter and with Christ's temptation in the wilderness through his extensive religious education both at home and at school. The originality of the poem lies in the linking of Christ and the scapegoat in His trial: 'the scapegoat of my juvenile poem', he wrote in 1945 to a lady researching 'Goats in History', 'was my own unhappiness' invention. In point of fact the Azazel Scapegoat of Jerusalem could not possibly have gone into the Galilean Wilderness of the Temptation, which is a great distance away.'[36] As Martin Seymour-Smith notes, Graves's poem 'makes Christ seem rather more like St Francis [of Assisi] than his traditional self',[37] though its impact does not depend on how the reader views Christ. There is also Graves's creation of a fantastic world of legendary creatures: 'Basilisk, cockatrice, / ... / With mail of dread device, / With monstrous barbèd stings, / With eager dragon-eyes: / Great bats on leathern wings ...'

Set in the context of war, the poem invites a range of allegorical interpretations – the wilderness as the Western Front, for instance, the 'comrade with ragged coat' a fellow soldier in the trenches, and the Christ-figure, as Miranda Seymour suggests, 'an idealized soldier comforting the wounded and the dying at the Front'.[38] The fluid rhyme scheme helps shape the poem without constricting it, and the predominantly two-beat line is handled with such varied line breaks that it never becomes monotonous. It may be that the conclusion of Graves's classical education encouraged a greater freedom in his verse, a willingness to experiment with 'Free Verse' (or at least freer verse) as he first called a poem also written during this period, subsequently retitled 'In Spite', in which he announces:

> I now delight,
> In spite
> Of the might
> And the right
> Of classic tradition,
> In writing
> And reciting
> Straight ahead,
> Without let or omission,
> Just any little rhyme
> In any little time
> That runs in my head;
> Because, I've said,
> My rhymes no longer shall stand arrayed
> Like Prussian soldiers on parade...[39]

Parades were very much on Graves's mind during his first few weeks of training at Wrexham. His time in the O.T.C. at Charterhouse, truncated though it was, enabled him to master the drill fairly easily, but he now had to learn how to drill others. His 'greatest difficulty', he remembered, was 'to talk to men of the company to which I was posted with the necessary air of authority'.[40] Another problem concerned army traditions and hierarchy, of which he knew nothing 'and made all the worst mistakes; saluting the bandmaster, failing to recognise the colonel when in mufti, walking in the street without a belt and talking shop in the mess'.[41] In addition, he had to master regimental history, musketry, field tactics, military law and organization, how to work a machine gun, and what both he and Sassoon recognized retrospectively as outdated 'Boer War field-tactics' of open warfare entirely unsuited to the very different conditions of the French battlefields. They dug no trenches, handled no bombs and were allowed to think of the company, rather than the platoon and section, as the smallest unit.

After only three weeks 'on the square' at Wrexham, Graves's training was interrupted when he was sent on detachment duty to an Internment Camp for Enemy Aliens at Lancaster. Sited in a disused wagon-works near the river Lune, it was a dirty, draughty place littered with old scrap metal and guarded with high barbed-wire fences. Graves's job was to command a detachment of fifty Special Reservists, most of them raw recruits from the Welsh border counties, a 'rough lot', according to him, who 'were constantly deserting and having to be fetched back by the police'.[42] It was a distinct anticlimax; though he had not expected to be actively engaged in the fighting, but be on garrison service at home while the regular troops were away, the camp was frankly 'horrid', he told his brother John, and his men difficult to control.[43] The German prisoners, on the other hand, were 'as quiet and peacable [*sic*] as little bleating baalambs' and gave 'no trouble at all'.[44] The place already held about 3,000 prisoners and more flooded in daily: seamen arrested on German vessels in Liverpool harbour, waiters from big hotels in the north, an odd German band or two, harmless German commercial travellers and shopkeepers. Even children were interned in the camp; more than a dozen little boys from the German bands were interned only 'because it seemed more humane to keep them with their friends than to send them to a workhouse'.[45]

It seemed an absurd situation in many ways and when Graves wanted to show how well he understood e. e. cummings's description of his bizarre life as a prisoner of war in *The Enormous Room*, he chose his time at Lancaster to illustrate the absurdity of some aspects of army life. His account was given in his Introduction to the English edition of cummings's book, which was published more than a year before it appeared in a slightly different form in *Good-bye to All That*. It opens by describing a column in *The Times* in which ridicule was poured on a story given to the Berlin press by an exchanged German prisoner:

He had described conditions at an internment camp at the Lancaster Wagon-works, alleging that in August 1914, so great was the prevailing panic, he with 39 others, waiters from the Midland Hotel, Manchester, had been taken to Lancaster handcuffed *and fettered*, by a force of sixty police armed with carbines under the command of the Chief of Police.[46]

The Times had protested that the 'fetters' were a bit too much to believe, but Graves added, with barely concealed irony, 'Well, they were true, for I was the officer at the camp who took the criminals over and gave the befrogged commander his receipt.'[47] As Graves also points out in his Introduction to *The Enormous Room*, war books are of two general kinds and his is nearer to the variety that resists depicting war as an exciting *Boy's Own* adventure of the wholly patriotic kind; in this he was undoubtedly influenced by cummings rather than Sassoon or Blunden, whose own memoirs were published the same year.

The chief absurdity of Lancaster for Graves was the fact that he had far more trouble with his men than with the prisoners. They had discovered a way to break out of their quarters through a sewer, to find themselves women in the town. Graves, still cherishing his ideal of chaste, homosexual love, found this particularly distasteful and in the one poem known definitely to have been written at Lancaster expressed his disgust in terms that reveal not just a revulsion from heterosexual physical love but also a snobbish and clichéd dismissal of working-class life:

> Down dirty streets in stench and smoke
> The pale townsfolk
> Crawl and kiss and cuddle,
> In doorways hug and huddle;
> Loutish he
> And sluttish she
> In loathsome love together press
> And unbelievable ugliness.[48]

His worst experience of Lancaster, however, came from an unexpected direction; it would distress him greatly and is worth relating because it throws light on his claim to have suffered from 'shell-shock' as a result of the war. The regimental telephone, unfortunately situated in an office where he slept on a sloping desk, rang late one night when he was half-asleep and in answering it he received an electric shock, probably from lightning in the storm raging outside. He was, he claimed, 'unable to use a telephone properly again until some twelve years later'.[49] His distress is understandable, but to imply, as he does, that this was a direct result of the war seems something of an exaggeration.

There were positive sides to life at Lancaster, however. He got on well with the commandant, a 'fatherly colonel of the Loyal North Lancashire Regiment', tolerated the assistant-commandant, 'who alleged that he had ten years more seniority than any other major in the British army and made wistful jokes about his lost virility', and the adjutant, Deane.[50] ('The doctor he dismissed as the 'mess-buffoon'.)[51] His closest friend there, the Secretary, C. B. Bull, had been a well-known figure at Oxford, 'owner of the *Isis*, and combined divinity, athletics and boxing-coach' at the University, with whom Graves boxed to keep fit, practice which would stand him in good stead. Bull also sponsored him for the local Lodge of the Royal Antediluvian Order of the Buffaloes, whose rituals appealed to Graves's growing appreciation of the absurd.

Nevertheless, guarding prisoners of war in England, especially such docile ones, seemed to Graves 'an unheroic part to be playing' in a war that by mid-October 1914 had reached a critical stage. His expectation of a 'short war' that would be 'over by Christmas' had been destroyed as early as 23 August,[52] when the British Army was forced to retreat at its first major battle of the war, Mons. The British suffered a further reverse at Le Cateau on 26 August. Although Paris was saved and the Germans forced to fall back at the Battle of the Marne in early September,[53] the British suffered further serious losses during the battle and the Germans would quickly return to the offensive just over a month later at the First Battle of Ypres.[54] The Allies' hope of support from what had been dubbed the 'Russian steam-roller' on the Eastern Front had been quickly dispelled by news of General Hindenburg's crushing victory over them at the Battle of Tannenburg in late August.[55] Combined with Turkey's entry into the war on the side of the Central Powers, this effectively put Russia out of the fighting until mid-1915 and released more German troops for the Western Front. By Christmas 1914 the opposing armies would have dug themselves in along a line from the Belgian coast to Switzerland, a line that was rarely to move more than ten miles either way during the next four hard, grinding years. Graves was clearly aware of the gravity of the situation and the scale of the losses when he wrote to Cyril Hartmann about the 'awful' Charterhouse casualty list at the end of October 1914. In the same letter he reported that the 1st Royal Welch Fusiliers, who were defending the Channel ports, had 'just been annihilated – except for two officers and a few men'.[56]

Graves now wanted to 'be abroad fighting' and was, therefore, greatly relieved to be recalled from detachment duty on 19 October to continue his Officers' Training Course at Wrexham. It had taken less than three months to convert him from his pacifist position at Charterhouse, a disturbing change he notes in his 'On Finding Myself a Soldier' in the curious image of a 'creamy rose' bud, which unfolds to reveal 'Twelve flamy petals ringed around / A heart more red than blood'.[57] Having acknowledged the need to fight, however, he was more conscious than ever of his calling as a poet and how threatened that now was by 'The Shadow of Death', as he called his poem on the subject:

> ... Oh my songs never sung,
>> And my plays to darkness blown!
> I am still so young, so young,
>> And life was my own...[58]

It would be another six and a half months after his return to Wrexham, however, before Graves was (in the words of his poem) in a position to 'fight and kill' in France. He was forced to watch his contemporaries being sent out one by one to France to replace casualties in the 1st and 2nd battalions, while he remained 'despondently at the depot'.[59] Although he had pleased his parents by looking 'flourishing and taller' when he arrived at Harlech in a short leave on 20 October,[60] once he returned to the depot his company commander reported him to Crawshay as 'unsoldierlike and a nuisance'.[61] Crawshay was especially critical of his uniform and untidy appearance, which Graves clearly cared little about. Sassoon had discovered, by the time he joined the Royal Welch Fusiliers in May 1915, that there was a great deal of snobbishness about one's choice of tailor in both the Hunt and the Army. ('You can't have your shirts too dark', his tailor had warned him when he went to be fitted for his uniform.) Graves, schooled by Amy, had certainly not gone to the best military tailor and his uniform had not been the most expensive available. Even so, he was reluctant to ask his parents for more money for a new outfit. He also blamed his batman ('palmed off on him', he believed) for failing to polish his buttons and shine his belt and shoes to the required brightness. He continued to care little about clothes and even less about etiquette, and would still be considered unsoldierlike in appearance by the time he met Sassoon at the end of 1915.

Crawshay's second criticism, that Graves was not a sportsman, was easier to rectify, especially after his boxing practice with Bull at Lancaster. But the chance to prove himself in this area did not come immediately and he began to feel very stale indeed, and life rather bleak. Recruit officers spent a great deal of their time in the Company and Battalion Orderly Room, learning how to deal with crime. The problem for Graves was that 'crime' meant any breach of army regulations, most of them petty. It seemed to him that he and other trainee officers wasted a good deal of their time dealing with the usual fairly harmless swearing and drunkenness common on pay-night. He had made 'pals', he told his mother when she visited him again in early December 1914, but one by one they were sent out to the 1st and 2nd battalions in France and had 'fallen or ... been wounded or captured in large numbers'.[62] He did not care much for the men who replaced them, 'rather horsey young Welsh squireens'.[63]

Leaves could not be relied on for a respite. They were uncertain, infrequent and short, overshadowed by the threat of an early recall. Christmas 1914, for instance, came and went with no sign of Robert in London, where his parents now occupied the house of Amy's brother, Robert von Ranke, the German Consul-General in London until the outbreak of war.[64] He was expected all day long on 28 December, but did not arrive home until five days later.

Robert did, however, manage to take one short break just before Christmas to visit an ex-Charterhouse friend, Ralph Rooper, at Gresford, a few miles from Wrexham. Fellow protégés of Mallory, they had shared a number of other interests at school, but Rooper was a year older than Graves and had won a scholarship to New College, Oxford, when war broke out. Rejected by the Army because of his weak heart, he had joined the Red Cross and drove ambulances at the Front. They would write to each other regularly during the war. Graves called Rooper 'quite one of the dearest and the best' and would count it 'one of the greatest sorrows of [the] bloody fourth year of war' to hear that 'dear old Ralph' was killed driving an ambulance near Rheims in May 1918.[65] However bleakly he represented his time at Charterhouse, he had clearly made some good friends there.

Graves's visit to Rooper in December 1914 had led to another positive experience during his time at Wrexham. Mallory's name had naturally come up in conversation, together with that of Marsh, and had given Graves an excuse to contact the latter: 'Last time I met you at George Mallory's,' he reminded him, 'you asked me to look you up in Town this winter.'[66] By the time his letter was written on 26 December, he knew that he was due a week's leave 2–9 January 1915, and he concludes: 'before I go out to the slaughter – a sort of respite like Jephthah's daughter had in which to bewail her virginity – and would like to look you up sometime then'. Alfred found his son's Biblical comparison of himself to Jephthah (which Robert repeated in a letter to Rosaleen at about the same time) 'charming',[67] and Marsh, whatever he thought of this gentle emotional blackmail, replied positively. An invitation to dinner with Marsh followed, giving Graves a renewed sense of direction since he intended to take some of his poems with him to discuss with the editor of *Georgian Poetry*.

Before that, on 2 January, came dinner with Rooper and a play, Shakespeare's *Henry V*, the first theatrical performance Graves had attended after a childhood more sheltered than most. It was a small sign of his growing independence from his parents, who raised no objections. As Alfred noted, he now looked 'every inch the young soldier' and could do more or less what he chose, returning home very late indeed by family standards after an 'excellent' evening.[68] His next evening, dining with Marsh at Raymond Buildings, Gray's Inn, continued what he looked back on wistfully as his 'mental debauch' in London, discussing his verse with Marsh and leaving more poems with him. Exhausted by such unaccustomed stimulation, he spent 4 January at home resting and polishing his buttons, going out only to do a little shopping in the afternoon, almost certainly in pursuit of some smarter equipment that might please Crawshay.

When Graves's early recall to the depot came on 5 January, he still managed to carry out one of his most important plans for his leave, a visit to Johnstone at Charterhouse. He was accompanied by yet another friend he had made at the school, a half-Portuguese youth, Henry Devenish, who, it seems, 'did not prepossess' Alfred.[69] After a delay in finding Johnstone and a three-hour talk with him, Robert missed the train back and had only an hour, albeit a 'happy' one, with his family before they saw him off at Paddington.

Alfred and Amy had had several talks with Robert about 'his affairs', but though they had found him 'very affectionate' and 'well disposed' towards them, he had also struck them as extremely 'reserved', leading his father to comment on 'the pathos of the situation'.[70] His parting words to his son were a classical maxim: '*Sis sollers ac fortis in armis*', or 'may you be both crafty / skilful and brave in arms'. Neither Robert nor his family knew when he would be sent to the Front, nor whether he would survive the war.

Back at Wrexham with the same uncertainty hanging over him and no respite in sight, Graves's main emotion was one of 'crushing boredom'.[71] It was in part a reaction to the excitement of his leave, he told Marsh, to whom he wrote on 22 January begging for a response to his poems, however brief and however 'cruel'. Although the early weeks of 1915 were an exceptionally busy period for Marsh, he made time to encourage the youngest of the potential 'Georgian' poets. His criticism, when it came, was similar to that he had given Sassoon nearly two years earlier: that his verses contained 'far too much of the worn-out stuff and garb of poetry'.[72] While assuring Marsh that he was 'not annoyed' as the older man had feared he might be, Graves laid most of the blame on his father for his 'obsolete' vocabulary, all the arrogance and condescension of untried youth apparent in his reply:

> Influences at work – first in my reading, the immense preponderance of the 'classical' over the modern, second, my dear old father, a dear old fellow who in young and vinous days used to write with some spirit and very pleasantly; but now his inspiration has petered out. He was hand in glove with Tennyson and Ruskin and that lot and has memories of Wordsworth: consequently since my earliest years he has been trying to mould me in the outworn tradition, and though I have struggled hard against this as you must see, the old Adam is always cropping up unnoticed...[73]

His uncle Charles of *The Spectator* exerted a similar influence, 'made stronger by his great avuncular kindness and generosity', Graves claimed, concluding quite reasonably that a 'boy' like himself, who had been 'so forlornly *sui generis* at home, school and now again in the regiment, would have to be a Hercules to struggle successfully against uncles, schoolmasters and the books he reads'.[74] By the time he replied to Marsh at the beginning of February 1915, he had already begun that Herculean effort to escape the 'outworn tradition' of his father's generation, having bought Rupert Brooke's poems at Marsh's suggestion.

It is significant that Marsh did not criticize Graves's handling of metre as he had Sassoon's. An outstanding classicist himself at Westminster and Cambridge, he would have appreciated Graves's great respect for metre, fostered in him not only by his study as a Classics scholar at Charterhouse but also by the father whom he so patronizingly dismissed. Another bond with Marsh was their love for a younger man; in Marsh's case it was Brooke, while Graves felt that he could discuss his feelings for Johnstone with Marsh and ask him to keep an eye on Johnstone once Graves had been posted to France.

There is no doubt that Marsh's friendship, coming when it did, was helpful to Graves, encouraging him to become more independent, to think for himself, to resist vagueness and poeticisms borrowed from others. His placing of one of his early war poems, 'The Dead Fox-Hunter', in both the *Westminster Gazette* (20 September 1916) and the *Saturday Westminster Gazette* (23 September 1916) was a boost to morale and the inclusion of eight of Graves's other poems in *Georgian Poetry 1916–1917* was an important step in his early career. Yet Marsh himself was already beginning to seem a little out of date to a new generation of poets in England, pre-eminent among them Ezra Pound, D. H. Lawrence, Richard Aldington, 'H. D.' and other Imagists, followed later by T. S. Eliot. To use the political terminology adopted by Graves himself in his later analyses of the Georgian era,[75] Marsh was to the 'right' of Pound, Aldington, Wyndham Lewis and their acolytes, but to the 'left' of the 'old guard', still represented by poets like Austin Dobson, Henry Newbolt and William Watson. Graves's later praise of Isaac Rosenberg as a 'born revolutionary', a poet Marsh found too challenging, emphasizes how wide the gap would become between his and Marsh's expectations of poetry. Meeting Marsh at a crucial point in his development may help to explain why Graves never became wholly Modernist in technique.

His attempts to follow Marsh's advice were a welcome distraction for him from the boredom he experienced at Wrexham, leavened only by the suspense of his wait for a posting abroad. Another of the few positive things to come out of his time there, he believed, was being taught how to compose field-messages by a young officer, Captain 'Shots' Jones, who gave him a useful 'formula ... cutting out everything not pertinent to the message'.[76] If he could be said to have a 'poetic style' by 1930, he claimed, it was 'a style of still further elimination of what is not pertinent; the message reduced to "who, how, why"'.[77] He would read some of his fresh poems to his family on a brief visit to see them in mid-March, leaving the collection with them in the hope that his father would be able to find a publisher for it.[78] The only event to break up his monotonous routine in the month following his London leave was the result of a bout of influenza in early February. When Crawshay went down with it next, Graves found himself in temporary charge of the battalion, marching 1,100 men 20 miles a day for two days, sufficient proof of his abilities for Crawshay to promise to put him on a draft for France.

It was a wake-up call and Graves now focused more seriously on his training, taking only two of the six days' leave granted to him a month later, in order to concentrate on it. He now began to learn more about the use of Lewis machine guns, rifles, hand grenades and mortars, added to the usual monotonous routine of section, platoon and company drill. With his strict academic training he had no trouble passing the Machine Gun and Rifle Range Musketry Course with first-class honours.[79] By 1 May he had been promoted to First Lieutenant and two days later was finally able to prove his worth to Crawshay, in an unexpected way. Johnny Basham, a sergeant in the Royal Welch Fusiliers, was training for the Lonsdale Belt welterweight title and offering to fight three rounds with any member of the regiment. He had already dispatched one challenger with insulting ease when Graves volunteered to go next. Through a characteristic mixture of ability, experience, bluff and luck he managed to survive the three rounds and was invited to train with Basham for the next five evenings as he prepared for the Championship.[80]

When Basham won his title on 11 May, Graves's name was put down for France, Crawshay now convinced of his worthiness. One day later Alfred and Amy received a telegram from 'dear Robbie': 'Starting France today. Don't worry, best love, Robbie.'

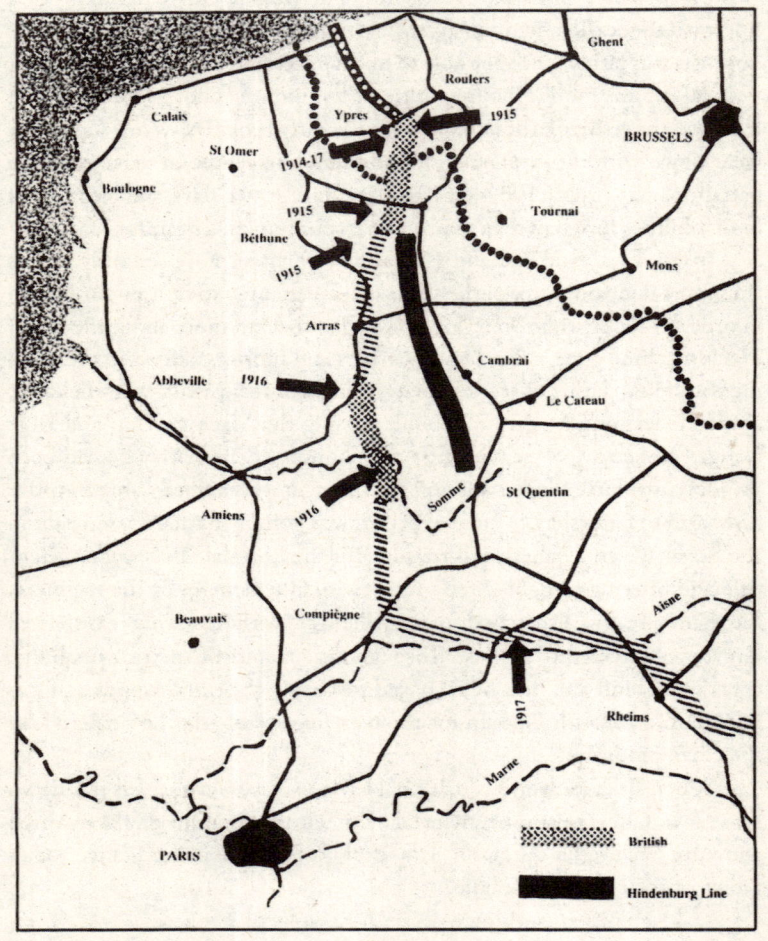

6

'THESE SOUL-DEADENING TRENCHES' (MAY–JULY 1915)

'Farewell' the Corporal cried, 'La Bassée trenches!
No Cambrins for me now, no more Givenchies,
And no more bloody brickstacks – God Almighty,
I'm back again at last to dear old Blighty.'

But cushy wounds don't last a man too long,
And now, poor lad, he sings this bitter song:
'Back to La Bassée, to the same old hell,
Givenchy, Cuinchy, Cambrin, Loos, Vermelles.'[1]

However entertaining Graves's boxing anecdote may be, it was not just his skill in the ring that had finally convinced his adjutant to send him to France in May 1915. By then the Allies were suffering from a severe shortage of men. In January, British troops had been sent out to Gallipoli in response to Turkey's threat to Russia; in the Middle East, British and Indian soldiers, having beaten off a Turkish attack on the Suez Canal, were preparing to invade Palestine; and another expeditionary force from India was fighting for possession of Baghdad.

On the Western Front the need for men was desperate. In the Allies' offensive at Neuve Chapelle, 10–13 March, the 1st Royal

Welch Fusiliers had lost yet more men, Robert told his parents when they visited him on 1 May. And a second German offensive at Ypres begun in April increased the urgent need for reinforcements. On 9 May there were more severe losses at the Battle of Aubers Ridge, an unmitigated disaster for the British Army. Crawshay put Graves's name down on a draft for France on 11 May, and just four days later the Battle of Festubert started claiming further victims, including men of the 1st RWF, which was 'all but annihilated' there, according to Graves.

By the time Graves set off for France the Germans and the Allies had reached a stalemate on the Western Front, the only hope of a rapid victory being to break through the enemy's line. All possible methods were used – bombardment with heavy artillery, surprise raids and mines. The month before Graves's arrival, the Germans at the Second Battle of Ypres had started to use gas on the unprepared Allies and only fear of their own weapon had prevented a major breakthrough. Each time an attack was repulsed trenches were dug and the stalemate increased – 'an unromantic sitting still 100 yards from Brother Bosch', as Sorley called it.[2]

When Graves set off for Liverpool on 12 May to join a troopship for Le Havre, he had been hoping to be sent out to France for so long that he had already anticipated what awaited him there. So convincing was his imaginative account of trench warfare – 'It's a Queer Time' – that it was taken, on publication, to be his first 'realistic' description of battle based on first-hand experience. Instead, he confessed later, it was written at Wrexham 'some weeks before I had a chance of verifying my facts'.[3]

The First World War produced an unprecedented outpouring of verse, both from civilians and participants, who faced experiences completely new to them. (As Blunden observed, England was no longer a nation of shopkeepers but of poets.) For those who had been practising poets before the war, which included virtually all the major names – Owen, Sassoon, Rosenberg, Brooke, Blunden, Sorley and Gurney, as well as Graves – finding the language and technique to write about war was as much of a challenge as a stimulus. While the increased intensity of their daily lives offered them a wide range of new subjects for verse, its very novelty seemed to call for a different approach. Sassoon, for instance, who had been dabbling mainly in what Edmund Gosse called his 'lutes and nightingale' style, turned quickly to satire after his first encounter with the trenches – and Graves – in late

1915, leading him to reject the powerful influence of Brooke's *1914* sonnet sequence.

Graves's initial reaction to his first imaginings (rather than experience) of the trenches was to write in 'the language I used to speak at the age of nine'.[4] Although the reference here, in his letter to Marsh of 22 May 1915, was to 'The Poet in the Nursery', also written at Wrexham earlier in 1915, it applies equally to the second poem included in that letter, 'It's a Queer Time'. This is a 'recent improvisation of mine', he tells Marsh, as he sends him the first draft of its final three stanzas. The fact that he does not send Marsh the opening couplet and first stanza of the poem suggests that he was still working on them. Since they are the most effective part of the poem, it may be that these opening lines were completed after he reached the trenches on 19 May:

> It's hard to know if you're alive or dead
> When steel and fire go roaring through your head.
>
> One moment you'll be crouching at your gun
> Traversing, mowing heaps down half in fun:
> The next, you choke and clutch at your right breast –
> No time to think – leave all – and off you go...
> To Treasure Island where the Spice winds blow,
> To lovely groves of mango, quince and lime –
> Breathe no goodbye, but ho, for the Red West!
>   It's a queer time.[5]

The simile Graves chooses to describe his first authenticated reaction to the trenches gives a clue to his initially puzzling decision to revert to the language and experience of childhood: 'I feel here,' he told Marsh, 'exactly like a man who has watched the "movies" for a long evening and then suddenly finds himself thrown on the screen in the middle of scalp-hunting Sioux and runaway motor cars.'[6] Searching for an equivalent to this first frightening yet exhilarating experience of trench warfare, Graves's imagination has reverted to 'Cowboys and Indians', a game he almost certainly played in childhood, as he lived life with great intensity. The second stanza of 'It's a Queer Time', for instance, recalls childhood memories of Laufzorn, 'digging tunnels through the hay / In the Big Barn,' cause it's a rainy day / ... / You're back in the old sailor suit again'.

Another section of Graves's first poetry collection, *Over the Brazier* (1916), is entitled 'Nursery Memories' and employs a similar technique. Although this can occasionally seem a little contrived and *faux-naif*, for the most part it succeeds in showing us the trenches in a fresh light. All the horror and revulsion he experienced there emerges powerfully, for instance, in 'The First Funeral', where the child-narrator recalls coming across the stinking corpse of a dog, which he and his sister then bury, an incident that had actually happened to Robert at Harlech:[7]

> He felt quite soft and horrid:
>   The flies buzzed round his head
> And settled on his forehead:
>   Rose whispered: 'That dog's dead'.[8]

Good-bye to All That has a significant number of references to bloated, rotting corpses and their smell.

Similarly, when Graves wants to suggest that perhaps not all claims of soldiers at the Front are to be believed, he simply presents, in 'The Adventure', a child boasting of impossible feats, such as 'killing a tiger near my shack'. The lively imaginings of children in a wood, pretending to be big-game hunters, are given sinister overtones all the more shocking for the implied contrast of war with innocent childhood games. Graves claimed in 'Babylon', a poem published in his second poetry collection, that 'The child alone a poet is', but would limit his use of the child's voice and viewpoint mainly to his war poetry. At the same time he would continue to visit the world of children, which he found curiously comforting. Whenever he went into billets from the front line, he told his parents, he 'staved off approaching senility' by 'mak[ing] for the nursery', where he got on 'splendidly' with French children.[9]

***

Setting out for the battlefield for the first time was inevitably a dramatic moment, one that a number of the war poets marked in verse. Rupert Brooke, for example, though he never reached the fighting at Gallipoli (dying at Skyros on the way), conveys the sobering effect of this journey into the unknown in 'Fragment', as he watches his shipmates and fellow soldiers through the cabin window:

> I would have thought of them
> – Heedless, within a week of battle – in pity,
> Pride in their strength and in the weight and firmness
> And link'd beauty of bodies, and pity that
> This gay machine of splendour' ld soon be broken,
> Thought little of, pashed, scattered...[10]

When Graves arrived at Le Havre in mid-May 1915, Brooke had been dead for less than a month and, though Graves assured Marsh that 'we can only be glad that he died ... in such a good cause',[11] it was another reminder of his own possible fate. A still starker warning of the dangers that threatened even before he reached France was the news of the sinking of the *Lusitania* on its way to Liverpool on 7 May 1915, less than a week before his own departure from the same port. But whether he felt fear or exhilaration or both is not known, since, unlike Sassoon and Edward Thomas, for instance, he left no diary for the period. His father's diary, however, gives an invaluable record of this period, sometimes conveying a more detailed and more accurate picture of Graves's activities during the war than *Good-bye to All That*. Robert's many letters to his parents between 1914 and 1919 are described and commented on by his father as they are received. According to Alfred, 'Robby ... had a pleasant journey to Le Havre', a 'good passage'.[12] Having set out from Wrexham on 12 May with five fellow officers, Graves had waited at Liverpool to join units of what he called, with a proud consciousness of his superiority in Special Reserve, 'Kitchener's New Army'. Made up from those who had responded to Kitchener's recruitment drive in August 1914, this unit was being sent out much earlier than Kitchener had originally intended, to help the struggling and depleted Regular Army. Its first serious engagement would be at the Battle of Loos, alongside Graves's regiment among others.

By Sunday, 16 May, Graves was in charge of a working party of over a hundred men at Le Havre, 'doing fatigue work down at the quay in the immense warehouse', he told his parents in the first of a series of letters that he would allow his father to 'furbish up' a little and publish in *The Spectator*.[13] The next morning of 17 May, Graves and his fellow officers, Robertson, McLellan, Watkin, Robert Hanmer Jones and Frank Jones-Bateman, were on their way to join the Welsh Regiment, to which they had been 'attached'. Graves was 'rather sick' at not being with his own regiment and was convinced that his 'attachment system' could not hope to be a 'success': 'It is merely a contrived source of annoyance to the men attached,' he told Marsh, 'and the men to whom they are attached.'[14]

Graves's journey to the trenches themselves could stand for that of many other soldiers in First World War France: a train ride which would have taken under five hours in normal circumstances took five times that length of time, though as his letter home shows, it had its entertaining side and had been a bonding experience:

> ... a great column of us marched to the station and entrained. We took twenty-five hours to go about as many miles, travelling, the five of us Flash Mob, in one carriage with packs and valises, which was cheery, but no good for sleeping. We had a rowdy dinner beforehand, with homards, pain d'épice, bully beef which isn't bad stuff – for a time – marmalade, tinned sausages, sang a lot of songs, and did the 'To-morrow comrades we' touch. When we arrived at the rail-head, a small town (ask no names), we disembarked feeling a bit like the bottom of the proverbial parrot-cage, and were told by the guide who met us that we were to go straight into the trenches.[15]

With his usual cavalier attitude towards facts, Graves has grossly minimized the distance, partly for purposes of style: the 'railhead', Béthune, is approximately 160 miles from Le Havre, not 25 miles as he implies. Nevertheless, he has made his point about the difficulties of transportation in those circumstances.

Graves's account of his subsequent march to the trenches at Cambrin 'by cobbled road and a mile and a half down a muddy communication trench in the dark, lit by occasional star shells' is equally graphic but less inaccurate: it was after six miles (he claimed five) that he was welcomed to C Company of the 2nd Welsh Battalion. Weighed down with his 'pack-valise' of about 60 lbs, revolver, field glasses, compass, whisky flask, wire-cutters, periscope and other equipment, he was grateful to be given a cup of tea, some cake and 'an Egyptian' (a cigarette), then sent off for a much-needed sleep.

Unlike his heightened version of events in *Good-bye to All That*, Graves's letter to his parents makes it clear that in real life he was allowed this first morning to sleep through the inspection, an hour before dawn, of 'stand-to', a less punishing introduction to warfare than he portrays. In fact, far from the 'baptism of fire' experienced by Sassoon, for instance, later in 1915, Graves was relatively fortunate in his first tour of the trenches. He got on well with his company commander, Captain Dunn, described by the adjutant as 'the soundest officer in the battalion'.[16] Two months younger than Graves, Dunn was nevertheless a reassuring presence, imperturbable in the face of danger. He had come straight from Sandhurst, according to Graves, but had none of the military stiffness Graves would encounter in other Regular Army officers later on. He conducted company business informally and in a democratic way, over a meal, in consultation with his four junior officers – 'a sort of board-meeting with Dunn as chairman'.[17]

To begin with at least, the meals over which they held their discussions – real eggs and bacon, coffee, toast and marmalade for breakfast, for instance – sound a great deal better than the tinned bully beef, Maconochie stew and hard biscuits served later, reminding the reader how early Graves arrived on the Western Front. He was also fortunate in his first experience of the trenches: his description of them to his parents makes them sound more like their German counterparts, sent back by envious British soldiers: 'palaces … wonderful places … clay walls – bomb-proof ceilings, pictures on the walls, straw-filled baths, stoves, chairs, complete with a piebald cat'.[18]

Trenches varied greatly in different parts of the line, but most were muddy, rat-infested passageways with primitive dugouts built into their earth sides. Graves's trenches at Cambrin had been dug by the French, but it was almost certainly Dunn's good sense in working his company hard at maintaining and improving them – 'not only for safety but for health' – that made them seem positively welcoming when Graves stumbled into C Company headquarters on the night of 18/19 May 1915.

He felt lucky too in his allotted batman, a man called Fry, who worked in a paper-bag factory in civilian life and whose skills went far beyond polishing buttons and belts: 'He is a good servant[19] but a bad man. What constitutes the good servant is the faculty of coming back with more than he sets out with: mine got hold of a new Webley revolver complete with lanyard, an excellent weapon.'[20] (This practice was known euphemistically as 'winning' in the Army.)

Graves even came to feel lucky in the men he had been sent to command, though they were neither smart in appearance nor disciplined in behaviour. But in other ways, he realized, they were 'not far removed from the [Royal Welch] Fusiliers: the men are recruited from the same class and district.'[21] Mostly miners in civilian life and used to death, they had 'a very limited morality', according to Graves: they would, for instance, 'rob anyone of anything, except a man in their own platoon'.[22] Still rather puritanical about sex, he also found them 'lecherous', the young ones at least, 'but without the false shame of the English lecher'.[23] Although not as senior in service as the Royal Welch Fusiliers, the 2nd Welsh Battalion had a distinguished service record dating from the eighteenth century. (The 69th of Foot, it eventually came to be known as 'the ups and downs', because the number reads the same both ways up: 'The 69 was certainly upside-down when we joined it', Graves cannot resist joking in *Good-bye to All That*.) Graves's reference to the 2nd Welsh battalion's 'peaceful attitude' and other remarks made by him, therefore, caused some offence and was commented on in their Regimental History. By the time Graves joined it, the 2nd Welsh had served continuously since landing at Le Havre in August 1914 and had lost most of its original men. From an initial position of slight scorn, Graves would develop a grudging respect for them. 'They would follow their officers anywhere,' he remembered, pessimistic though they were by this stage of the war.[24] And he would miss the openness and chattiness of the men when he rejoined the more formal 2nd Royal Welch Fusiliers at the end of July 1915.

Graves had quickly established himself with his own platoon, 30 or so men of C Company's 2nd Welsh, with a witty reference to a popular comic Welsh song, 'Crawshay Bailey': 'Crawshay Bailey's brother, Norwich, / for instance, was fond of oatmeal porridge, / and was sent to Cardiff College, / for to get a bit of knowledge': after that he had 'no trouble with the platoon at all'.[25] His love of music was another bond with his men, who were 'great singers', he reported home, and would sing even at their tiredest and most down-hearted, accompanied no doubt by Graves who had led so many family sing-songs in the past. Knowing his father's interest in song, he would often send home details of their repertoire, though what his mother made of one particularly suggestive one, Alfred does not record:

> *Woodpecker Song*
> I shoved my finger in a woodpecker's hole
> And the Woodpecker screamed GOD STRAFE your soul
>   Take it out!
>   Take it out!
>   Take it out!
> REMOVE IT.[26]

He got on well, too, with his platoon's Sergeant Eastmond, and mentions several of his men by name, in particular Private James Burford, whom he claimed was the oldest man in the regiment at 63, and Private Bumford, the youngster at 15. Graves still had a few men with him from the Royal Welch Fusiliers, one of whom, Frank Jones-Bateman, would become a good friend during their exile with the 2nd Welsh. Graves was never without friends. Jones-Bateman was 'honest and kind hearted', a 'quiet boy' of nineteen, fresh from Rugby, with a scholarship waiting for him at Caius (not 'Clare' as Graves claims) College, Cambridge.[27] Although nicknamed 'Silent Night', he and Graves found plenty to talk about, starting with his visit to Graves from an adjoining company on the first day. They would write to each other after they were separated, sending their respective poems, and Graves believed Jones-Bateman to be 'the best sort of critic', who did 'not try to force the poet away from his present moods on to paths that seem more suggestions how to improve what he has written'.[28]

He found him one of only 'three good critics of his poetry during the War' and would be very sad indeed to hear of his death at the same battle that killed Wilfred Owen, the Sambre, and on the same day, 4 November 1918. The four years that Graves spent in the Army would be full of what Sorley called these 'friendships of circumstance'.

The loss of friends in war was in the future, however, and Graves's first letter home from the trenches was a 'very blithe one', according to his father.[29] After only three days at Cambrin, a relatively quiet sector that the English had just taken over from the French, the 2nd Welsh were back in reserve billets at the coal-mining village of Labourse, approximately three-and-a-half miles from the Front. Graves's worst experience had been coming across a man who had blown his head off with his own rifle after hearing bad news from home about his 'girl'.[30] Labourse, situated near the road between Béthune and La Bassée, experienced nothing on the scale of Ypres, roughly 30 miles to its north, or the Somme battlefields, between 20 and 25 miles to its south, and Graves would realize how 'lucky' he had been in his 'gentle introduction' to the trenches when, after three days' rest, the 2nd Welsh were next sent to Cuinchy.[31] (Graves had used his rest to write to his father asking him to send him his copies of Keats and Butler's *Erewhon*.)

Cuinchy proved to be the 'baptism of fire' that Cambrin had not and a stark contrast. The trenches, set among the Cuinchy brickstacks, seemed to Graves to have 'made themselves rather than been made' and 'ran inconsequently in and out of the solid stacks of bricks, many about 18 feet in height over a base area of 35 square feet.' Allowing for a little excusable exaggeration, Graves's claim that one of the trenches was built with communication-boxes and corpses, with mud everywhere and everything 'wet and smelly', gives a fair picture of the dismal scene.[32] Another horror were the rats that came up from the nearby canal and, according to Graves, 'fed on the plentiful corpses and multiplied exceedingly'.[33] One officer new to the battalion, woken by the sound of scuffling on his first night at Cuinchy, had discovered two rats on his bed 'tussling for the possession of a severed human hand'.[34] Lice, too, though less obviously repulsive, caused great misery in these trenches and the men spent a lot of their spare time trying to free their clothing of them. Graves's poem on the subject of the 'little lice' ('The Trenches') may be jokey, but the nuisance was a serious one, marked again in verse by Isaac Rosenberg in 'Louse Hunting' and other of his poems.

It was an altogether nightmarish situation, with each side occupying half the brickstacks and sniping down from the top of them onto each other. Trench mortars and rifle grenades made even the shortest journey hazardous: it was here Graves experienced his first serious threat of death, when a German rifle grenade landed within six feet of him but failed to explode, having landed by sheer chance on its stick rather than head. Here also he learnt to judge danger by noise and discovered that he had 'extraordinarily quick reactions to danger'.[35] Most soldiers did after a time, though not always quick enough, Graves realized after another threatening incident. Hearing one shell 'whish-whishing' towards him, he dropped flat, his ears singing 'as though there were gnats in them' and his shoulder twisted in the fall.[36] His chest 'sang' too and he lost his sense of balance, ashamed to be discovered on all fours by his sergeant major. There was constant mining and counter-mining in the area and a very real fear on both sides of the line of being blown up by it.

The men, Graves noted, were 'much afraid', yet always joking, their humour of the most macabre kind.[37] One corpse, his arm still extended as it had been at the moment of death, had been brought back from No Man's Land and placed on the fire-step, his arm stretched out across the trench; some of the men would actually shake the dead hand as they passed, with the words, 'Put it there, Billy Boy.'[38]

Like Graves's own black humour in *Good-bye to All That*, it was evidently their way of coping, even mimicking the absurdity and horror of the situation. One memorable anecdote that Graves relates, true in essence he believed, though not something he had witnessed himself, was of two soldiers who had murdered their sergeant major. Their macabre explanation of why it was an 'accident' – they had meant to shoot their platoon sergeant instead – makes the reader laugh first but ask questions afterwards. (Both men were shot by a firing squad against the wall of a convent, Graves adds for good measure.)

Some experiences at Cuinchy were too gruesome for jokes, Graves realized, when he came across a man whose brains had been blown out:

> One can joke with a badly-wounded man and congratulate him on being out of it. One can disregard a dead man. But even a miner can't make a joke that sounds like a joke over a man who takes three hours to die after the top part of his head has been taken off by a bullet fired at twenty yards range.[39]

It was incidents like this which made him write to his parents early on to say that he could not 'stick those fellows who write home to say that war is adorable'.[40] The only real difference in attitude between himself and that more well-known protester, Sassoon, would be that Graves's protest occurred much earlier and that he believed that to protest publicly would not be the act of an officer and a gentleman.

Despite his horror of the trenches, however, Robert could not resist collecting souvenirs at Cuinchy to send home to his family – 'a hand grenade to be converted into a candle stick', together with 'snipers' and other bullets and bits of shrapnel, 'part of [a] shell which had killed a man, in a Ration Tin'[41] – which his father proudly showed to the V.C. hero, Michael O'Leary, at the Hyde Park demonstration on 11 July 1915, since they had been taken from the very trenches where O'Leary had won his Victoria Cross.

By the time these mementos had reached the Graves family on 4 June, Robert was already enjoying 'ten days safely with reserves' in the nearest fair-sized town, Béthune.[42] Seven miles or so behind the lines and still very little damaged, it had everything he had longed for in the trenches, 'a swimming bath, all sorts of shops, especially a cake-shop, the best [he'd] ever met, a hotel where you [could] get a really good dinner, and a theatre'.[43] (The dinner was particularly luxurious – 'fish, new potatoes, green peas, asparagus, mutton chops, strawberries and cream, and three bottles of Pommarol [sic]', highlighting the stark contrasts encountered in France.)[44] For Bernard Adams, a fellow-RWF soldier and friend of Graves, it was particularly wonderful to be able to get a luxurious shampoo and haircut, as he recorded in his posthumous account of the period in *Nothing of Importance* (1917).

The main meeting point for officers was the Café du Globe, a 'glorious institution' according to (purportedly) an ex-Carthusian, possibly Graves, who sent back an anonymous letter to the school magazine on the subject; it paints a colourful picture of the café reputed to be the 'favourite rendez-vous' of the Prince of Wales, based in the area with the 40th Siege Battery:

> Every officer's charger in at least 8 divisions knows the way to its front doors: from early dawn to the curfew toll they are lined up in the sunny square outside, chestnut, black, roan, bay, sorrel and mouse-coloured, waiting for their masters, that are drinking inside and rather resentful of the dirty little *gamins* who hold their heads, smoking cheap cigarettes and shouting obscene cosmopolitanisms at passers-by.[45]

Champagne cocktails at one franc (10d English money) a time were the order of the day.

But when Graves wanted to convey how civilized Béthune felt after life in the trenches, he illustrated his point by describing the 'very nice ... bourgeois family' with whom he was billeted in Avenue de Bruay, the Averlants. He was particularly taken by the children, a teenage girl and her two little brothers, and proud of having been able to help the girl work out the theory of decimal division – in French: 'Now you didn't think I was as clever as all that did you?' he asked his parents, though he had already been chosen as interpreter for his group of officers on landing in France. His ability with languages would mean that, unlike Sassoon, he was able to communicate with the French, and he was both shocked and fascinated to hear from the Averlants' daughter that the reason she had used so many abbreviations in her maths notes was that the teacher had been in such a hurry: heavy shelling by the Germans had meant that the pupils had to take shelter in the cellar – 'and when we came back each time was less and less time left,' she explained.[46]

The combination of all these experiences – the horrors of the trenches, the mud, the rats, the bombardments, and the enormous relief of coming out of them to civilization and the innocence and freshness of children – is brought out clearly in what is almost certainly Graves's first truly realistic war poem, 'Limbo':

> After a week spent under raining skies,
> In horror, mud and sleeplessness, a week
> Of bursting shells, of blood and hideous cries
> And the ever-watchful sniper: where the reek
> Of death offends the living ... but poor dead
> Can't sleep, must lie awake with the horrid sound
> That roars and whirs and rattles overhead
> All day, all night, and jars and tears the ground;
> When rats run, big as kittens: to and fro
> They dart, and scuffle with their horrid fare,
> And then one night relief comes, and we go
> Miles back into sunny cornland where
> Babies like tickling, and where tall white horses
> Draw the plough leisurely in quiet courses.

Even the gruesome detail that some parapets at the Cuinchy brickstacks had been built up with corpses was included in the first version of the poem, in which lines 9 and 10 originally read:

And the dying whisper: 'Parapet's too low.
Collect these bodies ... quick ... build them up there!'[47]

'Limbo' contrasts strongly with the majority of war poems of this early period, which still tend towards the patriotic and idealistic, full of abstract ideals of honour and duty, along the lines of Brooke's *1914* sonnet sequence. Although Graves's poem is also in sonnet form, it is one of unrelieved nastiness until the final four lines. It is not surprising that the initially Brooke-influenced Sassoon was to find Graves's early war poetry 'very bad, violent and repulsive'.[48] (It is doubtful, however, whether it shocked Robert's 'venerable sire' as Sassoon claimed;[49] Alfred was still making every effort to place each of his son's poems for publication as Robert sent them to him.) 'Limbo' was a brave and honest poem to write in the circumstances and makes Graves a pioneer among the war poets.

Graves's respite in Béthune was over all too quickly, and by 9 June he was back in the trenches, at a 'nasty little salient' to the south of Cuinchy brickstacks, where casualties were always heavy.[50] The first excitement of the 'baptism of fire' soon wore off, he told his family, and the 'joys of sniping fat Germans, though sweet, [were] seldom long-lived'.[51] The machine-gun fire, one of the deadliest features of trench-life, 'ripple[d] to and fro like a garden spray' and 'the snippy sniper gets snapped'.[52] Graves's new, expensive periscope, was hit too, an indication of how frighteningly accurate German snipers could be and an event which he marked in another 'realistic' war poem, which opens: 'Trench stinks of shallow-buried dead / Where Tom stands at his periscope'.[53] (This was sent at once to Edward Marsh, who evidently found it too repulsive and it was not published in Graves's lifetime.)

Despite the extreme danger, Graves's main feeling was of boredom, his daily trench routine striking him as 'aimless pottering'.[54] His title 'Limbo' sums up the sense of purposelessness he experienced that summer.

Graves's second break in this monotony came in the third week of June when the 2nd Welsh were transferred on 22 June to Vermelles, about three miles south of Cuinchy. Although the town lay only three-quarters of a mile from the British front line and had been taken and retaken eight times since the previous October, some semblance of normal life remained possible in Vermelles. Apart from night-digging, there was very little work to do. The troops could not drill since they were so near the front line, and there was no fortification work to be done there. So they strolled about in the deserted gardens of the town, where roses, lilies, cabbages and fruit trees grew indiscriminately. They also played cricket, officers against sergeants, Graves getting the top score, he was proud to report, in one of these games. Still in the same billets by 2 July, a cellar in the ruins of Vermelles, he reported to the relief of his anxious family:

> No work to do, plenty of sunshine, food and drink and flowers, and drawing 12/9 a day pay and allowance the whole time! In four days we have an 8 days rest and then come back for 16 days to the same sector which is a delightfully quiet spot. There is nothing eventful at all here except our games of nap and vingt-et-un and cricket (with a rag ball, a stump of charred wood for a bat and a parrot-cage for wicket – perhaps dear people the grisly dead object it contains would rather spoil your play).[55]

There was time also for poetry and, apart from a jokey verse about a hideous glass case containing artificial flowers, which he used for target practice, Graves also wrote at least one serious poem at Vermelles, 'Cherry-time at the Front', which he sent to his father in early July. As Graves noted on his own copy of *Over the Brazier*, this was a rewrite of a poem composed at Harlech in 1911 – 'but they were Wimbledon cherries'.[56] Emile Cammaerts, a Belgian poet who was writing his own war poetry at this time and to whom Alfred showed his son's poem, was 'delighted' with it, particularly the refrain that 'reminded him of one of the early Flemish folk-songs':[57]

> Merry, merry,
> Take a cherry;
> Mine are sounder,
> Mine are rounder,
> Mine are sweeter
> For the eater
> Under the moon.
> And you'll be fairies soon.[58]

Written in response to the abandoned gardens of Vermelles, where Graves could escape from the war for a time, this is another example of his attempt to define the ugliness of the trenches by contrasting them with something both lovely and natural. There is also a hint at another world:

> Cherries of the night are riper
> > Than the cherries pluckt at noon:
> Gather to your fairy piper
> > When he pipes his magic tune...[59]

Only the change in the last two lines of the final refrain introduces the possibility of death: 'When the dews fall. / And you'll be fairies soon.' But it is a faint hint only and the poem's original title, 'Cherry-time at the Front', was changed in *Over the Brazier*, with 'at the Front' omitted and the poem itself placed in the earlier, pre-war section. 'Slight' as it is, according to one critic Alfred showed it to,[60] Graves himself believed that it was 'good': 'Nobody else has the subtlety to see this,' he wrote to Cyril Hartmann who had praised it.[61]

Another poem that was almost certainly written under the influence of the cherry trees and deserted gardens of Vermelles – 'The Morning Before the Battle' – shows how widely Graves's early war poems varied in both content and technique as he struggled to find a way of describing his new, shocking experiences. In contrast to 'Cherry-time', he turns here directly to the fighting and its likely consequences. As Charles Mundye points out, Graves 'represents [his] divided self in two halves' of a Petrarchan sonnet.[62] Switching between the two is like reading Blake's *Songs of Experience* after *Songs of Innocence*, the latter represented by 'a deserted garden full of flowers' and trees. (Blake's poems were one of the few books Graves took to France in 1915.) The garden, Graves noted, was 'a garden in Béthune near the College des Jeunes Filles', but it is clearly also a symbolic place introduced, once again, to contrast with the ugliness of the trenches.[63] This is represented by the 'wraith' of the last six lines, 'His head all battered in by violent blows', the cherries of the first eight lines becoming 'clotted blood' in an implied comparison with the partaking of the body and blood of Christ at Holy Communion.[64] The narrator's conclusion, that 'dead men blossomed in the garden-close', though somewhat melodramatic, brings the two halves of the poem together and suggests that Graves himself was thinking of his fellow soldiers killed during this period. It also anticipates T. S. Eliot's corpses flowering in the first section of *The Waste Land*.

'A Renascence', too, shows the range of Graves's experimentation and feelings in 1915, though he later found the poem 'inexcusable' and omitted it from the second edition of *Over the Brazier* in 1920. In it he presents a positive view of the fighting, one that helps to explain the later decision by the government's Department of Information to use some of his war poems 'for propaganda in neutral and belligerent countries':[65]

> White flabbiness goes brown and lean,
>   Dumpling arms are now brass bars,
> They've learnt to suffer and live clean,
>   And to think below the stars...
>
> Learning to leap the parapet,
>   Face the open rush, and then
> To stab with the stark bayonet,
>   Side by side with fighting men.[66]

Yet at the same time Graves portrays the grim reality of war in poems that were never published in his lifetime, possibly because of their initial vetting by Edward Marsh, poems such as 'The Last Drop' ('Jusqu'au bout' in its first version) in which 'Old Age' has 'sentenced Youth to die', or 'Trench Life', which opens 'Fear never dies'.[67]

One of Graves's problems at this time was a lack of suitable models; his current favourite, Keats, gave him no real help in these uncharted waters. His next request to his father, A. E. Housman's *A Shropshire Lad*, would be far more suitable. But by the time it arrived, his circumstances had changed yet again, leaving him little time to write poetry. For at the end of July 1915 Graves and his fellow-RWF officer, Robertson, received orders to report to the 2nd Royal Welch Fusiliers, part of the 19th Brigade.[68] Another two of the original six, Jones-Bateman and Hanmer Jones, were posted to the 1st Battalion, and the remaining two had already returned to England, McLellan sick and Watkin with shrapnel wounds, a foretaste of what was to come.

7

The Battle of Loos
(August–October 1915)

The torn line wavers, breaks, and falls.
'Get up, come on!' the captain calls
'Get up, the Welsh, and on we go!'
(Christ, that my lads should fail me so!)
A dying boy grinned up and said:
'The whole damned company, sir; it's dead.'
'Come on! Cowards!' bawled the captain, then
Fell killed, among his writhing men.[1]

'Machine Gun Fire: Cambrin', (September 25, 1915)

When Graves and Robertson went to join the 2nd Royal Welch Fusiliers at the end of July 1915, the battalion was in the Laventie sector, approximately 17 miles north of Vermelles. But the two officers managed to make the journey last over two days, deliberately missing at least one of their train connections in order to spend another indulgent night in Béthune on the way, with a second at Berguette.

Graves had not been as delighted as he had anticipated to leave the 2nd Welsh, especially his men, who 'all crowded round to shake hands and wish' him luck.[2] Nor did he look forward to starting again with a new company and new customs, a justifiable fear as it turned out. One of the few regular battalions still more or less intact at that time, the 2nd Royal Welch Fusiliers seemed to him a hotbed of snobbishness and elitism and very tough even on Special Reserve officers, let alone New Army ones. Regular officers referred to all new subalterns as 'warts' for at least six months after their arrival, put them through gruelling riding lessons if they were not already first-class horsemen (Graves was not), and ran a battalion rather than a company mess as a sign of their distinction. This was of no benefit to junior officers, who were not allowed the usual whisky at meals and forbidden to talk. Even Robertson, a man of 42 and a solicitor in civilian life with a large practice, who had stood for Parliament in the most recent election, was snubbed when he attempted to do so.

As Graves also quickly realized, however, they were highly professional, extremely good soldiers and he grew proud of belonging to such an efficient battalion. Although their much stricter rules earned him punishment on occasions, he could see that they were well thought out and for the safety of the battalion, which lost far fewer men unnecessarily than the 2nd Welsh. They insisted on getting fire ascendancy in whatever sector they occupied and made it a 'point of honour' to be masters of No Man's Land, which turned Graves's first night with them into a terrifying experience. It was regimental custom to test new officers by sending them out on night patrol. Graves's company commander, Captain G. O. Thomas, followed the custom and his new officer found himself going out on night patrol for the first time in his army service. (He had never done so during his two months with the 2nd Welsh; anyone who did was considered 'mad'.)[3] Now, accompanied by his platoon sergeant, an ex-policeman called Townsend, and wriggling flat along the ground, Graves made a painful sortie into No Man's Land, which lay beneath the RWF's high-command trenches. The objective was a sap-head beyond the German wire, which involved a crawl of only 200 yards by Graves's reckoning, but which took about two hours to accomplish.

Captain Thomas was satisfied and even the colonel seemed impressed; personal courage in a young officer was highly respected in the battalion. After that Graves went out fairly often, indulging the daring, reckless side of him that relished danger. Responding on one occasion to the colonel's appeal for volunteers to investigate suspicious sounds in No Man's Land, he persisted even after the moon came out 'so bright and full it dazzled the eyes', he recalled.[4] Determined not to be accused of 'cold feet', he resisted the appeal of his (temporary) company commander, J. A. Childe-Freeman, to call things off. In the event Graves was lucky and survived, but the experience left him 'with a sense of nightmare' at the 'dangerously clear light of an evil-looking moon',[5] and helps explain one of his more puzzling poems:

> I hate the Moon, though it makes most people glad,
>   And they giggle and talk of silvery beams – you know!
> But *she* says the look of the Moon drives people mad,
>   And that's the thing that always frightens me so.
>
> I hate it worst when it's cruel and round and bright,
>   And you can't make out the marks on its stupid face,
> Except when you shut your eyelashes, and all night
>   The sky looks green, and the world's a horrible place...[6]

In this third of what Graves called his 'Nursery Poems' in *Over the Brazier*, the child's irrational fear of the moon, which seems to him threatening rather than projecting its usual associations of beauty or romance, conveys the terror Graves had experienced on his foolhardy night patrol, though this had been all too rational. He was to express a similar sentiment in similarly childish terms in 'The Cruel Moon' in his third verse collection, *Fairies and Fusiliers* (1917).

Graves's daring exploits helped offset his failure to live up to the 2nd Battalion's strict standards of etiquette and dress. He got on well with his fellow platoon officers in A Company, to which he had been assigned, 'the best company I could have struck,' he claimed.[7] Its commander, Captain Thomas, was a regular soldier of seventeen years' service, a well-known polo player and fine soldier – 'a great character', Graves told his parents; he had 'never known a man more sparing of his words or a better listener ... a good sort, and a silent humorist of the first water':

> When he first went home on leave in December he is reported to have been seen in Piccadilly wearing a British warm coat, with no badges of rank, over his uniform, goose-stepping down the pavement and giving an exaggerated salute to all officers and winking at all the Tommies and N.C.O.'s he met. This was a reaction against regimentation and pleased him highly. He did little else on his five days.[8]

Although Thomas, unlike the 2nd Welsh company commander Captain Dunn, never took his juniors into his confidence about company matters, he was most conscientious in taking his watch at night, unlike some of the other company commanders. He was also generous in sharing his weekly hamper from Fortnum and Mason.

Graves had been with the 2nd Royal Welch Battalion about three weeks when the 19th Brigade, to which it belonged, was moved down from the Laventie to the Béthune sector and he found himself back in familiar territory, the Cuinchy brickstacks. His battalion was ordered to the La Bassée canal bank only a few hundred yards to the left of his position with the 2nd Welsh Battalion at the end of May. 'Nasty trenches' though they were, he wrote to his parents, he felt more in touch with their methods than during 'the dull routine' of the previous weeks.[9] (Dull as it had been, however, it had allowed him to write some more poems and he had sent at least three new ones home during the respite.)

One new feature at Cuinchy was the Germans' wish to be sociable. As the well-known Christmas Truce of 1914 had suggested, German soldiers appeared to bear no ill-will towards their opposite numbers, and at Cuinchy they started sending friendly messages over in undetonated rifle grenades. Their most interesting missive for Graves was a copy of the *Neueste Nachrichten* (the 'Latest News', a German Army newspaper printed at Lille), which gave sensational details of Russian defeats around Warsaw and the capture of large numbers of prisoners and guns. He was surprised to find the sinking of a German submarine by a British armed trawler also reported, since no English newspaper would have been allowed to publish this kind of information if one of their submarines had been sunk. Although the fraternization went no further than this, Graves was keen to emphasize that the episode was 'not an emotional hiatus but commonplace of military tradition – an exchange of courtesies between officers of opposite armies'.[10]

Graves's move to the 2nd Royal Welch Fusiliers had delayed the home leave due to him by 24 July 1915, his twentieth birthday. So too had preparations for a coming offensive in the La Bassée area, news of which had started to leak out through younger staff officers. By 18 August the continuing Russian losses in the East, to which the German newspaper had alerted Graves and his fellow soldiers, had convinced an initially sceptical Kitchener that Britain and France must act vigorously on the Western Front. Just as Russia's plea for help against Turkey at the end of 1914 had led to the catastrophic attack on the Dardanelles, so Russia's losses on the Eastern Front in the summer of 1915 would be a catalyst for a new Anglo-French offensive in the West. There was also the continuing aim to break through the German defences in Artois Champagne and restore a war of movement; the recovery of the mining district around Lens and Loos was another motive. The British attack was planned initially for 8 September (but delayed until 25 September) at Loos, to the south of Cuinchy. The battlefield itself would extend almost as far south as Lens and as far north as Givenchy, the 2nd RWF's sector lying towards its northern limit.

By the end of August the extensive preparations for the battle made it obvious to the Germans, as well as French civilians, what was being planned, removing the element of surprise. Graves noted, for instance, batteries and lorry-trains of shells rumbling nightly up the Béthune-La Bassée road to his north and men sapping forward at his previous posts of Vermelles and Cambrin, where the lines were rather far apart, to make a new front line. Orders for the evacuation of hospitals in the area were issued and cavalry and New Army divisions began to arrive. The Royal Engineers started digging pits at intervals along the front line for gas cylinders, to be used for the first time in retaliation for the German use of gas at Ypres in May. Scaling-ladders for climbing quickly out of trenches were brought up by the lorry-load and dumped at Cambrin village. By 3 September it was clear to Graves that his division, 2nd Division, would be attacking on the Cambrin-Cuinchy sector, and so great was the general excitement that he was almost sorry to be given home leave shortly afterwards.

But it felt wonderful to escape wartime France, even if thoughts of it were never far away. Graves was struck, for instance, by the 'general indifference to and ignorance about the war' even in London, which was full of men in uniform.[11] The first patriotic fervour had died down, enlistment was still voluntary, and the universal catchword seemed to be 'Business as usual'. It all seemed rather 'unreal' to him and he escaped at once to Wales.[12] Life in the trenches had, if possible, increased his love of the area around Harlech, of which he had written nostalgically only two months previously at Vermelles in late June 1915, in response to the question 'what life to lead and where to go / After the war, after the war':

> I'd thought: 'A cottage in the hills,
>   North Wales, a cottage full of books,
>   Pictures and brass and cosy nooks
> And comfortable broad window-sills,
> Flowers in the garden, walls all white.
> I'd live there peacefully and dream and write.'[13]

Called 'Over the Brazier', this became the title-poem of his first verse collection, as well as a partially self-fulfilling prophecy.

When he arrived at Erinfa, he found his parents, Rosaleen, Charles, John and their half-brother Perceval waiting for him in a place that had always given him a sense of freedom. His own memory of his six days there was of 'walk[ing] about on the hills in an old shirt and a pair of shorts'.[14] In fact, apart from catching up on his sleep, he had involved himself far more in family life than this suggests, showing what a close-knit group the Graveses were. There were the usual evening sing-songs with 'Robby ... the chief Folk-Song singer', his father noted.[15] He joined in the swimming, played whist, and on the morning of 11 September, a Saturday, accompanied his father to Harlech village, where they read in the papers of the Zeppelin raid over the City of London and Wood Green. (Robert had passed some of the burning houses on his way to Wales.) His relations with his father had never been better; they took a long walk together discussing Robert's views on his younger brothers and his hopes for the future – 'an open air life – scientific agriculture with literature as his second string or schoolmastering on Abbotsholme lines'.[16] Alfred, with his usual concern for that future, had arranged tea with the President of St John's College, Oxford, Dr James, who was staying nearby, and Robert dutifully attended. He even went with his family to church the next day, despite his own religious waverings, and rejoiced with them when *The Spectator* arrived with extracts from his letters from the trenches in it.

Any spare time was spent walking on the hills behind the house with Rosaleen, to whom he seemed as close as ever. Inspired almost certainly by his letters home about the sufferings of men in France, Rosaleen wanted to join the Voluntary Aid Detachment (VAD), a group of women given basic nursing training to help in hospitals in Britain and abroad. Her interview was fixed for 17 September, the day after Robert's leave came to an end, which gave them even more than usual to discuss. Their half-sister Molly had already gone to France as a nurse and their half-brother Dick had been sent to the Dardanelles as an army interpreter. Of all Alfred's children of suitable age only Perceval, still trying to enlist, and Clarissa, recovering from a second nervous breakdown, were not 'serving their country'. One of Robert's cousins on the Graves side, Charles Massie Blomfield, had already been killed, at the Second Battle of Ypres.

On Tuesday 14 September Robert took the lunchtime train to London, again with his father, who drew great pleasure from the memory of 'Robby's dozing in the Railway carriage ... with his dear head' on Alfred's shoulder.[17] They also spent the next day together as Alfred helped Robert with last-minute tasks – correcting the typescript of a second 'Scenes from the Trenches' letter, visiting Cox's bank, where Robert found the large sum of £65 to his credit. They went shopping at the British army officer's great salvation, the Army and Navy Stores, for French long boots, a wristwatch, a new cap, well-lined waterproofs and a refill of Robert's medical supplies. Lunch was followed by a visit to the barber's for a shave and, finally, the opticians, leaving barely time for Robert to catch his train to Godalming for an overnight stay with the Mallorys.

Term had not yet started at Charterhouse, so Graves was not able to visit 'Peter' Johnstone again. He had received some 'bad news' about him at the end of June, when his cousin Gerald had reported that Johnstone was as 'bad as anyone could be' and 'not at all the innocent fellow [Graves] took him for'.[18] The clear implication was that Johnstone had been caught in homosexual practices, illegal in law and strictly forbidden at Charterhouse. Since Graves had found Johnstone's long weekly letters his 'greatest stand-by against the impermanence of trench-life ... and the uncleanness of sex-life in billets', and since he still regarded any physical expression of sexual attraction with some horror, it had come as a great shock.[19] But Johnstone's letter of explanation – that he had just been 'ragging about' and would stop it immediately – had mended matters. On 5 August, Robert had written him a loving letter, written against the eventuality of his death, telling Johnstone that he 'mean[t] infinitely more' to him than himself and leaving him 'all my friends and my books'.[20] His poem to Johnstone, written a few months later at Le Havre, '1915', confirms that his love for the boy had survived the Charterhouse incident:

> ... Dear, you've been everything that I most lack
> In these soul-deadening trenches – pictures, books,
> Music, the quiet of an English wood,
> Beautiful comrade-looks,
> The narrow, bouldered mountain track,
> The broad, full-bosomed ocean, green and black,
> And Peace, and all that's good.[21]

And in 1916 Graves would write more explicitly in 'The Fusilier – (For Peter)' of:

> ... the quiet one the poet the lover remaining
> Will meet you little singer and go with you and keep you
> And turn away bad women and spill the cup of poison
> And fill your heart with beauty and teach you to love...[22]

'The Fusilier' would be sent to Edward Marsh, himself a lover of young men, in December 1916, but it remained unpublished in Graves's lifetime, partly because by 1917 his sexual tastes were beginning to change and he no longer believed that Johnstone was the innocent creature he had imagined.

In September 1915, however, Graves was sorry to miss seeing Johnstone, although he enjoyed staying with George Mallory and Ruth Turner, the woman he had married in 1914. They were expecting their first child, an event that may lie behind Graves's 'To My Unborn Son', though the high risk of death in France and his homosexual tastes in 1915 probably also helped inspire it. In addition Graves visited Frank Fletcher, who sent Alfred a 'very nice' letter afterwards, saying that he had 'greatly enjoyed Robbie's visit' and had 'found him far more of the man than he would have been at the end of a year at Oxford'.[23]

By Fletcher's standards, Graves was about to increase his 'manliness' greatly, for on his arrival back at Cambrin preparations for the Battle of Loos were at their height. After a day's delay at Folkestone, he had resumed charge of his platoon on 18 September, only a week before the start of the battle. On 19 September the 2nd Royal Welch Fusiliers relieved their fellow battalion in the 19th Brigade, the Middlesex, at Cambrin, the trenches from which they were to attack on both sides of the La Bassée canal. On 20 September Robert wrote a letter to be sent to his family in the event of his death.

Graves had been introduced to the horrors of trench warfare in the rat-infested mud of the Cuinchy brickstacks, with its human corpses forming part of the parapet. He had been able to cope, to some extent, by treating it partly as a 'boy's own adventure', as his poetry shows. But he had experienced nothing on the scale of the Battle of Loos, where the number of dead, missing and wounded exceeded that of any previous offensive, 60,000 for only three days of actual battle on 25 and 27 September and 13 October. The 2nd Royal Welch Fusiliers lost almost half its number, 311 killed or wounded out of a battalion of approximately 700 men. For the first day alone the 'Roll of Honour' notices in *The Times* filled four columns.

Even before the fighting began Graves had started to question the wisdom of those in command. On 24 September, for instance, instead of being allowed to rest and prepare themselves for the battle, due to start at 5.30 a.m. the next day, Graves and his men were ordered to march the six or seven miles to Béthune to deposit their so-called 'spare kit' at Montmorency Barracks in the town. When, after a decidedly alcoholic dinner with the staff of a New Army division billeted there, Graves came to take his platoon back to the trenches, they found the Béthune-La Bassée road choked with troops, guns and transport and had to march miles north out of their way. Even then they were held up by massed cavalry on several occasions and it was not until 1 a.m. or later on the day of the battle itself that they reached Cambrin. They had marched approximately 20 miles in what seemed to Graves a completely unnecessary exercise: 'We were cold, tired and sick, not at all in the mood for a battle.'[24] They were also very wet, having been ordered to leave their waterproof capes at Béthune. Yet in only a few hours' time they were to follow the Middlesex Battalion over the top in support once the initial heavy bombardment and gas attack had been launched.

What happened next was, in the words of one of Graves's fellow officers, a 'bloody balls-up'.[25] The bombardment, designed to wipe out German defences, not only failed to offer adequate cover for the attackers through lack of shells but also fell short at times, and one of Graves's many nightmarish memories of Loos was of British soldiers being killed by their own fire. Another was of seeing gassed men stumbling back 'yellow-faced and choking ... their buttons tarnished green'.[26] Graves claimed that this was because the gas company lacked the correct spanners to unleash the gas at the right time, but only one thing is certain: that, despite the wind being in the wrong direction, the gas company had been ordered to deploy their 'accessory' (as it was euphemistically called) and it had, predictably, been blown back into the British lines.

Perhaps Graves's most harrowing experience at Loos was watching British soldiers being mown down by German machine guns. Although numerically far superior to their enemy, the British had too few of these weapons. (As Martin Gilbert notes, it was only five months since Field Marshal Haig had told the British War Council: 'The machine-gun is a much over-rated weapon and two per battalion is more than sufficient.')[27] The Germans were equally shocked at the carnage, christening the battle 'The Field of Corpses of Loos' (*Den Leichenfeld von Loos*). Graves's reaction was to write 'Machine-Gun Fire: Cambrin', describing a typical incident on the opening day.[28] Hardly the kind of poem to boost morale among soldiers or civilians, this poem remained unpublished during Graves's lifetime, though his prose account of the incident would be published 14 years later in *Good-bye to All That*.[29]

A second poem inspired by the first day's events, 'The Dead Fox-Hunter', paints a similarly grim picture of the carnage and courage of that day, though in less satiric tones. This may be because the officer described, Captain A. L. Samson of C Company, 2nd Royal Welch Fusiliers, was a friend of Graves. Despite its rather fanciful ending, in which Graves imagines the fox-hunting captain being welcomed in heaven by a hunt, its praise of Samson's heroic death, stifling his cries of agony to prevent his men from trying to reach him, chimed with the contemporary need for uplifting war poetry and it was published in 1916:

> ... We saw that, dying and in hopeless case,
>   For others' sake that day
> He'd smothered all rebellious groans: in death
> His fingers were tight clenched between his teeth.[30]

When the critic Herbert Palmer wanted to discuss this and similar war poems with Graves in 1925, Graves replied that 'he wanted to forget it, could not read it with composure'; even then, Frank Kersnowski concludes, ten years after Samson's death and seven years after the Armistice, 'Graves remained intensely troubled by the effects of his wounding, physical and psychological, in the war.'[31]

The most revealing lines Graves wrote about Loos are the final couplet he added to his July 1915 poem of belief in 'the wisdom of God's ways' and pious resignation to death in battle – 'Big Words'. Written after he had witnessed the slaughter at Loos, these later lines are in a very different vein:

> But on the fire step, waiting to attack,
> He cursed, prayed, sweated, wished the proud words back.[32]

In fact, Graves himself was not called on for a direct attack on 25 September. In all the confusion, the remains of A and D Companies had finally been assembled, ready to follow B and C Companies over the top, but Captain Thomas, now in charge of the greatly depleted battalion, refused to send them until he got specific orders from headquarters. At this point, Graves's 'mouth was dry, his eyes out of focus and his legs quaking' under him, a condition he treated with about half a pint of rum.[33] His men were silent and depressed as they waited, their platoon sergeant, Townsend, making 'feeble bitter jokes about the good old British army muddling through and how he thanked God we still had a navy'.[34] After a few hours the attack was officially called off.

Graves's memory of 26 September was a hazy one of getting the wounded down to the dressing station, spraying the stinking trenches and dugouts to get rid of the 'gas-blood-lyddite [from high explosives]-latrine' smells, and clearing away the earth where the trenches had collapsed and were blocked.[35] His company commander, Captain Thomas, had been killed and Graves found himself in sole charge of B Company. On 27 September the 2nd Royal Welch Fusiliers was again instructed to be ready to attack. And though, after a five-hour wait, the order was rescinded, the strain and exhaustion had been enormous and would continue until 3 October. Graves claimed to have kept 'awake and alive' through those six nightmarish days 'by drinking about a bottle of whisky a day'.[36] What sickened him most was his belief that the 2nd RWF's efforts had been nothing more than a diversionary exercise.[37] He and his fellow survivors had no blankets, greatcoats or waterproof sheets, and no time or materials to build new shelters. Every night they went out into No Man's Land to help bring in the dead, whose bodies swelled, stank and eventually burst open; unlike the children in his poem 'First Funeral', who buried the dead dog's corpse in fresh mint, there was nothing suitable on the devastated ground to disguise the revolting smell.

On 3 October, the 2nd Royal Welch Fusiliers were relieved by a scratch battalion made up of the 2nd Royal Warwickshires and 1st RWF. Neither Jones-Bateman nor Hanmer Jones was among the latter, both having been wounded in the fighting. The same day Graves wrote a letter to his parents, who had not heard from him since 24 September, Alfred noted, 'the day before the great battle on his front'.[38] Their only hope during the agonizing ten-day wait had been that 'no news is good news'.[39] They were extremely happy and greatly relieved, therefore, to hear that their son had 'escaped by a miracle ... hit in the boot by shrapnel – hand cut – nearly buried by a Black Maria [i.e. a German stick grenade], gassed in one lung', but horrified to learn that he had 'slept in the wet without coat and knees bare' and had had '10 sleepless days'.[40] While his mother's reaction was to send him comforts from home, Alfred's was to quote his son a passage from the Irish Cuchulain saga in which Cuchulain's father, Lug, takes Cuchulain's place in the war of Ulster versus the Four Provinces, allowing his son to sleep for three days, Alfred wishing he 'could be a Lug to dear Robby'.[41]

By the time Robert heard from his parents, however, he was resting safely behind the line, first at Sailly la Bourse, then further back at Annezin where he lodged with an old woman, Adelphine Heu, whom he described in 'A Rhyme of Friends', along with other French civilians he was to stay with in the course of the war. He was lucky indeed to be alive and unwounded; three times his company had been told to be ready to attack, and on each occasion the order had been cancelled at the last moment. He had also escaped any direct involvement in the final attempt to break through the German line at the Hohenzollern Ridge on 13 October. This had been another 'dud show', according to Graves, chiefly to be remembered for the death of Charles Sorley, a captain in the Suffolk Regiment[42] and 'the only great poet killed in this war', as he was to write to Sorley's father on 15 March 1917.[43] (Later he would expand this to include Isaac Rosenberg and Wilfred Owen, both killed in 1918.)

Graves had coped well at the Battle of Loos and had escaped physically unhurt. The fighting had brought out his strengths – his intelligence, his self-confidence, his daring, his cavalier attitude towards rules and his ability to get on with his men. But it is hard to believe that the carnage he had witnessed did not leave its mark on him psychologically. A highly imaginative young man of barely twenty, he would feel its effects for at least another decade, if not for the rest of his life.

8

SIEGFRIED SASSOON AND A RECIPE FOR RUM PUNCH (OCTOBER 1915–MARCH 1916)

> Roused from long slumber by the clash of War,
> John Bull leaps out of bed with startled roar,
> Unchains his bulldog Jack and Terrier Tom,
> And then goes back to bed for twelve months more.[1]
>
> *'Epigram on the First Year of the War', 1915*

By mid-October 1915 the 2nd Royal Welch Battalion, and Graves with it, was back in the same sector as before. Having lost heavily in the Battle of Loos, they reorganized at Annezin, with Béthune conveniently close for champagne cocktails at the Globe Café. Some of the lightly wounded were able to rejoin for duty and a big draft from the 3rd Battalion restored their numbers to nearly seven hundred, with a full complement of officers.

Graves had worked out his own chances of survival as three to one and considered himself extremely lucky to have 'come through the last show unhurt'.[2] But he felt more isolated than ever, he told Edward Marsh, among 'the type of regular officer who lives the sort of life I have always abominated ... whose sole topics of conversation are wine, women, racing, hunting and musical comedy'.[3] Apart from the occasional chance meeting with an 'educated' person, he regarded his fellow officers with a scorn that did not escape notice.

But he had acted bravely in the fighting itself and it may have been in acknowledgement of this that he was given a rest from the front line. Attached to the battalion's 'Sappers', pioneer or combat engineers who specialized in maintaining communications and reserve trenches, Graves himself was inclined to see such a posting as a way to get rid of him. Nevertheless he appreciated the benefits greatly, telling his ever-anxious parents that it meant 75 per cent less danger than in the trenches, comfortable billets and more congenial company, which included an officer he had got to know at Loos, Philip Hill of the Middlesex Regiment.[4]

Best of all, Graves now had time to write poetry again. In a letter enclosing four poems written in 1915,[5] he told Marsh, who had just brought out *Georgian Poetry 1913–1915*, that he was beginning to realize 'what the New Poetry is to be' and believed that 'given a good rest and congenial company to settle [his] shaken mind', he could write 'something really good'.[6] With his move to the Sappers those conditions had been partially fulfilled and he wrote at least one poem, sent home to his mother, about the 'Pickelhaube', or German spiked helmet.[7] Since this was never published, it is unlikely to have been the 'something really good' he was hoping for, but at least he was writing poetry again. More significantly, it would contribute to one of his best works of 1916, 'Goliath and David', in which line 19 had originally referred to Goliath as 'spike-helmeted, grey, grim'.[8]

He was not happy, therefore, to be recalled suddenly to the trenches in the first week of November. Although he told his parents that this was 'without any explanation',[9] he afterwards explained it as a punishment for failing to observe one of the many battalion orders, either through a characteristic absent-mindedness, or simple disregard for rules. He had, in any case, been hoping and plotting to wangle a transfer to the Reserve Battalion in England, asking his ever-willing father to use his influence in high places ('will ask Brigadier General Thomas to befriend Robby in the way he desired', Alfred recorded in his diary on 5 November 1915). His chief solace in all this continued to be Johnstone, who he had persuaded himself was 'still wholesome-minded and clean-living' – 'my best friend, a poet long before I'll ever be, a radiant and unusual creature whose age hovers between six and seventy'.[10] It was almost certainly during his more leisurely time with the Sappers in October and November 1915 that he had written his tribute to the boy, '1915'. Fully expecting to 'go west', he asked Marsh to 'be as good a friend' to Johnstone as he had to Graves himself.[11] For as he freely admitted in 'A Rhyme of Friends', he 'feared death each hour' in France.[12]

It may have been the constant fear of dying that prompted him to write an unusually appreciative letter to his parents in mid-November, expressing his gratitude for what they had done for him – 'the early teaching' and 'example set him at home', and (in direct contradiction to what he would later claim in *Good-bye to All That*) the help his father had given him with his poetry. Alfred joyfully reports this in his diary as a proof of the Biblical command: 'Cast thy bread upon the waters and thou shalt find it after many days', adding that 'living so near to death' had indeed been 'a quickener of the spirit' for his son.[13] Another incentive for Robert's sudden gratitude may have been the news that his father had finally persuaded Harold Monro of the Poetry Bookshop in London to read his son's poems, with a view to publication.

By mid-November, Graves was having 'a terribly rough time' in the damp trenches.[14] Although still 'loyal and willing' he had 'ceased to feel aggressive' and winter was fast approaching; he was growing all too accustomed to the 'continual experience of death' and patrolling had lost its initial excitement.[15] He was therefore 'delighted' to be transferred to the 1st Royal Welch Fusiliers in the second half of November; it seemed to him 'less old-fashioned in its militarism and more human', while equally 'efficient' and 'regimental'.[16] (The 2nd Battalion doctor, Captain J. Dunn, not normally given to gossip, repeated a rumour that Graves, who 'had reputedly the largest feet in the Army, and a genius for putting both of them in everything', had 'put one on a kitten' and that was the reason for his transfer.)[17]

A Regular Army battalion like the 2nd Royal Welch Fusiliers, the 1st RWF had suffered far greater losses in France and many of its original men were dead or wounded by November 1915. The battalion had landed at Zeebrugge with the 7th Division in 1914 and marched through Belgium to Ypres, where it had scored a decisive victory against the Germans. In its subsequent struggle to help keep the enemy from seizing the Channel ports, however, it had been reduced from 1,150 to 90 men in just 12 days, despite reinforcements. Restored by further drafts to its proper strength, the 1st RWF had again distinguished itself at the Battle of Neuve Chapelle in March 1915, but once more lost the greater part of its men at the Battle of Festubert two months later. In September it had suffered more high casualties at the Battle of Loos. Graves, who had been promoted to captain on his return to the 2nd RWF in November 1915, was being sent with officers from other RWF battalions to make up for the heavy losses in the Givenchy trenches. By the time he arrived, none of the 1st Battalion officers were Regulars, with the exception of the commanding officer, Colonel Minshull-Ford, and his second in command, the quartermaster Joe Cottrill, and a few subalterns who had come straight from Sandhurst.

Graves was again fortunate in joining the 1st RWF at Béthune, just over a fortnight before they were due for a long Divisional Rest in the back area, though his transfer meant that his next leave would be delayed from December 1915 to January 1916. He also felt lucky in being assigned to A Company, which he believed, in retrospect, to have been the best he ever served in. Since the battalion had already replaced the company commanders it had lost at Loos, he was made second in command to Captain Richardson, a young man fresh from Sandhurst whose death near Fricourt in March 1916 would fill him with particular sadness. He also liked and got on well with his platoon commanders, especially Edmund Dadd and C. D. Morgan,[18] and referred affectionately to 'Old Graves', Sassoon's commanding officer in C Company. The battalion, Graves told Marsh a few weeks after joining it, was 'full of delightful people' and Colonel Minshull-Ford was 'a brilliant soldier', a man of 'immense technical and practical knowledge, and a very kindly, tactful person'.[19] The younger officers struck him as 'an exceptionally nice lot'.[20]

At least one of these officers was already known to Graves by name through Marsh (dubbed by Edmund Gosse, rather pedantically, 'the Choragus' of the new poets) – Siegfried Sassoon. Marsh had befriended Sassoon, as he had Graves, just before the outbreak of war and followed both their careers in the Army carefully. It is evident from Graves's letters to him that Marsh had also mentioned them to each other, though virtually all his letters to Graves have been lost. So that while it is undoubtedly a coincidence that they both arrived with the 1st RWF within days of each other (Sassoon a few days after Graves), their meeting on 28 November

1. RG's mother, Amy Graves, carrying Charles (aged one), with (l. to r. front row) Clarissa (eight), Robert (three) and Rosaleen (seven).

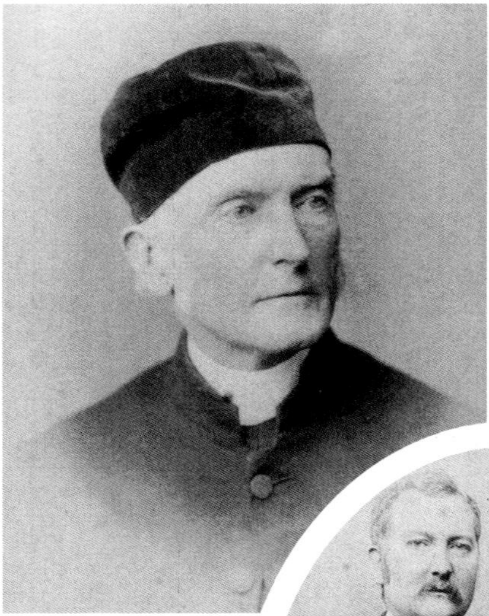

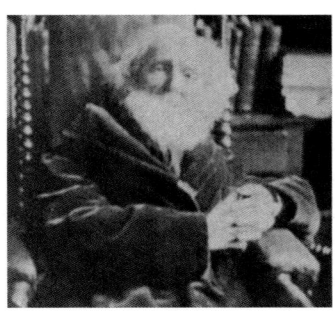

2. RG's paternal grandfather, Charles Graves, Bishop of Limerick.

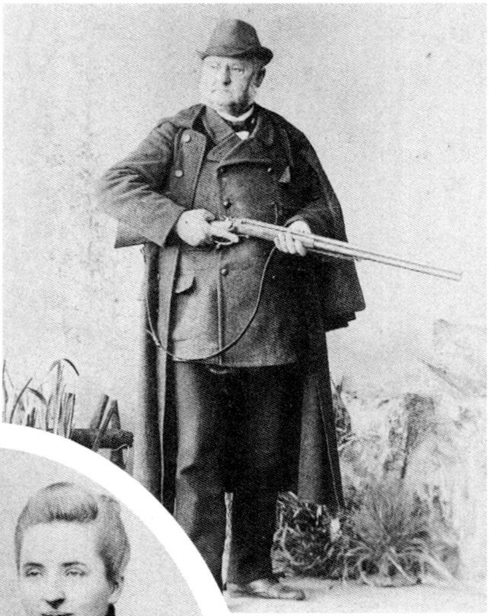

3. RG's maternal grandfather, Heinrich von Ranke.

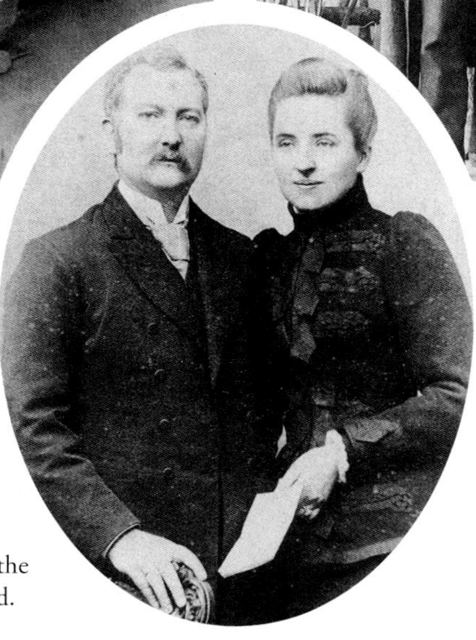

4. RG's parents, Alfred Perceval Graves and Amalie Elizabeth Sophie von Ranke in December 1891, the month they married.

5. RG's great-great-uncle, the historian, Leopold von Ranke in 1885.

Leopold von Ranke, the Historian, was my mother's great uncle

I found this picture when tidying up "Erinfa", Harlech, my parents' home & feel sure it was a late portrait of Leopold von Ranke. It was taken in 1885 by ROB. Wallich in Berlin

. Clarissa Janie Graves

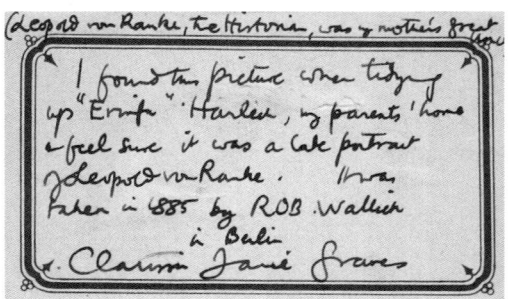

6. Clarissa Graves's note concerning her discovery of this hitherto unknown photograph of Leopold von Ranke.

7. Architect's drawing of Red Branch House, commissioned by Amy Graves in 1893/4.

8. The Graveses holiday home, Erinfa, Harlech, Wales, commissioned by Amy Graves in 1898, when RG was three.

9. RG's father, Alfred (seated centre), with the children of his first marriage, (from l. to r.) Mary (Molly), Perceval, Richard (Dick), Philip and Susan (centre front).

10. Alfred and Amy Graves in September 1908 with their children (from l. to r.) Charles, Clarissa, Rosaleen, John and RG, aged 13 and about to leave for Copthorne Preparatory School.

11. Copthorne Preparatory School, West Sussex, c. 1910.

12. RG shortly before leaving Charterhouse School in 1914.

13. George Harcourt Vanden-Bempde-Johnstone at Charterhouse School in 1913; known as 'Peter' at school and portrayed as 'Dick' in *Good-bye to All That*.

14. George Mallory

15. RG in uniform of the Royal Welch Fusiliers, inscribed 'Ever your loving son, Robbie'

16. Siegfried Sassoon at the Army School, Flixecourt, May 1916.

17. RG taken near the time he met Sassoon in November 1915.

18. A Graves family gathering in November 1917 to send Rosaleen off to France as a nurse: seated (l. to r.) RG, Amy, Clarissa; standing (l. to r.) Rosaleen, Charles, Alfred and John.

19. Edward Marsh, in 1912, the year before RG first met him.

20. Lady Ottoline Morrell, from Robert Gathorne-Hardy's photograph album.

21. Robert (Robbie) Ross in 1916, when RG first met him.

22. Charles Scott Moncrieff., in the uniform of the King's Own Scottish Borderers, on a visit to Durie in 1916.

23. Officer Cadet Wilfred Owen in 1916, the year before RG met him.

24. Captain W. H. R. Rivers, R.A.M.C.

1915, described in *Good-bye to All That* as a chance encounter in Sassoon's C Company mess over a copy of Lionel Johnson's essays, followed by a cream-bun tea in Béthune, may not be the full story. But it is an entertaining one and highlights what made them such close friends at the start, their devotion to literature. So too is the letter Graves wrote to Marsh about the problems this created:

> S.S. and I have great difficulty in talking about poetry and that sort of thing together as the other officers of the battalion are terribly curious and suspicious. If I go into his mess and he wants to show me some set of verses, he says: 'Afternoon Graves, have a drink ... by the way, I want you to see my latest recipe for rum punch.' The trenches are worse than billets for privacy. We are a disgrace to the battalion and we know it: I don't know what the CO would say if he heard us discussing the sort of things we do. He'd probably have a fit. His saying is that 'there should be only one subject for conversation among subalterns off parade'. I leave you to guess it. It's a great standby to have S.S. here in such society, though one or two of our brother officers are exceptionally nice.

By the time both men came to describe their relationship publicly, Graves in *Good-bye to All That* (1929) and Sassoon in *Memoirs of an Infantry Officer* (1930), their friendship was at an end. Sassoon would omit any mention of it from his 'memoir' covering this first meeting, *Memoirs of a Fox-Hunting Man* (1928), and Graves's account is not always entirely accurate: for example, the poem he claims Sassoon showed him on 28 November 1915, 'To Victory', was not written until 4 January 1916. Sassoon's later scathing comments about Graves in his own annotated copy of *Good-bye* (only recently come to light) would make it clear how hostile he felt towards Graves by 1929: when Graves describes himself as being 'delighted' by his own arrival with the 1st Battalion, for instance, Sassoon comments in the margin: 'The 1st Battalion wasn't'.[21]

Fortunately, Sassoon's diary entries for late November 1915 and Graves's letter to Marsh about their first meeting mean that we have an account of their feelings at the time. Both, it emerged, felt warmly but a little condescendingly about the other, Sassoon for example describing Graves as 'An interesting creature, overstrung and self-conscious, a defier of conventions', while also noting that he was 'very much disliked' in the unit.[22] In addition he told Marsh shortly afterwards that Graves was 'a strange person, full of ideas and originality', the main cause of hostility towards him, he believed.[23] He found Graves's poetry 'bad, violent and repulsive' and unfit for publication, '(like his face, which had a twist to it, as though seen in a slightly distorting mirror), his mental war-pictures' seemed to him 'a little uncouth and out of focus'.[24] Graves in turn confessed to Marsh that Sassoon's verses, 'except occasionally', did 'not please' him very much.

Despite some similarities of background and education – both were from cultured middle-class families that encouraged interest in the arts and had attended public schools, they shared an ambition to be a poet and an idealized homosexuality, and both had written for guidance to the high-minded sexual pioneer Edward Carpenter – they differed sharply from each other. In spite of being nearly nine years younger, Graves struck Sassoon as far more confident, the natural leader of the two. Where Sassoon was diffident about his talents, Graves bragged unashamedly of his modest achievements to date. While Sassoon was conventional and conformist in both social and artistic matters, Graves appeared to relish rebellion. Whereas Sassoon, who considered himself emotional and non-intellectual, was deeply suspicious of new ideas in the arts, Graves was assertively intellectual, revelling in the play of ideas often at the expense of emotions. He would go on to welcome the difficult, strange and modern in art, whereas Sassoon would continue to linger nostalgically in the past. Unlike Sassoon, who had been very careful indeed to conform to the highest Army standards in manners and dress, Graves struck his superiors as slovenly and careless in both respects. Colonel C. I. Stockwell, who took over the 1st Royal Welch Fusiliers not long after Graves and Sassoon joined it, and found Sassoon an 'excellent' officer, described Graves as 'an average officer who did his work neither well nor ill – but he lacked something – he did not instil confidence or moral [sic]'.[25] 'He's quite dotty', Sassoon was told by one of Graves's fellow officers: 'He used to sit up till one o'clock at night writing with dozens of candles lit all around his bed, and in the morning he used to shave with one hand and read a book with the other.'[26] They even differed physically, Sassoon's face smooth and conventionally handsome, Graves's made irregular by his badly broken nose (due to rugby and boxing at Charterhouse), a difference Sassoon viewed symbolically, as though Graves's inner irregularities were manifested in what

Sassoon called his 'twisted, grieving face'. Where Sassoon was normally graceful, Graves was often clumsy.

The difference between them showed itself most clearly in their work, even at this early stage in their development. Although both basically accepted the necessity of the war, Sassoon wanted war (at that time) to be 'an impressive experience – terrible but not horrible enough to interfere with [his] heroic emotions'.[27] Graves seemed to him to want the war to be 'even uglier than it really was',[28] as his numerous realistic trench-poems, subsequently suppressed, showed. But as Graves pointed out to Sassoon in his best 'old-soldier manner ... he would soon change his style' after time in the trenches[29] – which, of course, Sassoon did, inspired by his first tour of trenches at Festubert. The result, 'The Redeemer', was realistic enough to satisfy even Graves, who rejoiced to see the change. Graves, in effect, did for Sassoon what Sassoon would do for Wilfred Owen, that is, he emphasized the need to write honestly and, if necessary, to move beyond the Romantic tradition they had all three inherited and loved. (By March 1916 Graves would find Sassoon's war poems 'infinitely better than the first crop'.)[30]

Despite the consolations of Sassoon's friendship, Graves recalled the late-November nights at Festubert, working on a defence scheme in freezing hard ground, as a 'nightmare',[31] and welcomed the order to retire to the 'back area' in Picardy at the end of the month. But it involved a punishing journey, an even more 'laborious experience' for Graves's A Company, he claimed, than for Sassoon's C Company.[32] His pride in his company is evident in an account he sent home to his family of the move south: 'a wonderful piece of work' by his men, '3 hours loading train, 8 hours in train, 3 hours unloading. March on empty stomachs from Station to Camp – 21 miles – without one man falling out.'[33] Like Sassoon, Graves would describe this gruelling journey in more detail in his prose work. Later on he would give a verse account of one such night-time march, recreating both rhythmically and stylistically the initial excitement of change ahead, the invigorating effect of a large body of men marching together into the unknown. The influence of Sorley's 'All the Hills and Vales Along' almost certainly lies behind Graves's own effort:

> Soon with a roaring song we start,
>   Clattering along a cobbled road,

> The foot beats quickly like the heart,
>   And shoulders laugh beneath their load.
>
> Where are we marching? No one knows,
>   Why are we marching? No one cares...[34]

Twenty-three stanzas marked the 23 miles marched, perhaps one reason for this piece of verse remaining unpublished until his posthumous *Complete Poems* appeared in 2000.[35] For 'Night March', as Graves called it, is in some ways the 'wonderful thing' Sassoon pronounced it, Graves's 'most sustained effort' by 1916.[36]

By the time the 1st Royal Welch Fusiliers had reached their final destination in the Picardy uplands, Montagne le Fayel, 20 miles west of Amiens, they were exhausted. A journey of approximately 65 miles, which would have been a three-hour drive for the divisional general in his staff car, had taken them from 30 November to 6 December, underlining one of the less dramatic but pressing problems of the First World War again, the simple logistics of moving large groups of men and equipment even short distances.

Everyone, including Graves, however, appreciated the escape from an area of northern France overrun by the military. No troops had yet been billeted in Montagne and, though its inhabitants were understandably annoyed to be woken in the middle of the night by the advance guard to provide accommodation, they seemed to Graves 'much more likeable' than the jaded peasants of Pas de Calais.[37] He was welcomed into his billet by a retired schoolmaster, Monsieur Elie Caron, a committed vegetarian who hoped to live to a hundred. Graves, having heard rumours of a 'coming Somme offensive', was not so optimistic.[38]

In his own annotated copy of *Good-bye to All That*, Sassoon would later claim that the Somme offensive 'wasn't mentioned or thought of till the spring of 1916'.[39] In fact, the day the 1st Royal Welch Fusiliers arrived in Montagne, 6 December 1915, also marked the opening of the Chantilly Conference at Oise between the French and English staff to discuss such an assault, and rumours of it may have reached the 1st RWF during their six-week stay. While British casualties of over half a million since hostilities started were high, those of the French were far higher – nearly two million from a smaller population. When the Allies agreed at Chantilly on a strategy of combined offensives by the French, Russian, British and Italian armies against the Central Powers in 1916, a Somme offensive was the Franco-British contribution, with the French to undertake the main part and the 4th British Army in support on the northern flank. In February 1916 these plans would have to be revised dramatically with the onset of the Battle of Verdun.

Whether the rumour of a Somme offensive had reached the 1st Royal Welch Fusiliers by December 1915 or not, Graves was more conscious of the possibility of death than ever before. It made him even more appreciative of Johnstone, who continued to write long letters, some of fifteen pages, to him weekly. Determined to survive in poetry at least, it was in the peaceful surroundings of Picardy that Graves almost certainly began to plan his first poem to the boy, '1915'.[40] The completed poem would be the last addition he was able to make to his proposed first collection. For while Graves was still travelling to Montagne, Harold Monro had told Alfred that he was prepared to publish a 32-page volume of Robert's poems.[41] Robert worked throughout December on the typescript his father had prepared for him and by Christmas Eve Alfred had a corrected copy of it for Monro. More corrections would follow as Alfred, ever the poet himself, criticized some of his son's efforts. He strongly objected, for instance, to the 'Lines to Francis' that Robert had added, lines which may have been intended for a fellow soldier (Francis Jones-Bateman?), or for Johnstone under yet another pseudonym:

> It's not for the lewdness of the tale you told
>> That I'm so angry, dear,
> For who could be so foolish or so bold
>> As to hope virgins here?[42]

Alfred thought these lines frankly 'immoral', sending his son 'an absolute *snorter*' about it, and Robert dared not dispatch him another poem. The next one he sent, 'The Fusilier', to Monro this time, was addressed directly to Johnstone, though there was nothing in it, he argued, that could be judged 'immoral'.[43] So the lines to Francis were omitted from his first volume and, like 'The Fusilier', were never published in Graves's lifetime. Another poem based on his experience near the Cuinchy brickstacks, 'Through the Periscope', was also cut, possibly because lines such as 'trench stinks of shallow-buried death' were a little too realistic for Alfred.

Graves was already thinking of possible titles for his collection. His first idea, *Schoolboy Militant*,[44] would quickly be replaced by *C'est la guerre*, which seemed to him to express 'just what I want, an explanation, an excuse almost for the tremendous change in tone and method and standpoint' between the opening section of poems written at Charterhouse and the last parts of the 'verse-cycle' with its 'hardening and coarsening and loss of music'.[45] His main concern, he told Marsh, was to avoid anything that would make him 'ridiculous in the eyes of the Regiment and of Charterhouse'.[46] The final choice would be *Over the Brazier*, the title of the last poem in the collection, which steers well clear of anything too controversially realistic.

The trenches, in any case, seemed less real in Picardy, though a short visit to Festubert on arrival had brought them back briefly. Graves found the countryside around Montagne 'lovely', relishing its hilliness in particular after the flatness of the area around La Bassée, where 'the nearest approach to a hill was the canal bank or the sides of a mine crater'.[47] Like Sassoon he found Picardy like Arcadia in comparison. Although he thought Montagne itself 'dull' on arrival, Graves quickly grew to appreciate 'this delightful rest-cure village' and only four months after leaving it was enthusing to Sassoon, 'wasn't Montagne glorious?'[48] It was in such idyllic surroundings that he read and enthused about Brooke's poems, seven of which Marsh had included in the *Georgian Poetry 1913–1915* collection he sent to Graves, who succumbed to the lyrical seductiveness of poems like 'Tiare Tahiti' and 'The Soldier': 'I feel in reading them,' he wrote to Marsh, 'that his is exactly the language I am floundering to catch, musical, restrained, refined, and not cramped or conventionally antique, reading almost like ordinary speech.'[49]

He was not given much leisure to enjoy poetry, however. Colonel Minshull-Ford put the battalion through its training with peacetime severity, actually demanding that they 'forget the trenches' and 'fit [them] selves for the open warfare that was bound to come once the Somme defences were pierced'.[50] But even Graves who, like Sassoon, did not believe in the breakthrough and thought the training entirely inappropriate, 'thoroughly enjoyed' these daily field-days: the countryside was 'quite unspoilt' and though the guns could be heard, they were far in the distance.[51] He was above all grateful to learn that, with the promotion to divisional training school, the 1st Royal Welch Fusiliers would not be threatened with trench-work for some time and could look forward to Christmas out of the line; they could be sure of 'living and keeping well till February 1916 at least'.[52] He rejoiced too when Marsh, who had lost his position as private secretary to Winston Churchill when Churchill resigned from the government in November 1915, was appointed assistant private secretary to the prime minister, Herbert Asquith, shortly afterwards.

Even battalion drill and musketry seemed more enjoyable at Montagne and entirely unrelated to war as Graves had experienced it. Under Minshull-Ford these normally tedious routines now involved a lot of games, including inter-battalion rugby, which was encouraged on half-holidays and Sundays. Graves played full-back for the 1st Royal Welch Fusiliers, with his company commander, Richardson, in the scrum's front row, the battalion's trench-mortar officer Pritchard as fly-half and a young Welshman, 2nd Lieutenant David Thomas, playing inside three-quarter. Thomas ('Tommy') had come out to France with Sassoon and it was soon evident to Graves that Sassoon was deeply in love with the young man. Tommy, whom Graves remembered as a 'simple, gentle fellow and fond of reading',[53] quickly became part of the close friendship that developed between Sassoon and Graves.

Christmas 1915, the only one Graves would spend in France, came and went peacefully at Montagne. There was a special meal for 'the men', who were served by their officers to mark the occasion and allowed to enjoy what Sassoon called a little 'disciplined insobriety', which filled Montagne's streets with 'maudlin sergeants' and 'paralysed privates'.[54] He does not specify how the officers celebrated, but even a year later when wartime shortages were more severe, the 2nd Royal Welch Fusiliers would enjoy a meal of 'paté de foie gras, julienne [soup], curried prawns, roast goose, potato and cauliflower, plum pudding, anchovy on toast, dessert; Veuve Clicquot, port, cognac, Benedictine, coffee'.[55] Graves confirmed that they had done themselves 'proud' at Christmas and New Year's Eve 1915 and recalled having had to put his fellow officers to bed 'in batches' afterwards.[56]

By the beginning of 1916 Graves was looking forward to another two months at Montagne, 'consum[ing] vast quantities of the local cream' and feeling like an 'absolute caricature of the Happy Warrior': even 'the men', he told Marsh, had 'ceased to grouse'.[57] He felt luckier still when, in the middle of January, he was told to report to the Base Depot at Le Havre: two company officers from each divisional brigade had been chosen to instruct troops there and Graves, as one of those who had been in France longest, was chosen. It was, he noted, 'a gift of two months longer life'.[58]

Graves was attached to No. 6 Training Camp and his job involved teaching trench relief and trench discipline, the theory of it in an initial lecture, followed by the practice of it in a model set of trenches. Lecturing every morning to between 100 and 400 men, an initially daunting prospect, he quickly realized that it was well within his powers: he had a loud, clear voice and enjoyed telling people what to do. And when the commandant of the Bull Ring, as it was known, suddenly ordered him one rainy day to lecture to 3,000 Canadians in the camp's enormous concert hall, he realized that he was quite good at it. (He claims to have entertained them with 'the story of Loos, and what a balls-up it was, and why it was a balls-up', and that the commandant had taken such a subversive talk well.)[59]

On the whole, however, Graves found it a dull and repetitive job, varied only by the audiences to whom he lectured – 'regulars, terriers [territorial army], Kitcheners [New Army], colonials of every class and nationality from Welshman to Russian'.[60] He grew weary of having to be 'very staid and smart' and to remember his position at all times. Most of his fellow instructors were much older than he and he missed being among people of his own age and rank. In sheer self-defence, he maintained, he had learnt to worship his regiment, though in fact this was an attitude that had started long before January 1916 and that would continue to the end of his life. He seemed apologetic about the depth of his feelings for such a conservative organization as an Army battalion and appeared to need to justify himself, to his friends and fellow poets and perhaps to posterity.

The Base Depot itself was situated in the pleasant old port of Harfleur, overlooking the bay and approximately three miles from Le Havre. Although not as attractive as Montagne, it seemed to the still puritanical Graves a great deal better than Le Havre, which repelled him with its 'horrible painted women, cheap cinemas, Belgians, A[rmy] S[ervice] C[orps], slatternly French tradespeople and various kinds of embusqués [French for 'shirkers']'.[61] In addition, the town of Le Havre seemed 'dull' to him.[62] He spent most of his spare time at Harfleur in the Instructors'

Mess, where the chief subjects of conversation were morale, the reliability of various divisions in battle, the value of different training methods and war morality, with particular reference to atrocities. There is an affectionate description in 'The Fusilier' of 'the heated mess-room, the drinkers and card-players', his 'jolly brother officers all laughing and drinking', the 'gallant hearty company' and 'the sparkle of wine', a picture somewhat at odds with other impressions Graves gave of despising many of his fellow subalterns.[63] For, as his poem goes on to admit, the narrator himself has become one of them by February 1916 – 'the furious / The callous rough ribald-tongue the Fusilier captain / The gallant merry Fusilier that drank in the messroom [sic]'. Yet, as he is anxious to point out in this second poem addressed specifically 'To Peter', or Johnstone, 'the quiet one, the poet, the lover' has also 'remain[ed]'.[64]

'The Fusilier' is the only surviving poem known to have been written at Le Havre. (Graves sent another, 'The Airman', home to his parents, which Alfred thought 'good', but this has not been found.)[65] Kept busy by his duties and still dealing with corrections to the Monro typescript, Graves may have had neither the time nor the energy for new verse. He was also distracted, not from poetry but from writing his own verse, by the discovery of Charles Hamilton Sorley, whose *Marlborough and Other Poems* was published in January 1916. *Marlborough* was a revelation to Graves, who wrote excitedly to Marsh a month later about the 'brilliant young poet' with whom he had 'fall[en] in love', 'ridiculous' though that seemed.[66] Sorley, he claimed, was a man 'entirely after [his] own heart in his loves and hates'.[67] He compared Sorley, politely, to Marsh's great love, Brooke (of whom, ironically, Sorley had been highly critical), implying that Sorley spoke that 'musical, restrained, refined' language, 'reading almost like ordinary speech', that he had praised in Brooke. But, as Graves later confessed to Edmund Gosse, he had been initially 'repelled by what sounds more like Modernist than Georgian features – Sorley's carelessness of metre and unmodulated harshness', the sort of sound that reminded him of the rooks' cries in two of the poems.[68] It was more Sorley's 'austerity and spirit and wholesomeness' that had attracted him at the start.[69] These were the qualities Graves admired in the two poems from which he quotes in his letter to Marsh, 'All the Hills and Vales Along' and one of Sorley's two sonnets on death. Living as he was with the constant fear of death, even behind the lines, Graves appreciated the Marlburian's stoic attitude toward it, revealed so clearly in the sonnet that opens:

> Such, such is Death: no triumph; no defeat:
> Only an empty pail, a slate rubbed clean,
> A merciful putting away of what has been.[70]

Graves began to identify closely with Sorley, whose indirect approach to war in poetry started to appeal to him more than his own largely realistic descriptions of it up to 1916. In his letter to Sorley's father of March 1917 praising Sorley's 'greatness', he claimed that his son's 'clean brave words are the best inspiration possible for the people who are trying like me after a new and vigorous poetry, and like rain and wind and freedom'.[71] He would pass on his enthusiasm not just to Marsh but also to Sassoon, who would, like Graves himself, pay a pilgrimage to the Sorleys at Cambridge during the war. For both living poets, Sorley would become a standard of excellence in their own attempts to tell the unsentimental truth about the war.

Graves's most intriguing reference to Sorley occurs in a letter to Sassoon of May 1916, when his uncle Charles is reviewing Sorley's *Marlborough and Other Poems* for *The Spectator*, and reveals more about the living poets than the dead one. Questioning Sassoon about his conversation with a contemporary of Sorley's at Marlborough, Graves ends 'and was he "so"?', using a then-current euphemism for homosexuality.[72] Since Sorley's poetry contained no conventional love lyrics by the age of twenty, Graves assumed that he must be 'so', clearly wanting to include one of his favourite poets in a category with which both he and Sassoon identified in 1916.

It was at Le Havre in February 1916 that Graves first read Sorley, one of a number of pleasures he enjoyed there. But by 1 March he was writing to Marsh from the Café Normandy in Le Havre, where he had agreed to take the chair at a St David's Day celebration with six other patriotic officers. Although he was having 'a very jolly time',[73] he was longing to get back to his battalion, despite freezing temperatures, six inches of snow and the threat of a coming offensive. Whilst he had been cheered by news of a Russian victory against the Turks at Erzurum in mid-February, he had also heard by 24 February of the start of the Germans' fierce attack on the French at

Verdun. As increasing numbers of French divisions had to be diverted to Verdun, it had become clear by March that the supporting role of the British Army at the Somme would have to become the principal effort. Less than a week after expressing a wish to rejoin the 1st Royal Welch Fusiliers, Graves was ordered to do so.

9

THE ROAD TO HIGH WOOD
(MARCH–JULY 1916)

> I never dreamed we'd meet that day
> In our old haunts down Fricourt way,
> Plotting such marvellous journeys there
> For golden-houred 'Apres-la-guerre'.
>
> 'Familiar Letter to Siegfried Sassoon'[1]

When Graves rejoined the 1st Royal Welch Fusiliers in the second week of March 1916, after a brief stay in hospital in Le Havre with a bout of flu, they were busy preparing their section of trenches near Fricourt for the Somme offensive. The battalion had been assigned to the Bois Français sector, about three miles east of Albert, with billets five miles away at Morlancourt, a village five miles south of Albert. Untouched by shell-fire in March 1916, Morlancourt would later be devastated by fierce fighting between German and Australian troops.

As Graves reported to Marsh on 15 March, his first day back in the trenches, it was 'rather trying' to have to return to them 'after a three months holiday', especially to such violent conditions:

> ... I have to get used to all the old noises, from the crack!
> Rockety-ockety-ockety-ockety-ockety of a rifle bullet, to the

boom! ... swish ... swish ... Grr ... GRR! ... GRR! ... *ROAR*! of a fifteen-inch shell and there are a lot of new terrors since last December. The *specialité* here is 'canisters', round, tin, barrel-shaped trench-mortars filled with about twenty pounds of the highest explosive. About ten or twelve times as much stuff is handed round now than when I first came out, but I always enjoy trenches in a way, I must confess: I like feeling really frightened and if happiness consists in being miserable in a good cause, why then I'm doubly happy. England's is a good cause enough and the trenches are splendidly miserable: my company firing-line averages 30 yards from the Bosches, the mud is *chronic*, there are few parts of the trench where one can stand upright without exposing oneself, and not a single canister-proof dug-out. If only it was blowing sleet and a gas attack was due tomorrow my cup of happiness would be full.

Two other major changes Graves found were the replacement of Colonel Minshull-Ford, whom he liked, with Colonel C. I. Stockwell, whom he thought a 'swaggering bully', though 'a very capable fellow', and Sassoon's new role as transport officer.[2] Sassoon, known for his skill with horses, had been the obvious choice to replace Lieutenant Ormerod, who had been sent back to England, and Sassoon's friends, including Graves, rejoiced in his relatively safe position. The move brought Sassoon nearer to Joe Cottrill, the colourful quartermaster in charge of the rations taken daily to troops in the trenches, and Graves enjoyed getting to know Cottrill too.

Stockwell, a strict disciplinarian with very high standards, had been shocked by the state of the 1st Royal Welch Fusiliers' section of the front line when he joined the battalion at the end of February 1916. His first report in late February read: 'Wire rotten; parapet everywhere bad and nowhere bullet-proof.'[3] He immediately ordered the whole of the battalion's front line to be rewired. This meant extra work for the already exhausted men, who had to go out nightly on wiring-parties in addition to their usual duties. On 18 March, Graves's fourth night in a 'perfectly disgusting lot of trenches, muddy, tumble-down, and with very low parapets', he had been leading A Company up to the line when they were overtaken by C Company, with David Thomas bringing up the rear.[4] The habitually cheerful 'Tommy' seemed to Graves 'unusually glum and serious'.[5] A few hours later, as Graves and his men were reinforcing the chalky, crumbling parapets with sandbags – and forced to stand on top of them only 30 yards from the Germans with the feared exposure to the moon behind them – news came from C Company to their right that Thomas had been hit by a sniper. Reassured by the fact that he was able to walk to the dressing-station, Graves's initial reaction had been to rejoice that the man he called his 'best friend' in the battalion 'would be out of it long enough perhaps even to escape the coming offensive and perhaps even the rest of the war'.[6] Dr Kelsey Fry, a dental surgeon in civilian life, who would go on to specialize in injuries of the jaw with the pioneering plastic surgeon Sir Harold Gillies, was also optimistic about Thomas, as long as he lay still for a while. But Thomas had insisted on raising his head to find a letter to his girlfriend, and choked to death as a result. To Graves and Sassoon, both attracted sexually more to men than to women at that time, it deepened the irony and the tragedy. Sassoon, who had hoped to protect his beloved Tommy from such a fate, had been due to rejoin C Company in the line in only two days' time.

Sassoon had already written what Graves thought 'a perfectly ripping' poem about Thomas, 'A Subaltern'; following his death, he would write at least three more. Graves's own efforts to pay tribute to David began the day after he died and the result, 'Not Dead', was sent to Marsh on 4 April 1916. It was Marsh's favourite from the collection in which it would appear, *Goliath and David*, and described by Edmund Blunden as 'that unforgettable almost-epigram' and 'the pick of them all'.[7] But tastes have changed greatly and Patrick Quinn's description, 'escapist pastoral' (in which the 'rough bark of friendly oak', the 'brook' that goes 'bubbling by', the chaffinches and primroses represent 'all that is simple, happy, strong' in his lost friend), seems nearer the mark a century later.[8]

But Graves's second attempt to pay tribute to the youth he described to his mother as 'one of those sunshiny delightful boys whom everyone loves at first sight and who never made an enemy in his life', would produce his best poetry to date and remain one of his most effective comments on the war.[9] When 'Goliath and David', as it was called, appeared in a slim, privately printed volume of that name in early 1917, Scott Moncrieff rightly observed that it was 'inspired by a muse who has shaken off her fetters'.[10] And Alec Waugh would claim two years later that it was 'the most subtle thing' Graves had written.[11]

Graves said in *Good-bye to All That* that 'Goliath and David' was written just over six months after Thomas's death, but there is an early draft in the

RWF Archives which suggests that it was started much earlier in the trenches while his anger and grief at the death of his 'best friend', together with his memory of it, were still intense. For this earlier version opens specifically in the trenches with the death of a young soldier called David:

> A crash a cry a sudden shout
> And running feet by my dugout.
> A wild face torn from cheek to chin
> Spurting the blood in jets broke in/
> Spurting long jets of red breaks in
> And gurgling blood, I'm killed he cried/s
> Throws forward blindly, choked/s & died/s
> David's clean beauty ripped away
> The man who wrote the Bible lied/s...[12]

The only trace in the final version of Graves's original intention to set the poem in the trenches are the words 'Out between the lines he went'. Other significant omissions from this early draft – such as 'the Bible lies' or 'God's a liar' – were almost certainly made in order not to offend his devout parents. Even as it stands, 'Goliath and David' must have made them fear for the faith of a son who, in reversing the triumph of God's champion David against the Philistine Goliath, implied (indeed, actually stated outright) that 'God's eyes are dim, His ears are shut'.[13]

From the reversal of the expected order of names in the title onwards, the reader is being prepared for what Graves specifically stated was 'the biblical order being reversed', though the ending when Goliath kills David still comes as a shock.[14] This deliberate setting up, then thwarting of expectations, as Peter Howarth points out, anticipates Graves's 'many debunkings of history', from *My Head! My Head!* (1925) to *King Jesus* (1946), in which *Good-bye to All That*, he claims, should be included.[15] Graves's message in 'Goliath and David' not only questions belief in God, however, but also belief in a war where, it is implied, youth, beauty, idealism and extreme, if foolhardy, courage are no match for brute strength, cold steel and violence. By removing his initial setting of the poem in the trenches and avoiding any direct reference to David Thomas, Graves can convey his essentially anti-war message indirectly and even more effectively as the reader herself makes the connection. He can also pay tribute to Thomas without appearing sentimental, gushing or valedictory. As Peter Parker has noted, this is 'an extremely effective poem, both on a personal and public level', with 'the grief and horror' the poet feels expressed fully in the ending where the Biblical David dies in an equally shocking manner to the later one:

> Steel crosses wood, a flash, and oh!
> Shame for beauty's overthrow!
> (God's eyes are dim, His ears are shut),
> One cruel backhand sabre-cut –
> 'I'm hit! I'm killed!' young David cries,
> Throws blindly forward, chokes … and dies.
> Steel-helmeted and grey and grim
> Goliath straddles over him.[16]

In case there is any doubt as to Graves's anger at the war after Thomas died in March 1916, he included in *Good-bye to All That* the ironic marginal note he made originally in 'Goliath and David', which opens:

> War should be a sport for men above forty-five only, the Jesse's, not the Davids. 'Well, dear father, how proud I am of you serving your country as a very gentleman prepared to make even the supreme sacrifice. I only wish I were your age: how willingly would I buckle on my armour and fight those unspeakable Philistines!…[17]

'Goliath and David' universalizes, through myth, the tragedy of all the brave and beautiful young men who died fighting in a war they believed in, initially at least. Graves's company commander, Richardson, for instance, was killed on the same night as Thomas, together with the trench-mortar officer Pritchard, deaths that strengthened Graves's superstitious attitude towards life. Only the evening before he had been talking to all three subalterns and the battalion adjutant, who had told them that 'not a single officer' had been killed since Loos. Graves was convinced that he was the only active combatant present to survive the following evening because he had been the only one to 'touch wood' (his pencil). Brought up in a family full of superstitious practices, the war reinforced his belief in powers above, beyond or outside the rational. His poem 'Corporal Stare', for instance, describes a celebratory dinner he had given at Béthune in June 1915, when he quite clearly 'saw' the ghost of a corporal who had been killed a month earlier at Festubert.[18] It was a belief that would feed into his theory of the White Goddess and the importance of the irrational element in poetry.[19]

Graves found life particularly 'gloomy' after the deaths of Thomas and Richardson, a depression that was not dispelled even by the news on 19 March of his long-deferred leave.[20] Nevertheless he planned to get his leave extended by having the nose operation recommended to him by Dr Kelsey Fry, the battalion doctor. British gas masks had become more sophisticated by 1916 than their crude early models, but they still required the wearer to be able to breathe freely through his nose, which Graves's displaced septum would not allow. His father got to work at once pulling strings, as usual; on Marsh's advice he wrote to Sir Alfred Keogh, Director General of the Army Medical Services, who arranged for Robert to be operated on free of charge at the Queen Alexandra Military Hospital, Millbank, by a first-class surgeon, Mr Potter, on 4 April.

Graves arrived back in England on 27 March and spent the intervening week visiting central London with his sisters, on one occasion meeting Edmund Gosse, 'an awfully nice old man', he wrote to Sassoon, who may have arranged the meeting.[21] He spent his evenings singing with Rosaleen and also visited his brother John at Copthorne and 'Charlie' at Charterhouse. The latter institution gave him 'two golden days', he told Marsh, 'everybody wept on [his] neck', and he contrived, 'through fulfilling all [his] social obligations, to spend most of [his] time in Peter [Johnstone]'s study'.[22] (He would be amused later by the headmaster's 'extraordinary comment' to the younger boy after reading Robert's '1915' poem to him: 'Your friend Graves is a silly fellow: he pretends he is in love with someone when he isn't.')[23]

The letter to Marsh was written in early April as Graves waited for his operation, which was finally carried out on 6 April. He had expected an easy recovery, filled with idle days and poetry-writing. Instead he bled badly and took far longer to recover than expected, feeling ill and depressed. He was not allowed out of hospital until 26 April. In those three weeks he had managed to write only one poem, 'The Lady Visitor in the Pauper Ward'. 'Old Skin and Bone', he told Marsh who admired it, was 'the Squire's gaunt maiden aunt who used to love visiting paupers in the Almshouse and unsettling them.'[24] Everything was grist to his mill, the 'old cool peace' of the Almshouse ward, undoubtedly inspired by the Queen Alexandra Hospital, so restful after the front line. Patrick Quinn sees the Lady Visitor as 'representing the war which has broken into a calm world of peacetime England' and the poem itself as evidence that Graves was 'growing tired of the patriotic civilian response of his countrymen'.[25]

When Robert arrived home, he was still looking 'very pale' and two days later, on 28 April, his mother put him on a train for Wales with Clarissa, to convalesce. 'I went up to Harlech to walk on the hills,' he remembered. It was on this occasion that he met his future wife, Nancy Nicholson (though he did not know it at the time), who was staying at Harlech with her father, the artist William Nicholson, and her painter brother Ben. Robert also took possession of a cottage from his mother, who owned considerable property in the area – a small two-roomed affair on the hillside away from the village in the hamlet of Llechwedd. Amy had been reluctant to part with it but, anxious about his health and fearful for his future, she finally sold it to him for 29 pounds and 19 shillings on 12 April 1916. From 1913 onwards she had allowed her older children to write and paint there away from the bustle of family life and Robert, like Clarissa and Rosaleen, had grown to love 'Gweithdy Bach'. By May 1916 it represented for Graves a future in defiance of the war, 'something to look forward to when the guns stopped'.[26] Gweithdy Bach would feature in at least four of his poems and inspire both the lyricism and humour of his letter to Sassoon in early May from his 'small, white-walled cottage ... that once belonged to a consumptive coachman, then to a drunken carpenter, then became a brothel, then a Sunday school', looking out on 'bright sun and misty mountains and hazy seas and sloe blossoms and wild cherry and grey rocks and young green grass'.[27] The thought of his cottage would comfort Graves on the Somme, where he would write again to Sassoon after their brief meeting at Mametz Wood:

> In Gweithdy Bach we'll rest a while,
> We'll dress our wounds and learn to smile
> With easier lips; we'll stretch our legs,
> And live on bilberry tart and eggs,
> And store up solar energy,
> Basking in sunshine by the sea,

> Until we feel a match once more
> For *anything* but another war.[28]

After almost a fortnight of Harlech, Robert felt much stronger and could walk the mountains with ease, able to breathe freely at last through both nostrils. His uncle Charles had come to join him and apart from a distinct difference of opinion about two of Robert's idols, Samuel Butler and Edward Carpenter, was good company – 'a ynarc [cranky] but pleasant old scarecrow' – and full of literary talk.[29] Best of all, Robert believed he was doing 'decent work' in poetry again, including a few poems he thought good enough to show Marsh. One of these may have been 'Sorley's Weather', inspired by the review his uncle was writing of *Marlborough and Other Poems* during his stay and the bleakness of the landscape on occasions; another, 'Careers', about memories of sibling rivalry that Gweithdy Bach had brought back, and a third, 'A Pinch of Salt', in which the opening stanza (admired particularly by Gordon Bottomley) contemplates the delicate nature of poetic composition and the importance of dreams, an area he would explore again later with Dr W. H. R. Rivers:

> When a dream is born in you
>   With a sudden clamorous pain,
> When you know the dream is true
>   And lovely, with no flaw nor stain,
> O then, be careful, or with sudden clutch
> You'll hurt the delicate thing you prize so much.[30]

Graves had resigned himself to missing the publication of his first collection, *Over the Brazier*, during his stay at Harlech. But, planned for 1 May 1916, the date had been put back to 15 May and he returned to London from Wales a day early for the occasion. The book's cover had finally been designed, from a picture of the Menin Gate, by Claud Lovat Fraser. It was a choice that Graves approved of (though his family did not), since Lovat Fraser had been to the Front and would not make any technical mistakes in the design: he had, in Graves's opinion, been drawing 'awfully well' in early 1916.[31] In addition, as a fellow Old Carthusian, Lovat Fraser might help the book's appeal at Charterhouse. *Over the Brazier* had no dedication, Graves told Marsh, because if he dedicated it to his father, Johnstone might be hurt, and vice versa.

Graves was 'overwhelmed' by the reception his first book received, much of it due, had he known it, to his father's many letters to his 'poet friends' about it.[32] The reviews were for the most part, and unsurprisingly, kind and positive, his uncle's editor at *The Spectator*, John St Loe Strachey, giving it a particularly enthusiastic and selling one, which opened: 'Mr Robert Graves's verses have a quality which renders them memorable.'[33] And the anonymous critic of *The Times Literary Supplement* referred to 'a complete sincerity which allows no hint of the imitative: if its rawness is sometimes repelling yet as the writer has an ear for musical cadence he often lays a spell on the reader and achieves something like true beauty.'[34] Sales would be healthy enough to print a second impression in 1917, then a second edition in 1920, with the omission of 'On Finding Myself a Soldier' and 'A Renascence'.

With just over a week left before his Army Medical on 24 May, Graves filled his diary with pleasures as well as duties. Beside a final check-up at Queen Alexandra Hospital, he attended as his father's guest a dinner of the Honourable Cymmrodorian Society, a Welsh literary club that included some of the greatest Welshmen of the day, David Lloyd George and the Australian Prime Minister W. M. Hughes among them. Again with his father, he visited Harold Monro, who was pleased with the sales of *Over the Brazier*, at the Poetry Bookshop. The same day he had lunch with Edward Marsh, an occasion slightly marred for him by the addition of three literary ladies and a 'dull diplomatist' instead of the young poet, Robert Nichols, Marsh had hoped would come. But Marsh did manage to arrange a meeting on this same leave with another writer Graves was longing to meet, Samuel Butler's friend and biographer Henry Festing Jones. Graves took to 'Enrico', as his friends called him, at once, detecting 'a queer Butlerian frankness about him'. ('"My father was an illegitimate, y'know," he said at dinner quite abruptly.')[35] He was thrilled to be allowed to examine Butler's papers. He even managed to see Johnstone again on his last visit to Charterhouse in late May before rejoining his regiment.

The medical board passed Graves fit on 24 May and the next day Amy was seeing him off at yet another station, Euston, for his train to Liverpool to rejoin his regiment. The 3rd battalion Royal Welch Fusiliers had been moved from Wrexham to what Graves called the 'dank grimness' of one of its suburbs, Litherland: it puzzled him that 'a beautiful name like Litherland' had not succeeded in evolving something better than what it stood for to him, 'factories, puddles, tramlines, dingey [*sic*] shops and a deformed and crooked minded population'.[36] Set in a rash of recent housing developments near Seaforth and Litherland Station in the wilderness of an industrial estate, it could not have been a greater contrast to the wild beauty of Wales he had so recently left, or even the attractions of Wimbledon Common.

The tin huts of Litherland Camp were set dismally between the 'hell-workshop' (Sassoon's words when he arrived there the previous year) of Brotherton's Ammunition Factory and a large Roman Catholic cemetery, with the smoking chimneys of Bryant and May's match factory only half a mile away. Liverpool, four miles off, seemed equally 'ghastly' to Graves, who did not appreciate the casual delights of the Adelphi Hotel and visited it as little as possible.[37] Another depressing feature of the depot was finding himself with so many of his contemporaries who were 'hobbling about ... hopelessly crippled by Active Service', an aspect of war that, ironically, he forgot about in France, where people were 'cleared away so soon either to hospital or under the poppies'.[38]

Fortunately, a number of Graves's friends were in the camp. Frank Jones-Bateman and 'Father' Watkin from his time with the Welsh Regiment and Aubrey Attwater, assistant adjutant of the camp, who had joined the 2nd Royal Welch Fusiliers early in 1915 and been severely wounded. Attwater, who had come straight from Cambridge at the outbreak of war, was known as 'Brains' in the camp. He was something of an exception among officers made up mostly of country gentlemen with estates in Wales, according to Graves, who did not get on easily with men who 'had no thoughts in peace-time beyond hunting, shooting, fishing and the control of their tenantry'.[39] In addition, Graves still felt oppressed by an atmosphere of what he called, rather priggishly, 'moral and actual smut'. He longed to 'go home' to France.[40] It was because of this 'want-to-get-back-to-the-boys-ish[ness]', he believed, that he managed to offend most of those he called 'the more considerable people' at Litherland, including his commanding officer, Colonel H. R. Jones-Williams, the adjutant and even his friend Attwater.[41] But as a fellow officer at Litherland told Sassoon, Graves:

... fairly got on people's nerves with his hot-air about the Battle of Loos, and his brain-waves about who really wrote the Bible ... The Blighter's never satisfied unless he's turning something upside down. I actually heard him say that Homer was a woman ... And ... he had the damned sauce to give me a sort of pi-jaw about going out with girls in Liverpool.[42]

Graves could cope with a certain amount of hostility, even thrive on it, but he was greatly depressed by news from Johnstone that his mother, having discovered Graves's letters and finding them sexually suggestive, had forbidden any further correspondence between them. It was an injunction that gave rise to an initially puzzling poem in Graves's third verse collection, *Fairies and Fusiliers* (1917), 'Marigolds', which he started possibly at Litherland, and certainly by September 1916.[43] Originally marked 'This for Pierrette[44] who writes "Forget"', then amended to 'who wants me to forget', 'Marigolds' is Graves's declaration to 'Peter', that his love for him can never be destroyed, whatever attempt is made to root it out, the central metaphor taken from Graves's early experience of gardening at Red Branch House, the marigold symbolizing both passion, grief and jealousy:

> Look: the constant marigold
> > Springs again from hidden roots.
> Baffled gardener, you behold
> > New beginnings and new shoots
> > Spring again from hidden roots.
> > Pull or stab or cut or burn,
> > They will ever yet return.[45]

Graves had little time to dwell on his troubles, however, since he was kept busy with his duties, the daily training of recruits that had grown more intense than ever in the build-up to the Somme. In his fourth (and final) week at the camp, for instance, beside the extra duties he accrued as 'Captain of the Week', he continued to be responsible for the 'trained men' course with 'night ops three days a week ... sweating about the country at all hours'.[46] At the same time his 'bloody verses insist[ed] on forcing themselves' to be written: 'they flock on me in shoals,' he told a sympathetic Sassoon, 'and I can't refuse them'.[47] The inspiration for at least one poem came from

Sassoon himself, who had sent Graves a verse-letter from France, composed in the relative peace and quiet of the Army Training School at Flixecourt in May – 'quite one of the nicest' poems Graves had ever received.[48]

Another less elevated distraction was an 18-year-old subaltern, whose vitality and personality charmed Graves so much that he was angry to see the youth dancing with a woman of dubious reputation at the Adelphi Hotel, proof that he did not entirely resist the lure of Liverpool. But his main preoccupation remained poetry. His hopes of having time to write it during his hospital stay and convalescence had not been as productive as he had hoped; ironically, it was during his most strenuous period at Litherland that he completed at least two more poems, 'The Last Post' and 'Babylon'. Sent to Rosaleen, originally under the title 'The Bugler', at the beginning of June, 'The Last Post' reveals how much Graves's thoughts were focused on his return to France and his likely fate there, as well as what might be called the reverse influence of Brooke. Like Sorley and Sassoon before him and Edward Thomas after, he conjures up Brooke's stirring appeal to patriotism in sonnets such as 'Blow out, you bugles, over the rich Dead', only to reject it:

> The bugler sent a call of high romance –
> 'Lights out! Lights out!' to the deserted square.
> On the thin brazen notes he threw a prayer,
> 'God, if it's *this* for me next time in France...
> O spare the phantom bugle as I lie
> Dead in the gas and smoke and roar of guns,
> Dead in a row with the other broken ones
> Lying so stiff and still under the sky,
> Jolly young Fusiliers too good to die.'[49]

Graves later wisely omitted a final, rather melodramatic couplet, which read:

> The music ceased and the red sunset flare
> was blood about his head as he stood there.

'Babylon', written the day after Graves left Litherland, on 25 June, highlights his growing tendency to identify poetry with children. Inspired almost certainly by his recent return to Harlech, a place filled with memories of childhood experiences of fairies and the supernatural, in it the narrator laments their passing:

> None of all the magic hosts,
> None remain but a few ghosts
> Of timorous hearts, to linger on
> Weeping for lost Babylon.[50]

But it would be some time before Graves could return in verse to that childhood world he yearned for: orders to leave for France took him back to Wimbledon on 25 June. He spent the next day again with his father, being shepherded from bank to dentist, to the Waldorf Hotel, where he treated Alfred to a good lunch. He also visited some of his relatives and Marsh, who introduced him to Margot Asquith, the wife of the prime minister and Marsh's new employer. But he did manage to have tea alone with his half-brother Philip, on leave from Cairo where he worked in military intelligence with a man Robert would get to know well a few years later, T. E. Lawrence. By 27 June, Graves was back in France.

When, four days later, the Battle of the Somme began, Graves was still in transit to join the 2nd Royal Welch Fusiliers, to which he had been assigned. Although he was extremely disappointed not to be rejoining the 1st Battalion, this transfer, combined with his nose operation, may have saved his life; together they meant that he had missed the opening of an offensive in which three-fifths of his fellow officers would be killed.[51]

As it was, Graves's journey to join the 2nd Battalion at Givenchy across the canal near the Cuinchy brickyards was delayed in Rouen by a new rule which decreed that all officers had to pass 'a certain gas-helmet test'.[52] When he arrived at his battalion on 5 July, it was in the middle of a successful raid, which Colonel 'Tibbs' Crawshay, fresh from Wrexham and knowing Graves, asked him to describe in detail for the regimental records. While welcoming this acknowledgement of his literary ability, Graves was surprised by the generally chilly reception he received. The main reason, he learnt later, was a rumour (based on his middle name which had become the nickname 'von Runicke') that he was a German spy. It was unlucky that a notorious German spy caught in England in 1911 had used the pseudonym Dr Armgaard Karl Graves and was assumed by some to be Robert's brother. Only Robert's established courage in the line could eventually end the suspicion.

A contributory factor to the men's dislike of him must have been Graves's evident scorn for most of his fellow officers, as at Litherland: 'seldom have I met a less cultured and more close-hearted lot,' he wrote to his mother on 14 July, 'so absolutely different' from the 'darling first batt[alion]'. But he did make an exception of the battalion doctor, Captain J. C. Dunn, a hard-bitten, rather dour Scot who had served as a trooper in the Boer War, was 'a born soldier', according to Crawshay, and 'should have had a Brigade'.[53] Graves thought Dr Dunn 'a great character, a bit crabbed in his Scottish way, but my God *dependable*'.[54]

By 7 July 1916 Graves reported, with some irony, to his mother: 'Safe back in the *trenches* again ... very frightened at first more than I have ever felt before; but the feeling wore off in a couple of hours.' He found little changed in the area: 'La Bassée plain is still red with those hateful poppies and the shelling heavier than ever.'[55] Having heard of the 1st Battalion's 'usual wiping out' in the fighting, he may even have felt lucky not to have been with them. But four days after his arrival with the 2nd Royal Welch Fusiliers, they too were ordered to the Somme battlefield. Marching through Béthune to Fouquières, they boarded a train to the Somme railhead near Amiens. Then, in easy stages, they marched through Cardonette, Daours and Buire until they reached the original front line, close to where David Thomas had been killed at Fricourt. Marching another two miles along the Méaulte-Fricourt-Bazentin road, nicknamed 'Happy Valley' originally because it had for a time been safe from German fire, but 'Death Valley' once the Germans overcame that problem, they arrived at the most recent battle area. It was littered not only with human corpses but also with dead mules and horses, which Graves felt strongly should not have been 'dragged into the war' in that way.[56]

Graves was pleased to discover on arrival at Mametz Wood that the 1st Royal Welch Fusiliers were bivouacked close by and even more delighted to learn that Sassoon and his other friend in the battalion, Edmund Dadd, were still alive. Sassoon had kept in close touch with Graves during Graves's stay in England and had been as disappointed as he was to hear of his transfer back to the 2nd RWF, so welcomed the possibility of a meeting greatly. After missing each other on 13 July they finally met the next day, when Sassoon found Graves as 'whimsical and queer and human as ever', making him long for a life of 'travels and adventures, and poetry; and anything but the old groove of cricket and hunting, and dreaming in Weirleigh garden'.[57] Curiously, Graves either forgot or deliberately omitted this meeting from *Good-bye to All That*, though he gave vivid details about Sassoon's daring, single-handed raid on Quadrangle Trench, not all of them accurate. He also mentioned the rhymed letter he sent in response to Sassoon's about the times they were going to have together when the war ended: 'how, after a rest at Harlech we were going for a visit to the Caucasus and Persia and China':

> ... And doing wild tremendous things
>   In free adventure, quest and fight,
> And God! what poetry we'll write![58]

In a letter to his family describing their talk which had so excited both men, Graves claimed that it was his 'very dear friend', Sassoon, who had 'broached [the] project for a joint tour [of] foreign parts' and had offered to 'finance the operation'.[59]

Neither Graves nor Sassoon expected to have time for poetry at Mametz Wood, but it was to provide the germ of one of Graves's best-known and most shocking poems, 'A Dead Boche'. Returning from a foraging trip to the wood, which had witnessed fierce fighting between the big men of the Prussian Guards Reserve and the little men of the South Wales Borderers, Graves had to pass by a German corpse, its back propped up against a tree:

> To you who'd read my songs of War
>   And only hear of blood and fame,
> I'll say (you've heard it said before)
>   'War's Hell!' and if you doubt the same
> To-day I found in Mametz Wood
> A certain cure for lust of blood:
>
> Where, propped against a shattered trunk,
>   In a great mess of things unclean,
> Sat a dead Boche: he scowled and stunk
>   With clothes and face a sodden green,
> Big-bellied, spectacled, crop-haired,
> Dribbling black blood from nose and beard.[60]

Graves's description of the event in *Good-bye to All That* some 13 years later – of the Prussian's 'green face, spectacles, close shaven hair' and the 'black blood ... dripping from the nose and beard' of the 'bloated and stinking' corpse – must be a rare example of a prose piece being based on a poem rather than vice versa, since he kept no diary at the time.[61] The stark realism of 'A Dead Boche', which still had the power to shock in July 1916, made it particularly memorable and came to represent for many a typical war poem by Graves, an irony probably not wasted on a poet who already favoured childhood innocence, myth and legend as the more effective way of conveying his horror at the war.

Poetry was quickly forgotten as the 2nd Royal Welch Fusiliers prepared for action. General Rawlinson, commanding the 4th Army, frustrated by the 38th Division's failure to take Mametz Wood, had devised a plan to break through the German defences along a four-mile front between Delville Wood on the right and Bazentin-le-Petit Wood on the left. Since direct attack had proved ineffective, he decided on a surprise night attack, which succeeded, the 1st RWF helping the 7th Division clear Bazentin-le-Petit Wood and push up the slopes beyond towards High Wood. By 15 July, Sassoon could report: 'The 7th Division have reached their objective.' Graves, who had just arrived at the new front line, had to wait in shell-holes for the next stage of the battle. Apparently unperturbed by the fighting raging around him, he found time to write to his family to thank them for some kippers and to report on 'two queer things' he wanted, in his whimsical fashion, to record, the kind of detail which makes *Good-bye to All That* such an entertaining read. One of them had occurred in his dugout during 'the hell of a bombardment' as a small mouse bolted for cover down his neck: he managed to kill it with a punch in his back and 'fish it out'.[62] The other concerned a 'tame magpie very friendly and conceited' he had encountered in a German gunner's post.[63] Both incidents he seems to have regarded as good omens. For he felt 'very confident' that he would 'come through this lot without being killed or severely wounded', a statement which must have struck his parents as deeply ironic when they received Colonel Crawshay's letter of condolence for the death of their son a week later.

By 19 July, Graves's 19th Brigade had established its headquarters in Mametz Wood, their target to recapture High Wood. But the 2nd Royal Welch Fusiliers, reduced by casualties to 400 men, was pulled out of the line and placed in reserve for the major assault on High Wood the next day. At midnight it was moved to a position in front of Flatiron Copse, less than two miles south-west of High Wood and the site afterwards of a large cemetery, another irony not lost on Graves. Although heavily shelled from 3 a.m. to 8 a.m. on 20 July, then intermittently till noon, the 2nd RWF was in a relatively safe position: Graves had certainly been in far more dangerous ones. The 800-yard south-west face of High Wood was to be attacked by the 5th Scottish Rifles and the Cameronians, with the 20th Royal Fusiliers and Public Schools Battalion in support.

How the battle itself went Graves was unable to say since, in retreating from a heavy barrage put down by the Germans along the ridge where the 2nd Royal Welch Fusiliers were waiting, he was wounded. The line of his wounds, through his left thigh near the groin, and another two inches below the point of his right shoulder and out through his chest two inches above his right nipple, made it clear afterwards that he had been wounded by a shell exploding just behind him as he ran: 'I must have been at the full stretch of my stride to have escaped emasculation'.[64] His other wounds were slight, one over his eye and two small cuts on his left hand which, since they matched ones on his right hand received at Loos, he took superstitiously as a sign that he would survive.

But Dr Dunn, who dressed his chest wound and sent him down to the old German dressing-station at the north end of Mametz Wood, believed that it was the kind of injury 'few recover from'.[65] (When Crawshay had first told him of how severely Graves had been wounded, Dunn remembered replying 'Is he? Well, I'm not surprised', such was Graves's daredevil reputation.)[66] Graves, who was given the customary morphia, possibly a little more than usual, had only the vaguest memory of being put on a stretcher and winking at the stretcher-bearer sergeant who was saying 'Old Gravy's got it all right'.

Heavily drugged and unconscious, Graves lay in a corner of the overcrowded dressing-station, given up for dead, until the next morning when he was found to be still breathing and put on an ambulance for the nearest field hospital at Heilly:

The pain of being jolted down the Happy Valley, with a shell-hole at every three or four yards of the roads, woke me for a while. I remember screaming. But once back on the better roads I became unconscious again.[67]

Shortly afterwards Colonel Crawshay sent his letter to Graves's parents, informing them that their son had died of wounds and conveying the usual praise and condolences. But Graves, like his von Ranke ancestors, he believed, was made of sterner stuff and survived an even more painful, nightmarish train journey from Heilly to the no. 8 Base Hospital at Rouen a few days later. It seemed to him propitious that he arrived there on the eve of his 21st birthday, 24 July 1916. His survival had not only strengthened his superstitious belief in portents but also his belief in himself and his poetic vocation. There was in his own eyes something mythic in his survival: he firmly believed that he had come back from the dead. And his first feeling was one of enormous gratitude.

10

THE SURVIVOR (JULY 1916–FEBRUARY 1917)

To die with a forlorn hope, but soon to be raised
By hags, the spoilers of the field, to elude their claws
And stand once more on a well-swept parade-ground,
Scarred and bemedalled, sword upright in fist
At head of a new undaunted company:

Is this joy? – to be doubtless alive again,
And the others dead? Will your nostrils gladly savour
The fragrance, always new, of a first hedge-rose?
Will your ears be charmed by the thrush's melody
Sung as though he had himself devised it?

And is this joy: after the double suicide
(Heart against heart) to be restored entire,
To smooth your hair and wash away the life-blood,
And presently seek a young and innocent bride,
Whispering in the dark: 'for ever and ever'?[1]

'The Survivor'

Graves's survival seemed all the more miraculous, both to himself and to his family and friends, because of the misinformation and misunderstandings that initially surrounded it. Alfred Graves's diary, the most reliable source for the details of what became tragic and comic in turn,[2] shows that his son was convinced he would live by the time he was put on the train to no. 8 Hospital, Rouen, though the doctor who put him on it regarded his case as hopeless. Robert's first letter home, written to his mother from the hospital train, seemed to confirm his optimism: it played down the seriousness of his wound and was in his usual firm hand, so that his family were 'not unduly anxious' about him when they received it on 24 July 1916, his 21st birthday.[3] But when Alfred called on Marsh that same evening, having failed to get any further information from either the Officers' Casualties Office or the War Office, he found him seriously concerned about Robert. The following day, 25 July, three more letters arrived for Amy, one of them from Robert, which she opened first. He was sleeping better, haemorrhaging less, and enjoying being 'treated like a prince', though not to the extent of being fed the melon ('nice juicy ear-cooling, round, Harlech-dessert melon') which his 'whole soul lust[ed] after'.[4] Amy's second letter, from the hospital matron in Rouen, was cautiously reassuring, but the third, from Colonel Crawshay, announced unequivocally that Robert had 'died of wounds'. A telegram from the War Office the same day 'regretted' to inform them of his 'severe gun shot wound'. Since his parents could find no evidence of which letter had been written first, they feared the worst.

This see-sawing of emotions was to continue until the end of the month. On 27 July another cheerful letter from Robert arrived, wishing his father a belated happy 70th birthday and reporting a visit from his aunt Susy, a Cooper aunt who had married a Frenchman and was visiting another wounded nephew at the same hospital in Rouen. He was also visited by a representative of Cox's Bank, asked by Alfred in London to investigate through their 'Enquiry Agency', and although Robert was annoyed by the visit, his parents were reassured by a telegram from Cox's on 27 July informing them that his 'progress' was 'good'.[5]

But on 28 July a long telegram from the Army Council appeared to confirm Crawshay's report of his death. It was too much for Amy who, in emotional turmoil as she watched her German relatives and her British sons and nephews fighting each other, had lost her faith in God for a time and now viewed Robert's supposed death as a 'punishment' for it.[6] Alfred, who wept with her, refused to give up hope, however, and at 10.30 that same evening took her into central London, to the Officers' Casualties

Office again. Here they were greatly reassured to learn that the telegram confirming his death had come from the Front, not the hospital. They were further heartened by another letter from Robert, who was writing daily at this point, to report real progress; his heart, which had been forced out of place, was returning to normal as the blood from his lung was absorbed. (The doctors would drain the lung of three ounces of blood on 29 July.) He now felt like 'a young lion', he reassured them.[7]

Just as they were finally convinced that Robert was safe, however, a 'fresh horror' hit them on 31 July, a letter 'stating definitely that he had died of wounds' and that his personal belongings were being sent back to them.[8] Only when Alfred studied the letter more carefully did he realize that it had not come from the hospital but from Robert's batman at the Front. 'Amy fairly jumped for joy', a joy increased shortly afterwards by a wire from Rouen: 'Captain Graves progressing favourably transferred to England shortly'.[9] Even an official announcement of his death in *The Times* of 3 August would have failed to disturb them, had they seen it, since they were expecting him home on a hospital train at Waterloo that very day.

Alfred was at the station to catch a glimpse of his son, who confessed himself 'embarrassed' at the sight of his father 'hopping about on one leg, waving an umbrella and cheering with the best of them'.[10] Robert was relieved to escape to the ambulance, but his determined father, advised by a helpful ambulance man, followed by Underground to Kentish Town, then by tram to Parliament Hill Fields, where he managed to stop the ambulance on West Hill and travel the rest of the way with his son to Queen Alexandra's Hospital for Officers in Millfield Lane.

There, in a comfortable room of his own with views over the hospital's extensive grounds overlooking Hampstead Heath, Robert told his father of the 'first terrible three days' before he reached Rouen.[11] He also told Alfred of the announcement of his death in *The Times* and on his way back to Harlech the next day Alfred wired the paper, contradicting the report. On 5 August the paper published his correction in their 'court circular' at their own expense:

> Captain Robert Graves, Royal Welch Fusiliers, officially reported dead of wounds, wishes to inform his friends that he is recovering from his wounds at Queen Alexandra's Hospital, Highgate, N.

The effect of these two contradictory statements within two days of each other was immediate: 'Such millions and billions and squadrillions of letters came,' Graves told Marsh, 'condoling, inquiring, congratulating – I never knew I had so many friends.'[12] Some correspondents he found rather tedious, others distinctly amusing: people with whom he had been on the 'worst terms' during his life – his housemaster, Mr Parry, for instance – wrote 'the most enthusiastic condolences' to his parents.[13] Graves had already written to one man he believed did not like him, Colonel Crawshay, in response to Crawshay's polite letter of sympathy to his parents, to announce his survival gleefully: 'Now Graves writes to the C.O.,' Captain Dunn noted with amusement, 'that the shock of learning how much he is esteemed has recalled him from the grave, and that he has decided to live for the sake of those warm feelings he has misunderstood!'[14]

Among the many letters, however, were three that Graves treasured greatly. The first was from Sassoon (whom he now called 'Sassons' since the death of David Thomas had brought them so closely together); the second from his Charterhouse friend, 'dear old Ralph Rooper', who having believed him dead for at least a week, wrote: 'Oh my dear, dear Lazarus'; and the third from Marsh, worried at not hearing from him since 26 July and probably fearing a relapse. Graves's letter to Marsh is of particular interest, setting out in prose as it does Graves's fanciful account of his 'evasion' of death in terms which the classically trained scholar Marsh would well understand. In it there is a deliberate and playful mixture of the ancient and the modern. After assuring Marsh that he 'did die' on his way to the Army's field ambulance, he switches to the River Lethe, celebrated by Latin poets as the river of forgetfulness or oblivion, guarding the underworld Hades, but just as abruptly Graves switches back to the present: 'I had only just time to put on my gas-helmet to keep off the fumes of forgetfulness'. The 'old Rhadamanthus', the judge of the dead, takes us back to Greek mythology, only to be jerked out of it by Graves telling Marsh that the Greek judge wanted 'a court-martial of British officers' and 'chuck[ing] a Mills bomb' which (in a direct quote of Sorley) 'scattered millions of the mouthless dead'. Graves next commandeers the boat of Charon, in Greek myth the ferryman who conveys the dead across the river Styx to Hades, by holding a 'revolver' to his head, and giving him an equally modern and anachronistic 50-centime note left over from Rouen. Faced by his last obstacle, the monstrous three-headed dog Cerberus, Graves substitutes the classical 'sop' of 'honeyed cake and poppy seeds' with a very modern British 'Army biscuit smeared with Tickler's "plum and apple" jam and my little morphia tablets carefully concealed in the appetizing conserve'.[15] Once past Cerberus the narrator wakes to find himself back firmly in the twentieth century 'being lowered on the floor of the 99th Field Ambulance': 'The doctor was saying "hopeless case" (and this part of the tale is true, truer even than the rest) and I winked at him and said "dear old doctor" and went off to sleep again.'[16]

This prose account to Marsh echoes Graves's verse version in 'Escape', with a few mythological additions such as 'the Lady Proserpine' (Persephone), who 'cleared [his] poor buzzing head and sent him back / Breathless, with leaping heart along the track' shouting 'Life! Life! I can't be dead! I won't be dead!'[17] The poem's subtitle – 'Aug. 6th 1916 – Officer previously reported died of wounds, now reported wounded. Graves, Captain R., Royal Welch Fusiliers' – suggests strongly that the correction in *The Times* of 5 August had prompted the poem in reply:

> ... But I *was* dead, an hour or more.
> I woke when I'd already passed the door
> That Cerberus guards, half-way along the road
> To Lethe, as an old Greek signpost showed.
> Above me, on my stretcher swinging by,
> I saw new stars in the subterrene sky...[18]

It is a witty opening, universalizing the experience of death with its allusions to ancient beliefs, but placing the narrator's own experience of it firmly in the present with its reference to his army stretcher. Frank Kersnowski compares this way of using classical myth in a contemporary context to what W. H. Auden would later do in 'The Shield of Achilles', or what T. S. Eliot would do repeatedly, though most notably in *The Waste Land*, both of whom, he argues, found themselves 'accounting as best they could for the dissociation between past and present that culminated in the violence and politics of World War I'.[19] It is a comparison which the much slighter 'Escape' hardly merits – Graves himself described it as an 'escapade that *attempts* at poetry'[20] – yet it is true that, like Eliot and Auden, Graves's mind moved easily, almost instinctively, between the mythological and the realistic, between the ancient and the modern, as his retelling of the Greek myths, *The White Goddess* and other works would show. Despite the apparent gravity of its theme, 'Escape' shows Graves at his most exuberant, conveying a sense of euphoria at being alive, especially evident towards the end of the poem as Cerberus gains on the narrator and the rhythm changes as the narrator crams the monster's mouth 'with army biscuit smeared with ration jam' and stuffed with morphia pills:

> He crunches, swallows, stiffens, seems to grapple
> With the all-powerful poppy ... then a snore,
> A crash; the beast blocks up the corridor
> With monstrous hairy carcase, red and dun –
> Too late! for I've sped through.
>   O Life! O Sun![21]

The light, almost facetious tone of 'Escape' disguises deep dreads and anxieties.[22] So too does its jokey rewriting of mythology, which allows Graves to convey what seemed to him almost mythical events in his own life.

Graves completed an illustrated version of 'Escape' for Sassoon on 9 August as another of the verse-letters they had started sending to each other, with Sassoon's name added to the opening line ('But Sassons I *was* dead, an hour or more') and addressed 'To S.S. Who Mourned Me Dead'.[23] He had written to Sassoon several times from hospital at Rouen, but the letters were never delivered, since Sassoon himself had been sent back to England with suspected 'spots' on his lungs shortly after Graves left the Front. Instead of joining the 1st Royal Welch Fusiliers at Ginchy, Sassoon had found himself first on a train for Rouen, then on a hospital ship for Southampton. By an extraordinary coincidence, when he arrived at Rouen on 30 July 1916 Graves was still there, though in a different hospital: they also landed at Southampton within a day of each other, Sassoon on 2 August, Graves on 3 August. Yet Sassoon still believed that Graves was dead, and was devastated. Thinking back on their brief but intense friendship, he tried to sum up the curious appeal Graves held for him: 'There was something of a bitter charm in him,' he wrote to a friend, Edward Dent, 'a sort of sallow, victimised, faithful Jester in the storm ... queer twisted smile – ungainly lankiness – rather goggling eyes ... His rare gaiety was like a young animal hopping in a daisied field.'[24] When Marsh telegraphed the news to his hospital bed in Oxford that Graves was alive and progressing well, Sassoon could barely contain his joy: 'I'm so glad in my heart that Robert has come back!' he wrote again to Dent. 'Isn't that wonderful and splendid?'[25] While Sassoon was writing joyfully to Dent on 4 August, still believing Graves to be in Rouen, Graves was addressing a letter to him in France from his hospital bed in Highgate, misunderstandings that were quickly cleared up by Marsh. By 7 August Graves was pressing Sassoon to accompany him to Harlech when he was released from hospital:

> Advantages besides those already enumerated – sea air; skilled and certificated nurses – (my sister and mother); a piano not too much out of tune and my sister plays exquisitely and so do you, don't you?; some younger brothers to liven things up; Snowden; the complete works of Samuel Butler and [Richard] Middleton and other amusing books; Gweithdy Bach, oh and lots more.[26]

Graves's exuberant verse followed two days later (though not sent to Sassoon until 18 August) and by the middle of August they had agreed on a convalescence together in Wales.

But Graves's recovery took longer than expected – it was more than a fortnight before he was allowed to sit on a chair rather than lie flat on his back – and his initial euphoria began to give way to darker thoughts as he relived his recent experiences in France. Was it really 'joy? – to be doubtless alive again, / And the others dead?'[27] It was the beginning of a sense of guilt that would recur throughout his life, a well-known syndrome for many who survive traumatic events. In August 1916 the long lists of casualties published daily in *The Times*, some of them known to him personally, would not allow him to forget, and when he was eventually able to travel up to Harlech on 26 August, he spent the journey in tears. Fortunately, he was escorted by Rosaleen, whose nursing job reminded her daily of the cruel effects of the war. The flag-bedecked car his delighted mother had ordered to meet him at the station seemed to him a mockery and he tore the flags down himself. And when he set out in search of his usual pleasure, walking, even the hill country behind the family home failed to offer its usual consolations: 'the immediate horror of death', he recalled, was 'too strong for the indifference of the hills'.[28] By the time Sassoon joined him three days later, he had already started planning and possibly writing 'The Survivor Comes Home', a poem written when he 'had the horrors' upon him.[29] A startling, tortured account of his mood by September 1916, it was nevertheless 'too long to get [the] harrowing effect' aimed at, in Sassoon's opinion.[30] Almost certainly in response to Sassoon's comment, Graves produced a shorter version, with the original stanza order changed, while still preserving the ominous repetition of key words in the poem – 'stirs', 'dead', 'Death', 'night', and the insistent alliteration of a harsh 'd' in 'drenching', 'drags', 'drip, drip, drip', heralded in the first sonorous verse:

> Despair and doubt in the blood:
> Autumn, a smell rotten-sweet:
> What stirs in the drenching wood?
> What drags at my heart, my feet?
> What stirs in the wood?[31]

Poetry was the main topic of conversation when Sassoon joined Graves at Harlech on 29 August. Alfred thought Sassoon 'a fine, tall, manly, modest fellow' who reminded him of Joseph Conrad,[32] but Graves viewed him rather differently as a fellow survivor, as the opening of 'The Bough of Nonsense' shows, Sassoon being the 'elder' of the second line:

> Back from the Somme two Fusiliers
> Limped painfully home; the elder said,
> 'Robert, I've lived three thousand years
> This summer, and I'm nine parts dead'...[33]

Subtitled 'An Idyll', the poem quickly turns into 'Nonsense to cheer up a brother-officer, after our experience in the Somme fighting', according to Graves;[34] they were both 'beginning to wonder whether it was right for the war to be continued',[35] so they agreed to collaborate on a verse collection in which they would make contrasted definitions of peace: 'With Siegfried it was hunting and nature and music and pastoral scenes', with Robert it was chiefly children.[36] Later on they would disagree as to how their unhappiness about the conduct of the war should express itself, but for the moment they were in complete agreement that something must be done.

Most of Sassoon's fortnight at Harlech was spent with Graves in his refurbished cottage, Gweithdy Bach, although he also enjoyed games of golf with Charles Graves and several outings into the hills with the whole family. In conscious emulation of two poets they both admired, Wordsworth and Coleridge, they were working on their joint publication along the lines of *Lyrical Ballads*. Having considered Marsh's copious comments on their respective contributions and suggested numerous emendations to each other, they aimed to have a manuscript ready for the inspection of Robbie Ross, literary journalist and art critic, by the time they returned to London in mid-September. They also tried their poems out on Graves's family just before they left in mid-September for Oxford and London.

Graves had ended his verse account of their anticipated visit to Wales among other places, 'And God! what poetry we'll write!'[37] But when they showed their joint manuscript to Ross on 13 September 1916, he rejected their proposal outright, wisely as it turned out. Sassoon, he pointed out, needed a publication of his own (apart from the collections he had had privately printed at his own cost) and had enough strong poems to warrant one, despite having been turned down by Harold Monro. Ross also believed that Graves had put most of his worthwhile verse into *Over the Brazier* and needed more time to build up another collection, advice that Graves accepted, albeit regretfully: 'I'm sorry, rather, because old Sassoon's such a dear and we took some pains over coordinating the two sets of verses.'[38] Yet Graves could not have been unaware that at least two of his most recent compositions, 'Goliath and David' and 'Babylon', were among his best work to date, a conviction he must finally have shared with Ross, who helped not only to place Sassoon's poems with Heinemann but Graves's as well. It was an ideal solution, since Graves needed something more substantial and more commercial than the Poetry Bookshop's 32-page pamphlet. Sassoon's collection, *The Old Huntsman and Other Poems*, would appear a few months later, but Graves's not until late 1917, allowing him time to build up a body of verse he would call *Fairies and Fusiliers*. Ross's role in Graves's life would not be extensive, but it would be a crucial one, launching him as he did into the mainstream through his approach to Heinemann.

Sassoon had known Ross since autumn 1915, but this London meeting was Graves's first with a man still associated with Oscar Wilde and moving openly in homosexual circles. Ross had stood by Wilde throughout his trial and imprisonment, and still worked tirelessly to promote his works. Ross had been joint-owner of the Carfax Gallery with More Adey for many years and by 1916 was an acknowledged connoisseur of the arts. His exquisite apartment at 40 Half Moon Street, Piccadilly, where Graves and Sassoon stayed on 13 and 14 September, was a glimpse into another world for Graves and he greatly enjoyed the 'mental and moral stimulation' of his 'two very jolly days' there.[39] His ostensible reason for this London visit, like Sassoon's, had been an appointment with his army chest specialist on 13 September, but his stay with Ross had been far more important to him.

It had been a particularly exciting few days for Graves, following as it did on another visit he and Sassoon had made on their way back from Wales, to Lady Ottoline Morrell, the half-sister of the Duke of Portland, wife of the MP Philip Morrell, and a generous patron of the arts. Whilst being uncomfortable with the pacifists whom Ottoline welcomed to her manor at Garsington – Graves would later blame them for Sassoon's anti-war protest – and almost certainly finding her theatrical dress and manners as extraordinary as Sassoon did, Graves got on well with her. He would visit Garsington frequently the following year while stationed in Oxford and periodically after that, and could truthfully say after knowing her for six years that she had always been 'very good' to him personally.[40] But then their friendship had not been threatened by Ottoline's amorous intentions, which had complicated her relationships with a number of the younger men she met; in September 1916 these seem to have been focused on Sassoon. Graves's irregular features evidently appealed less to her than Sassoon's more conventionally handsome ones.

Graves's looks appealed more to Lytton Strachey, also attracted to young men, who, glimpsing him across the room at Garsington in 1917, would describe him to Dora Carrington as 'attractive – tall and olive-brown complexioned, with a broken nose and teeth ... with dark hair and eyes'.[41] When they talked, Strachey was aware of 'strange concealed thoughts which only very occasionally poke up through the schoolboy jocularities'.[42] Although Graves would use the nickname given to Ottoline by her homosexual friends, 'Lady Utterly Immoral', he also insisted to Sassoon that she was 'such a ripper'.[43] His more considered opinion about her later would be that she was 'a kind charming mad woman and a notorious breaker up of homes; to be dined with only using a long ladle'.[44]

Both Ottoline and Ross were influential figures in their respective areas and Graves would benefit from Sassoon's introduction to them. But Sassoon's third introduction – to his mother, that same week – would not be so successful and would contribute indirectly to the end of their friendship over a decade later. For Graves's description in *Good-bye to All That* of Theresa Sassoon, whom Sassoon took him to visit at his family home at Matfield in Kent on 15 September, seemed to Sassoon 'unforgivable'.[45] Mrs Sassoon, who had been abandoned by Siegfried's father Alfred when Siegfried was less than five and Hamo, the youngest of her three sons, only three years old, was very close to her children. She had been fiercely protective of them and completely devastated when news of Hamo's death in the Gallipoli Campaign reached her in November 1915. Refusing to accept his death as final and comforted by the writings of the spiritualist Oliver Lodge, she had tried to keep his memory alive by preserving his room exactly as it had been and her attempts to contact his spirit nightly had kept Graves awake at Weirleigh. Sassoon knew this to be true and himself despaired of his mother's pathetic clinging to the dead, but was appalled by what he saw as Graves's disloyalty in retailing such private matters to the world. Graves, who named neither Sassoon nor his mother in the passage concerned, could not understand Sassoon's anger. But he did admit to Ross that he was 'a tactless sort of looney' at this time.[46] And there is no doubt that he exaggerated matters in *Good-bye to All That*. Far from announcing to his friend (i.e. Siegfried), 'I'm leaving this place. It's worse than France', as he claimed in that book, he stayed for nearly another week in September 1916. He also described it to Ross (*after* his first night there) as 'a congenial atmosphere'.[47] Having accepted Ross's rejection of the *Lyrical Ballads* project, he was starting on a novel based on his war experiences and evidently found Weirleigh the right place for it, despite Mrs Sassoon's nightly vigils.

In contrast to the many drafts Graves went through with his poems, he would write most of his prose works at great speed, and this novel, the first of them, was almost finished when his leave ended on 18 November. After parting from Sassoon in Kent, he had travelled to Wales, where his father and his uncle Charles were 'taking the waters' at Llandrindod Wells, near the Shropshire border. The three of them formed a plan to have Robert sent to Egypt, so that he could winter abroad as the lung specialist had advised. Robert duly wrote a letter to his uncle Robert Windham Graves, a British career diplomat stationed in Cairo. He also did some writing, completing another poem he claimed was 'ingenious', 'Died of Wounds', written 'into the shape of a funeral urn, as George Herbert might have done', but not one he felt succeeded.[48] By 2 October he had reached the sixth chapter of his novel, when he became 'a bit weary'.[49] Ten days later, however, having walked 51 miles from Ruthin to Harlech and full of a sense of energy, he was ready to take it up again with 'renewed zest'.[50] So that by the time he was back in London on 25 October, he had completed fourteen of his projected seventeen chapters. He thought the novel 'good' but could see no way of making it acceptable to the British censor; America was his only hope. There was, therefore, no need to hurry and he was, in any case, busy with other things by then, focusing on the poetry collection Ross had proposed to Heinemann. The novel was left unfinished and all but one page of its manuscript eventually destroyed. But that one page, which shows that Graves was sticking closely to his own experience at least until the end of 1915, suggests that this early attempt lay firmly behind his later non-fiction one, since it is repeated almost word for word in *Good-bye to All That*.[51] It clearly helped him greatly in writing his memoir in a short time in 1929.

One practical reason for abandoning his novel in late October 1916 was Graves's determination to indulge his various other interests while he waited for his next medical board examination that had been deferred by a week until 17 November. He spent a weekend at Charterhouse at the end of October, staying with Ruth Mallory in her husband's absence in the Army and enjoying a long, now forbidden talk with Johnstone, lunched with Sassoon and Marsh on 2 November, spent three days getting to know Ross better at Half Moon Street and visited Oxford on 13 and 14 October with his father, who was anxious to ease his son's future there. Alfred arranged several useful introductions and Graves met Ross there unexpectedly, which probably explains why he spent time in Oxford recasting five or six of his older poems that he and his willing father 'fished out of the big grey typescript to give Heinemann' with 'two more new ones'.[52] One of the new poems was called 'The Cubicle Window'; 'it's exactly how it happened and the exact words I'd have used,' he told Ross, but the poem itself is lost, possibly destroyed after Ross's lukewarm response to it.[53] Graves was delighted to be able to visit Raymond Rodakowski, who had written to him unexpectedly from Somerville College Hospital. Rodakowski's atheism no longer disturbed Graves; they were now in agreement especially over the hated 'unsettled' feeling most soldiers experienced on returning from France.[54] Both would rather be back with their men, despite the dangers and discomfort of the Front. News of British success on 13 November, the opening day of the Battle of the Ancre, made it seem more imperative than ever to return to the fighting.

Sassoon expressed very similar feelings to Graves during this stay in England and by December 1916, when he joined Graves at the Litherland camp, they had agreed that 'since everyone was mad', it was no use making a protest. Robert remembered Siegfried saying that:

> ... we had to keep up the good reputation of the poets, as men of courage, he meant. The best place for us was back in France away from the more shameful madness of home service. Our function was not to kill Germans, though that might happen, but to make things easier for the men under our control.[55]

Graves was resolved to return to France as soon as possible, and by 24 November, a week after rejoining the 3rd Royal Welch Fusiliers, was feeling 'disgustingly military', he confessed to the very anti-war Ross.[56] He was certainly not tempted by the thought of remaining in Litherland, though in the event it proved more enjoyable than he had expected. In any case, his extended sick leave, combined with the number of officers available for active duty, made a posting to France before Christmas unlikely. Despite the intense cold of the Liverpool suburb that affected his damaged lung and being 'overworked at so-called light duty', life was far from unpleasant.[57]

It had taken Graves some time to 'settle down to the life of a sojer [sic]', he told Ross, and he had still done no writing at all six days after his arrival, partly because of 'professional duties'.[58] Whether his job as editor of the *Regimental Magazine* could be counted as one of these duties or not, he seems to have enjoyed it. He also found the Officers' Mess more attractive than he had during his first stay, undoubtedly because of the addition of someone Sassoon had described to him in glowing terms, Robert ('Bobbie') Hanmer. Graves, still sexually attracted to young men of a certain type, thought Hanmer 'one of the dearest people [he had] ever met'.[59] Sassoon, who had known 'Bobbie the Beautiful' from hunting circles before the war, had been delighted when he joined the 3rd Royal Welch Fusiliers at Litherland, viewing him as he had David Thomas, as the very model of English youth, cheerful, bright-eyed, fair-haired, shining-faced, healthy, simple and true. Graves's slightly more objective view was of 'a perfectly charming boy of a rather conventional type but absolutely unlike the usual run of Sandhurst subalterns in his nice manners and simple tastes';[60] conventional, but not nearly as conventional as he had expected, 'only rather charmingly ignorant in certain subjects'.[61] Although he enjoyed sharing a hut with Bobbie, who was in C Company with him, he was even more anxious to see Sassoon again and prepared to sacrifice his place in the hut for Sassoon. It was an offer that provoked a note on Graves's letter in Sassoon's hand – 'get thee behind me Satan...'[62] Other inducements to return that Graves offered were old friends, such as C. D. Morgan, 'Bill' Adams and 'Tommy' Black, and a man who played the piano 'quite pleasantly'.[63] Even though he had had to turn down an invitation from Ottoline to a weekend at Garsington, Graves himself was feeling 'thoroughly happy, happier than [he] ever remember[ed] being in the army', with the possible exception of their shared 'rest' at Montagne.[64] For in deciding to return to France for the fourth time, he had been relieved of any further need to make decisions. As Sorley wrote (and Graves was reading in the privately printed volume of *Letters from Germany and from the Army*, which Professor Sorley had sent to him earlier in the year): "'Tis sweet, this pawn-being: there are no cares, no doubts: wherefore no regrets. The burden ... [of] the making up of one's mind is lifted from our shoulders'.[65] Like Sorley a reluctant volunteer, Graves could nevertheless not feel happy in England while the war went on.

Graves was among friends at Litherland and had never been prouder of his regiment, a feeling that brought to mind a poem written by Lovelace in the seventeenth century – 'To Lucasta, Going to the Wars' – with its well-known conclusion:

> I could not love thee (Dear) so much,
> Lov'd I not Honour more.

Graves's own 'Lucasta', the Honourable George Harcourt Vanden-Bempde-Johnstone, though of a different sex from Lovelace's, came from a class steeped in notions of honour and patriotism. The narrator's motives for going, shared by Graves, did not include a belief in the righteousness of the war itself, as Graves makes clear:

> It doesn't matter what's the cause,
>   What wrong they say we're righting,
> A curse for treaties, bonds and laws,
>   When we're to do the fighting!
> And since we lads are proud and true,
>   What else remains to do?
> Lucasta, when to France your man
>   Returns his fourth time, hating war,
> Yet laughs as calmly as he can
>   And flings an oath, but says no more,
> That is not courage, that's not fear –
> Lucasta he's a Fusilier,
>   And his pride sends him here.[66]

Opening in the same common measure as Lovelace's poem, so popular among hymn- and ballad-writers, Graves quickly branches out into his own variations, in much less formal language, as he tries to analyse his motives and at the same time impress Johnstone, the last close friend he would visit before leaving for France again:

> Let statesmen bluster, bark and bray
>   And so decide who started
> This bloody war, and who's to pay
>   But he must be stout-hearted,
> Must sit and stake with quiet breath,
>   Playing at cards with Death.
> Don't plume yourself he fights for you;
> It is no courage, love, or hate
> That lets us do the things we do;
>   It's pride that makes the heart so great;
> It is not anger, no, nor fear –
> Lucasta he's a Fusilier,
>   And his pride keeps him here.[67]

As the last line suggests, the final version of this poem was written in France, but the ideas behind it were inspired in England by Sassoon's declaration that they had 'to keep up the good reputation of poets' by returning to the Front. Sassoon had joined Graves in Litherland by 2 December and together they worked out ways of dealing with the tedium of camp life until they left. Although neither was able to devote much time to poetry, they pursued their distractions. Sassoon's weekends and some of his afternoons were spent at Formby Golf Club, which had granted free membership to RWF officers. And though Graves refused to take golf seriously, partly as a defence against his golf-mad and highly competitive family, he would often accompany Sassoon on the train to Formby for a little light fooling around on the course. (He had given up golf when he realized that it was 'bad for [his] temper'.)[68] Like Sassoon he was disgusted by the excess of good food in the Golf Club House, while the poorer classes suffered real deprivation. But neither of them, however scornful they might be in private, managed to resist the lure of expensive cocktails or dinner at Liverpool's Adelphi Hotel.

Graves did not share Sassoon's pleasure in hunting, but almost certainly joined in games like football and rugby organized at Litherland. He was proud of the speed of his recovery, which he attributed largely to long walks in the Welsh mountains, and regarded his ability to play football again with some complacency. A visit from his father and Rosaleen on 12 December, when Alfred had been invited to give a lecture to the Liverpool University City Society, was one of the few variations to his routine; Graves, still the dutiful son, persuaded several of his fellow officers to attend it with him.

Sassoon, sadly, had the flu on this occasion and, despite his pep talk to Robert about maintaining the honour of poets at the Front, he was determined not to leave England until the harshest weather had passed. Ironically, it was the initially reluctant Graves who kept the faith, persuading the medical board on 18 December to pass him fit for overseas. He feared what he might find in France. Knowing of the Royal Welch Fusiliers' heavy losses on the Somme and confronted daily by the raw, often physically inadequate conscripts who had been drafted in since early 1916, Graves was apprehensive of what he called, in a note to a poem written at this time ('The Legion'), 'The effect of untrained drafts on a Line Battalion'.[69] By setting his poem in another time and place (ancient Gaul in the first century BC), Graves avoids direct comment on the present war; at the same time, by naming the Roman 'legion' of the poem 'the Three-and-Twentieth', he invites comparison with the Royal Welch Fusiliers, known as the 23rd Regiment of Foot, presenting the reader with an ambivalent view of the situation through the two speakers, who differ. Like one of the two, Strabo, Graves could see that the soldiers of late 1916 were, like those of the Roman legion:

> 'Unsoldierlike, slovenly, bent on loot,
> Grumblers, diseased, unskilled to thrust or shoot.
> O brown cheek, muscled shoulder, sturdy thigh!
> Where are they now? God! watch it straggle by,
> The sullen pack of ragged, ugly swine!
> Is that the Legion, Gracchus? Quick, the wine!'...[70]

At the same time, Graves had grown to admire many such soldiers as they had gone into action together and had, like his second speaker Gracchus, kept his pride in his regiment:

> 'The Legion is the Legion, it's all right.
> If these new men are slovenly, in your thinking,
> Hell take it! you'll not better them by drinking.
> They all try, Strabo; trust their hearts and hands.
> The Legion is the Legion while Rome stands,
> And these same men before the autumn's fall
> Shall bang old Vercingetorix out of Gaul.'[71]

Wilfred Owen, who thought this poem 'glorious',[72] equated Graves's position unhesitatingly with that of Gracchus. But there are so many ambiguities in both the poem and its setting that it is unlikely to be quite so straightforward. For instance, the Roman Army, which was the invading force in Gaul (modern France), could be taken to represent the courage of the Allies and their resistance, or the ruthlessness of the German invaders, its soldiers seen as pitiless invaders or courageous warriors fighting for their country's honour. What *is* clear, however, is that, as in so many of his so-called war poems, Graves is writing not so much about the war itself but about related issues, in this case loyalty to the regiment. By using Roman history, as he had used Biblical legend in 'Goliath and David', he not only avoids direct comment but also universalizes his theme.

Graves dated 'The Legion' to late 1916, which suggests that it was written during a break from his duties on Christmas leave, for one slight and unexpected benefit of putting himself forward for France was a week in Wimbledon with his family, from 22 to 29 December. In his efforts to fit everything in before he left England, however, he so exhausted himself that he spent Christmas Day itself lying in bed and was unable to accompany his parents to help entertain Rosaleen's patients at her Denmark Hill hospital. He was sufficiently recovered to do his usual last-minute replenishment of equipment, typical of many British officers on leave, at the Army and Navy Stores, including a revolver, a covering for his steel helmet (a recent addition), waterproofing and a torch. The waterproofing was particularly important, since the Somme area was experiencing one of its most severe winters of the war. According to the historian of the 40th Division, it was 'the most God-forsaken and miserable area in France, bar, possibly, the salient of Ypres. The whole countryside was a churned-up, yeasty mass of mud, as a result of the vile weather and of the battle [i.e. of the Somme] which even yet had not petered out.'[73] Still expecting to leave for France at the end of the year, Graves spent his last day of leave with his Charterhouse friends Rooper and Devenish and his last evening with his family, singing folk songs to Rosaleen's accompaniment.

One of the most familiar aspects of army life, however, was waiting and Graves remained in Litherland for another three weeks until orders came for him to join the 2nd Royal Welch Fusiliers on the Somme. After another, surprise visit to his family on 19 January 1917 and a last dash to see Johnstone, Graves finally sailed for France on 22 January, leaving Sassoon to send out copies of his privately printed *Goliath and David*. (Heinemann wanted a bigger book than Graves could supply at this point and Sassoon had persuaded him to print ten of his poems with the Chiswick Press as Sassoon himself had done.)

In this particular case the delay in leaving was fortunate since the weather continued to be appalling, according to Dr Dunn. The new year had opened for the 2nd Royal Welch Fusiliers at Vauchelles near Abbeville, he recalled, 'with three weeks of frost ... rain or snow all the time' and only two fine days in the first fortnight; five times the average number of men reported sick with the flu and bronchitis, beside the usual trench-fever.[74] When Graves eventually joined his unit on 25 January 1917 at Bouchevesnes, where it had taken over the section of the Front to the left of Cléry, it was suffering its eleventh day of frost. Dunn, a hardened soldier, could not remember being so cold since nights on the African veldt during the Boer War. Graves's 'Sorley's Weather', written shortly afterwards at Suzanne in February, was almost certainly inspired partly by this severe weather.

Being housed in tents did not improve matters, nor did having a seriously weakened lung, and when Graves arrived he was asked 'with kindly disapproval' by Dunn 'what [he] meant by coming back so soon'.[75] Colonel Crawshay had been badly wounded the night before his arrival, so it was the acting commanding officer to whom Dunn reported that Graves was unfit for trench service. Instead he was put in charge of the headquarters company, consisting of regimental clerks, cooks, tailors, shoemaker, pioneers and others, and went to live with the transport back at Frises. Their dugouts, next to the solidly frozen Somme, were an improvement on tents but still incredibly cold; Graves shuddered to think what the trenches themselves must be like as he helped deliver rations to their unfortunate inhabitants.

Nothing was as it had been. Crawshay had been invalided back to England along with many others, the quartermaster, Yates, was sick and everything seemed different to Graves: 'It was a very different Second Battalion. No riding-school, no battalion mess, no Quetta manners. I was more warmly welcomed this time; my suspected spying activities were forgotten.'[76] Graves appreciated the change greatly, as well as his relatively safe job. But in Yates's absence he was helping with transport, which meant a long trek daily to help deliver food and supplies to the trenches. Conditions in Reserve billets at Suzanne, where the battalion was transferred at the end of January, turned out not to be billets in the usual sense but dugouts and shelters in the ruined town. The weather had become so bitter that the men were able to play football on the Somme, now frozen two feet thick in parts. The meals, though leaving the nearby kitchen hot, were cold by the time they arrived on the plate. Worst of all for the majority of men was an order from the teetotal divisional commander stopping their daily issue of rum. The impression that remained with Graves afterwards was one of desolation: 'In all this area there were no French civilians, no unshelled houses, no signs of cultivation. The only living creatures that I saw except soldiers and horses and mules were a few moorhen and duck in the narrow unfrozen part of the river.'[77]

Graves's miseries were increased by a common problem among soldiers, bad toothache, which meant a ride of 20 miles to see a dentist and a painful, bungled extraction. Another potential threat was that of having to serve on a court-martial panel, which he avoided by persuading another officer to replace him. But he was unable to find a replacement for a second, even more onerous duty, thrust upon him when the acting commanding officer, James Cuthbert, fell ill and Graves, as next most senior officer in the battalion, had to stand in for him at the Commanding Officers' Conference at brigade headquarters. There was a plan by the brigadier to 'bite ... off' a German salient opposite the 2nd RWF's trenches, 'as proof of the offensive spirit of his command', which seemed entirely unrealistic to those who would have to carry it out.[78] Graves, who was proud of his outspokenness at the meeting, claimed to have played a significant part in the attack being called off, though Dr Dunn, the battalion diarist, makes no mention of him in this respect.

There was time, however, to write at least one poem in early February, addressed to Robert Nichols, who would become one of the best known of the young poets during the war with his *Ardours and Endurances* (1917). It had been Nichols's request to dedicate the last section of this to Graves, combined with his praise of *Over the Brazier* and their shared admiration of Sorley that had started their friendship.[79] Graves had finally tracked Nichols down, during his January 1917 leave, to a private hospital in London. Officially invalided out of the Army with shell shock after only three weeks in action, Nichols confirmed to Graves that he was actually suffering from syphilis, for which he was being treated. Once Graves had rationalized Nichols's sexual relations with women, still a distasteful thought to him personally, he 'liked him in a way', he wrote rather condescendingly to Sassoon: 'quite enthusiastic about the right things – very well-read – so I gave him a hell of a lecture on his ways and, finding he took it well, made friends with him'.[80] Graves's confidence in his own judgement, his sense of knowing better than others, makes him sound like Nichols's father or schoolmaster rather than a man two years his junior.

It was in response to Nichols's letter to him in France that Graves's poem was written in the form of a verse-letter. Nichols, who had composed a popular poem about a faun, had asked Graves somewhat whimsically to 'feed his faun with cherries'.[81] 'The Somme and the Hippocrene [a spring on Mount Helicon sacred to the Muses] are both frozen over hard and white with snow above,' Graves replied: 'But I'll try to break a hole in the ice and sing dolorously like a sad bittern or an orphaned pismire [ant].' The result is an early version of 'To R.N.', which contrasts Nichols's 'sleek fauns and cherry time, / Vague music and green trees, / And life born young again' with existence on the Somme, where 'Ice grips at branch and root / And all the birds are mute',[82] an echo of Keats's 'No birds sing', no doubt. Nichols's readiness to listen to Graves and his evident admiration for him encouraged another of Graves's tendencies, to hold forth on subjects about which his listener might have been expected to know as much, if not more, than he did. For at the age of only 21 he now proceeded to define what a 'poet' should be ('besides a mere craftsman') to someone who would become a far more successful poet than himself within the year:

> Lofty without being pompous, hard without being cruel; also soft without sentimentality ... a woman suffering all the hardships of a man; hardening her weak softnesses; healthy and clean, loving the elements, loving friends more than life itself, proud, whimsical, wise, simple. But appreciating the refinements of Life as much as the harshnesses – warm sun on the bare chest, comfortable armchairs, a good fire, a jolly red Burgundy or claret, music above all and colour and sleep, and mountains seen from a distance as well as from the precipice face of Lliwedd.[83]

In that same letter of 2 February 1917, Graves had told Nichols that he could not be 'happy in England ... while the War lasts'. He was still writing to him in a positive mood about France sixteen days later, even after a 'devil' of a night trying to find the horses and some mules that had bolted when their limber-carts were badly shelled. As the officer in charge Graves had had to pursue the animals from four in the afternoon until one o'clock the next morning. A thaw had set in, but conditions were equally bad, with fog, mud and water-filled craters replacing the ice and snow. Graves became chilled through, his weakened lung eventually succumbing to bronchitis. By the end of the month he was back in England, with strict instructions from a doctor who had examined him at Rouen on his way home *not* to attempt to return to France. Writing to Ottoline Morrell from, 'of all delightful places', Oxford, where he was sent to convalesce at Somerville College Hospital, Graves claimed that his month in France 'broke [his] heart altogether' and that he had accepted the doctor's injunction.[84] It was the last active service he would see in the war.

11

A Change of Direction (March–June 1917)

> And have we done with War at last?
> Well, we've been lucky devils both,
> And there's no need of pledge or oath
> To bind our lovely friendship fast,
> By firmer stuff
> Close bound enough.
>
> By wire and wood and stake we're bound,
> By Fricourt and by Festubert ...
>
> *'Two Fusiliers'*[1]

Dated August 1916, 'Two Fusiliers' suggests that Graves had not expected to return to the Front after being invalided home from France that same month. Addressed to Sassoon, the poem also shows how close Graves felt to him at this point. They had spent nearly seven weeks together at Litherland, from early December 1916, but by the time Graves's bronchitis struck on 18 February 1917, Sassoon was already on his way back to France to join the 2nd Royal Welch Fusiliers, just as Graves was about to leave it. Sassoon may even have passed Graves on the journey, as he had once before. It would be another five months before they met again and when they did so, it would be under circumstances that bound them even more closely together.

As early as March 1916, when Graves had witnessed the death of David Thomas and other close friends, he had felt that his 'breaking point was near'.[2] And it is clear from 'A Child's Nightmare' that his experience at High Wood had brought back the 'horror bristling round the head' of his childhood nightmares, horrors intensified by his return to the Somme area in January 1917. By the time he arrived at Somerville College Hospital, Oxford, a month later, he was in a precarious state mentally as well as physically, attacked by what he called his 'fiddle-stick shell-shock feeling'.[3] Added to his fear of telephones was a terror of train journeys, which brought back memories of his nightmare ride to Rouen in July 1916. He also reacted severely to certain smells, a phobia originating almost certainly in the gas attacks at Loos. However the fear of gas had started, by 1916 it had become 'an obsession, even a sudden strong scent of flowers in a garden' was 'enough to set [him] trembling'.[4] Sudden loud noises would have a similar effect, evoking heavy shelling in the trenches and sending him flat on his face or running for cover.[5] His nightmares too continued. Although the worst effects would die down after ten years or so, in 1935 he was still dreaming of trying to save people, with his 'lieutenant', from a burning house, in which dead bodies with army identity discs would figure.[6] Another symptom noted by Alfred Graves was his son's sudden mood swings when the 'horrors' were on him.

It was in one such mood that Graves had written 'The Survivor Comes Home', he noted, the 'despair and doubt in the blood' strong upon him.[7] 'Mentally and nervously', he claimed, he remained 'organized for war' long after it was over.[8] To begin with these attacks occurred every two months and lasted two days: '*You* know,' he wrote to a fellow sufferer, Ross's friend, Charles Scott Moncrieff with whom he had become friendly, 'the bursting shell and dead men in holes'.[9] Graves himself generally called his condition 'neurasthenia', a diagnosis arrived at by army doctors, who would award him a disability allowance for it after the war. (Nowadays we should probably call it Post-Traumatic Stress Disorder.) He also used the term 'shell shock', though he was never officially diagnosed with this condition, which was only slowly being recognized by the military in 1917 and was, in any case, notoriously difficult to define precisely.[10] If Graves did suffer from 'shell shock', however, it was not in its most acute form, which displayed symptoms of conversion disorder, including mutism and amnesia. Nevertheless, his condition would be severe enough to make everyday life, including personal relationships, difficult for him for over a decade.

By 1924 Graves would conclude that the 'only possible cure' for his 'neurasthenia' was to have 'no leisure time' on his hands at all, with his writing the main beneficiary.[11] Between 1917 and 1926, when the chief effects began to diminish, he would produce nine collections of verse and five prose works. The poetry itself became part of the cure as he exorcised his demons through disturbed poems such as 'Raising the Stone', 'The Gnat', 'Forgetting War', 'Incubus', 'Ghost Raddled', 'Haunted', 'Dicky', 'The Pier-Glass', 'Down', 'A Letter from Wales', 'The Presence' and many others. He viewed poetry at this period as 'first, a personal cathartic by the poet suffering from some inner conflict'.[12]

This process of exorcism had already started at Somerville College Hospital, where he finally had time for poetry, and the promise of publication by Heinemann to encourage him. His ten privately printed pieces in *Goliath and David*, together with the five that Harold Monro agreed to let him include from *Over the Brazier* and at least nine more written since late 1916, gave him a good start, but Heinemann wanted a more substantial collection. By October 1917 Graves would have added over twenty new compositions.

The poems of this period are deliberately upbeat, Graves told Gosse, who had written to congratulate him on *Goliath and David*, published early in 1917. It seemed to him his duty, while the war continued, to keep up his 'brother soldiers' morale' as far as he could. He completely disagreed on this point with Sassoon who, according to Graves, considered himself 'best employed by writing poems which [would] make people find the war so hateful that they [would] stop it at once whatever the cost'.[13]

The conflagration of war must burn itself out, whatever I might write about the wickedness and horror of war; and who knows but that I might help on a decent peace by cheering up my friends and encouraging them to fight more happily. I suffer all that S[iegfried] S[assoon] suffers, or nearly all, I'm only hiding it till after the war: now I have to laugh and make merry, however much it hurts[14]

One way of keeping some of the 'wickedness and horror of war' out of his poetry, yet at the same time not ignoring the subject completely, was to continue to approach it less directly through myth, legend and history. Approximately a quarter of his next collection, *Fairies and Fusiliers*, would appear on the surface to have little to do with contemporary events, 'The Assault Heroic' being a case in point. Although its opening lines could (and did) refer to his own experience in the trenches, Loos in particular:

> Down in the mud I lay,
> Tired out by my long day
> Of five damned days and nights,
> Five sleepless days and nights...[15]

the body of the poem takes the form of a Bunyanesque dream allegory, with echoes of Browning's 'Childe Roland to the Dark Tower Came', in which the narrator and protagonist faces the 'dungeon of Despair', the 'Desolate Sea' and a castle filled with 'foes', who boast:

> We've murdered all your friends;
> We've undermined by stealth
> Your happiness and your health.[16]

We could, of course, be back in the trenches here, but the weapons directed at the speaker – stones, spears and boiling oil – are decidedly non-contemporary and converted into the 'lumps of gold' of poetry. As his dream ends, the narrator captures the castle 'keep'. Only when he blows his horn triumphantly in victory is the reader taken back to the Western Front, as the sound becomes the familiar wake-up call of the trenches, and to the very different, equally grim, reality of another 'assault', the 'heroic' of the title being deliberately ironic:

> ... *Stand to! Stand to!*
> *Wake up, sir! Here's a new*
> *Attack! Stand to! Stand to!*[17]

The poem itself becomes another attempt to deal with the carnage of war through the power of words.

An important aspect of Graves's 'cheering up' strategy was to write about the world he had chosen as his contrasted definition of peace, that of children. At the same time as he was writing the extra poems Heinemann had called for, Graves had discovered the late fifteenth- and early sixteenth-century poet John Skelton and had enjoyed his 'peculiar quality of joyous foolery' that he also recognized in English nursery rhymes (a subject he would explore later).[18] In addition to 'The Poet in the Nursery' and 'Cherry-Time' from *Over the Brazier* and 'Babylon' and 'Careers' from *Goliath and David*, nearly a quarter of the poems in *Fairies and Fusiliers* were written either from a child's point of view[19] or were on subjects traditionally reserved for children.[20] An early poem revised for this collection, 'Love and Black Magic', a story of wizards and spells likely to appeal to children, shows an overlapping with Graves's growing belief in the supernatural or non-rational aspects of life, demonstrated in that poem based on his own experience of ghosts, 'Corporal Stare'. It was an area that would become increasingly important to him as he tried to clarify his poetic theories.

Fairies and Fusiliers opens with an address 'To An Ungentle Critic' and a defence of his own method, which by 1917, he realized, might seem old-fashioned to readers of avant-garde magazines such as Alfred Orage's *The New Age*:

> But what reads new or curious there
> When cold winds fly across the air?
> You'll only frown; you'll turn the page,
> But find no glimpse of your 'New Age
> Of Poetry' in my worn-out words.[21]

The volume closes with a poem repeated from *Over the Brazier*, 'Free Verse', which suggests that while Graves was not ready for the more extreme experiments of Modernism, nor was he happy with the more formal technique of his father's generation. As Charles Mundye points out, 'this is the start of a long-term debate for Graves and for 20th century poetry as a whole about the relationship between traditional form and the modern poetic tradition' and consistent with the later position that he and Laura Riding would explore in *A Survey of Modernist Poetry* (1927).[22]

Another form favoured by Graves in *Fairies and Fusiliers* is the verse-letter or 'epistle', a tradition stretching as far back as Homer and Ovid at least, and kept alive through the ages by such poets as Samuel Daniels and Alexander Pope, whose 'Epistle to Dr. Arbuthnot' tackles serious subjects in a more personal way. In Graves's case the letter form would allow him to write about the war whilst avoiding direct description, or moral judgement of it. His 'Familiar Letter to S.S.', written in response to Sassoon's 'A Letter Home', which had initiated the dialogue, focuses on what Graves hoped would follow the war rather than the war itself. Turning to the ancient Welsh landscape and legend he valued so much, he imagines in easy rhyming couplets a world where two poets can 'rest a while' and 'dress [their] wounds and learn to smile / With easier lips', before setting out for foreign places, including Sassoon's 'ancestral' home of Baghdad, where they will 'catch the Persian rose-flower scent, / And understand what Omar meant'.[23] Above all, he envisages 'what poetry we'll write!' He also includes an actual dialogue between himself ('R') and Sassoon ('S') in 'The Bough of Nonsense', first published in *Goliath and David*, and would combine the verse-letter tradition with the dialogue form in 'Bazentin 1916' and 'A Letter from Wales' in later collections.[24]

In the comfort of Somerville College Hospital at the beginning of March as he quickly recovered his health, it was a pleasure for Graves to work on his poems, which had seemed difficult to write in the icy conditions of the Somme a month earlier. To add to his sense of well-being, perhaps as a result of it, he 'allowed' himself to 'fall in love with' a 'most charming person' called Ken Barrett from the 1st Dorset Regiment, writing to Sassoon rather breathlessly: 'I can't tell you much about him except that he's got dysentery and a horrible brother ... whom he dislikes and a nice mind and second sight and is most intelligent and aged 19 and rather Iberian looking (what a sentence!).'[25]

Communications with Johnstone had become increasingly difficult as his mother was determined to prevent any attempt to contact him and Barrett appears to have filled the gap. Wilfred Kenyon Tufnell Barrett, the son of a clergyman, who had trained at Sandhurst and would become a regular soldier after the war, was assertively heterosexual, in pursuit of one of the nurses at Somerville. He differed from Johnstone in everything but his youthfulness and sensitivity. But he shared one important interest with

Graves, a belief in the supernatural. There are frequent references to 'ghosts' and 'magic' in Graves's 37 surviving letters to 'Ken', the first of which opens 'Dear old Evil Eye' and ends 'Beaucoup ghosts here' (that is, Harlech). He was greatly attracted to the younger man's 'tremendous electric energy', those 'powers' that kept him writing to Barrett over a period of 44 years or more, letters that were not discovered until 1995.[26] Just as Rosaleen Graves believed her brother to be 'psychic', so Barrett's daughter would claim the same for her father. She would also suggest that one long break in their letters in the 1930s would be brought about by Laura Riding. Their contact at Somerville College Hospital lasted less than three weeks, but was followed by a profound change in Graves for which Barrett was at least partly responsible.

Before his stay at Somerville was over Graves was feeling well enough to go out to tea with 'all the young Oxford poets', by which he meant in particular Aldous Huxley, Thomas Earp and Wilfred Childe, the joint editors of *Oxford Poetry 1917*, almost certainly introduced to him at Garsington, which he visited frequently during his convalescence.[27] He may also have met them through his Charterhouse friend Cyril Hartmann, who was still at Oxford. Ottoline Morrell and her friends were 'charming' to him and the poets 'exceptionally nice', but he found them 'faintly decayed', he confessed to Edward Marsh, and did not expect much of 'a startling nature' from them.[28] Marsh was beginning to put together *Georgian Poetry 1916–1917*, in which he would include eight of Graves's poems but nothing by Huxley, Earp or Childe. Yet Graves was pleased to be asked to contribute to *Oxford Poetry 1917* and supplied the editors with 'Dead Cow Farm' and 'Double Red Daisies'.

Ironically, Graves was becoming increasingly attached to the city he had been so anxious to avoid when he enlisted and was sufficiently recovered by mid-March 1917 to apply for a job at Oxford, an instructorship in No. 4 Officer Cadet Battalion, 'on the strength', he claimed, 'of a chit from the Bull Ring commandant at Havre'.[29] By the time he left Somerville College Hospital on 17 March the position was almost settled and, after a flying visit to Litherland for the final seal of approval from his commanding officer, he could look forward to at least eight months more in England in congenial surroundings. Following a hectic week in London 'seeing people', especially Robbie Ross and his friends at Half Moon Street – 'great fun', he told

Sassoon[30] – he set off for yet another convalescence at Harlech. Conscious that Sassoon was now on the Somme with the 'bloody battalion' he had so recently left, he hardly dared tell him how wonderful Wales was in late March: 'absolute peace and quiet; soft colours, sheep, stolid peasants, rough old rocks. Heaven!'[31] A great deal of his time was spent walking in the hills by day and learning to play the harp at night, helped no doubt by Rosaleen, who was with him: 'If I succeed,' he wrote to Ottoline, '... I'll be the first bard who really did play the lyre though they all talk about it.'[32] He had written very little verse there by the end of March, except an 'appreciation' of John Skelton, the poet he had recently discovered. Skelton seemed to him 'a true Englishman and a man after [his] own heart', who wrote 'beautiful doggerel nonsense and thoroughly irresponsible and delightful jingles, though "the first scholar in the land" according to Erasmus'.[33] Graves's own aspirations as a poet emerge quite clearly in the conclusion to his defiant defence of a largely unread poet, whom he had unwittingly echoed in 'Free Verse':

> ... angrily, wittily,
> Tenderly, prettily,
> Laughingly, learnedly,
> Sadly, madly,
> Helter-skelter John
> Rhymes serenely on,
> As English poets should.
> Old John, you do me good![34]

While Graves continued to enjoy himself, first in Wales, then back in Oxford, by 2 April Sassoon was setting off with the 2nd Royal Welch Fusiliers for Arras and the Front. The year 1916 had ended in a sense of defeat for the Allies: the Somme offensive had failed, Russian morale was at a low ebb, Roumania (as it then was) had been overrun and, at sea, Jutland had not been the decisive engagement hoped for. Only the capture of Baghdad could really be counted as a victory and this seemed to most people too far away to be of much interest, with the exception of Sassoon who identified with it as his ancestral home. One result of the growing dissatisfaction had been a change of political leadership in England, where Lloyd George's government replaced that of Asquith on 7 December 1916, and a switch in military leadership in France, where General Nivelle (of Verdun fame) replaced Marshal Joffre as Commander-in-Chief of the French Armies. While Lloyd George and his fellow politicians were rejecting German peace proposals in December as insincere, Joffre had been drawing up plans for one more great battle at Arras, in the belief that this would finally end the war.

On the day the Battle of Arras began, 9 April 1917, Graves was writing to tell his family that his staff appointment at Oxford had been confirmed.[35] On 11 April he returned home to pick up clothes and manuscripts to take back to the 'rather fine rooms' he had been given at Wadham College, where his instructorship was to take place. His letter of thanks to Ross for a 'magnificent' edition of Skelton and his description of his rooms reveals a more aesthetic side than his rather careless physical appearance would lead one to expect, evidence perhaps of some influence from Ross's own beautifully decorated apartment at Half Moon Street: 'I've got together quite a serviceable library: and some jolly pictures ... Two of those, aren't they called 'Kokka' prints?, two Medici's and some silver prints of old statues, one or two pleasant watercolours of home by my sister, and school groups and maps of the Somme.'[36]

Graves enjoyed his time at Wadham, where he was a member of the Senior Common Room with access to the college's famous brown sherry. His commanding officer, Colonel Stenning, the university's Professor of Hebrew, was a fellow of the college, a disruption of the normal order of things Graves clearly relished. He particularly enjoyed the dislocation of the social system in which the St John's don destined to be his moral tutor was a corporal in the General Reserve, obliged to salute his future student, Graves, whenever they met. A former college 'scout', or servant, had a commission and was instructing one of the other cadet battalions.

By the time Graves was 'comfortably settled down' at Wadham on 21 April, Sassoon was back in England at the 4th London Hospital, Denmark Hill, with a near fatal wound from the Battle of Arras. Welcoming him home on 22 April, Graves told him that his sister Rosaleen was nursing there. He also encouraged his father to visit Sassoon and review Sassoon's first trade publication, *The Old Huntsman and other Poems* in *The Observer*. (Alfred was 'really delighted' with the book, he told Sassoon when he received his review copy in late April.)[37] Graves also persuaded his uncle Charles to review it in *The Spectator* and E. B. Osborn to do so in the popular *Morning Post*. In addition he went round all the Oxford booksellers to 'get them to buy large stocks'.[38] Such efforts over a book that had replaced his own planned joint volume with Sassoon show a generosity of spirit which would make up in his friends' eyes for his frequent tactlessness and occasional arrogance.

His duties with No. 4 Battalion were demanding, since it was one of a number of battalions recently formed from a pressing need to train more officers for the Front as quickly as possible. Graves's platoon was part of D Company, commanded, according to one of its cadets, Lester Pearson, by a 'timid-looking, very English, donnish type, Captain Morrell, of a wealthy brewing family'; it was a 'rough and rowdy bunch', Pearson recalled, himself included.[39] The introduction of conscription and the urgent need for soldiers at the Front had changed the nature of the men entering the Army and those becoming officers by 1917. Although fewer officer-cadets were now 'gentlemen', from the Regular Army's point of view, their 'deficiency in manners' seemed to Graves 'amply compensated for by their greater efficiency in action'.[40] His own platoon consisted largely of men from the colonies – Australians, New Zealanders, Canadians, South Africans and two men from the Fiji Islands – plus an English farm labourer, a Welsh miner and only two or three public school boys.

The other two platoons of D Company were made up mainly of English youths just out of public school and the choice of Graves to command the less genteel colonials suggests that he was still seen as somewhat irregular and tough enough to handle them. Most of his cadets were non-commissioned officers who had already served at the Front for some time; one or two of them were old enough to be his father. Pearson thought him an 'unlikely choice' to manage their 'unruly and high-spirited' platoon but claimed that he had 'enough good sense to give us our heads' and to accept their somewhat unconventional ideas of spit-and-polish and military discipline.[41] Graves found them 'a good lot' and they got on well together.[42] Pearson, who would go on to become prime minister of Canada, remained in touch with Graves after the war and became a friend of the family.

The four-month cadet course was strenuous for both cadets and their instructors. Much of the training was drill and musketry, but Graves believed that the important part was 'tactical exercises with limited objectives', for which the instructors used the Army textbook *Instructions for the Training of Platoons for Offensive Action, 1917.* This treated the platoon rather than the company as the chief tactical unit and seemed to Graves 'perhaps the most important War Office publication' of 1914–18.[43] He took his duties seriously and all the cadets in his platoon would pass their final examinations, though he would not be with them by then.

By mid-May he was beginning to feel 'seedy' and started dosing himself on a 'dry strychnine tonic'.[44] After seven or eight weeks in his job Graves fainted and fell downstairs one evening, cutting his head open. Back in Somerville College Hospital in early June, he explained his relapse to Marsh as 'a collapse after too much work with my battalion'.[45] To other friends he blamed his 'nerves'[46] and to yet others he offered a purely physical explanation, his lungs, for which he thought the damp Oxford climate unsuitable.

There were other possible factors at work. The need for more poems for Heinemann, for instance, though it produced 'a good many decent ones' at Wadham, according to Graves,[47] it did so perhaps at the cost of his health. And one of the poems included in the eventual collection, 'Strong Beer', suggests that there was a less serious side to his time at Oxford which might also have taken its toll on his constitution. For by mid-April, when he started his instructorship, his circle of friends had widened considerably. He continued to visit Ottoline and her friends at Garsington nearly every Sunday for tea and his initial hostility towards the pacifist circle he met there diminished as he got to know a number of its members, among them Clive Bell, Lytton Strachey and Bertrand Russell, in addition to Aldous Huxley. He also became friends with the Irish poet and novelist, L. A. G. Strong, who would keep in touch with him regularly until the advent of Laura Riding. Graves met new people, too, through Cyril Hartmann at University College, the most significant, or at least the most eccentric of whom was Evan Morgan. Two years older than Graves and a product of Eton and Balliol College, Morgan, son of the 1st Viscount Tredegar, was already known to Graves by name through Morgan's cousin, Raymond Rodakowski. Moving in a privileged world of wealth and deference more akin to that of the Renaissance than twentieth-century Oxford, Morgan was a larger-than-life figure, not unlike Sassoon's musician friend, Lord Berners. A flamboyant homosexual, practical joker, gourmet and music lover, who surrounded himself with beautiful works of art by Michelangelo, Donatello and Leonardo da Vinci, he was also a convert to Roman Catholicism who would become a Privy Chamberlain of the Cape and Sword at the Papal Court. Later on he would fill the grounds of the family home he inherited with exotic animals and birds.

When Graves met him in 1917 he was private secretary to the Conservative government's Minister for Labour, W. C. Bridgeman, a contact Graves would find useful not long afterwards. Although he seemed an unlikely friend for Graves, they evidently enjoyed canoeing on the Isis together, on one occasion falling over a weir in their boat. More importantly, they shared a passion for poetry and an interest in magic, though Morgan's involvement was more sinisterly rumoured to be in the 'black arts', an interest that would bring him close to the occultist Aleister Crowley later on. Graves's praise of 'strong beer' and frequent references to 'good ripe burgundy' at this time suggest that he may have been drawn into Morgan's riotous way of life temporarily, with the fall down the stairs simply a matter of being drunk.

There is yet another possible explanation for Graves's collapse, however, and one which may also explain the extraordinary event that followed his second admission to Somerville College Hospital, when he fell in love with a woman for the first time in his life. On 22 April 1917, Graves's second day as an instructor at Wadham, Johnstone had been arrested on Godalming Station late at night for soliciting a corporal in the Military Police, who brought charges against him. After an initial hearing the next day, Johnstone was tried in Godalming Magistrates Court on 26 April. With the help of a leading barrister, Sir Richard Muir, and the eminent psychiatrist Dr Henry Head, the charge was dismissed. But the local newspaper had already reported it and it was eventually picked up by the well-known journalist, Horatio Bottomley, who on 2 June 1917 fulminated self-righteously in the *John Bull* magazine against the unequal treatment meted out to commoners and aristocrats, naming Johnstone and the dismissal of his charge as a case in point.

The main interest of the story is the way Graves presented it to the world. In 1917 he made no mention of having heard of it until nearly three months after it occurred, though it must have caused an enormous scandal at Charterhouse. And though Graves appears initially to have accepted

Johnstone's absence from school in May (when he planned a visit) being due to illness, he is less likely to have escaped hearing of Bottomley's irate article, naming Johnstone, on 2 June. It is, of course, possible that he did not see, or hear of, the *John Bull* piece until 12 July, as he told Marsh, despite the fact that both his father and his uncle Charles wrote for the magazine.

But if Graves did see the article before he went to Somerville College Hospital for the second time, it might explain his abrupt change of sexual direction more convincingly. When he came to write about this period himself in 1929, he pre-dated this whole Johnstone incident by two years, so that his falling in love with a woman was not seen to be connected to Johnstone's behaviour. Yet he had written to Robert Nichols in 1917: '*Since* [my italics] the cataclysm of my friend Peter [i.e. Johnstone], my affections are running in the more normal channels.'[48]

Three years of army life had, in any case, broken down Graves's puritanical fear of sex that had made a platonic male relationship so attractive at the start. It is also significant that it was at Somerville College Hospital, where Graves had witnessed Ken Barrett's strong attraction to one of the nurses, that Graves himself was to fall in love with a woman, Marjorie Machin. Writing to Barrett in 1919 about being happy with marriage, Graves tells him 'but for you I would never have been where I am now and God bless you for it'.[49] The only person he confided his love of Marjorie to initially was Barrett, who had first met her, like Graves, during their March stay in hospital. Like all the other women at Somerville, she was a nurse with the Voluntary Aid Detachment Service, but she differed from them in other ways. A skilled pianist, like Robert's sister Rosaleen, she also shared with him the difficulties of having a German parent (her father) during a war against Germany. Although 'not beautiful', according to one of her friends, she was 'lively, intelligent, tall and neat'.[50] Interestingly, another friend described her as 'almost masculine', perhaps making Graves's transition from male to female love easier. Whatever attraction she held for him, Graves did not talk to her directly of his feelings, but would write to her about them after leaving Somerville for the second time in late June 1917. When she replied that she was 'fond of someone else', he stopped writing at once: he 'had seen what it felt like to be in France and have somebody else playing about with one's girl'.[51] But as he admitted to Barrett, he was relieved that, having proved that he had 'the power of falling in love with a girl', he could 'now ... safely and happily return unto my friends of my own sex and be happy'.[52] He was still not fully prepared for such a radical change and there is no evidence in his poetry of this period of the strength of feeling displayed towards Johnstone in '1915' and 'The Fusilier'; in fact no love poetry at all by Graves has survived from 1917. And he could still sound immensely condescending about women, writing to console Barrett on 5 August 1917 about the behaviour of the girl he was in love with, for example:

> But of course it's not a girl's fault if she encourages people: she doesn't know she's doing it, living as she always does by the heart rather than by the head, and will quite honestly deny that she's been flirting. It's her temperament and men don't understand it, expect her to be reasonable like themselves. But I actually believe that a man can always get a girl he wants by taking a firm line.[53]

It is ironic to consider that the two significant women in Graves's life for the next two decades, Nancy Nicholson and Laura Riding, were both strong feminists who would quickly cure him of such male chauvinist views. Even his useful, if obvious insight that 'one can't treat girls as though they were boys' sounds a little arrogant to modern ears, particularly since it is followed by the claim that he could have 'won' Marjorie if he had chosen, despite her 'love for another'.[54]

Overall Graves seems to have regarded Marjorie as a useful stage in his sexual conversion, writing to Barrett six months after the event, as he announced his plans to marry Nancy:

> I met her just at the time that I felt the approach of a real person to love, and for two or three days mistook her. Then, half realised and fortunately found she was fond of someone else: then wholly realised and bad [sic] her my adieux. The sad part came later when it appeared that she was at least as fond of me as the other chap. Her fault?[55]

His 'flibbertigibbet state' at Somerville College Hospital when he first met Barrett he viewed later as 'just announcing that Nancy was about to appear and make life something worth living'.[56] Poor Marjorie became 'one false scent' in such a scenario, later a single paragraph in *Good-bye to All That*. She never married.

12

A Protest, Craiglockhart and 'A Capable Farmer's Boy' (June–July 1917)

> Personally I think [Sassoon's] quite right in his views but
> absolutely wrong in his action ... It would be true friendship for
> me to heap coals of fire on the head of the dog that bit me by
> turning pacifist myself but you can be quite assured that I'm a
> sound militarist in action however much of a pacifist in thought.
>
> *Robert Graves to Edward Marsh, 12 July 1917*

By the time the possibility of a relationship with Marjorie Machin ended, Graves was convalescing in Queen Victoria's former palace of Osborne on the Isle of Wight.[1] Arriving at Osborne House on 19 June 1917, Graves would remain there for just under a month, living in some style. (His bedroom, for instance, had once been the royal night-nursery of King Edward VII and his siblings.) Having been in a state of great emotional turmoil at Oxford, he welcomed the variety of pleasant distractions that Osborne offered:

> This was the strawberry season and fine weather; the patients
> were able to take all Queen Victoria's favourite walks through
> the woods and along the quiet sea-shore, play billiards in the
> royal billiard-room, sing bawdy songs in the royal music-room,
> drink the Prince Consort's favourite Rhine wines among his

Winterhalters, play golf-crocquet and go down to Cowes when in need of adventure. We were made honorary members of the Royal Yacht Squadron. This is another of the caricature scenes of my life; sitting in a leather chair in the smoking-room of what had been and is now again the most exclusive club in the world, drinking gin and ginger, and sweeping the Solent with a powerful telescope.[2]

Whether Graves's facts are entirely accurate or not – he was always seduced by his love of a 'good' story – his feeling of relief and renewal is convincingly conveyed. So that it is no surprise to read his father's diary report on 30 June 1917 of a letter Rosaleen had sent from Robert: 'He is much better of rest, sea air, and good food.' Another, more serious diversion at Osborne that contributed to Graves's recovery was his friendship with the Cistercian monks at nearby Quarr Abbey. Driven from Solesmes in France by the anti-clerical laws, they had settled on the Isle of Wight and built a new abbey on the foundations of the one demolished in 1546 during Henry VIII's dissolution of the monasteries. Their special mission from the Vatican was to collect and edit ancient church music. Listening to the fathers at their plainsong proved a welcome escape from the war for Graves and the man who had introduced him to the Abbey, Vernon Bartlett.

Although Bartlett was not the journalist of that name as Graves had initially thought, his appreciation of the Cistercian monks' plainsong suggests that he was a person of some sensibility. He may also have enjoyed the fathers' splendid library of 20,000 books, as Graves did, though the latter was disappointed that these did not include poetry. (Fortunately, Graves had brought his own favourite poets with him – Keats, Sorley, Skelton, and his book of ballads, together with Latin prose by his 'dear Apuleius'.)

Bartlett became Graves's closest friend during his month at Osborne House and a fellow conspirator in his attempts to liven up the place, which he found rather gloomy due to the large number of neurasthenic patients. One of these was A. A. Milne, 'very depressed' according to Graves, and 'in the least humorous vein'.[3] Significantly, Graves does not include himself among the neurasthenics; he was evidently feeling much better. He and Bartlett, deciding that 'something must be started' to offset the gloom, inaugurated the Royal Albert Society, for reasons Graves explained to Robert Nichols with some relish: 'Here we live among decaying royalty and the mouldered memories of Prince Albert Great and Good, in whose honour I and ... Bartlett have formed a rag society; now very strong and hilarious after two meetings. We affect Albert chains and side-whiskers and invent monstrous yarns about our hero.'[4] Other absurd features included the rules governing membership which, apart from admirers of the Prince Consort, included 'those who had resided for six months or upwards by the banks of the Albert Nyanza.'[5] Another 'rag' with more sinister overtones was their 'discovery' of a so-called corpse on the beach, which they reported to the coastguard, though it was in reality an old ship's fender, with a frayed rope at the top serving as hair. The incident, though slight, may help explain a puzzling poem in *Fairies and Fusiliers*, 'I Wonder what it Feels like to be Drowned', ostensibly inspired by taking a bath.

Meantime Graves continued to be 'nonsensical', as he acknowledged, with Bartlett his willing accomplice in such pranks as changing all the labels of the pictures in the galleries; 'anything to make people laugh'.[6] His spirits were raised even further by letters of praise for *Goliath and David* from Arnold Bennett, John Masefield and Robert Bridges, to all of whom he had sent copies, and a message from Nichols at the beginning of July reporting Masefield's statement that 'Nichols, Graves and Sassoon are singing together like the morning stars'.[7] A week later Marsh wrote to say that he wanted to include eight of Graves's poems in *Georgian Poetry 1916–1917*. None of the pieces would be new by the time they appeared there in December 1917, but Graves welcomed their publication as yet another acknowledgement of his growing importance as a poet.[8]

With such a positive start to July, it was even more of a shock to hear from Robbie Ross on 9 July of Sassoon's written protest against the conduct of the war, which he had sent to his superior officers at Litherland and planned to make public. Graves was already slightly worried about Sassoon's state of mind after reading his letter of 25 June, but had thought it nothing serious until he received a second letter from him on 30 June, which caused him to reply: 'what characteristic devilment it is'. But it was not until he heard from Ross, who had received a copy of Sassoon's protest, that he realized the gravity of the situation, replying to Ross on the same day: 'It's so awful about Siegfried: and he did it without consulting his friends, or saying anything about it to anyone sane.'[9] This was not strictly speaking true; Sassoon had discussed his protest in some detail with the Garsington pacifists in June and, through Ottoline's influence, had been helped to draft it by Bertrand Russell, who would later go to prison for his anti-war beliefs. But then Graves was coming to regard the Garsington circle as neither 'sane' nor as Sassoon's true 'friends'.

Sassoon had been growing increasingly unhappy about the conduct of the war since he had first witnessed the suffering of the men in the trenches in November 1915. The beginning of friendships with two well-known pacifists, Ross and the Cambridge musicologist Edward Dent, and the death of his younger brother Hamo in the Gallipoli campaign, had started the process. Then the deaths of close friends in 1916, especially David Thomas, followed by the carnage Sassoon had seen on the Somme in July 1916 and at Arras the following April, had strengthened his doubts. Further heavy losses in the 1st and 2nd Royal Welch Fusiliers in April and May had added to his despair and anger. The warm reception of *The Old Huntsman* in May 1917 had given him confidence that his views would be taken seriously and his subsequent convalescence in the privileged surroundings of Chapelwood Manor had done nothing to change his mind. Rather than enabling him to forget the sufferings of the soldiers, his stay with Lord and Lady Brassey made him even more enraged at what seemed to him the complacent unawareness of civilians in England. A lunch with H. W. Massingham of the *Nation* in June convinced him that the Allies were not fighting the war in good faith, but that their aims were entirely acquisitive. After a spectacular success at the Battle of Messines in early June, the war was not going well for the Allies, with Field Marshal Haig's preparations for the Third Battle of Ypres ('Passchendaele') looking ill-fated to many.

Sassoon had continued to satirize the war heavily in his poetry, but by June 1917 that had begun to seem inadequate. An impulsive as well as a courageous man, he decided finally that he had no choice but to send a strongly worded protest to his superior officers, which he did on 6 July. The reason he did not consult Graves, Ross or Marsh was almost certainly because he feared that they would try to stop him. While he knew that Graves and Ross both shared his criticism of the conduct of the war by July 1917, he rightly suspected that they would not approve of his action because of the very real threat it brought of a court martial and imprisonment, possibly even death. Graves himself spelt out his position in a note added to his letter to Ross of 9 July, making it clear that though he sympathized with Sassoon's condemnation of the war he did not think it right for the professional pacifists to make a cat's paw of him when he was in so shaky a state of health. Ross was also a pacifist, but agreed with Graves that Sassoon's gesture was inadequate and that it would be absurd for him to get himself cashiered and imprisoned because of it. This may explain why Graves was one of the last to be sent Sassoon's protest, not receiving it until 12 July.

But by then Graves had already done his best to limit the damage, writing to the 'dear old Senior Major at Litherland' [Major Macartney-Filgate], imploring him not to 'let the Colonel [Jones-Williams] take S[assoon] seriously but to give him a special medical board and more convalescent home [leave]'.[10] His aim was to delay any dire consequences until he could find 'an opportunity for getting hold of him [Sassoon] to stop him disgracing himself, his regiment and especially his friends'.[11] He also contacted Bobbie Hanmer, knowing how fond Sassoon was of the young subaltern, and asked him to write to Sassoon 'in the same strain'.[12]

Graves's own account in *Good-bye to All That* is not entirely accurate: he claims, for example, not to have seen the actual text of the protest until the end of July, when Sassoon sent him a copy of it published in the *Bradford Pioneer* of 27 July, yet Sassoon's own annotated copy of *Good-bye to All That* confirms that he sent it to Graves on 10 July. But his account of his feelings about Sassoon's actions in the same book is completely authentic, since it was a point of view he repeated to Sassoon himself at the time:

> I entirely agreed with Sassoon about the 'political errors and insincerities' and thought his action magnificently courageous. But more things had to be considered than the strength of our case against the politicians. In the first place, he was in no proper physical condition to suffer the penalty which the letter invited: namely, to be court-martialled, cashiered and imprisoned. I found myself bitter with the pacifists who had encouraged him to make this gesture. I felt that, not being soldiers, they could not understand what it cost Siegfried emotionally.[13]

Graves did not hesitate to point out to Sassoon, however, that it was not 'good form', nor was it the act of 'an officer and a gentleman', a piece of emotional blackmail Sassoon managed to resist, though he realized that most of their fellow officers would endorse it. To their mutual friend, Edward Marsh, Graves wrote on 12 July, 'It's an awful thing – completely mad – that he has done'. Whilst Graves thought Sassoon's actions quite wrong, he was sympathetic to his views and was relieved to learn that Marsh did not regard him as a criminal. He desperately wanted to help Sassoon, and Marsh's attitude made it easier to ask his advice. Like Ross, Marsh regarded the War Office as their best hope, though he was unfortunately no longer working for it. Graves claimed in *Good-bye to All That* that he wrote immediately to his recent Oxford friend, the Honourable Evan Morgan, in his capacity as private secretary to a government minister, though in fact this letter was not sent until the crisis was over. Meantime he received a sympathetic reply from Major Macartney-Filgate at Litherland, assuring him that Sassoon would be ordered to face a medical board rather than a court martial.

So Graves persuaded his own doctors to pass him fit for home service, despite the fact that he was not yet fully recovered, and was back in London on 16 July. After meeting with both Marsh and Ross next day to discuss the situation, he was at the Litherland depot of the Royal Welch Fusiliers on 18 July. In the interim Sassoon, determined to martyr himself if need be for the pacifist cause, refused to take the face-saving medical board examination arranged for him. In this context Graves's arrival was crucial, his method simple but effective. In order to take away Sassoon's motivation for continued rebellion, he lied to him about the consequences, assuring him, on an imaginary Bible, that if he refused to be medically boarded the military authorities would shut him up in a mental hospital for the rest of the war. There would be no martyrdom. Thoroughly defeated by the prospect of such an anti-climactic end to his dramatic gesture, Sassoon finally gave in and agreed to attend a medical. Ignoble as his capitulation seemed to him, he was nevertheless aware of a huge sense of relief, since he had fully expected to be sent to prison. Even after he learned of Graves's lie much later, he was still able to write appreciatively of his act and to admit: 'No doubt I should have done the same for him had our positions been reversed.'[14]

The new medical board, instantly arranged for the next day, had almost certainly been fixed, not because of Graves's letter to Evan Morgan as he claimed, since we now know that this was sent later, but probably because of Ross's efforts at the War Office, where he had a contact. Graves's tearful evidence to the board itself – he was 'in nearly as bad a state of nerves as Siegfried', he recalled – must also have helped, and the board conveniently found Sassoon 'shell-shocked' and in need of treatment.[15] By the kind of coincidence Graves enjoyed, the most helpful member of the board, Captain McDowall, a morbid psychologist, would advise Graves later on his own mental state in 1921.[16] That same day, 19 July, Graves was able to write to Marsh with evident relief, 'It's all right about Siegfried.' To his parents he boasted that he had 'squared up' Siegfried's case and to Ross that, after 'superhuman struggles', he had 'arranged everything about Siegfried quietly':

> Result: he is suffering from nerves and the medical board are sending him to some unpronounc- or spell-able place in Edinboro' under the charge of a Doctor Rivers, a nerve man. He is quite reconciled and is going cheerfully. I wish to Hell I could go too. I'm quite worn out. His views on the War of course are unchanged.[17]

It is important to remember that by the time all this took place and Sassoon was on his way to Craiglockhart War Hospital for Neurasthenic Officers on 23 July 1917, Graves was still only twenty-one. Julian Dadd, a fellow officer from the 1st Royal Welch Fusiliers, believed that Graves had been 'master of the situation' and that 'for a man of his age, his ability and tact were wonderful', one of the few occasions on which Graves was praised for his tact.[18]

Sassoon and Graves would celebrate Robert's 22nd birthday on 24 July in Edinburgh: 'great fun', Sassoon reported to Marsh, '[we] ate enormously'.[19] Having been detailed to escort Sassoon to Craiglockhart, Graves missed the train, arriving four hours after Sassoon with his fellow escort, S. W. Harper, but stayed on for a few days. Set into the side of Wester Craiglockhart Hill, 400 feet above sea level, to the south-west of Edinburgh, the hospital was a healthy spot, enjoying magnificent views of the Forth Valley and the Pentland Hills, though the building itself, converted from a 'hydro', or hydropathic hotel, into a military hospital in late 1916, was rather gloomy – a heavy, Italianate-baronial affair of decayed grandeur. Sassoon thought it an unsuitable place to house 300 or so depressed and often traumatized officers.

Fortunately, Sassoon took instantly to his case doctor, William Halse Rivers Rivers [sic], whom he met shortly after his unescorted arrival, a tall, heavy-jowled man of 53 in wire-rimmed glasses with a thick moustache, bushy eyebrows but thinning hair. Graves, who was introduced to Rivers during this first stay, claimed that he and Sassoon had heard of 'Doc Willie', as he was affectionately known, before their arrival at Craiglockhart. By the time war broke out he was already eminent in the several fields of anthropology, neurology and psychology. A fellow of St John's College, Cambridge, he had continued to expand his research during the war, finding his true vocation, many believed, in a remarkable aptitude for treating psychoneuroses. He had been transferred from Maghull War Hospital, only a few miles from Litherland, in 1916 and such was his reputation that he had been placed in charge of over 100 of Craiglockhart's 300 or so patients. The other three doctors, Captain Brock, Major Ruggles and Lieutenant MacIntyre, shared 200 patients between them (Brock, however, had the distinction of treating Wilfred Owen, whose time at the hospital overlapped with Sassoon's).

Graves, who was to get to know Rivers better over the next four years and to learn a great deal from him, was particularly impressed by his practice 'of taking up a new department of research every few years and incorporating it in his comprehensive anthropological scheme'.[20] It was an approach to knowledge that appealed to him and that he would himself adopt.

By 1921 Graves would believe that Rivers was 'by far the greatest living psychiatrist'.[21] In 1917 at Craiglockhart he was already impressed by Rivers's approach to his patients whom he diagnosed and treated, Graves noted, 'largely through a study of their dream-life', his method recorded in some detail in his posthumous publication, *Conflict and Dream* (1923).[22] The similarity with Graves's theories on poetry was to forge a strong link between them, helping the younger man develop his own literary-critical technique, which would lead to the practice known as 'close reading'. Both methods involved a rigorous delving into the subconscious in an attempt to locate the origins, in one case of a dream, in the other of a poem; both, Rivers believed, originated in conflict. As Peter Haworth has argued, Graves adapted Rivers's broadly Freudian ideas about dreams into a theory about poetic creativity.[23] 'The nucleus of every poem worthy of the name', Graves claimed, 'is formed in the poet's mind during a trance-like suspension of his normal habits of thought, by the supra-logical reconciliation of conflicting emotional ideas'.[24] The first of Graves's books on poetic theory, *On English Poetry* (1922), would be dedicated to Rivers, and the next two, *The Meaning of Dreams* (1924) and *Poetic Unreason* (1925), deeply indebted to him. Rivers also seems to have taught Graves to see his war traumas in a positive light and persuaded him that they gave him certain advantages as a poet.[25] In addition it may have been Rivers who introduced him to Sir James Frazer's *The Golden Bough* and two other important writers on primitive cultures, Jane Harrison, author of *Prologomena: A Study of Greek Religion*, and Johann Jakob Bachofen, author of *Mother Right*. Graves's opportunity to discuss such matters with Rivers during his first visit to Craiglockhart was limited; by 29 July he was back with the 3rd Battalion in Litherland. But he made sure to keep in touch, sending 'that excellent man' a copy of his *Goliath and David* 'as a token of esteem and regard'.[26] A month later he sent his 'love', via Sassoon, to 'your Doctor Rivers: on whom be peace.'[27]

Meanwhile Graves was 'having a good time at Litherland among friends'.[28] He was busy, with 325 men and 35 officers to drill, while at the same time, in his usual energetic way, enjoying squash, racquets and tennis. The hope of being sent to Egypt by his next medical board may partly explain his cheerfulness; he was not looking forward to Litherland in the winter, especially with his weakened lung. He knew what it would be like: 'with the mist coming up from the Mersey and hanging about the camp full of T.N.T. fumes. When I was there the winter before I used to sit in my hut and cough and cough until I was sick. The fumes tarnished all our buttons and made our eyes smart.'[29] By 21 August his expectations were for Salonika, but the possible destination changed constantly as the Allies' fortunes changed. Much as he dreaded another winter in Litherland, however, he knew how relatively lucky he was: 'Poor devils at Pilkem!' he wrote to Sassoon on the opening day of the 3rd Battle of Ypres.[30] By diverting the main weight of his offensive northwards to Flanders after the failure of the Battle of Arras, Haig hoped to distract the enemy's attention from both the trouble-ridden French and the Allies' submarine campaign at sea. But the fighting would drag on and long before his empty 'victory' of 4 November 1917, when the British finally reached their objective, Passchendaele, the battleground had become a swamp of mud and blood. In pressing on to the bitter end, Haig used up valuable reserves which might have saved the Allies from the humiliating reverse at Cambrai that was to follow.

When orders arrived for Graves of a posting to the Welsh borders in late September, he was still hoping to be sent to Egypt but grateful at least to get out of Litherland for the winter. The 3rd Garrison RWF was under canvas at Oswestry, about to transfer to Kinmel Park, Rhyl, on the north coast of Wales itself. As someone who had seen active service and was already a captain at 22, Graves was once again allotted a position and responsibility that would have been unthinkable in peacetime. After his first job of giving 'further instructions' to 60 or so officers sent from other cadet battalions, he found himself by November in charge of 30 young officers, 400 to 500 men, and another draft of 200 trained men under orders for Gibraltar, when the rest of the battalion was sent to Cork. There was great unrest in Ireland after the Easter Rising of 1916 and the colonel entrusted Graves to look after those left behind. He also asked him to 'keep an eye on his children', according to Graves, who enjoyed 'playing about a good deal with them' under the nickname 'Georgy giraffe'.[31]

Graves never hesitated to emphasize his achievements, few of which can now be verified, but there is no doubt of his ability to get on in the Army, partly through his quick wits and his self-confidence. Although he may not have endeared himself to all his fellow soldiers, he was clearly trusted by his superiors in a difficult situation.

Graves's position at Rhyl would allow him to work on the final revisions to *Fairies and Fusiliers*, still planned for publication in late autumn 1917. He had received Heinemann's contract by 9 August. The publisher's initial doubt as to whether there was sufficient material for a book had been quashed by Ross, to the relief of Graves, who feared having to 'put in too much, like Siegfried did'.[32] And Ross continued to help throughout the proof stages. Graves was able to send Sassoon the first set of proofs, though by the time they arrived they were already in need of correction, partly because of Graves's habit of continual revision. His average number of drafts for a poem was seven or eight, but sometimes he made a great deal more. 'Corporal Stare', he told Sassoon, had for instance been 'materially improved and corrected' since its first draft.[33] Only one of the poems offered to Heinemann failed to please the publisher, 'To My Unborn Son', as 'supposedly too erotic',[34] a criticism that both Sassoon and Ross endorsed. ('It practically describes a wet dream', Sassoon had written frankly to Graves when he and Ross, with Marsh's agreement, had rejected it previously for *Goliath and David*.)[35] Looking back from a less repressed age, 'To My Unborn Son' seems more interesting than 'The Caterpillar', which replaced it, suggesting that as far back as late 1916 when it had been written, Graves was already beginning to realize the consequences of a homosexual relationship at that time, a particularly serious one for someone who enjoyed children as much as he did. This may be one of a number of reasons why he was beginning to find a relationship with a woman rather than a man increasingly attractive by late 1917.

'It was at this point I remembered Nancy Nicholson,' he wrote of his arrival at Rhyl at the beginning of October.[36] In fact, his romantic interest seems to have begun over a month earlier on leave in Wales, when he had visited the Nicholsons at their rented house in Harlech, 'Llys Bach'. Nancy had been about to leave for a fancy-dress party in a bandit costume, and the intriguing combination of a slim, pretty 17-year-old girl dressed in male clothes may have been the reason that Graves decided to accompany her. Too restless to think of sleep on his return, he persuaded Nancy's older brother, Ben, to drive him on afterwards to other neighbours, the Stuart Wortleys. It was 3 a.m. before he got home and the next day he was back at the Nicholsons, playing with the youngest of Nancy's three brothers, Christopher ('Kit'), then having supper with Ben.

It was through Ben that Robert had got to know the Nicholsons better, when he allowed the young painter to use his cottage as a studio, in return for a few improvements to it. His first distinct memory of Nancy was in April 1916, when he was in Harlech recuperating from his nose operation. She was 16 and on holiday from school. But Graves's interest had been in Ben, whose asthma had kept him out of the Army and who was working hard on the paintings that would make him even more famous than his distinguished artist father, William Nicholson. His mother Mabel Pryde was also an artist, as was Nancy herself. Although never formally trained, by the age of 16 Nancy had already been asked to design a cover for *Vogue* and was determined to succeed in her chosen profession with as much fierce determination as Graves himself.

Still completely committed to Johnstone in 1916, however, Graves had not seen Nancy as a potential love interest. His next clear memory of her, waving to him in January 1917 from the door of the Nicholsons' London house (where he had called to say goodbye to Ben), is more romantic: he 'remembered her standing in the doorway in her black velvet dress'.[37] At 17 she still seemed to Graves 'ignorant', by which he probably meant that she had not had as conventional an education as he had. But he found her 'independent minded, good-natured, hard' and, of particular importance to him, 'as sensible about the war as anyone at home could be'.[38]

The fancy-dress party at the end of August, coming as it did after news of Johnstone's court case and 'shortly after the episode of the Somerville nurse', Graves is careful to remind the reader,[39] was almost certainly a turning point in their relationship. Anxious to dissociate himself from what now seemed to him a sordid world, Graves was clearly out to prove himself solidly heterosexual in his tastes, the only 'wholesome' state to be in, he now argued.[40] Both still very young and sexually inexperienced as they were, however, the relationship went no further at that time.

It was not until October 1917 that their real intimacy began. Graves had been spending a busy leave in London catching up with friends, having lunch with Ross at the Sesame Club for instance, or lunching with Henry Festing Jones and visiting Edmund Gosse with him afterwards. On his next to last day, 11 October, he had visited the Nicholsons, a visit that went so well that he missed his last train home to Wimbledon. He then returned on his last day for dinner and a musical revue with them, before catching the night train to Edinburgh to visit Sassoon again. Everything conspired to make the evening memorable. Brought up by strict though loving parents, Graves had not been to a revue before, and 'Cheep' at the Vaudeville Theatre was a perfect introduction to the genre. Sentimental, funny and satiric by turn, it was set in the trenches of the Somme with one of the greatest musical stars of the period, Miss Lee White, in soldier's uniform, taking the lead as 'Old Bill', a popular character created by the cartoonist Bruce Bairnsfather. Her song, 'Where did that one go?', was a huge hit, but the song Graves remembered from the show, also sung by Miss White, was 'of Black eyed Susans, and how "Girls must all be Farmers' Boys, off with skirts, wear corduroys"'.[41] Nancy had now become a land-girl herself to help in the war effort. She wore her corduroy breeches whenever possible and it is clear that Robert was attracted by a certain sexual ambiguity in the situation; when trying to overcome Sassoon's initial resistance to her, he described her as being not only 'young, kind, strong, nice-looking and a consummate painter', but also 'a capable farmer's boy', with reference to the revue.[42] In addition, he told Sassoon that she had 'a man's brain', a description that would have enraged Nancy who was already a militant feminist, as she warned Robert.[43] John Masefield's wife, Constance, would later note in her diary that Nancy was 'a strange, shy, boyish girl, very clever with her fingers and quick in brain', though she also added that Nancy did not have 'enough adventure in her to be a poet's wife'.[44]

One thing Nancy would have taken as a compliment, however, was Robert's remark that she had 'a child's heart'.[45] For during the course of the evening Nancy had shown him her illustrations for Robert Louis Stevenson's *A Child's Garden of Verses* and he recognized that 'my child-sentiment and hers – she had a happy childhood to look back on – answered each other'.[46] They were both 'quite mad on toys', for instance, and would later put together a collection of 'toys, soldiers and wooden animals and ivory men and silver buddhas and coloured boxes of plaited straw'.[47] This shared love started a correspondence between them about Robert's children's rhymes, which Nancy offered to illustrate.[48]

An added attraction for Robert was his affection for the whole Nicholson family: in particular her mother Mabel, 'a beautiful wayward Scotch melancholy person', her father, William, a witty, charming, exuberant man and something of a dandy, who was also very generous, as well as Nancy's brother Ben. Robert had less contact with her second brother, Tony, who was a gunner waiting to go out to France, while her third brother, 'Kit', was still a child. It is evident that Graves also appreciated the fact that the Nicholsons were well connected and more colourful than his own family, and that they moved in a far less conventional world; Nancy's parents counted among their friends such distinguished figures as Max Beerbohm, J. M. Barrie, Rudyard Kipling, Ellen Terry and Edward Lutyens.

Nancy's 'ignorance', far from being a barrier, was reassuring. Although Graves professed admiration for her independent-mindedness, her lack of academic qualifications combined with her youth made her less of a threat to someone still unsure of himself beneath his surface confidence: she 'needn't be taken too seriously', he told one friend early in 1918.[49]

There were other possible reasons for this whirlwind romance, one of which was identified by Clarissa Graves as the need that men in war had to 'propagate themselves before sudden death',[50] a theory supported by Robert's poem 'To My Unborn Son', which his homosexual friends Sassoon, Marsh and Ross had so disliked. Graves's own, related explanation for the relationship was 'the desire to escape from a painful war neurosis into an Arcadia of amatory fantasy'.[51]

But perhaps the strongest, though most hidden reason of all for this sudden romantic attachment to a woman was Graves's need to dissociate himself from Johnstone and any connection with homosexuality.

13

THE FAIRY AND THE FUSILIER (OCTOBER 1917–JANUARY 1918)

> ... Now your brief letters home pretend
> Anger and scorn that this false friend
> This fickle Robert whom you knew
> To writhe once, tortured just like you,
> By world-pain and bound impotence
> Against all Europe's evil sense
> Now snugly lurks at home to nurse
> His wounds without complaint, and worse
> Preaches 'The Bayonet' to Cadets
> On a Welsh hill-side, grins, forgets.[1]
>
> *'Letter to S.S. From Bryn-Y-Pin'*

Graves's evening with Nancy on 12 October 1917, the start of his 'Arcadia of amatory fancy', ended with him catching an overnight train to Edinburgh, where he was to witness a romantic attachment of a different kind.[2] For on this second visit to Sassoon at Craiglockhart he was met at Waverley Station by another patient at the hospital who had fallen in love with Sassoon, Wilfred Owen. Owen, who had gone through 'seventh hell' on the Serre/Beaumont Hamel front in January 1917 and further unspeakable experiences at Fayet and Savy Wood near the Hindenburg line, had been diagnosed with 'shell shock' and sent to the Scottish War Hospital for Neurasthenic Officers at the end of June, a month before Sassoon. But it had taken him nearly another month to pluck up the courage to introduce himself to a poet whose recently published *The Old Huntsman* he admired greatly. His hero-worship of the man he regarded 'as Keats & Christ & Elijah & my Colonel & my father-confessor & Amenophis IV in profile',[3] had quickly spilled over into a romantic love not reciprocated by Sassoon.[4] But Sassoon liked Owen and was quite ready to accept his hero-worship. So when Graves's arrival on 13 October threatened to interrupt his daily round of golf, he sent Owen as his substitute to meet him at the station and bring him on to Baberton Golf Club. It would not be the last time Owen appeared as Sassoon's substitute to Graves.

Owen had already seen and admired some of Graves's poems and was surprised to find him 'a big, rather plain fellow, the last man on earth apparently capable of the extraordinarily delicate fancies of his books'.[5] But then, not only was Owen's poetry still unpublished by October 1917, he was also suffering from a strong sense of social and, at 5 feet 5½ inches, physical inferiority to the other two poets. Both had responded in a somewhat condescending manner to him. Sassoon, for instance, freely admitted that at their first meeting he had felt superior to Owen, who struck him as a 'rather ordinary young man, perceptibly provincial, though unobtrusively ardent in his responses to my lordly dictums about poetry'.[6] Graves in turn dismissed Owen fairly briefly in *Good-bye to All That*, ending with the comment that he was 'a quiet, round-faced little man'.[7] Sassoon, in his own annotated copy of *Good-bye to All That*, would write indignantly 'This is an outrage' beside Graves's words; but this may have been in reaction to the preceding remark that 'Owen had been accused of cowardice by his commanding officer. He was in a very shaky condition.'[8] Graves's own recent distancing of himself from homosexual entanglements may help to explain why Sassoon was so much more enthusiastic about Owen at the start. Graves had already told Sassoon of his brief 'love' for Marjorie Machin, which may have felt like a betrayal to Sassoon, and was now talking fondly of Nancy Nicholson. Whereas Graves would urge Sassoon to form a 'triangle' with the heterosexual Robert Nichols, Sassoon would favour the homosexual Owen as 'the third' in the triangle.[9] Peter

Parker suggests that had Owen not been homosexual, Graves would have valued his work more highly.[10]

There was no disagreement between Sassoon and Graves over the latter's claim that 'it was meeting Siegfried ... that set [Owen] writing his war-poems.'[11] It was certainly seeing Owen's 'Disabled' that same day that began to modify Graves's patronizing attitude to Owen. 'It's a damn fine poem,' he wrote to him a few days later, though he could not resist including a long list of suggested changes, with a lecture about metrical irregularities – 'One has to follow the rules of the metre one adopts.'[12] In doing so he revealed his own conservatism still in matters of technique. A few of Graves's suggested changes were adopted by Owen, who nevertheless bridled a little at the detailed advice, telling his mother that Graves appeared to consider him 'a kind of *Find*!!', adding 'No thanks, Captain Graves! I'll find myself in due time.'[13]

By December 1917 Graves would indeed be boasting to Marsh that he had 'just discovered one, Wilfred Owen: this is a real find ... the real thing', though he could not resist adding, with a touch of his old arrogance, 'when we've educated him a trifle more. R[obert] N[ichols] and S[iegfried] S[assoon] and myself are doing it.'[14] Despite thinking Owen 'too Sasso[o]nish in places', Graves became a great admirer of his work and would name him as one of only three 'poets of importance' killed in the First World War, as well as in his *Survey of Modernist Poetry* (1927).[15] Owen for his part would pay tribute to Graves as well as to Sassoon in his epigraph to 'The Next War' and by January 1918 could describe Graves's technique as 'perfect'.[16] By May he was glorying openly in the 'silent and immortal friendship of Graves', as well as Sassoon.[17] *Fairies and Fusiliers*, published shortly after their first meeting, would remain one of Owen's most treasured books.

Dr Rivers had returned from a fortnight's much-needed rest two days before Graves's second visit to Craiglockhart, but they had little time to discuss the dream theory that fascinated them both, since Graves had to return almost immediately to Kinmel Park Camp at Rhyl. There was time for one long talk with Sassoon, however, about the latter's protest, in which Graves continued his attempts to convince Sassoon to be 'proud and true' and to 'act like a gentleman'.[18] For, while Sassoon was growing increasingly unhappy at what he felt was his desertion of his men in France, he still believed that he had no alternative but to protest. 'If you had any real courage,' he told Graves, 'you wouldn't acquiesce as you do.'[19] Graves, for once, refused to take the bait; while regretting that Sassoon should think him a coward, he spelled out his own attitude towards the war once again:

> I believe ... in keeping to agreements when everybody else keeps them and if I find myself party to principles I don't quite like, in biding my time till I have a sporting chance of rearranging things. One must bow in the house of Rimmon occasionally.[20]

There were a number of reasons for Graves's unusually mild response. His exchange of letters with Nancy was going so well that by the end of November he would be contemplating marriage; his reputation was beginning to rise, with his appearance in *Oxford Poetry 1917* achieved, the assurance of eight of his poems in *Georgian Poetry 1916–1917*, and the publication of his *Fairies and Fusiliers* now fixed for 8 November. E. B. Osborn had chosen his verse for particular mention in *The Muse in Arms* and Edmund Gosse had given him a good puff in the *Edinburgh Review*.

When *Fairies and Fusiliers* duly appeared on 8 November it was dedicated to the Royal Welch Fusiliers Regiment rather than to Sassoon as originally intended. Graves's explanation to Sassoon, possibly with Nancy in mind, was the wish to avoid jealousy 'among friends and lovers.'[21] It could also have stemmed from a reluctance to be associated publicly with someone who had protested openly about the continuation of the war.

Fairies and Fusiliers was published by Heinemann in an edition of 1,000 copies in the same format, Graves was proud to note, as that of the far better-known poems of John Masefield. Bound in wine-red cloth with a blue-grey dust jacket and issued from a much larger publishing house than *Over the Brazier*, it attracted a respectable amount of attention. Since Graves frankly admitted that he had 'squared nearly all the reviewers' and relied on 'allies like Gosse and Masefield to push the book', this was hardly surprising.[22] His own favourite reviews were in *The Times Literary Supplement*, the *New Statesman* and, less predictably, the conservative *Morning Post*. The book would go into two editions but only, according to Graves, because 'it was published in the war-years when people were reading poetry as they had not done for years.'[23] Knopf would publish an American edition in 1918 and Graves would be invited to give a lecture tour of the United States by

Pond's Agency in 1919. Although Graves doubted that it was a 'big success', he did concede that it was 'quite a good show'.[24] Despite what Paul Fussell judged to be 'the melodramatic dichotomy', the 'fatal lack of subtlety' in both its title and its contents, it was almost certainly the contrast described by Fussell between 'pastoral and anti-pastoral, the "home" of Spenser and Shakespeare and Herrick *versus* the "France" of Haig and Ludendorff', which gave *Fairies and Fusiliers* a wide appeal.[25] It was certainly a dichotomy Graves experienced himself during the war and the most efficient way he could convey it to others. His nursery teas and games of tiddlywinks with the colonel's children at Rhyl, for instance, were all the more precious and meaningful to him as a contrast to his experiences in France, his 'Songs of Innocence' to set beside his 'Songs of Experience'.

Underlying all the poems in *Fairies and Fusiliers*, Graves believed, was 'a frank fear of physical death'.[26] Although no longer in the fighting himself, he was kept informed by men he had served with in both the 1st and 2nd Royal Welch Fusiliers and horrified by high casualties in the two battalions in such engagements as the Battle of Polygon Wood or the Third Battle of Ypres, many of them good friends of his. And despite the first meaningful use of tanks at the Battle of Cambrai in late November and early December 1917, the war would seem no nearer its conclusion by Christmas. On the contrary, the Bolshevik Revolution of late 1917 and subsequent Russian armistice negotiations with Germany in December 1917 would allow the Germans to move large numbers of troops from the Eastern to the Western Front.

Graves continued to be 'haunted' by the war, with ghosts of his dead friends invading his everyday life and his poetry:

> ... I meet you suddenly down in the street,
> Strangers assume your phantom faces,
> You grin at me from daylight places,
> Dead, long dead, I'm ashamed to greet
> Dead men down the morning street.[27]

Nevertheless, by the end of November 1917 Graves was also extremely happy, for on Thursday 22 November he and Nancy had become unofficially engaged. Their letters, which started with her offering to illustrate his children's rhymes, had rapidly become more intimate. Longing to see her again, Robert had seized the first chance to do so, cutting short a family visit and the opportunity to wave Rosaleen off for Voluntary Aid Detachment (VAD) service in France. A close-knit unit, Amy and Alfred's children had gathered at Wimbledon for the occasion, Clarissa from Cheshire, Charles and John from Charterhouse. As acting commanding officer of his camp, Robert had granted himself a short leave. But he had annoyed his usually tolerant and long-suffering parents when he left suddenly, cutting short a family photograph session at a local studio, not even waiting to see his favourite sibling off to France at Charing Cross Station. Only after he had departed, when a telegram arrived for him from Nancy ('Hoorah! meet me at St Ives') did his parents realize the reason for his abrupt departure. 'Sly dog!' his father commented with some amusement.[28] His mother was not so sympathetic and was 'furious', according to Robert, until he 'smoothed her down'.[29] Nancy, with her land-girl breeches, smock, cropped hair and strong feminist beliefs, was not the kind of daughter-in-law Amy was hoping for. In writing to apologize to Rosaleen for 'not actually coming to the station with the rest of the caravan', Robert gave her some idea of his visit:

> ... She was in great form and we chopped mangold wurzels and groomed cart horses together: she's the only girl on the farm ['Hilton Hall', the farm bought by the writer and publisher David Garnett] and it's a rotten life for her: the hours long, the work hard, the farmers disagreeable kind of folk, and nothing of the better things of life to cheer her up.[30]

There were consolations, however, particularly after three years of wartime shortages: the food was plentiful, even 'superabundant', and Robert was treated to 'an immense 1913 tea ... about fifteen different cakes', even though his visit had not been expected.[31] He was introduced to her black poodle, Smuts, and they spent some time discussing a collaboration on a children's book of rhymes, stories and games. Although few of their plans would be realized and Nancy failed to complete the planned illustrations, it is clear that she had a significant effect on Robert's poetry for some years, leading him further into a world of nursery rhyme and song.[32]

Curiously, for a poet who declared himself in love and who would go on to become one of the greatest love poets of the twentieth century, there was no immediate outpouring of love poetry to Nancy, nor would there be much written to her at all during their eight years together, in striking contrast to his time with Laura Riding that was to follow. Despite his excitement, Graves does not give the impression of someone deeply in love. Writing to Charles Scott Moncrieff, now a friend, a few weeks after his engagement to Nancy and questioning the source of his renewed poetic energy, he asks: 'Because I am in love?', then answers his own rhetorical question: 'Not altogether. But largely.'[33] And of these few love poems to Nancy, a number point to difficulties in their relationship. 'Fastidious', for example, written almost certainly during the first year of their marriage, but unpublished until 2016, hints at a lack of spontaneous enjoyment of each other physically, particularly on Nancy's part:

> If we could speak, if we could think
>   In common talk of hand and lips,
> So that your mouth would never shrink
>   And my hands float on you like ships,
> If unfastidious of fine words
> Or careful gesture, like two birds
>   We might find love.[34]

The 'cold silence' of the woman in the second stanza has a chilling effect on the narrator, who concludes: 'Oh, poetry is no friend to love.'[35] The explanation may lie in Robert and Nancy's youth and sexual inexperience; it may also have stemmed from Nancy's ardent feminism. She had warned Robert early on to be 'very careful' what he said about women; the attitude of the local farmers kept her in a continual state of anger.[36] Robert had accepted 'the whole patriarchal system of things' (as he saw it at work in his family) unquestioningly until he met Nancy. But his mother had also taught him respect for strong-minded women, and his reading of Samuel Butler had encouraged him to rebel against conventions.

Previous biographers have suggested that Nancy's feminism was in reaction to her mother's role in the family. Mabel Nicholson had had to put aside her own painting career when she had children and to live with a husband who more or less openly carried on affairs with other women. But Nancy was by nature independent and had grown up at the height of the Suffragette movement; she may simply have been attracted to it on her own account. Although Robert seems to have had no difficulty in accepting her position, it would cause problems for him in the future.

Graves gives the impression overall that his 'love' for Nancy was more of a product of his will than of his emotions. After his meeting with her in September, he had already resolved to 'keep an eye on her in case she becomes lovable'.[37] Even before his visit to her at Hilton Hall, when they became unofficially engaged, he had referred to 'getting married shortly' in a letter to Sassoon, as though anxious to make quite clear his change of sexual orientation.[38] (This may also have been in the nature of a warning to Sassoon, whom he believed was attracted to him sexually.) It was in a letter to the heterosexual Nichols that same month he had insisted that his 'affections [were] running in the more normal channels'.[39]

However anxious Graves was to marry, there would be no formal announcement of his engagement until nearly a month later. Meanwhile, he returned to the remnants of the 3rd Garrison Battalion at Rhyl. He was still hoping to be posted to a warmer climate, the reason he gave for refusing the post of adjutant, a safe job guaranteeing that he would remain in Britain until the end of the war on increased pay. He had set his sights on Egypt or Palestine and, when he was ordered to Gibraltar, pulled strings at the Foreign Office, probably through Marsh or Moncrieff, to have the order cancelled.

One consolation of his Rhyl posting was that it left him time to write poetry and this would increasingly be about the world of children. Of over 40 poems written between autumn 1917 and the end of 1918, and brought together as *The Patchwork Flag*, approximately half would relate to the private world of nursery rhymes, ballads and allegories that he and Nancy now inhabited together. As he confessed rather apologetically in his 'Letter to S.S. from Bryn-y-Pin':

> ... now he rhymes of trivial things
> Children, true love and robins' wings
> Using his tender nursery trick...[40]

Although *The Patchwork Flag* would remain unpublished as a collection until 2016, half of its poems would appear in Graves's next trade edition, *Country Sentiment* (1920). Significantly, fewer than half of the war poems in *The Patchwork Flag* would be included, the rest remaining unpublished in his lifetime, largely on the advice of friends. 'Book seems short of guts somehow,' Sassoon noted on the manuscript: 'I don't like the few grim things mixed up with the irresistible nursery and semi-serious verses.'[41] As Charles Mundye suggests, in an edition that includes *The Patchwork Flag* in full, its author's decision not to publish the collection was 'the beginning of a much more long-term tendency to suppress nearly all of his war poetry from his own canon'.[42]

Nancy had encouraged Robert to escape further into a world he found unthreatening, but it may not have been the most helpful direction for him in psychological terms. His 'Letter to S.S. from Bryn-Y-Pin' shows that he was still deeply haunted by the war, 'hourly yet confused and sick / From those foul shell-holes drenched in gas', and that 'the least chance / Of backward thought beg[an] a dance / Of marionettes that jerk[ed] cold fear / Against [his] sick mind'.[43] A public expression of his haunted state of mind may have strengthened the cathartic effect of poetry, which he fully acknowledged. As it was, his painfully realistic poems about the effect of war on those who fought in it, such as 'The Survivor Comes Home', remained unknown and therefore excluded from considerations of his war poetry and First World War poetry generally, until at least 1988 when William Graves published his edition, *Poems About War*.

Excluded, too, from *Country Sentiment* would be the 'Foreword' to *The Patchwork Flag*, in which Nancy's world of domestic pursuits such as sewing is contrasted tellingly with Robert's experiences in France, through the simple image of a patchwork quilt:

> Here is a patchwork lately made
> Of antique silk and flower-brocade
> Old faded scraps in memory rich
> Sewn each to each with feather stitch.
> But when you stare aghast perhaps
> At certain muddied khaki scraps
> And trophy fragments of field-grey
> Clotted and stained that shout dismay
> At broidered birds and silken flowers;
> Blame my dazed head, blame bloody war.[44]

Nancy herself appears not to have realized the extent of Robert's trauma, or his evident need by November 1917 to marry. As a feminist, she disliked the idea of marriage and attached no importance to the ceremony, according to Robert, who claimed not to do so either. Fortunately for him, since his parents would have been horrified by the two young people living together outside of marriage, Nancy did not want to disappoint her father, who 'liked weddings and things'.[45] And there were more practical reasons for it; Robert was still expecting to be posted to Egypt, then Palestine, and marriage would make it much easier for Nancy to accompany him.

They would announce their engagement formally on Robert's next leave, which occurred in mid-December. His arrival home, unexpectedly, on Saturday 15 December marked the start of a dramatic few days for the Graves family. Charles had also arrived unannounced the evening before on his way back from taking scholarship exams at Oxford. He had caught his family finishing their supper, but Robert's dawn arrival the next day found them all asleep and he had had to throw pebbles at the window to be let in. The following day he had gone to see Nancy in central London, a reunion that had evidently gone well since he had missed the last train back to Wimbledon again and been forced to walk the last few miles home in a blizzard. Monday was equally exciting when a telegram arrived at Red Branch House to say that Charles, like Robert, had won an Exhibition to St John's College, Oxford. Although relations between the two brothers were rarely easy and Robert was almost certainly relieved that Charles had not outdone him with a scholarship, it may explain why Robert waited until the family had celebrated Charles's triumph the next day before he announced his own news. He and Nancy had already shared the news of their engagement with the Nicholsons the previous evening and Mabel thought him 'the one person good enough' for her daughter, but was almost as upset at the thought of losing her as William, who claimed he had been 'in love with' Nancy since the day she was born.[46] 'Of course I think if anyone could be worthy of my Nancy it is he Robert,' he wrote to Ben, but he had spent a sleepless night nevertheless.[47]

Lunch with the Graves family the next day alerted both the Nicholsons to another problem, the differences between the two families, the artistic and rather unconventional Nicholsons with their mixture of bohemian and aristocratic friends on the one hand and the 'grave Graveses', as William called them, on the other, Robert's earnest, religious, worthy parents and their hearty world of family sing-songs and parlour games; 'Can't you see Mrs Graves and I,' William asked Ben, 'lying under a sofa playing sardines and heaven help us when they found us and sat on us.'[48] While Mabel confessed to finding the family 'a bit trying especially the old man ... He's awful', she predicted correctly that Nancy would 'be a match for them'.[49] Like William, she preferred Amy despite what seemed to them her regrettable taste, particularly in clothes. 'But really she had dignity in spite of her profile and green velvet outfit,' William concluded after the wedding itself.[50] Alfred's fussing over every detail would almost spoil William's very real pleasure in arranging it all.

Alfred Graves, however, had found the Nicholsons 'delightful' when they arrived at Red Branch House for lunch on 1 December 1917: 'Mr N[icholson] most witty and charming[;] Mrs N[icholson] a very capable and wise woman.'[51] Nancy, fortunately, had 'grow[n] on' him, despite staying in her 'male attire' for tea.[52] Amy's views on her future daughter-in-law are unlikely to have been so positive, but she joined in the celebrations when, after the Nicholsons had left, her youngest son John came in 'as Cupid', to announce Robert and Nancy's engagement, and when Robert threw the family ring with an ancient eagle on it and she caught it.[53] The engaged couple left soon afterwards for the theatre, another sign of the Nicholsons' influence.

Robert was due at Rhyl the following day, 19 December, but waited until the evening to catch his train back, unable to resist the Nicholsons' invitation to Kit's birthday party, which included such celebrated figures as Max Beerbohm, Edwin Lutyens and the writer E. V. Lucas. Life was always, as Alfred noted, 'a very messy' affair at the Nicholsons. He was, fortunately, unaware that William found him 'a dreadful bore of the third water'.[54] But William liked Robert greatly – 'the more we see him the more we love him'[55] – and despite his reluctance to part with his only daughter, he approved of the marriage. His wife, 'Prydie', and 'the Captain', as they nicknamed Robert, quickly became 'closest friends'.[56]

Not everyone approved, however, as Graves learnt when Sassoon came to visit him at Rhyl a few days later; Graves felt obliged to apologize for his engagement. Another of his homosexual friends, Robbie Ross, also made his disapproval clear, hinting at African blood in Nancy's family and warning him of the possibility of a 'coal-black' child.[57] A meeting with Nancy would reconcile him to her, but Sassoon was not so easily placated and relations began to cool between them.

None of this deterred Graves, who wrote to his family from Harlech, where he was spending his three-day Christmas leave with the Nicholsons, to announce an early date for the wedding, 23 January 1918. His ostensible reason was the possibility of a posting to Palestine, but he was almost certainly anxious to make his sexual position clear. Nancy's parents had agreed to a speedy wedding, with the proviso by her mother that her son-in-law should consult a lung specialist to establish whether he was fit for service in Palestine. When he visited Sir James Wheeler on 9 January, the doctor gave him a reasonably good report on his lungs, though the damaged one still had only a third of its normal capacity and there were bronchial adhesions. He did warn, however, that Graves's 'general nervous condition made it folly for [him] to think of active service in any theatre of war'.[58] This was greatly to Mrs Nicholson's relief: her son Tony was already serving in France and she did not want to add to her worries.

The marriage could now go ahead and William was in his element, inviting all his most entertaining as well as famous friends to join them for the ceremony at St James's Church, Piccadilly. Robert and his family added their own guests – 'half a hundred startled Graves friends,' William reported to Ben.[59] The result was a mixture of some of the best-known names from the artistic and literary worlds, with a fair sprinkling of 'society' figures and some eminently sober and respectable Graveses. All William's closest allies were there, including Ellen Terry, J. M. Barrie and Augustus John, as well as Lutyens, Lucas and Beerbohm, whose sister Agnes had designed Nancy a wedding dress in a romantic pale-blue and white check silk quite unlike the breeches and smock she usually favoured. Beside his numerous relatives, Robert's guests included Marsh, Ross, Heinemann and his publishing partner Sidney Pawling (also Nancy's godfather), Scott Moncrieff, Roderick Meiklejohn (Ross's eminently respectable senior civil service friend), Harold Monro and Wilfred Owen, who sacrificed a visit to his adored mother to be there. 'Graves pretty worked up but calm,' Owen wrote to his sister Susan the day after the wedding: 'Bride ... was pretty, but no wise handsome.' Charterhouse was represented by George Mallory, now convalescent from the war, who had agreed to be best man, and Nevill Barbour and Henry Devenish. Robert was delighted when Masefield and Arnold Bennett came too. A significant absentee was Sassoon, now in Ireland, who had encouraged Owen to attend but had given the rather flimsy excuse of a Gas Training Course at Cork as the reason for his own absence. Rosaleen Graves, whose leave from France had not come through in time, was also much missed.

Although St James's was only a few hundred yards from the studio flat in Apple Tree Yard, where Nancy spent the night on a sofa, William arranged for her to arrive in style with him in the splendid car of his friend Lady Sackville. William remembered her looking very beautiful in her pale-blue silk dress, with the bouquet he had lovingly composed for her, and her turning to him during the brief journey to say 'Father, this is fun',[60] a puzzling detail in light of what Robert himself recalled. Having described Nancy's feminist outrage when she read the marriage service, apparently for the first time that morning, with its promise among other things to 'obey' her husband, he claimed that 'she all but refused to go through the ceremony at all', despite Robert's arrangement for it to be 'modified and reduced to the shortest possible form'.[61] The result, he recorded, was:

> Another caricature scene to look back on: myself striding up the red carpet wearing field-boots, spurs, and sword; Nancy meeting me in a blue-check silk wedding dress, utterly furious; packed benches on either side of the church, full of relatives; aunts using handkerchiefs; the choir boys out of tune; Nancy savagely muttering the responses, myself shouting them out in a parade-ground voice.[62]

William, on the other hand, described Nancy and Robert's voices as 'fine firm unashamed'.[63] And whereas Robert rather proudly described his new wife grabbing hold of one of the bottles of champagne her father had generously supplied for the reception with the words, 'Well, I'm going to get something out of this wedding at any rate', and changing back into her land-girl clothes after three or four glasses, William focused on the gaiety of the wedding guests crammed into Apple Tree Yard.[64] Amy, who had already been shocked by Nancy's refusal to take her husband's name and resolutely signing the register 'Nancy Nicholson', was further dismayed by the reappearance of the breeches and smock, catching hold of her neighbour E. V. Lucas and exclaiming 'Oh dear, I wish she had not done that.'[65]

Fortunately, Nancy left her own account of the day, which shows that she enjoyed most of it greatly. Since her medium was the visual rather than the verbal, her account is teasingly brief. It might have been entertaining to know what she thought of the poem Alfred spent many days writing for the event, 'The Fairy and the Fusilier', or alternatively, 'The Fusilier and his Fairy' (an unfortunate *double entendre*). And though she noted their numerous wedding presents, it is only to complain of how many thank-you letters they would entail. But she does reveal that her main feeling at the wedding service itself, which she continues to object to in principle, was one of amusement rather than fury: 'Everybody was awfully solemn except us two,' she told her brother.[66] When Robert made his comment about how flat the choirboys were, for instance, Nancy says she 'winked at them and they went flatter'.[67] And while she did indeed change back into breeches at the reception, she thought her wedding dress 'ripping' and the cake and 'phiz [*sic*]' 'lovely'.[68] The language is that of a mischievous schoolgirl. Like Robert, she seems to have regarded it as 'great fun', rather than an affair of high romance: 'The most amusing thing about getting married (especially me),' she said, was 'the surprise of everyone.'[69] It was not the most solid foundation for a marriage.

14

BABES IN THE WOOD (JANUARY 1918–JANUARY 1919)

... in such cushioned ease I live
With Nancy and fresh flowers of June
And poetry and my young platoon,
Daring how seldom search behind
In those back cupboards of my mind
Where lurk the bogeys of old fear,
To think of you, to feel you near
By our old bond, poor Fusilier.

Letter to S.S. From Bryn-y-Pin[1]

However much 'fun' Robert and Nancy's wedding turned out to be, neither of them enjoyed their first night together at Garland's Hotel, not far from Apple Tree Yard. Both were virgins, and highly embarrassed at the idea of sex. Robert, for one, was grateful for the distraction offered by the constant air-raid warnings. The sexual side of their marriage would never be satisfactory, according to Nancy, who found Robert both too demanding and rather clumsy.

But once installed in William Nicholson's house in Harlech, a place where both of them had spent the best times of a happy childhood, they were able to retreat back into a shared world of toys, fairy tales and make-believe. Robert reverted to childhood language – the affectionate term 'wingle' is a particular favourite – and planned to compile a map of Harlech marking all his favoured places as a child – 'for the use of our children when they live there'.[2] According to Nancy, they had a 'ripping time' in 'gorgeous weather'.[3] 'Am I enjoying myself and this life? Ask me!' Robert wrote, not very tactfully, to Sassoon during the honeymoon.[4]

When Nancy returned to David Garnett's 'Hilton Hall' to complete the last month's farming there, however, and Graves to Rhyl, his 'horrors' returned, with 'a nervous attack of sleeplessness that [came] with hideous recollections of France every two months'.[5] He kept himself busy, deliberately writing an average of ten letters a day, one always to Nancy, and with the help of Scott Moncrieff he arranged to get a job as instructor in an Officers' Cadet battalion at the same camp, at Kinmel Park. And when Nancy came to share his lodgings at Terfyn Bungalow, Abergele, not far from the camp, they started to make plans for their life after the war.

Their priority for the future was to allow time for their own work, to be carried out ideally in collaboration. Robert's increased focus on nursery rhymes and ballads was partly to provide Nancy with material to illustrate. They decorated 'nursery' plates together, Nancy's central picture illustrating Robert's verse running around the rim. Another idea was to create a book of songs to be set to music. With the enormous success of 'Keep the Home Fires Burning' in mind, Robert approached Edward Marsh, who knew Ivor Novello well, and by March 1918 reported to Sassoon that the young Welshman was setting a series of poems that he had written for the purpose to music.[6] Graves confessed frankly to 'admir[ing] a man who can amass thousands by a song like "Keep the Home Fires Burning" and also write really good music besides'.[7] (Sassoon himself wanted to murder the man who wrote it!) The plan petered out when Novello lost interest and even the local doctor, J. R. Heath, a talented but far from great composer, failed to deliver the music for the project. *The Penny Fiddle*, as it was called, would not be published until 1960.

Other equally unrealistic plans involved farming, first in California where they could join Nancy's brother Ben, then on the Sussex Downs, with all their friends brought in to help:

> You would manage the office [he told Scott Moncrieff, still at the War Office], S[iegfried] S[assoon] the horses, I and Nancy the ploughing and

sowing and spuds, Bob Nichols the sheep with an oaten pipe. Robbie
Ross would hang the pictures and act as mess president. Alec Waugh
perhaps the ducks and hens with his Barbara [Jacobs] – A repertory
theatre and printing press on the premises and a bar parlour more famous
than any Mermaid Tavern.[8]

Like most of these youthful plans, this turned out to be an entirely unrealistic
proposition, since Sassoon declined to provide the necessary finance for the
farm. Written on 24 March 1918, only three days after the opening of the
great German offensive of which Graves was well aware, this letter shows how
hopeful as well as happy he felt in the early months of his marriage despite the
war. He had his worries: Ross, hounded by Noel Pemberton Billing as one
of the group of prominent homosexuals whom Billing was trying to destroy
with his 'black book' and conspiracy theory; Sassoon, who was now back
on active service though in the less dangerous theatre of war in Palestine;
his sadness at the death of his cousin Adrian Graves at the Front. But life
seemed full of possibilities to Robert. If the farming 'commune' of friends
failed, he and Nancy planned to start a 'crèche for homeless poets – Helicon
Hostel' at a lovely old house in Woodstock, where Nancy – and reputedly
Chaucer – had been born.[9] In it Robert planned to include the Australian
poet and music critic W. J. Turner (of 'Chimborazo, Cotopaxi' fame).

The spring of 1918, though not quite as 'disastrous' for the Allies as
Robert viewed it, gave no real cause for hope; it even appeared to him for a
time that he would be obliged to go back to the Front, whether fit or not,
before the year was over. Nevertheless he continued to be happy, especially
once they discovered in late spring that Nancy was pregnant. Although
forced to find new lodgings in mid-March, since his landlords disapproved
of Nancy's trousers and her dog, Smuts (and probably also her refusal to
take her husband's name), their new rooms at Bryn-y-Pin farm, St Asaph,
were an improvement on Terfyn Bungalow. Situated on the hill just above
the camp, the farmhouse had panoramic views for miles around. Nancy had
secured work in the area at once and Robert found his new job instructing
cadets 'the only live job left in the army in England [sic]'.[10] A 'plain platoon
commander' again, he was 'yet allowed to row [his] own boat'.[11] He liked
his company commander, an old friend from the regiment, and had a high
success rate with his candidates.

There were also diversions: a training course at Berkhamsted, for instance, in April, was rewarded with leave in London, where the rising artist Eric Kennington drew Graves's head in pastels, the first of a number, and Graves wrote the Introduction to Kennington's June 1918 Exhibition catalogue. Kennington would also use Graves as one of the three soldiers in his war memorial at Battersea. William Nicholson had been an early admirer – and purchaser – of Kennington's work and almost certainly brought about the meeting. Graves would, in turn, introduce both Sassoon and T. E. Lawrence to Kennington. Later he and Nancy would become good friends of Kennington's wife, Celandine, too.[12]

Graves was also busy that summer planning his next collection of poetry, which he proposed to call *The Patchwork Quilt*, later changed to *The Patchwork Flag*, a title he explained in his 'Foreword' to it, sent in a letter of thanks to Sassoon for an advanced 23rd birthday present of £23. Like his life by 1918, Graves wrote, the collection would be made up of the extremes of his existence, of 'occasional corpses that blunder up among the nursery toys'.[13] He included the poem 'The Patchwork Quilt' in the letter.

By the end of June, Robert and Nancy were enjoying Robert's leave in a house lent by the Nicholsons' friend, Edie Stuart-Wortley, at Maes-y-Neuadd, 'a quite ideal place near Harlech', Robert told Sassoon, 'an old manor house with a ghost and a farm and an orchard and heaps of rooms and everything perfect'.[14] Tony Nicholson and Rosaleen Graves were on leave at the same time and joined Robert, Nancy and her parents for the 'temporary heaven' of a week's leave, spent 'eating blackcurrants and gooseberries in the kitchen garden, and climbing about on the rocks and talking about before and after the war and playing the piano (real music) and lying in the hay and smoking'.[15]

An added frisson for Robert were the ghosts rumoured to haunt the fourteenth-century house; 'invisible except in the mirrors', they would 'open and shut doors, rap on the oak panels, knock the shades off lamps, and drink the wine from the glasses at our elbows when we were not looking'.[16] Maes-y-Neuadd and its haunted mirrors would almost certainly appear as the setting for 'The Pier-Glass' later. He firmly believed that the one visible ghost, 'a little yellow dog that appeared on the lawn in the early morning to announce deaths', had been a herald of Mabel Nicholson's unexpected death shortly after this June visit.[17] Anxious not to miss a moment of her middle son

Tony's leave, she had refused to allow Spanish flu to keep her in bed and had consequently developed pneumonia, which proved fatal. Nancy's mother was a 'far more important person' to her than Robert, according to him, and he was alarmed at the effect that the shock of her mother's death might have on Nancy's pregnancy. The baby survived, however, but the further death a few months later of her brother, so recently with them at Maes-y-Neuadd, was an added strain that Robert feared would be too much for her.

Meantime, Robert was suffering his own losses. By the time he heard of the dreaded telegram bearing the news of Tony's death in France which had arrived at Apple Tree Yard on 8 October, Robert had lost two more friends in the fighting, Raymond Rodakowski at Ypres in October 1917 and Ralph Rooper at the end of May 1918. In his letter to Cyril Hartmann about 'dear old Ralph's death while driving an ambulance near Rheims', his feelings about the war by this point emerge clearly: 'This is one of the greatest sorrows of this bloody fourth year of war and as the poor Rooper parents have lost two sons in 6 months I somehow feel they'll agree with me that it's about time we all stopped killing.'[18] Robbie Ross's unexpected death in London on 5 October 1918 was another blow.

In this context Robert's claim that marriage had saved him from 'going off his rocker or getting killed foolishly' and his need for 'feather top rhymes and songs' is convincing.[19] Back in Kinmel Park with Nancy, he was convinced that if he ever made any name for himself as a poet, it would be with 'the children's stunt'.[20] When Sassoon accused him of escapism, he felt it necessary not only to explain but to apologize to him yet again:

> I say I'm awfully sorry I'm such a swine to be happy and I swear to you that if I only had myself to think about I'd change places with you at once despite my hellish fear of the La Bassée country and my waking terror of poison gas, which is my most awful nightmare whenever I feel ill and think about the line. As for my not 'writing deeply' blast you, you old croaking corbie, aren't I allowed for the honour of the Regiment to balance your abysmal groanings with my feather top rhymes and songs? And I have written croakingly too lately but I haven't sent you specimens because I think it's bad taste and most ungrateful when God's so nice to me. I've almost got the new book together and I forbid you to get the posthumous VC till it's published.[21]

Shortly after this letter was sent, only days after Mabel Nicholson's death, Graves was alarmed to hear of Sassoon's own narrow escape from death as he returned from one of his 'Mad Jack' raids on the Germans. Once Graves knew that Sassoon would recover, and even after Sassoon had repeated his criticism of *The Patchwork Flag* collection, he continued to be 'bloody happy', reminding his older friend that he was also 'bloody young'.[22] Sassoon responded with another verse-letter to put beside Graves's to him from Bryn-y-Pin, a letter that would cause great trouble between the two men over a decade later. (Lying wounded in a London hospital, Sassoon's epistle had opened: 'Dear Robert, / I'd timed my death in action to the minute...')

Sassoon's comments on *The Patchwork Flag* convinced Graves not to publish it, but they were not entirely negative; he offered suggestions and some praise too. He liked 'The Leveller', for instance, not surprisingly since, as Graves points out, it is as good a skit on Sassoon as Sassoon's *The Daffodil Murderer* was on Masefield. Graves based it on the death of two men he had known who were killed by the same shell: 'one a sodden Anglo-Argentine and t'other a boy of 18, very young-looking; the first called out "mother, mother" and the other cursed God and died.'[23] The last verse, Graves admits, is 'pure Sassons [*sic*]':[24]

> Old Sergeant Smith, kindest of men,
> Wrote out two copies there and then
> Of his accustomed funeral speech
> To cheer the womenfolk of each.[25]

When Graves included 'The Leveller' in *Country Sentiment*, he added a sixth stanza in his own copy later that is even more purely 'Sassonish' in its mordant irony:

> *'He died a hero's death; and we*
> *His comrades of "A" Company*
> *Deeply regret his death, we shall*
> *All greatly miss so true a pal.'*[26]

Apart from 'The Leveller', Sassoon also approved of 'Foreword' ('Here is a patchwork lately made...'), 'Night March' and Graves's glimpse back to the terrors of his childhood in 'The Picture Book'. But Sassoon continued to dislike the mixture of light verse and war poems; he found 'Sospan Fach' 'sentimental' and he hated the didacticism of the final poem, 'The Patchwork Flag', with its insistent praise of 'VIRTUE'.

Ross had supported Sassoon's reservations, calling for a collection that would be more homogeneous, either Fairies or Fusiliers, preferably the latter. But however anxious Graves was to win the approval of his two close friends, he was unable to comply, and not only because he was so 'bloody happy'. In the first place his most successful poetry is quite different from Sassoon's and copying it did not appeal to him. Secondly, he needed money quickly and could not simply or easily replace his nursery poems and ballads with war poems. Last, but not least, with his marriage to Nancy and a child on the way, his priorities had changed:

> Worrying about the war is no longer a sacred duty with me: on the contrary, neither my position as a cadet instructor nor my family duties permit it. I am no longer fit to fight and I am out to get as healthy as possible for the good I can do in England. Curse me to hell: I shall hate it: but I must be honest according to my lights however dim they have grown ... My occasional reminders are quite enough ... Please be kind to me Sassons, for the sake of Fricourt.[27]

For the time being, the war had receded in his mind, though it would return to trouble him further and inspire poems of a very different kind in his attempts to exorcise it.

By late August, in any case, the conflict was approaching its long-drawn-out end. Events had begun to shift in the Allies' favour early that month, with Canadian and Australian troops breaching German defences on 8 August. On 9 September the advancing British forces entered Cambrin, and from there pushed onwards into Lille. By the time Robert and Nancy moved into their own house at the end of September – a modest cottage at Rhuddlan within biking distance of the camp[28] – the peace process had started in earnest. On 28 and 29 September, when Messines and Passchendaele were recaptured by the British, the German General Ludendorff had urged Field Marshal Hindenburg to seek an immediate armistice.

Bulgaria had been forced to accept defeat by the Allies on 30 September and when General Allenby finally took Damascus and the British prepared to break through the Hindenburg Line on 1 October, Ludendorff begged the Kaiser in person to issue a German peace offer immediately. Political unrest in Germany was adding to her problems and by 4 October the Chancellor, Prince Max, finally telegraphed Washington requesting an armistice. He made it clear, however, that this was not a surrender, only an attempt to end the war without preconditions. President Wilson rejected his advance. A first condition of any armistice, he insisted, must be the evacuation of all occupied territories. The start of the second Battle of Cambrai on 8 October and the final breakthrough of the Hindenburg Line the next day forced Germany to accept Wilson's terms and on 11 October German troops began to withdraw from France and Belgium, though the fighting continued.

Another important move towards peace occurred on 19 October when all German U-boats were ordered to return to their bases, bringing a virtual end to submarine warfare. By 22 October, however, the German Chancellor was not yet ready to accept what he called 'a peace of violence', but the following day he was ordered to prepare realistic armistice terms by Wilson. Even on 24 October, Ludendorff and Hindenburg were still unwilling to acquiesce in what was now clearly a *fait accompli*. Their 'fight to the finish' telegram to all Army Group commanders alarmed the German government, which threatened to resign, and Ludendorff was forced to do so instead. By 25 October the Turks had been routed from their northernmost stronghold, Aleppo, and the following day began their own armistice talks with the Allies.

A day later Germany's last great ally, Austria, resolved to seek a separate peace and German sailors mutinied. It was clear that Germany was now on her own. But fighting on the Western Front continued, even after war on the Middle Eastern and Italian Fronts had ceased and even after the Allies had agreed on 3 November to a formal German request for an armistice. Ironically, Wilfred Owen, who believed that the Allies had deliberately 'thwarted' earlier peace efforts, died the day after this formal request was made, and many more were to die needlessly in the week of negotiations that followed. For in spite of General Groener's warning to the Kaiser that the armistice must be signed by 9 November at the latest, delegates did not arrive at the armistice meeting in the Forest of Compiègne until 7 November. The Kaiser himself was still refusing to abdicate and it was not until 9 November that he finally accepted the inevitable. The next day the German government formally accepted the Allies' stringent terms, though the legal documents were not signed until 5.10 a.m. on the morning of 11 November. The Armistice itself was set for 11 a.m. that day, the eleventh day of the eleventh month.

It was a huge relief for the majority of the British, now into their fifth year of war, and the event was marked throughout the country in a series of euphoric, often riotous celebrations. Even in North Wales, where it was viewed largely as a 'foreign war', according to Graves, 'little boys banged biscuit tins and a Verey light or two went up at the camp'.[29] But Graves, like Sassoon, was still haunted by memories of dead friends and unable to join in. The death of Ross had upset him greatly; there would 'never be another Robbie', he wrote to Sassoon, 'cynical, kindhearted, witty, champion of lost causes, feeder of the fatherless and widowed and oppressed'.[30] He 'felt his loss more than people could suppose'.[31] Ross's help in placing *Fairies and Fusiliers*, then preparing it for publication, had brought him close to the man Sassoon had compared to 'a benevolent and impulsive bachelor uncle'.[32]

Then, on Armistice Day itself, news arrived of Wilfred Owen's death on 4 November at the same Battle of the Sambre in which Graves's 'dear old butty' from the 2nd Royal Welch Fusiliers, Frank Jones-Bateman, had died on the same day. Both deaths, only a week before the cessation of hostilities, seemed particularly needless and hard to bear. Graves had grown closer to Owen in the letters and poems they had exchanged after Owen's return to France and had hoped that he would be transferred to Rhyl on his next leave. His last postcard to Graves had been written the day before his death.

Instead of celebrating, therefore, the announcement of the Armistice sent Graves 'walking out alone along the dyke above the marshes of Rhuddlan ... cursing and sobbing and thinking of the dead'.[33] He also wrote two poems on the subject, the shorter of them ('a little squib') in which his disgust at the rejoicing is balanced movingly with a reminder of the dead still lying out in the battlefields:

Why are they cheering and shouting
    What's all the scurry of feet
With little boys banging on kettle and can
    Wild laughter of girls in the street?

O those are the froth of the city
    The thoughtless and ignorant scum
Who hang out the bunting when war is let loose
    And for victory bang on a drum.

But the boys who were killed in the battle
    Who fought with no rage and no rant
Are peacefully sleeping on pallets of mud
    Low down with the worm and the ant.[34]

Graves's extended version of the same thought in 'Armistice Day 1918' was an even more scathing attack, which remained 'unprintable' according to him until the 'Jubilee celebration' of 1968, when it appeared in the *Daily Express* under the title 'November 11th, 1918'.[35] Here his scorn is nearer to despair as he describes the mindless rejoicing of 'the kids whom we fought for', who will themselves dream of 'another wild "War to end Wars"'. His pity in this longer version is not only for the men who died but also for the wounded who survived – 'the armless and legless and sightless'.[36]

***

Life must go on, however. For someone as positive as Graves, who considered himself 'much more of an optimist than any of [his] friends',[37] there were positive things to look forward to. He began to appreciate how 'extraordinary' it was that 'the War was won at last', putting a small Union Jack at the stairhead to remind himself of it and keep him from grousing at the 'petty annoyances of peace'.[38] His first child was expected in less than two months and Nancy was 'very well and full of cheerfulness'.[39] He was putting together another collection, based partly on *The Patchwork Flag*, which he hoped would answer Sassoon's reservations about that book, to be called *Country Sentiment*. 'Instead of children as a way of forgetting war', he was using Nancy, to whom the book is dedicated.[40] He planned to make it 'a collection of romantic poems and ballads', with a concluding section of 'pacifist war-poems'.[41]

By November 1918 Graves was also collaborating with his father-in-law on a magazine of literary and artistic contributions drawn mainly from their respective friends or, as Graves put it more frankly to Ken Barrett, 'a 10/6 literary and pictorial paper for the very rich'.[42] William Nicholson undertook the crucial matter of finance, Nancy promised to help with the artistic side, and Graves's recent friend (Sassoon's future landlord) W. J. Turner was appealed to for help on the literary side:

> I am thinking with my father-in-law who is intimate with Barrie, Kipling, Max Beerbohm, Lucas and all the best people of that sort, of getting out an annual to include the young people too, to the satisfaction I hope of both.
>
> The chief difficulty of getting the people is overcome at the start by the fact that they are all friends of ours and would be only too pleased to give us the right stuff. My father-in-law also knows all about reproductions for paintings etc. and where to get this done really well – seldom does one get a miscellany with the art as good as the writing... Anyhow it's a good scheme and has no flaws at present.[43]

J. C. Squire, who had left the *New Statesman* and was about to start his own magazine, the *London Mercury*, was also brought in to help.

William had been inspired originally by a seventeenth-century Staffordshire slipware plate he had come across in the summer of 1918, depicting an owl surrounded by seven little owls. By adding in his own whimsical fashion a rat caught in the owl's claws, he produced an intriguing as well as striking design, which struck him as an ideal cover for a little magazine. Graves would later explain the significance of both the owl and the rat in a verse on the back cover of the third and final issue:

> Athenian fowl with feathered legs
> Stand emblem of our will
> To hunt the rat that sucks the eggs
> Of virtue, joy and skill.

He would also add a gnomic comment by Lewis Carroll: 'All owls are satisfactory.'

A mixed bag of contributions from the impressive circle of friends they boasted between them, *The Owl* did not have a specific agenda and was essentially traditional in nature, unlike the Sitwells' more avant-garde *Wheels*, T. S. Eliot's *The Egoist* or Herbert Read's *Art and Letters*, all well under way by the time the first of *The Owl*'s three issues appeared in May

1919. 'It mustn't be controversial,' Graves warned Sassoon when soliciting his contribution.[44] *The Owl's* editors were anxious to spell out their intentions in their first editorial (almost certainly written by Graves): 'It must be understood that *The Owl* has no politics, leads to no new movement and is not even the organ of any particular generation ... But we find in common a love of honest work well done, and a distaste for shortcuts to popular success...'

Despite this opening declaration, shortly after the first number appeared and possibly under the influence of the increasingly socialist-minded Sassoon, Graves was sharing his 'secret dreams' of making *The Owl* 'the organ of Labour', by which he meant 'art and letters in the good old days after the [Russian] Revolution'.[45] It was not what the basically conservative Nicholson had in mind, however, and *The Owl* remained, as it started, a pleasant mixture of non-political, essentially traditional if quirky contributions. In one number, for instance, Graves looked forward to including 'part of [T. E. Lawrence's] Arabian story, Lady Jekyll's ... recipe for plum pudding, Max [Beerbohm] ... writing on Hall Caine and an Indian philosopher [Basanta Mallik] ... presenting a new philosophic system in brief which is going to have a shattering effect on the philosophical dovecots'.[46] It was 'merry company' for Graves and 'rather fun', especially when he was able to find some unpublished material by Herman Melville.[47] Not only did it bring him into closer contact with some of the best-known writers and artists of the period – Max Beerbohm, John Galsworthy, Thomas Hardy, John Masefield, William Orpen and W. H. Davies among them – but it allowed him to help friends such as Sassoon, Nichols and Turner with an outlet for their work, as well as a generous remuneration. It played to his strengths as a clear-headed critic of literature and gave him some practical experience in the magazine market.

Graves's own contributions to the first number of *The Owl* would be two poems already written for his projected *Country Sentiment*. Whereas Thomas Hardy's contribution that opened the magazine, 'The Master and the Leaves', was gently melancholy, Graves's 'Ghost-Raddled' and 'A Frosty Night' are full of a more menacing foreboding. 'Ghost-Raddled', retitled 'A Haunted House' in *Country Sentiment*, harks back to Maes-y-Neuadd, to a period before the war ended, when ghosts past and to come dominated Graves's neurasthenic dreams and he felt compelled to write:

> Of a night so torn with cries,
>> Honest men sleeping
> Start awake with rabid eyes,
>> Bone-chilled, flesh creeping...[48]

Perhaps, as Patrick Quinn suggests, the haunted house represents England. 'A Frosty Night', a ballad about a mother's concern for her 'dazed and lost and shaken' daughter Alice, is equally disturbing, hinting at possible tragedies to come and the duality of love:

> Your feet were dancing, Alice,
>> Seemed to dance on air,
> You looked a ghost or angel
>> In the star-light there.[49]

By mid-December, Graves had ample opportunity to work with his father-in-law on *The Owl*, as well as time for his own work, when the cadet-battalions were disbanded and their officers given leave. He had tried to get another job, without success, and was now faced with orders to report to the 3rd Royal Welch Fusiliers in Limerick. Nancy had already left for Apple Tree Yard by the time he travelled to London on 17 December and he joined her there. He was determined not to leave England until their child was born, and deliberately overstayed his leave. He was confident of his powers of talking himself out of any situation and on this occasion he would use the excuse of having to have a piece of 'shrapnel' (which proved to be a chip of flint from the cemetery where he was wounded) removed from his eyebrow.

On the advice of Edie Stuart-Wortley, who had become increasingly close to William since Mabel's death and the confirmation that her own husband had been killed in action, William had rented a large house on the south coast at Hove for the birth. It was here that Nancy and Robert spent Christmas and here, to the sound of waves beating on the shore, that Jenny Prydie Nicholson was born on Twelfth Night, 6 January 1919. Nancy had insisted that any girls born to them would take her name and was delighted that their first child was a girl. But she had been told nothing of what to expect and, slightly built as she was, did not give birth easily. According to Robert it took her years to recover from it. Curiously, he says little of his own feelings except to express relief that the birth was safely over. His letter to Sassoon the day after the birth is hardly that of a proud first-time father, though affectionate enough: 'It is a good sort of baby looks quite human not the peaked old man variety.'[50] He assured Sassoon that he was 'not going to tickle baby's toes except occasionally'. Reminding him that he had agreed to be Jenny's godfather, he promised Sassoon that his duties would not be onerous, since Nancy, beside insisting that Jenny take her surname, refused to have her christened. There would be little about his first child in *Country Sentiment*, despite his recent focus on children.[51]

Graves's attitude toward children would remain enigmatic: while he adored them and felt sorry for anyone without them, he seems almost entirely detached from his own at times. Writing to Nancy a decade after Jenny's birth, to explain how he was able to leave the four children they had had by then, he would tell her:

> The children are yours; you are their mother. I am their father, but they are not my charges, I feel, only my friends. I hate being away from them but I do not feel anxious about them in a paternal way. I will always help you with them.[52]

Detached though this makes him sound, however, being a father would dictate his life in a number of important ways. The process started with the birth of Jenny.

15

A POET ON PARNASSUS
(JANUARY–OCTOBER 1919)

> Now I begin to know at last,
> These nights when I sit down to rhyme,
> The form and measure of that vast
> God we call Poetry, he who stoops
> And leaps me through his paper hoops
> A little higher every time.[1]

When Graves left the Army officially in February 1919, he was 23, an age at which he would normally be expected to support himself. But the intervention of war had delayed the need to decide how best he might do this; the Army had guaranteed him accommodation and a regular income, both of which he now had to find for himself. Although he and Nancy had planned a number of ways in which they might earn a living, they had no practical ideas in place by the start of 1919. Robert was sure of two things only: that after thirteen years of school and more than four in the Army he was determined 'never to be under anyone's orders' again, and that his main aim in life was still to be a poet. The formula that would allow him to write poetry as well as support himself and a family, however, would elude him for years.

It was a problem faced by many of his poet friends, except for those like Sassoon fortunate enough to have a private income or, like Walter de la Mare and W. H. Davies, possessing a Civil List pension. Edmund Blunden would turn initially to journalism; Robert Nichols would accept a lectureship in Japan (as Blunden, in turn, would do), before trying his luck in Hollywood; and T. S. Eliot would work in a bank rather than accept the money his friends and admirers had raised for him.

Graves's father had resolved the dilemma by working as a Schools' Inspector by day, writing his poetry at night, and he expected his son to take an equally practical line. He made every effort to help, engineering at least two offers of a school-teaching post for Robert in 1919, and was puzzled and frustrated when Robert turned them both down, even more so when, a few years later, he refused the prestigious post of the Sandhurst Professorship of English. When, after another six years, Robert finally capitulated (as he saw it) to the system and took a paid job in Egypt, the experiment would be a failure. The answer lay in another direction and one much nearer to home. Meanwhile he and Nancy would experience years of severe financial difficulties, exacerbated by their own fecklessness and high expectations as the indulged children of reasonably well-off parents.

***

With the war at an end, Robert believed that he had a 'new loyalty' to Nancy and Jenny, concluding his verse-letter to them from the Royal Welch Fusiliers regimental headquarters at Limerick, as the brigade band played 'The British Grenadier' outside his window:

> Some speak of Alexander,
> And some of Hercules
> But where are there any like Nancy and Jenny,
> Where are there any like these?[2]

Graves left for Ireland on 15 January 1919, a week after Jenny's birth, his first visit since he was a baby himself. He found Limerick 'a lovely place': 'I feel absolutely part of it already,' he wrote to Rosaleen a fortnight after his arrival, 'and it provides the explanation of a great deal in me I could only guess before.'[3] It seemed like 'native air', he told his father, who had continued to return to the place of his birth regularly over the years.[4] Despite the lure, however, Graves was determined to get himself demobilized at the first opportunity. With the help of Edward Marsh and by entering 'student' on his form (a priority 'trade' for demobilization – as long as you were not 'a wuzzer, hambler, fluker, boober-up or bogeyman', Graves told Sassoon),[5] he felt confident of his chances.

But when the War Office telegram for his release came through on 3 February 1919, trouble with Sinn Féin had flared up again and the Army was ordered to stop all demobilization among troops in Ireland the following day. Convinced that he was sickening with the dreaded Spanish flu, however, Graves was determined to get back to England on the last train, leaving that evening: he 'did not intend to have [his] influenza out in an Irish military hospital with [his] lungs in their present state'.[6] But with the adjutant unwilling to let him go until he had helped with battalion theatricals on St David's Day, 1 March, and the battalion demobilization officer 'hand-in-glove' with him, Graves managed to get only one of two signatures needed to authorize his papers – from his unsuspecting colonel. Although still without the vital secret code-marks from the demobilization officer, he decided (ever the gambler) to risk it and caught his train as it was moving out of the station. The Army might refuse to demobilize him in England, he reasoned, but at least his flu would be treated in an English hospital.

It is tempting to dismiss what came next as one of his many 'tall stories' in *Good-bye to All That*: that he happened by chance to share his taxi from Paddington to Waterloo with a demobilization officer from the Cork district who, in gratitude for the lift, added the necessary 'secret code-marks' to Graves's demobilization papers.[7] But in this case the account is confirmed by Alfred Graves, who welcomed his son home on 4 February and accompanied him to Wimbledon Camp to start the demobilization process, which was completed in Brighton.

By the time Robert stumbled into 11 Seaside Villas, Hove, to rejoin Nancy, Jenny, William and Edie that evening, his flu had turned into an even deadlier septic pneumonia in both lungs, from which a gloomy, overworked doctor predicted little chance of survival. With both Nancy and Edie in bed with flu the next day, though in a much milder version, William decided that nurses were needed. But with the flu epidemic at its height, nurses were hard to find and he had to settle for two who had already retired. 'One was competent but frequently drunk', if Robert is to be believed; 'the other sober but incompetent'.[8] It was one of the two, however, who kept him alive, Alfred believed, by 'riling' him so much that he rallied again after the doctor had given him up for dead.[9] Robert regarded it as a further miraculous escape from the grave, writing in yet another verse 'Letter from Wales' to Sassoon:

> I died at Hove after the Armistice,
> Pneumonia, with the doctor's full consent.[10]

Graves's own explanation for his survival was the determination to perfect one of his own favourite poems, 'The Troll's Nosegay', which had already gone into several drafts by the time he fell ill. In his efforts to 'make a sonnet read as though it were not a sonnet, while keeping the rules', he amassed some 35 drafts.[11] If 'The Troll's Nosegay' did save his life, as he claimed, it seems an appropriate account of his own relation to poetry, one that anticipates his creation of the fickle, demanding 'White Goddess', though some critics have identified 'my lady' in the poem more probably with Nancy:

> A simple nosegay! was that much to ask?
> (Winter still nagged, with scarce a bud yet showing.)
> He loved her ill, if he resigned the task.
> 'Somewhere,' she cried, 'there must be blossom blowing.'
> It seems my lady wept and the troll swore
> By Heaven he hated tears: he'd cure her spleen –
> Where she had begged one flower he'd shower fourscore,
> A bunch fit to amaze a China Queen...[12]

By 7 March, Robert, Nancy and Jenny were in London, staying with William at Apple Tree Yard, and Robert was sufficiently recovered to accompany Nancy to lunch with his parents at the Sesame Club. He had emerged from the war 'very thin, very nervous' and with 'about four years' loss of sleep to make up',[13] a condition made far worse by his near-fatal illness. He was in no state to deal with the practical problems that faced him and was grateful for his father-in-law's offer of Llys Bach, the large, stone, pillared house William had rented near Harlech, until its lease ran out in the autumn. It would allow him seven months to recover and was a perfect place to convalesce, the area he described in 'Rocky Acres' as 'beloved by me best'.[14]

Gradually, as his health returned, Graves began to think more seriously about the future. Having initially rejected taking up his Exhibition at St John's College in favour of a few months studying Agriculture, Oxford now started to seem 'a convenient place to mark time until [he] felt like working for [his] living'.[15] Sassoon was already installed there, studying Political Economy at Rivers's suggestion, and had written enthusiastically to Graves about the fun they could have together, founding 'a splendid debating society and dining club' and other tempting ideas.[16] 'My God, we'll have fun at Oxford, old frump!' he wrote again.[17]

Graves had also discovered that ex-servicemen would be excused the intermediate examinations ('Mods') in the Oxford honours degree and since he had already been excused the preliminary examination ('Smalls') because of a certificate gained at Charterhouse, this would reduce the usual three-year degree to two years and a term. An added incentive was the government grant of £200 a year in addition to his Exhibition grant of £60, if he took up his place at St John's, together with his disability pension of £60. Even before he started at Oxford, he had more money than ever before. By March 1919 he had £150, saved from his army pay and invested in war bonds, and the government's gratuity of approximately £200 for ex-servicemen. He also earned occasional sums for his poetry and reviews.

But as Robert himself admitted, neither he nor Nancy knew the value of money and started to live 'as though we had an income of about a thousand [pounds] a year'.[18] They hired a full-time nanny (Margaret Russell) for Jenny and a 'general' servant (Barbara Morrison) for the housework, which left them both free for their own works. While Nancy devoted most of her time to producing illustrations for a small, privately printed book of nine of Robert's poems, *Treasure Box*,[19] he was busy preparing *Country Sentiment* and *The Owl* for publication. He was also writing occasional reviews, including among others Alec Waugh's *The Prisoners of Mainz*, Daisy Ashford's *The Young Visiters* [sic] and Butler's *The Way of All Flesh*.

Once *The Owl* was published, slightly later than announced, in May 1919, Graves was free to concentrate on *Country Sentiment*. Although he had decided not to publish *The Patchwork Flag*, he believed half of its 43 poems worth including in his new volume, which gave him a good start.[20]

With over half his collection already in place he was free to concentrate on what he called 'nursery stuff', together with 'romantic poems and ballads' inspired by Nancy.[21] Both kinds of verse were written in an attempt to forget the war, yet both suggest that beneath his happiness at being with Nancy and the birth of Jenny, darker thoughts still troubled him. 'Allie', for instance, reads at first like a simple children's rhyme as Allie, in an echo of de la Mare's 'Melmillo' that Graves had read, calls in first birds, then beasts, then fish and finally children. But its final stanza leaves a lingering sense of mystery, even menace; Blake's 'The Echoing Green' is evoked when Allie calls the children 'from the green', and we know that 'Songs of Innocence' are followed by 'Songs of Experience':

> Allie, call the children,
>   Call them from the green!
> Allie calls, Allie sings,
>   Soon they run in:
> First there came
> Tom and Madge,
>   Kate and I who'll not forget
> How we played by the water's edge
>   Till the April sun set.[22]

'Allie' has a distinctly elegiac feel to it, Graves's indirect acknowledgement, perhaps, of all the friends lost in the war.[23]

Although *Country Sentiment* is dedicated to Nancy, the love poems in it are hardly more upbeat, telling largely 'of deceit, failure and haunting'.[24] A dialogue between a mother and her daughter, who wants to give 'Apples and Water' to the hungry, thirsty soldiers marching to war, points to the consequences of a love too freely given, as the mother warns:

> Once in my youth I gave, poor fool,
>   A soldier apples and water;
> And may I die before you cool
>   Such drouth as his my daughter.[25]

It is the world of a poet Graves admired greatly, Thomas Hardy, and his country-dwellers, learning from experience how harsh life can be. Hardy's own favourite from *Country Sentiment*, 'The Cupboard', makes a similar point as a daughter finally reveals to her mother what her 'cupboard' holds:

> White clothes for an unborn baby, mother,
>   But what's the truth to you?[26]

It is a world where 'love' brings suffering and punishment. Incompatibility is also hinted at in 'Vain and Careless'. Even when the love poems do not end disastrously ('Loving Henry', 'Pot and Kettle'), they are curiously impersonal. And the one direct lyric about love, 'One Hard Look', points toward the problems rather than the joys of love in a series of simple but striking metaphors of the power of small things to disturb – gnats lodging 'in sleeping ears', mice scratching in the silence of the night, a straw adding to the intolerable weight on a camel's back:

> One smile relieves
> A heart that grieves
> Though deadly sad it be,
> And one hard look
> Can close the book
> That lovers love to see.[27]

'With the love-theme', Graves wrote, 'went the old fear-theme, sharpened rather than blunted by the experiences of peace.'[28] Although he is referring specifically to the development after *Country Sentiment*, the 'old fear-theme' is already present in that collection. It was over two years since he had been at the Front and he claimed that war poetry was 'played out' by 1919, yet *Country Sentiment* contains some of his most effective poems on the subject. Apart from 'Night March', 'Haunted' and 'The Survivor Comes Home', one of his new pieces, 'Retrospect: The Jests of the Clock', shows how vividly he still remembered, and could recreate, his time in the trenches. His use of the third person for what is clearly a first-hand experience gives the impression of the narrator having to detach himself from such harrowing experiences before he can describe them:

> ... When noisome smells of day were sicklied by cold night,
> When sentries froze and muttered; when beyond the wire
> Blank shadows crawled and tumbled, shaking, tricking the sight,

When impotent hatred of Life stifled desire,
Then soared the sudden rocket, broke in blanching showers.
O lagging watch! O dawn! O hope-forsaken hours![29]

And yet, 'he' knows full well, despite a resolve never to repeat such torment:

... That he'll be ready again if urgent orders come,
[...]
Ready once more to sweat with fear and brace for the shock,
To greet beneath a falling flare the jests of the clock.[30]

Neither pro- nor anti-war, Graves's war poetry 'tells it as it is', though the introduction of 'gods' (rather than 'God') and 'ghosts' in the first stanza distinguishes it from entirely realistic war poetry. 'The old gods' and 'ghosts' appear again to disturbing effect in 'Outlaws', which ends:

... Proud gods, humbled, sunk so low,
     Living with ghosts and ghouls,
And ghosts of ghosts and last year's snow
     And dead toad-stools.[31]

Graves was still happy with Nancy, however, and it was to please her, by supplying her with texts for illustration, that he had focused more on 'nursery stuff' as well as love poems in *Country Sentiment*, as he explained in the final piece of the collection, 'A First Review'. Here the Nancy-figure, Kate, urges the narrator to 'Cut that anger and fear, / True love's the stuff we need! / With laughing children and the running deer',[32] while the Sassoon-figure, 'Tom', 'a hard and bloody chap, / Though much beloved' by the narrator, tells him to 'have done with nursery pap' and 'write like a man'.[33] Urged on the one hand to get rid of 'Toys, [and] Country Lovers' and on the other of 'Hate and Fear', the poet-narrator is left with a sense of failure:

Everything they took from my new poem book
     But the flyleaf and the covers....[34]

The narrator is wrong, however. For Graves outwitted both of his advisers and *Country Sentiment* is 'haunted by images of fear and fury, sometimes emerging in a nursery setting, and even the lightest song may hint at death or nightmare'.[35] This conflict is faced and to some extent resolved in another poem carried over from *The Patchwork Flag*, 'The God Called Poetry':

> ... To-day I see he has two heads
> Like Janus – calm, benignant, this;
> That, grim and scowling: his beard spreads
> From chin to chin: this god has power
> Immeasurable at every hour:
> He first taught lovers how to kiss,
> He brings down sunshine after shower,
> Thunder and hate are his also,
> He is YES and he is NO.[36]

'Poetry to me at this time,' Graves claimed, was 'neither a formal muse nor a familiar deity, but a hidden Janus ... whose unpredictable behaviour made the poet's task an impossible one.'[37] The deity would change sex later on, but the 'unpredictable behaviour' would remain the same, in the person of the White Goddess.

* * *

While Graves struggled with the two-faced God of Poetry, he also carried on an outwardly untroubled, highly convivial life in a place he loved. Llys Bach enjoyed uninterrupted views across Harlech Castle to the Lleyn Peninsula with the mountains of Snowdonia to the north. Like Sorley on the bare Wiltshire Downs, Graves loved the harsh, craggy mountain scenery and the feeling that 'Time' had 'never journeyed to this lost land':

> ... Crakeberry and heather bloom out of date,
> The rocks jut, the streams flow singing on either hand,
> Careless if the season be early or late,
> The skies wander overhead, now blue, now slate...[38]

A few other poems in *Country Sentiment*, like 'Baloo Loo for Jenny', also reflect his life in the spring and summer of 1919; but on the whole his poetic life was separate from the life going on around him.

Once settled in William's luxurious six-bedroom house in March, Robert and Nancy had a succession of visitors to stay – his brother Charles for a night, sister Ros for a week and, at the end of the month, William and his youngest son Kit for a longer stay. By mid-April Alfred and Amy had joined the community, which by this time had become something of a 'Mutual Improvement Society', according to Alfred: Ros was teaching Nancy music, Nancy was instructing Robert in 'home duties and gardening' and Ros in gardening. Nancy was also learning to drive, which Robert would never do. Charles was teaching Ros golf and being taught 'domestic work' by her in return, while Charles's friend Richard ('Diccon') Hughes, now at Oxford with him, was having singing lessons and instructing the rest of the group on 'considerateness'.[39] Under Nancy's influence Ros had taken to breeches and – to Amy's further dismay – cropped hair. She had quickly become fond of Nancy and they would remain friends long after the separation from Robert.

By the time Amy and Alfred swelled the circle, Amy had put her Wimbledon house up for sale; they now set about making Erinfa their permanent home. With their usual hospitality, invitations to lunch, dinner, sing-songs, picnics, walks and fruit-picking expeditions began and filled the rest of the summer. Edie Stuart-Wortley, closer than ever to William, also arrived to stay in her own house at Maes-y-Neuadd a few miles away, adding to the social occasions still further.

Robert joined in with most of the festivities and was particularly keen on the musical evenings. By the end of April, having abandoned all hope of Ivor Novello setting his verses to music, he had asked the composer Dr Heath of Barmouth to take over the scheme. Consciously or not, he was following in his father's footsteps and it may explain his suggestions that he and Nancy should bring out 'the cream' of Alfred's lyrics, chosen by himself and Ros, with a cover design by Nancy.[40] Robert may also have been starting to recognize how unselfishly his father had helped him with his own poetry, which they discussed at length on the same occasion.

By June, Robert was asking his father to write on his behalf to a lecture agency about a lecture tour in America, a possibility he had discussed with John Masefield, who had recently returned from one. With Sassoon's sudden departure from Oxford in March to become literary editor of the *Daily Herald*, the university may have lost its appeal again. Robert's idea may also have been prompted by competitiveness since Sassoon himself accepted an invitation that year to lecture in America. Robert Nichols's tour there had been a great success and both Sassoon and Graves viewed it as a lucrative undertaking. But both would be disappointed: in Sassoon's case the market had been sated by a flood of British writers and in Graves's case he had, encouraged by Masefield, simply demanded 'too much' money, according to the representative from the Pond lecture agency who met Alfred at the Athenaeum Club to discuss the idea in mid-June.[41] Another poet, John Drinkwater, was 'formidable competition' for Robert, it seemed.[42]

Graves's version of events to friends was that he had decided against a lecture tour in favour of Oxford. If this was the case, it was a decision arrived at partly under the influence of Sassoon, who came to stay at Llys Bach for nearly three weeks in late August and early September. While Graves cared little for his uncle Charles's disapproval of the American plan, he found it more difficult to ignore Sassoon's opinion, which was also against accepting the school-mastering offer engineered by his father. Despite recent difficulties they both valued their friendship and it was on this occasion that Sassoon finally began to accept Nancy as a fixture in Robert's life. But he was still jealous of her and the fact that she was pregnant again could not have helped matters, underlining as it did the sexual side to her relationship with Robert. Sassoon declared himself still passionately attached to Robert, Robert still believed sexually so. Later, in an ironic twist, Robert would come to think that Nancy was sexually attracted to Sassoon.

Nevertheless, Sassoon could honestly thank them both for an enjoyable stay when he left in mid-September. Alfred, whose fears of Sassoon 'bolshevizing' his son had been calmed with Marsh's help, now thoroughly approved of him again and made sure he was given temporary membership of the local golf club, with he and Charles enjoying the chance to play against Sassoon again. Edward Marsh, who arrived with Lady Juliet Duff and her new husband, was another diversion for Sassoon, as was a visit to Gosse at Llandudno. But the main pleasure of this stay had been the opportunity to talk poetry again with Robert, who told him he had recently been 'so happy doing things in poetry' he had 'tried at unsuccessfully for weeks'.[43] Still full of appreciation for Sassoon's advice *not* to publish *The Patchwork Flag*, he valued his opinion of *Country Sentiment*, which was almost ready for publication. They may also have discussed Sassoon's contribution to the second *Owl*, now in active planning.

The decision finally to settle for Oxford helped to resolve Robert and Nancy's financial position, which was again bad despite Amy's generous gift of £100 when she found them (in Alfred's quaint phrase) 'at the pin of their collar'.[44] Robert solved the problem of finding accommodation in an Oxford crowded with returning servicemen as well as the normal intake of students, with a combination of his usual string-pulling and his ability to argue his case. When his first contact, Ottoline Morrell, failed to find him anything at Garsington, he took advantage of his slight friendship with Masefield, introduced to him by Gosse in April 1917. Knowing that Masefield had recently moved to Boars Hill, five miles outside Oxford, Graves wrote to ask whether he knew of any accommodation near him, perhaps already aware from Ottoline or Sassoon that Masefield had a large cottage in his grounds to let. Although Oxford University stipulated that students must live within three miles of the city centre, Graves was confident that, by playing on his damaged lung, he could get an exemption. He and Nancy, with Jenny and her nurse, visited the Masefields on 23 September, returning two days later, Alfred reported, with 'good hope of garden cottage at the Masefields, though others before them'.[45] Graves believed that Masefield's 'liking' for his poetry had swung the balance.[46] His exemption from the three-mile rule swiftly followed and by 10 October 1919 he and Charles were riding across country to Oxford with a lorry-load of the furniture William Nicholson had generously given him and Nancy, as the lease of Llys Bach came to its end.

Graves's gratitude to his father-in-law had been put to the test when William asked him to be best man at his marriage to Edie Stuart-Wortley on 6 October at Portmadoc. Not only was it less than 18 months since Mabel Nicholson's death, but William's son Ben had been unofficially engaged to Edie on his return to England in 1918. Not surprisingly Nancy, who still missed her mother terribly, and the aggrieved Ben refused to attend the wedding, but Robert's liking for William and his gratitude to him made it impossible to refuse the invitation. Although Ben would remain friends with Robert long enough to paint a striking picture of him, which Graves admired sufficiently to reproduce in part as the frontispiece to *The Pier-Glass*, their friendship would suffer from what Ben viewed as Robert's disloyalty and he later destroyed his portrait of Robert, on the pretext of improving it.

By the time Robert and Nancy moved into Masefield's cottage on 11 October 1919, they were already in debt again, and Amy once more came to their rescue with a loan of £140. Nancy was pregnant once more and, though impractical in the circumstances, it may have been a deliberate decision. (Since she and Robert were members of the Constructive Birth Control Society, it would have been ironic if the pregnancy was a mistake.) She had decided, in her determined and theoretical way, to have four children and quite quickly. But it was far from ideal timing and a second child would add to the strains of Robert's time at St John's. Amy's reaction to the news may be imagined.

To begin with, however, they were very happy indeed on Boars Hill, known as 'Parnassus' because of the number of poets living there when the Graveses arrived. Although Robert came eventually to think there were 'too many' poets in the area, he always exempted Masefield from his criticism.[47] He regarded the older, more established poet 'without any reservation' as 'an angel dropped straight from Heaven' and 'an awfully good friend'.[48] He would look back fondly on Masefield's 'shy morning smile and hello' as he 'used to trudge by his garden workshed half-hidden among gorse-trees'.[49] Although he became more critical of Masefield's poetry in time, he continued to admire the way he wrote 'from the heart' and, with *The Everlasting Mercy*, had created 'a fresh wind that carried English poetry clear out of the Edwardian doldrums' with his 'pungent, urgent, violent lines'.[50] Masefield, he argued, was a 'Chaucer's man', as 'obstinately rooted' in the early English tradition as he felt himself to be. For Masefield's part, he believed Graves to be 'the most likely young man in literature' by mid-1919.[51]

Graves was less enthusiastic about Masefield's very protective wife, Constance. Constance for her part had her own reservations, finding Graves 'tender-hearted, rather vain, very domestic' and disapproving of his readiness to confide in her all the details of his life with Nancy – 'he tells me more than he should' – and his 'garrulousness'.[52] She was even more critical of Nancy; beside claiming that she had 'not got enough adventure in her to be a poet's wife' and that she was 'very clever with her fingers and quick in brain', she found her:

> Affectionate too, but spoilt in a sort of artistic way, ready to find fault with anyone else's work. I quite like her, but wish she weren't so mulish. For some reason she insists on calling herself Miss Nancy Nicholson.[53]

Graves himself was already critical of the one other poet he knew on Boars Hill on arrival, Robert Nichols. Nicknamed 'Crikey' because of his repeated use of that exclamation, Nichols now struck Graves as rather affected; he appears to have tired of his apparently boundless confidence and manic energy, finding him instead 'still another neurasthenic ex-soldier, with his flame-opal ring, his wide-brimmed hat, his flapping arms and "mournful grandeur in repose".[54] Although grateful to Nichols for his promotion of his poetry in America, by late 1919 Graves was far less admiring of the poet and his work than he had been in 1917.

He spent more time with a third poet, Edmund Blunden, who had just arrived on Boars Hill like himself to take up his place at Oxford after serving in the Army. Like Graves, too, he was suffering from damaged lungs and would choose to study English rather than his original choice of Classics. They had been in contact by letter since early June 1919, when Sassoon had suggested Blunden as a possible contributor to the second number of *The Owl*. Graves had admired the poems Blunden sent him and took an immediate liking to the man himself when they met in October. To begin with theirs would be a respectful as well as an affectionate friendship ('dear old sock', Graves is addressing him by 1921, 'Blest, and best, Robert', Blunden replies), in which each would promote the other as a poet – Graves by helping Blunden complete *The Waggoner* and recommending it to literary friends, and Blunden with positive reviews of Graves's work when he started to write for the *Athenaeum*. Both had married young and had children early, though Blunden's first child with his wife Mary would die in infancy. Dingle Cottage, where Graves lived in some comfort in Masefield's garden, opened out onto Ridgeway and a short way along it, down a winding lane, was Mona Cottage, where Edmund and Mary lodged with Delilah Baker, known locally as the 'Jubilee Murderess'. Rumour had it that she had killed her husband under extreme provocation, a situation Graves evidently relished since he made it the basis for his poem 'The Coronation Murder', in which the murdered husband, 'Old Becker', crawls nightly up the stairs from 'his grave at the stair-foot'.[55] Graves, who grew fond of Delilah, christened her 'Angel Heavens' and made her various presents of tea and tinned plum pudding. By 1927 Blunden would look back nostalgically on their 'ancient commonwealth, when it was so pleasant and quick a walk between Angel's Heavens' hut and "that Maäsful's" even Dingle Cottage'.[56] Graves would collect Blunden daily from Mona Cottage as he cycled down to his lectures. It was, Graves wrote to his brother John shortly after their arrival, 'a heavenly life on Boars Hill'. Reverting to the childhood language he still used with John, he described Dingle Cottage as a 'glubshious place' with 'a double view from the top of the garden, as wide as Slip Back [i.e. Llys Bach], one way over Oxfordshire, the other over Berkshire'.[57]

Boars Hill was an altogether colourful place to live, quite apart from Nichols's flame-opal ring and wide-brimmed hat. There was for instance the Poet Laureate, Robert Bridges, at Chilswell House, with his bright eyes, abrupt challenging manner and flower in his buttonhole. Although Graves would not get to know him well, he already admired him as one of the first men of letters to have signed the Oxford recantation of hatred against the Germans, which Bridges had also helped draft and possibly written. Graves was less enthusiastic about Bridges's poetry and after an initial involvement in Bridges's 'Society for Pure English', had little further contact with him.[58] Bridges's *The Spirit of Man* (1915) anthology, which had been enormously popular during the First World War, struck him as 'an act of genuine if misapplied creation'.[59] *The Chilswell Book of English Poetry* (1924) would similarly fail to impress him. His greatest interest in Bridges appears to have been his tenuous link to Samuel Butler, whose sister had married Bridges's older brother.

Graves's relationship with another illustrious member of the community, Gilbert Murray, was a little closer since Murray was not only a poet but also Regius Professor of Greek at the university. As one of the scholars associated with Jane Harrison, he was involved in the myth-ritual school of mythography, with a deep interest in the psychic, both areas attractive to Graves. They clearly got on well together, since when Alfred and Amy visited their son at Boars Hill, Robert would be invited to bring them to tea with Murray and his aristocratic wife, Lady Mary, daughter of George Howard, 9th Earl of Carlisle. (It would be through Lady Mary and her sister-in-law, the Honourable Mrs Michael Howard, that Nancy's brother Ben would meet his future wife, another painter, Winifred Roberts, almost certainly while painting Robert's portrait in the summer of 1920.)

It was among such august company that Graves set out to establish himself more securely in the literary world.

16

OXFORD AND 'PIER-GLASS HAUNTINGS'[1] (OCTOBER 1919–MARCH 1921)

> Edmund [Blunden] and I found ourselves translating everything
> into trench-warfare terms. The war was not yet over for us. In the
> middle of a lecture I would have a sudden very clear experience
> of men on the march up the Béthune-La Bassée road ... These
> day-dreams persisted like an alternate life.[2]

In taking up his Exhibition at St John's College, Oxford, in
October 1919, Graves now faced the prospect he dreaded and
had sworn to avoid: two or three years of organized learning, of
finding himself under someone else's 'orders' again. Being four
years older than the average undergraduate and having his younger
brother Charles two terms ahead of him at St John's could not have
made the situation easier for him. Unlike Charles, who believed
that the 'great thing' at university was 'to be alive, play games,
avoid the Progs [i.e. Proctors, the University policemen] and
show hospitality', especially at breakfast, Robert took little part
in undergraduate life, seldom visiting his college except to draw
his government grant and Exhibition money.[3] He refused to pay
the college games subscription, 'having little interest in St John's'.[4]
The few undergraduate friends he had were at other colleges, like

Blunden at Queen's, and in any case he felt that Wadham had 'a prior claim' on his loyalty, due to his time there as an instructor in 1917.

There was still one link with Wadham that amused Graves, the fact that his moral tutor at St John's, J. V. Powell, had been his subordinate at Wadham, a corporal to his captain. He now no longer saluted Graves when they met, but fortunately he remained a friend and prevailed on the college to allow Graves to change his course from Classics to English Language and Literature without sacrificing his Classical Exhibition.

Graves claimed to find the English syllabus 'tedious', especially the eighteenth-century poets favoured by the dons, though not the ex-soldiers who were mostly anti-French and detected their influence at work. Like his personal tutor, Percy Simpson, editor (with C. H. Harford and Evelyn Simpson) of the Clarendon *Ben Jonson*, he compared writers like Alexander Pope unfavourably with the Romantic poets. Simpson, whom he found 'a darling', did, however, also manage to infect him with enthusiasm for Elizabethan and Jacobean literature, John Webster in particular, and would influence several of his books of criticism in the 1920s; beside quoting him in *Poetic Unreason* (1925), Graves would draw heavily on Simpson's *Shakespearian Punctuation* (1911) for his own influential analysis of Sonnet 129 in *A Survey of Modernist Poetry* (1927), one of a number of reasons to doubt Laura Riding's claim to have written most of that book. Simpson was also almost certainly responsible for Graves's familiarity with such arcane matters as the two versions of Thomas Wyatt's 'They Flee from Me', which Graves would analyse in *A Pamphlet Against Anthologies* (1928). Simpson had a high opinion of Graves's talents, though he found him, as Sassoon and others had done, 'greatly wanting in literary perspective', calling him 'a silly young ass' for attacking Thomas Burke and Pope, for instance, and warning him not to do so in his final exams.[5]

The compulsory course in Anglo-Saxon proved more of a challenge for Graves, who had previously found that languages came easily to him; he now found it hard to concentrate on the cases, genders and tenses of Old English, though Simpson assured his father that he had mastered it sufficiently to pass the exams. But Graves enjoyed Anglo-Saxon poetry, especially 'Beowulf' and 'Judith'. He would emerge from Oxford with a much wider and more detailed knowledge of English literature, as well as an increased skill in analysing it. On the whole he experienced in retrospect 'a warm feeling' for Oxford, which he believed had been 'extraordinarily kind' to him.[6] Its rules and statutes, though apparently set in stone, seemed to him 'ready for emergencies'; and in his case at least, he argued, 'a poet was an emergency'.[7]

Another great comfort and support was the Head of the English School, Sir Walter Raleigh (another resident on Boars Hill), whom Graves named 'the prince of dons'.[8] Raleigh, who had a great respect for the Graves family and admired Robert's poetry, made even more allowances for him than he did for all his ex-servicemen. He agreed to be Graves's tutor 'on condition that he should not be expected to tutor' him, an ideal arrangement as far as the younger man was concerned.[9] They met, therefore, as friends, free from the usual formalities of student-teacher relationships. It would be Raleigh who encouraged Graves, after he gave up working for his B.A., to put in for the slightly higher degree of a B.Litt., believing that his books 'would do' as a thesis and that he would get the B.Litt. as easily 'as a cat has kittens'.[10] It was also Raleigh's influence at this early stage that fostered Graves's belief in the importance of the irrational element in poetry. ('How awful it will be when poetry is explained!' Raleigh wrote to him on one occasion.)[11]

Raleigh was not the only one at Oxford to treat Graves as a special case. There were a number of people ready to sit at his feet.[12] His was not the normal undergraduate experience, though he did have to work hard at his course. When, only two months after starting it, six more of his poems were published in *Georgian Poetry 1918–1919*, with two more in the second number of *The Owl* the same month, followed by Secker's publication of *Country Sentiment* in March 1920, his stock rose even higher. Although reviews and sales of *Country Sentiment* were disappointing – 'praised for fancy, blamed for slightness', his father noted on 6 April 1920 – Graves was now an established poet. He was offered the prestigious job of editing *Oxford Poetry 1921* with Richard Hughes, asked to speak at various Oxford societies and allowed to organize his own poetry events, notably a recital by the American poet Vachel Lindsay, known as the travelling bard and founder of modern singing poetry.

The most important event of Graves's first undergraduate year at Oxford, however, owed nothing to Raleigh, or his glowing list of influential literary friends, but to his father. Although Robert was inclined to dismiss Alfred's achievements, he was nonetheless a respected figure in the academic world. On his first visit to Robert in November 1919, for instance, his father was invited to dine at All Souls College, where his friend from Trinity College Dublin days, Francis Edgeworth, was Professor of Political Economy, and to bring Robert with him. So on Sunday, 16 November, within a month of starting at the university, the new undergraduate found himself sitting at All Souls' High Table, together with T. E. Lawrence, who was working at the college on his second draft of *Seven Pillars of Wisdom*. When Alfred was introduced to 'Colonel Lawrence of Arabian fame', Lawrence asked whether he was any relation of Philip Graves, with whom he had worked at the Arab Bureau in Cairo. Alfred was delighted to be able to reply 'Only his father' and felt encouraged to introduce another of his sons, Robert, to him.[13] When Lawrence asked Robert in turn whether he was 'Robert Graves the poet', Robert was 'embarrassed' but highly flattered.[14] Lawrence, it transpired, had read his poems on one of his flying visits to Cairo.

A friendship between the 24-year-old Graves and the 31-year-old Lawrence developed rapidly from this first brief meeting, Graves often visiting Lawrence's rooms in All Souls between lectures. The little Hejaz colonel became a replacement of sorts for Blunden, who had been forced by financial need to leave Oxford by the end of the first year. Robert could boast to his brother John that he spent 'most of [his] time' with Lawrence.[15] By 1919 Lawrence's military achievements in Arabia and Palestine had turned him into a legendary figure, thanks largely to the American journalist Lowell Thomas. While far from dismissing his extraordinary exploits, however, Graves was more anxious to emphasize that Lawrence was also 'a great man on poetry, pictures, music and everything else in the world'.[16]

Lawrence himself wanted to be seen as a cultured man, above all, and had an exaggerated respect for creative artists, especially writers. Graves enjoyed Lawrence's belief in him as a 'resounding literary name' initially, though he 'never encouraged it'.[17] But he found it 'sad' that Lawrence should have 'reckoned himself a failure by such standards'.[18] It seemed to him that Lawrence's inability to be 'healthy in his attitude to writers and painters' lay at the root of his undoubted problems by the early 1920s.[19] Whilst he could be business-like and factual with someone like the military historian Basil Liddell Hart, with Graves one has the feeling that he is trying to impress. Graves, who was dazzled by Lawrence, was certainly trying to impress him, concluding some of his early letters to him in an elaborate style quite unlike his usual direct manner. Following a number of discussions on Lawrence's sexual problems after his flogging and alleged rape at Dera'a, for instance, Graves replied portentously:

> Prince,
> out of it seems a salty and desolate kingdom, Prince, you terrify me that such things can silently happen to princes and the world go wobbling contentedly on, and other princes contrive to drink each other's healths as if all was well and Nemesis had ended the reign of Croesus.

He avoids telling Lawrence that he thinks his attempts at poetry a failure by calling them 'poetic quartz in which the veins of metre run'.[20]

Sassoon's initial impression of Lawrence, to whom he had been introduced in 1918, was of a reticent, rather scholarly man, quite different from the military type he had expected. Graves's conclusion, after a friendship of many years, would be that Lawrence, 'for all his internal sufferings', remained 'a warm, generous, essentially truthful friend'.[21] He was not blind to Lawrence's 'manifest failings', his secretiveness, his neuroses, his possible fabrications: Lawrence, like Winston Churchill, he believed, 'had a devil', but like Churchill he 'kept it in check'.[22] Ultimately, he judged Lawrence 'an intuitive, affectionate, Galahad-like man of action'.[23] And while he thought Lawrence's decision to become a member of the Irish Academy of Letters 'the queerest thing he did', he found this assertion of his Irishness 'significant', in ways that are applicable to Graves himself, who had come to recognize his own 'Irishness' only recently by late 1919:

> He had all the marks of the Irishman: the rhetoric of freedom, the rhetoric of chastity, the rhetoric of honour, the power to excite sudden deep affections, loyalty to the long-buried past, high aims qualified by too mocking a sense of humour, serenity clouded by petulance and broken by occasional black despairs, playboy charm and theatricality, imagination that over-runs itself and tires, extreme generosity, serpent cunning, lion courage, diabolic intuition, and the curse of self-doubt which becomes enmity to self and sometimes renunciation of all that is most loved and esteemed.[24]

Lawrence viewed Graves, more succinctly, as 'a most excellent and truthful person'[25] and would be of great assistance to him, even after Lawrence had left Oxford to join the air force in 1922. He would help Graves out of at least three financial crises and, even more importantly, encourage and inspire him as a poet. Graves was grateful, for instance, for his positive response to a poem about the increasing sexual problems in his marriage, 'Song of Contrariety', while 'Children of Darkness' was inspired directly by Lawrence's remark about 'the futility of being' and 'parental difficulties', as well as their frank discussions of sex:[26]

> We spurred our parents to the kiss,
> Though doubtfully they shrank from this –
> Day had no courage to pursue
> What lusty dark alone might do:
> Then were we joined from their caress
> In heat of midnight, one from two...[27]

Graves valued Lawrence's opinion greatly as he worked on his next collection of poetry, *The Pier-Glass*, in 1920, adopting a number of his suggestions. When the book was published in February 1921, it would be dedicated (like *Country Sentiment*) to Nancy, but contained a head-note dedication 'To T. E. Lawrence, who helped me with it'.

Although Graves settled well to his academic work, earning a good report from Powell, the war was still with him. In the middle of a lecture disturbing memories, mainly of his first four months in France, would return to break his concentration and renew his sufferings. Many of the poems in *The Pier-Glass* reflect the 'haunted condition' he was still in by 1920 and few people could have been more suited to appreciate them than Lawrence, who continued to fight his own demons.[28] Graves told Blunden that half of the poems in the collection were 'a reaction *against* shell-shock',[29] a series of love poems and imaginings 'indulging in a sort of dementia praecox[30] of fantastic day-dreams' in pieces such as 'The Troll's Nosegay' and 'The Hills of May', but it was his attempt to 'stand up to the damned disease and write an account of it' in the other half that is of greater interest, according to him.[31] He believed the '*pièce de résistance*' of *The Pier-Glass* to be 'the set of four dramatic pieces of which "The Gnat" and "The Pier-Glass" form part'.[32] ('Reproach' and 'Down' are the other two.) Rivers, who also lies behind this book, had enabled him to see his neurasthenia as rich material for poetry and all four poems are 'war poems' of a kind. They were not easy to write and Graves had to revise each piece at least eight times before even he understood what they were to be about.

The imagery, particularly in 'The Gnat' and 'The Pier-Glass', is mysterious and troubling, reflecting Graves's state of mind as he wrote them. In 'The Pier-Glass', for instance, he uses the suggested rape of the servant-narrator by her master as an objective correlative for his own state of mind in relation to the war. The servant's reaction to having murdered her rapist in self-defence can be seen to mirror Graves's own guilt-ridden memories of the enemies he has killed in the war. The explanation for her haunted condition in a final stanza of the original version was added at Lawrence's suggestion but later removed, since Graves sensed rightly that the uncertainty and mysteriousness of the poem was increased without it, giving a more faithful reflection of the narrator's (and Graves's) disturbed state of mind. After wandering aimlessly but compulsively about a 'lost manor', visiting the 'master'-bedroom with its 'huge bed of state' and peering into 'a sullen pier-glass cracked from side to side', the narrator paints a final picture of her (and Graves's) despair and blankness:

> Is there no life, nothing but the thin shadow
> And blank foreboding, never a wainscot rat
> Rasping a crust? Or at the window-pane
> No fly, no bluebottle, no starveling spider?
> The windows frame a prospect of cold skies
> Half-merged with sea, as at the first creation –
> Abstract, confusing welter. Face about,
> Peer rather in the glass once more, take note
> Of self, the grey lips and long hair dishevelled,
> Sleep-staring eyes. Ah, mirror, for Christ's love
> Give me one token that there still abides
> Remote – beyond this island mystery,
> So be it only this side Hope, somewhere,
> In streams, on sun-warm mountain pasturage –
> True life, natural breath; not this phantasma.[33]

The servant's staring eyes suggest that she is sleep-walking, condemned to this eternal nightmare, her 'Death in Life' reminiscent of Coleridge's Ancient Mariner and his punishment. There is also a more direct reference to Tennyson's 'Lady of Shalott', though in Graves's poem 'the sullen pierglass' is already 'cracked from side to side', reflecting distortedly a face that is 'melancholy, / And pale, as faces grow that look in mirrors'.[34] (Mirrors in folklore are cracked to convey calamity, or a tragically fractured identity.) The epigraph to Graves's whole volume, taken from John Skelton, underlines the enigmatic nature of 'The Pier-Glass', referring as it does to a mirror 'as transparent as glass darkly'.[35] Biographically, there is a clear link between the 'lost manor' of 'The Pier-Glass' and Maes-y-Neuadd; Talsarnau, where Robert and Nancy spent their holiday in the summer of 1918. Both looked out on 'a prospect of cold skies / Half-merged with sea'. More significantly, Robert remembered Maes-y-Neuadd as 'the most haunted house I have ever been in',[36] where the ghosts were invisible except in the mirrors.

'The Gnat' also has its origins in Graves's wartime experience, though its transformation into a striking allegory gives it more than biographical interest. In a letter to his parents of 28 May 1915 Graves had written from the Cuinchy brickstacks about the effect the noise of various weapons and ammunition had on him – rifle grenades, 'sausage' mortar bombs, machine guns, shells of various sizes – and reported that when one shell had burst over the trench, just missing him, his 'ears sang as though they were gnats in them',[37] a simile that his subconscious evidently stored for later use. 'The Gnat' is a deeply ironic poem from its opening stanza onwards, in which the protagonist, shepherd Watkin, misinterprets the nature of the threat presented by the gnat, believing it to have entered his brain through his ear:

> The shepherd Watkin heard an inner voice
> Calling 'My creature, ho! be warned, be ready!'
> Calling, 'The moment comes, therefore be ready!'...[38]

Convinced he is about to die, he kills his faithful companion, the sheepdog Prinny, which he fears will be ill-treated after his death. With the dog's death, the gnat leaves him, but to a 'dead dream' of life, another 'Death in Life', a condition Graves felt himself to be in at times, even though the war – like the gnat – has departed. Whether the gnat is real or simply a delusion lodged in Watkin's brain is not specified, but there is certainly a parallel with Graves's debate on the value or otherwise of psychoanalysis, as Graves himself explains:

> ['The Gnat'] is an assertion that to be rid of the gnat (shell shock) means killing the sheep-dog (poetry) and when the sheep-dog is dead, the shepherd ceases to be a shepherd and must become a labourer; in fact I would have to give up being a poet and become a schoolmaster or a bank-clerk.[39]

The irony in his own situation lay in the fact that if therapy succeeded, he might be 'too completely cured' and unable to write poetry.[40] By choosing to be a neurasthenic poet, he was refusing to kill the thing he loved most.

Graves's is a neat explanation, but 'telling' his readers what 'The Gnat' meant is not the same as 'showing' and does not make it automatically successful as a poem. It owes its success to the vividness with which Graves conveys his disturbed state through the damage inflicted on the brain by such a small thing, in Watkin's case a gnat, in Graves's case what many might regard as his unnecessary reaction to a 'necessary' (in his opinion) war:

> On the next night
> The busy Gnat, swollen to giant size,
> Pent-up within the skull, knew certainly,
> As a bird knows in the egg his hour was come...
> ...
> He must out, crack the shell, out, out!
> He strains, claps his wings, arches his back,
> Drives in his talons, out! out![41]

The gnat used already in 'One Hard Look' becomes the symbol of the claustrophobia, violence and destructiveness of the war itself, its visitation a chilling reflection of Graves's own state in 1920, as are the other two poems he lists in his 'dramatic quartet', 'Reproach' and 'Down'.

The love poems with which Graves intended to balance such dark poems of despair seem lightweight by comparison. Each is charming in its own way, particularly 'The Patchwork Bonnet' in which the narrator 'throw[s]' 'his silent love' across the room:

> ... Where you sit sewing in bed by candlelight,
>   Your young stern profile and industrious fingers
> Displayed against the blind in a shadow show,
> To Dinda's grave delight...[42]

This gives us a glimpse of the happiness Graves still experienced, though less frequently, in his relations with Nancy, here busy at a favourite occupation, sewing.

Since only one child (Dinda/Jenny) appears in 'The Patchwork Bonnet', it is reasonable to assume that it was written just before the birth of Robert and Nancy's second child on 7 March 1920, (John) David Graves. Welcomed joyfully into the family, especially by Amy, who made it clear (to Nancy's extreme irritation) that her first male grandchild was a particularly important addition to the family, David nevertheless added to the increasing strains on Robert's life on Boars Hill. Only someone of his remarkable energy could have coped with juggling his academic work for St John's with all the other responsibilities of his life by March 1920. His first term at Oxford had been relatively free of pressure, with his various grants and loans from his parents relieving him briefly from financial worries. Nancy had been pregnant then, but not heavily so, and was able to cope with the absence of their 'general' [servant] whom they had 'let go' in the interests of economy. With the decoration and furnishing of Dingle Cottage as an outlet for her creative talents, she seems to have been less angry and frustrated with Robert than usual. They still had their nanny, Margaret, and Robert was able to attend lectures regularly, see his tutors and complete the work required of him. Although his essays were judged 'a trifle temperamental' by the college board,[43] the senior tutor, Powell, 'reported well' of his work.[44]

With the arrival of David in March 1920, however, domestic life became more demanding and Graves's second and third terms went less smoothly. In addition to his academic work, he was obliged to take on many of the household chores, blacking grates, cooking meals and washing dishes, as well as jobs he enjoyed such as gardening, making jam and bottling fruit. He and Nancy were in debt once more, partly because they had counted on the sale of his Welsh cottage that fell through, so he also gave paid talks to literary clubs and submitted poems and articles to various magazines. Even after William Nicholson, with his customary generosity, cleared their debts for them shortly after David's birth, they struggled financially. In June, Graves appealed once more to Edward Marsh for money from what he mistakenly thought of as the 'Rupert Brooke Fund'.[45]

Poetry, the thing that mattered most to Robert, had somehow to be fitted into the brief periods left to him between his chores, his academic work and paid literary undertakings. Fortunately he discovered that, although the addition of children to his marriage meant more domestic responsibilities, his poetry did not suffer: when he was working at a poem nothing else mattered; he went on doing his mechanical tasks in a trance until he had time to sit down to write it out. At one period he only allowed himself half an hour's writing a day, he claimed, but once he did write he always had too much to put down. Attempting to explain his poetry-writing to Malcolm Muggeridge many years later, he would compare the process to 'a sort of cloud descend[ing]' on him:

> It's as though the poem has already been written but you are trying to reconstitute it – you regard the poem as something there and you've got to get back to the original ... your original view of it.[46]

It was, Graves maintained, a 'mystical' experience. Yet at the same time it was always 'a painful process of continual corrections and corrections on top of corrections and persistent dissatisfaction', making it almost easier to work under pressure as he was forced to do in these early years of family life.[47]

Nancy, on the other hand, found that her work suffered badly in these conditions, though she persisted with her plans for four children in quick succession. The way in which the strain told most clearly on them both was on their health. Nancy was constantly ill, eventually with an underactive thyroid and ringworm, a fungal skin infection, and even though Margaret took over the domestic chores in Robert's third term at Oxford, he was overworked and often unwell.

Two months at Harlech from mid-June 1920 helped them recover their physical health, but Nancy insisted on a complete break for them both from the family and responsibilities. Leaving Jenny and David with Margaret, they set off on bicycles in mid-August for a fortnight on their own, intending to sleep out at night to save money. It is some measure of their impracticality that they failed to pack blankets and ended up sleeping in the relative warmth of the day, cycling at night. As they travelled westward over Salisbury Plain, they passed several deserted army camps that had a ghostly look at night, an unintentionally romantic, if eerie, result of their fecklessness. According to Robert their route had not been planned in any detail, but it is hard to believe that someone who admired Thomas Hardy as much as he did should simply 'find' himself near his house at Dorchester. He knew that Sassoon, now absent in America, had made his own magical visit to Hardy in late 1917 and there may have been an element of competitiveness in his own visit on this occasion. Did he really just happen to have a copy of *Country Sentiment* with him and suddenly decide, as he claims, that Hardy might like it?

When Graves arrived unannounced at Max Gate, however, he had an entrée of sorts, having met Hardy in February that year, the month the older poet visited Oxford to receive his honorary degree and attend a performance of his drama in verse *The Dynasts*. They had also corresponded over Hardy's contribution to the first number of *The Owl*. The welcome could not have been warmer and an invitation to tea was followed by the offer of dinner and a bed for the night. The whole visit went well, with Hardy noticeably gayer and more active than at Oxford, anxious to discuss a whole range of topics with two people he viewed as representatives of the post-war generation who might be able to enlighten him about such current mysteries as the Bolshevik regime or the 'Red Terror'.[48] His lively curiosity extended from a discussion of Nancy's daringly 'bobbed' hair and decision to keep her maiden name (which Hardy found 'old-fashioned') to why Graves had given up his title of 'Captain'. ('I would certainly keep my rank if I had one,' Hardy assured him, the reason Sassoon would later give for keeping his army rank in civilian life.)[49] Hardy's interest in church matters, though he no longer attended much, led to talk of his restoration of a Norman font in the neighbourhood and a debate on baptism, when it emerged that Robert and Nancy had not baptized their children. Hardy also entertained them with imitations of some of the pompous bishops he had witnessed at the Athenaeum Club, though he strongly disapproved of a recent visitor, Sir Edmund Gosse's 'breach of good taste in imitating [Hardy's] old friend Henry James, eating soup. Loyalty to his friends was always a passion with Hardy.'[50]

Finally, they turned to literature when Hardy asked to see some recent poems by Graves. They failed to agree on different writing methods, with Hardy confiding that he rarely went beyond three or four drafts of a poem for fear of it 'losing the freshness'. However, like Graves he found that he could write prose 'to a time-table', while 'poetry was always accidental' and, perhaps for that reason, 'prized ... more highly'.[51] They also discussed Hardy's dislike of autograph-hunters and critics, especially when the latter accused him of pessimism. His conclusion, with which Graves's own technique suggests he half agreed, was that 'All we can do is to write on the old themes in the old styles, but try to do a little better than those who went before us.'[52]

When Robert and Nancy left, it was with a pressing invitation to return. From Dorchester they cycled another 60 miles to Tiverton to visit Nancy's old nurse, who kept a 'fancy-goods' shop in the neighbourhood. Nancy, so fanatical about the visual that she would walk out of a room if a new visitor's clothes failed to harmonize with her decor, instantly reorganized the shop window. She also advised framing the prints for sale. Extremely house-proud herself, she gave the shop a thorough spring-clean and took her turn behind the counter. When, as a result, the weekly takings went up, she became convinced that a shop of their own on Boars Hill was the answer to their chronic financial problems. Undaunted by lack of funding or experience, she returned to Dingle Cottage at the end of August determined to put her plan into practice.

Robert himself offered no resistance. He had been made to feel guilty simply for being male and rarely rejected any of her ideas, however difficult they threatened to make life for him. By 7 October, just before the start of his second year at St John's, he was 'worn out from much work', he told Marsh, 'helping Nancy with her shop'.[53] Fortunately, Marsh had just sent him 'a large and timely cheque', as his share of royalties for *Georgian Poetry 1918–1919*, since setting up the shop had been a costly business, for which they had, as usual, to borrow money.[54] Nancy, in her theoretical way, had decided that a second-hand army hut would be ideal as premises and, when that proved impossible, opted for a custom-built shed designed by herself. Her stepmother, Edie, lent the money for it and William Nicholson painted the shop sign for them without charge.[55] Money was also needed for the rent of a corner of a field opposite the Masefields' garden, and yet more for an extensive stock of 'confectionery, groceries, tobacco, hardware, medicines and all the other things one finds in a village shop'.[56] It may have been partly to raise more capital, or perhaps because Nancy, like her father, was impressed by the aristocracy, that she decided to take their neighbour, the Hon. Mrs Michael Howard, into partnership. However they became partners, Norah Howard was not a wise choice, since she had no more knowledge of shop management than Nancy, not even in her chosen area of responsibility, the shop's bookkeeping.

Nevertheless, Boars Hill Shop got off to a good start. Robert, who was proud of his ability to manage the press, ensured that the enterprise was well advertised. The *Daily Mirror* carried a charming set of photographs, including ones of Nancy, Mrs Howard and a small child in the doorway of the wooden shed under the headline 'SHOP-KEEPING ON PARNASSUS' on its opening day, 7 October 1920, and the *Daily Mail* ran an interview with the two ladies the following day. Although Nancy may have been irritated by Norah Howard's claim to have been equally responsible for the original idea, she and Robert were both pleased with the initial response, when 'crowds came up from Oxford', Robert recalled, to visit a shop where you might just see a poet serving behind the counter.[57]

To begin with, the shop went 'at a terrific pace, gross takings about £200 a month' and increasing weekly, Graves reported to Ken Barrett.[58] Victims of their own success, or hubris, however, they decided to expand and turn it into a large general store to compete with the Oxford tradesmen. By the time the building had been enlarged and a further two or three hundred pounds of stock purchased, any initial profit had been eaten up.

It was at this point that Mrs Howard, perhaps anticipating financial disaster from her dealing with the accounts, quarrelled with Nancy and withdrew. 'Mrs Howard, Nancy thinks a fool,' Graves wrote to Blunden; 'I know her for a knave, crooked as Angel's [i.e. Mrs Delilah Baker's] little brick path, or the windings of the Isis ... intent on ruining us!'[59] Borrowing yet more money from his patient parents, he and Nancy had managed to buy Mrs Howard out by January 1921 and settle outstanding bills with their wholesalers. But Robert, whose fourth term had now started, found himself serving in the shop several hours a day instead of attending lectures and writing essays, while Nancy cycled round the big houses for the daily orders:

> Another caricature scene: myself, wearing a green-baize apron this time, with flushed face and disordered hair, selling a packet of Bird's Eye tobacco to the Poet Laureate with one hand and with the other weighing out half a pound of brown sugar for Sir Arthur Evans' gardener's wife.[60]

Robert almost certainly charged Robert Bridges the full price for his tobacco, while lowering the cost of brown sugar for the gardener's wife, since neither he nor Nancy could resist 'playing at Robin Hood', an indulgence of conscience they could ill afford.[61] Their comfortable, relatively spoilt upbringing had conditioned both of them to expect their parents to come to their rescue financially if need be.

By the end of February 1921, in Robert's fifth term at Oxford, it was clear that they could not manage without more help and after a failed attempt to persuade Barrett's artist wife to be their shop assistant, they hired a shop-boy to cycle round for orders in place of Nancy. The shop-business finally ousted everything they valued from their lives, Nancy's painting, Robert's writing and university work, and what Nancy considered her 'proper supervision of the house and children'.[62] As highly theoretical about childcare as everything else, she had 'always practised the most up-to-date methods of training and feeding children'[63] and was becoming increasingly unhappy with Margaret's handling of Jenny, now two, and David, nearly a year old. The nanny's devotion was not in question, but she was failing to follow Nancy's strict instructions as to diet and daily routine. Undeterred by the difficulties Mrs Howard was experiencing without a nanny – her ostensible reason for leaving – Nancy decided that Margaret must go. (Robert, knowing that Nancy 'put the children before everything' else,[64] offered no resistance, but the fact that he would hire Margaret later to look after the two eldest children of his second marriage suggests that he did not share Nancy's criticisms of her.) Instead of giving her notice in person, they took the more cowardly course of sending her to Robert's parents, on the pretext of a holiday, then expecting Amy to give Margaret a letter of dismissal from them.

One immediate consequence was that Nancy abandoned the shop to look after the children, leaving Robert to work behind the counter virtually full-time. He had only recently recovered from a severe bout of flu in December 1920 and in his exhausted state he now succumbed to another, followed by a bad attack of neurasthenia. The political situation in Europe seemed to him to be going from bad to worse. Added to trouble in Ireland, Russia and the Near East, 'the papers promised new and deadlier poison gases for the next war', one of the things he had most feared in the last one.[65]

An attempt to carry on the shop with a manager failed, mainly because it was the personal touch that had so appealed. Although Graves wrote with some bravado to Blunden on 10 March 1921 that ' "the shop" qua shop is flourishing', he admitted that 'qua anything else' it was 'in a bad way'. By the end of March, only six months after its hugely optimistic opening, Boars Hill Shop shut down completely, leaving Robert and Nancy with large debts. A big Oxford firm had offered to buy the shop from them, but Mrs Masefield had persuaded the owner of the field in which it stood to refuse to rent the land to them, thinking it much too near her house. Even the shed failed to bring Robert and Nancy more than about a tenth of what they had paid for it, since it could not be moved intact and had to be sold as timber. The stock was also sold off at a considerable loss and they were left with debts of £500, reduced after their lawyer's efforts to £300. Robert's attempt to pay some of this off with a series of articles on his 'adventures in trade' was also a failure.[66] William Nicholson, who immediately sent them a £100 note in a matchbox, was glad they had had to give up the shop: neither of them were 'shopkeepers by birth' and 'Nance ... should stick to her brush,' he told Robert, 'and you to your pen.'[67]

Robert and Nancy may secretly have agreed with William, but they were 'disgusted' by the whole affair. Robert gave a number of reasons for their decision to leave Boars Hill on 21 June, the next quarter-day when their rent to the Masefields was due – 'We can't afford to live on the hill,' he told Marsh on 13 April 1921, 'our cottage is unhealthy and our neighbours are not neighbourly' – but it was undoubtedly their neighbours who dictated their decision. There were just 'too many B[loody] B[astards?]'s (chiefly female)' for his taste, Constance Masefield among them.[68] Her blocking of their efforts to sell the shop had made him extremely bitter. Lawrence, who approved their decision to move, referred more politely to their 'overpowering neighbours', including Mrs Howard and Robert Bridges among them. He would also, more practically and with great generosity, send four chapters of his already legendary *Seven Pillars of Wisdom* for the sale of serialization rights in America, enabling Robert and Nancy to pay off the final £200 of their debts.[69]

The damage for Graves was far more extensive than financial debts or a house move, however. His physical health had suffered, his neurasthenia had returned with a vengeance, and his university studies were brought to an abrupt end. Although Graves attributes this last to advice given by the psychiatrist Dr McDowall (consulted in April on Rivers's recommendation), it is more likely that he had already decided to abandon his degree course. Once his debts were cleared and the shop closed there was nothing to prevent him returning to St John's. But he was conscious of the fact that he was at least a term behind in his work and that final exams were only a few months away. In any case he was far more interested in doing his own work. He had written nine poems in quick succession after the end of the spring term and was already collecting material for his next collection, *Whipperginny*. He had also submitted a more or less final draft of his first prose book, *On English Poetry*, to his typist.

Alfred Graves was predictably 'upset' at his 'chucking' his degree,[70] but Professor Raleigh was more optimistic. He encouraged Graves to believe that a thesis for the slightly higher degree of Hon.B.Litt. could be achieved by submitting another short prose book, thus avoiding the need to complete his course. This appealed greatly to Graves, who had almost certainly feared failing in an exam with candidates much younger than himself. His failure to win a full scholarship to St John's had left him feeling vulnerable in that area.

In any case Graves's recurrence of neurasthenia had left him in no fit state to continue a regular course of studies. While he thought he 'perhaps owed it to Nancy to go to a psychiatrist to be cured',[71] his fear that psychoanalysis might destroy his ability to write poetry prevented him from undertaking it seriously. (Discussing his problems informally with Rivers, or having one consultation with McDowall, did not count.) 'The power of writing poetry,' he claimed, 'was more important to [him] than anything else.'[72] So, with his usual confidence, he resolved to cure himself. He had already learned the rudiments of morbid psychology from Rivers and his colleague, Dr Henry Head (with whom Rivers had gone to work after Craiglockhart), and the rest, Graves believed, could be learnt from books. Paradoxically, however, it would be more through the writing of the very thing he thought it threatened – poetry – together with his prose book on the link between poetry and psychology, *On English Poetry* (dedicated in part to Rivers), that he would begin to recover from the effects of war, using his verse to explore psychological trauma. *Whipperginny*, started in 1921 once *The Pier-Glass* was safely in the press, would be the first obvious sign of his recovery.

17

'ROOTS DOWN INTO A CABBAGE PATCH'[1]
(1921–5)

> Nancy wants to draw again; I want to get all the accumulated
> stuff off my chest that a too strenuous life has piled up. And also
> to make jam and sweets and dig potatoes...[2]

By mid-1921 Graves's life was one of sharp contrasts, like
the decade he had recently entered, in which the Bright
Young Things with their hedonistic lifestyle flourished against
a background of hardship and severe unemployment. Even those
fortunate enough to find work suffered from low wages and poor
working conditions, which would lead to a series of strikes by miners,
railway- and other transport-workers, culminating in the General
Strike of 1926. Politically, too, it was a period of strong contrasts,
with Lloyd George's 1918 coalition government of Liberals and
Conservatives replaced by a Conservative government in 1922,
which was ousted briefly by Labour in 1924, then reinstated for
another five years until Labour regained power in 1929.

Robert and Nancy 'still called [them]selves socialists' during the
first half of the 1920s, but Robert's interest in politics was never very
strong. It was mainly through the more committed Nancy, Sassoon
and Rivers that he was kept aware of the political situation during

this period, when Rivers, for instance, agreed to stand as a Labour Party candidate for London University. Robert himself was far more concerned with his own private battle to reconcile his overriding urge to write poetry with the practical demands of family duties and the need to make money.

In March 1921 the practical concerns dominated as he began his search for a replacement for Dingle Cottage. Undeterred by the failure of her shop and determined to leave Boars Hill for somewhere very different, Nancy had given Robert specific details of the house she envisaged. Like him she wanted to live in 'true country sentiment', not what they both now dismissed rather absurdly as the 'suburban squalor' of the far from squalid Boars Hill. So her first demand was for a village five or six miles away from Oxford in the opposite direction. By laying a ruler across the Oxford ordnance survey map, Robert immediately narrowed the choice to four or five villages. Several of these were eliminated by another of Nancy's specifications. Her further demand that it should have a church with 'a tower, not a spire', made Islip the only option. According to Robert who may well have embellished the details of this unlikely story in retrospect, this was not the end of her requirements: the house must be a little removed from the village, with six rooms, indoor sanitation, a beamed attic, a walled-in garden, must be near the river and cost no more than ten shillings a week in rent. In his entertaining version of events the first estate agent he visited recognized the house immediately: 'Oh, you mean the World's End Cottage? But it is for sale, not renting.'[3] Nancy approved of it on sight, however, and when Robert protested that they had not got the £500 to buy it – they were in fact still in debt to that amount at the time – she replied airily: 'If we could find the exact house, surely to goodness we can find a mere lump sum of money.'[4] In the event it was Amy, as so often, who provided the money, persuaded to do so by her soft-hearted husband. She rented 'World's End' to them at the peppercorn rent of ten shillings a week, as Nancy had specified. Neither Robert nor Nancy seemed especially appreciative of her generosity. Nancy was more interested in plans for improving the house inside and out. Robert was simply happy to be living in a village where Abbot Islip, a friend and patron of one of his favourite poets, Skelton, had been born.

It was the start of another four years of financial crises. Nancy was already pregnant for the third time when they moved into 'World's End' on 15 June 1921: 'Most injudicious, I know', Robert admitted to Ken Barrett, 'but three isn't much worse than two, and the two are such shocking sturdy great lumps that a tiny one will be a change.'[5] Although this tied Robert even more firmly to his household duties, he continued to produce poems and was already working towards his next collection, *Whipperginny*. But it was becoming increasingly clear that his poetry would not earn him enough to live on. Even his father, normally so ready to praise and encourage, had been 'disappointed' with his son's last collection, *The Pier-Glass*, finding it 'too fantastical'.[6] More importantly, in terms of sales, the critics too had been less positive. Graves's adherence to the traditional forms and metres, together with his belief in rhyme, was beginning to make him seem old-fashioned by comparison with more experimental poets such as T. S. Eliot, whose *Poems* (1919) and *The Waste Land* (1922) would revolutionize expectations in poetry. Nor would any of Graves's prose books of the first half of the 1920s enjoy popular success.

Once again Robert and Nancy would appeal to the people who had come to their help continually since the birth of their first child, Jenny, in January 1919. Amy, despite her firm words about it being good for them to have to manage on their own, would repeatedly invite them to Harlech for holidays and send money for train fares too; William Nicholson would start paying Nancy an annual allowance of £120; Sassoon would give presents of money and offer loans – 'Why keep a Jewish friend unless you bleed him?' he asked – and Marsh would continue to pay generous royalties from *Georgian Poetry* as well as gifts from the private money Graves still insisted on calling his 'Rupert Brooke Fund'. *Georgian Poetry* was becoming seen as tired and lacklustre by 1921 and Graves's agreement to 'serve again in the old ship in spite of storms, squalls and barnacles' and appear in *Georgian Poetry 1920–1922* (which Sassoon and Turner among others had turned down) probably stemmed from a combination of loyalty to Marsh and the need for any royalties he could earn.[7]

Graves looked back on his four years at Islip as 'spent chiefly on housework and being nurse to the children'.[8] But he insisted that he 'liked [his] life with the children', and he was clearly happy there at the start.[9] 'Islip is Heaven,' he wrote to Blunden, just as he had once written to his brother John about Boars Hill:

> Stone houses. Cricket. An old stone bridge where was a Civil War skirmish. Flowers. River. Four public [houses]. A famous molecatcher.

A square church. Gossips. The Rectory where Dr South the Divine used
to powder his nose or was it his wig, I quite forget. Edward Confesssor's
birthplace. Not Edward Carpenter oh dear no! The quarry from which
Westminster Abbey came ... What else? Immmemmorial elmms as the
bees say when they're not too hot.[10]

The house itself, a little way from the village centre, was equally
attractive. Two seventeenth-century cottages made into one and turned into
an inn, it was built of local stone and roofed with stone tiles. It had three
bedrooms, a large attic workroom and a pump in the scullery, but outside
sanitation (which worried Amy) and, like Dingle Cottage, no electricity.
Its walled garden, in which herbaceous borders of old-fashioned flowers
flanked a long lawn, reminded Robert of something out of Kate Greenaway's
books, and he was grateful for a vegetable patch to cultivate. Twenty yards
away the River Ray ran between willows and poplars just before it joined
the Cherwell. Robert's favourite place became:

> The old cleft pollard willow leaning
> Where two streams flow together, tributary
> To little boastful Thames; where buttercups
> Streak the white daisy pasture and moor-hens
> Cluck in the rising sedge...[11]

He and Nancy 'loved the cottage, despite its damp and draughts, and the
muddy and cow-frequented lane leading to it'.[12] They were particularly
charmed by the massive oak beam that supported the former tap-room
of the inn, the low window seats and the stout doors. Nancy's father once
again supplied the furniture, all of it in keeping with the house, as might be
expected, and some of it rescued from a bonfire in the grounds of Blenheim
Palace. Robert was proud of 'World's End', of its twinkling brass ornaments
and 'holy-stoned' front doorstep.[13] Nancy instantly started redesigning the
house, 'painting the stairs all colours in the semi-darkness', according to
her husband.[14] By Christmas 1921, he told Blunden, she had 'thoroughly
converted it with her pick-axe and hammer into a Moddle [*sic*] Cottage'.[15]

The village itself suited them 'splendidly' to begin with, its inhabitants
'much the nicest-mannered lot' Robert had ever encountered.[16] He and
Nancy professed relief at its greater social mix after the elitism of Boars

Hill. And despite Alfred and Amy's efforts on their first visit there in June to establish themselves with the vicar (Carter), the rural dean (Colson), the schoolmaster (Brooke) and a landowning farmer (Young), Robert was boasting a month later to Blunden of his friendships with the more working-class postman and a retired sergeant major. It was perhaps in an effort to prove his egalitarian credentials that he immediately joined the village football team, which he was careful to point out was democratic, unlike the cricket team. Whereas he played regularly for the football team, becoming their chief (if rather rough, by their standards) scorer, he soon left the cricket team for this reason, he implied.

Yet he had evidently introduced himself as '*Captain* Graves' to the villagers, who addressed Graves respectfully by this title. And his friends at Islip included a clergyman, his neighbour the Rev. Thompson, and the writer John Buchan, who would become Governor General of Canada and the 1st Baron Tweedsmuir. His efforts to help the working classes as a Labour councillor lasted only a year. However vehemently he criticized the social system and considered himself outside it, he continued to mix largely with the middle and upper classes.

Once settled in, though still without running water in the house, Robert and Nancy began to entertain. Rosaleen, still studying medicine at Merton College, Oxford, and John, now at St John's on a scholarship, would often join them for Sunday lunch with other friends. One of their first and most important visitors was Dr Rivers, who came for lunch on Monday 29 August. Since Robert's brief visit to discuss his neurasthenia with the doctor in March 1921, he had sent Rivers an early draft of what he had first jokingly called *Pebbles to Crack Your Teeth On*, then, more soberly, *An Anatomy of Poetry*, followed by *The Making of Poetry* and *On Poetry*. Finally and more specifically the title became *On English Poetry*. As a neurasthenic, Graves explained in his introduction, he was interested in the newly expounded Freudian theory, but only 'when presented with English reserve and common sense' by Rivers, 'who did not regard sex as the sole impulse in dream-making or assume that dream symbols are constant'.[17] By applying Rivers's case-history method of accounting for emotional dreams, he hoped to come nearer to the understanding of romantic poems, his own included. His application of this method to Keats's 'La Belle Dame Sans Merci' was particularly successful, though E. M. Forster's favourite was his analysis of

A. E. Housman's 'The Carpenter's Son' and Rivers himself preferred Graves's interpretation of four of his own poems, including 'The General Elliott' and 'The God Called Poetry'. Graves's method seemed to Rivers 'thoroughly in agreement with the best psychology'.[18] His only fear was that the book might fall 'between two stools' – 'the psychological dry-as-dust and the literary critics'.[19] From Rivers's surviving letters to Graves (his to Rivers are lost), it is clear that Graves continued to seek guidance throughout from the man who had originally inspired it. For Graves's argument that all poems have their origin in a conflict of one kind or another is closely related to Rivers's 'Conflict and Dream' theory.[20] Since at least half of *On English Poetry* covered an area in which Graves for once did not consider himself an expert, it seemed important to have Rivers's opinion at every stage. He asked him, for instance, whether he believed that there were any ' "sexual" differences in dreams'.[21] Rivers believed there were, as did his neurologist friend Henry Head; and, like Robert, they both argued that the dreams of women are 'far simpler and easier to interpret than those of men'.[22]

Graves's more than usually tentative approach is hinted at in the book's slightly apologetic subtitle: 'An Irregular Approach to the Psychology of This Art, from Evidence Mainly Subjective'. It was not all one way, however; Rivers's response to Graves's stay with him at St John's College, Cambridge, from 26 to 28 November 1921, thanking him for the chance 'to talk symbolism', suggests that he too found the relationship fruitful. He was delighted to hear that *On English Poetry* would be dedicated jointly to 'T. E. Lawrence of Arabia and All Souls College, Oxford, and to W. H. R. Rivers of the Solomon Islands and St John's College, Cambridge...', since Lawrence was one of his heroes of the war. One of Rivers's last letters to Graves shows him 'absolutely in agreement ... as regards nothing being haphazard or accidental'.[23]

Graves described *On English Poetry* as a 'series of "workshop notes" about the writing of poetry', containing much he later found 'trivial but also much practical material' and centred around the concept of poetry as 'first a personal cathartic for the poet' then for 'readers in a similar conflict'.[24] He divided his observations up into 61 sections, some only a page in length, a result perhaps of his necessarily spasmodic working habits. Blunden, whom Graves had invited rather half-heartedly to contribute a section, put his finger on both the book's strengths and weaknesses. While admiring it as a 'singular collection of straight tips about poetry', he thought it a pity Graves had not produced a 'more sustained work'.[25] And though he found its basic premise, 'that poetry is the result of conflicting emotions ... sound enough', it did not account in his opinion for a poet like Robert Herrick, 'or the tranquil utterance of ripening character in Wordsworth, or a sort of wild paean like Whitman's'.[26] But he greatly enjoyed its 'quips and jest and wanton wiles', its reminiscences of Sassoon and 'the continual unconscious autobiography throughout'.[27] It is particularly interesting, for example, to hear Graves's comment on war poetry:

> I have definite evidence for saying that much of the trench-poetry written during the late war was the work of men not otherwise poetically inclined, and that it was very frequently due to an insupportable conflict between suppressed instincts of love and fear; the officer's actual love which he could never openly show, for the boys he commanded, and the fear, also hidden under a forced gaiety, of the horrible death that threatened them all.[28]

The influence of Coleridge's *Biographia Literaria* is clear throughout as Graves attempts to define poetry and his own poetic practice, but also that of Sir James Frazer's comparative study of mythology and religion, *The Golden Bough*, in which poetry is portrayed, as it is in Graves's book, as a kind of primitive magic with the poet as its priest. Most of Graves's favourite poets are brought in, from Chaucer, Skelton and Shakespeare, through the Romantics, to Hardy, Housman and Sorley. There is also a long passage, almost certainly autobiographical, to the reader on 'The Necessity of Arrogance' in the poet.

Although Graves would later judge *On English Poetry* 'very badly written and inaccurate', he also pointed out that by the time he started writing it in 1920 he had 'already planned a line that [he] had been following ever since'.[29] *On English Poetry*, for all its immaturity, is important, the first book of its time to take a truly psychological approach to poetry using modern psychological methods.[30] It was the inspiration for a far better-known study of what would be called 'close reading' in poetry, *Seven Types of Ambiguity*, according to its author, William Empson. Empson was particularly struck by Graves's insistence on the importance of 'the underlying associations of words, rather than their surface meaning', allowing for ambiguity and equivocacy in language.[31] Graves's most striking example of this theory, from Webster's *The Duchess of Malfi* (when Ferdinand, gazing at the dead duchess through tears, says ambiguously 'Mine eyes dazzle'), had almost certainly been pointed out to him by Percy Simpson, his tutor at St John's, in his introduction to Elizabethan and Jacobean literature.

Although Blunden had tried to persuade John Middleton Murry, for whom he now worked on the *Athenaeum*, to serialize *On English Poetry*, he failed, and when it was published, first by Knopf in America in May 1922, then four months later by Heinemann in England, it was not a commercial success. Graves, who had already revised it nine times before sending it to press, had also to pay for the further extensive corrections he made in the proofs, eating up what few royalties he might expect.

When the book came out in England in September 1922, Rivers was no longer alive to see it, having died of a strangulated hernia in June that year at the age of 58. It was the second unexpected death of a valued friend in less than a month: Walter Raleigh had died of typhus fever, aged only 60, on 13 May.[32] Graves found these two deaths particularly hard to bear. He had already begun planning a new book of criticism that he had intended to dedicate to both men, since both had helped to inspire it. Based on Raleigh's suggestion for a B.Litt. thesis, 'The Illogical Element in English Poetry', and drawing partly on what Graves had learned of psychology from Rivers, *Poetic Unreason* (as it became) focused on the 'supra-logical element in poetry', which the author believed could only be fully understood 'by close analysis of the latent associations of the words used'. Rivers is quoted and referred to on a number of occasions in the book. It was in part a continuation of Graves's ideas in *On English Poetry*, which would also develop into yet another work inspired by his discussions with Rivers, *The Meaning of Dreams* (1924), an introduction of sorts, Graves claimed, to *Poetic Unreason*.[33] *Poetic Unreason* would demonstrate even more convincingly the breadth of Graves's reading when it was published in 1925; admiration for most of the major writers is mixed with passages on less well-known writers such as the Earl of Rochester and Francis Quarles. It would also consolidate the theory of 'close reading', another refutation, if one were needed, of Laura Riding's later claim to have invented the concept.

The deaths of Raleigh and Rivers by early summer 1922 ended the first year of the Graves family's time at Islip on a note of loss, which would be repeated frequently throughout their four years there and which would cause Robert to describe it as a period of 'many deaths and a feeling of bad luck'[34] despite its optimistic beginning. One of the few positive things to emerge from Rivers's death had been a reconciliation with Sassoon, who was as devastated as Graves. But their old closeness had gone, leaving Graves rather isolated. He had already quarrelled with Ottoline Morrell and there would be a temporary rift with Richard Hughes, despite their work together on *Oxford Poetry 1921*, which had appeared successfully in the autumn of 1921. More recent friends, who might have filled the gap, had left or were about to leave Oxford, Lawrence chief among them.

Lawrence, who had been advising Winston Churchill on the situation in the Middle East since early 1921, enlisted in September 1922 in the Royal Air Force as 'Aircraftsman T. E. Shaw', but would be forced to leave for the Army Tank Corps until his reinstatement in the RAF in the mid-1920s. Graves would bring out the extraordinary nature of Lawrence's choice in 'The Clipped Stater', in which the god-like Alexander the Great chooses to become an ordinary soldier:

> He is enrolled now in the frontier-guard
> With gaol-birds and the press-gang's easy captures;
> Where captains who have felt the Crown's displeasure,
> But have thought suicide too direct and hard,
>
> Teach him a new tongue and the soldier's trade,
> To which the trade *he* taught has little likeness.
> He glories in his foolish limitations:
> At every turn his hands and feet are stayed.[35]

The sacrifice demanded of Alexander is having to receive his meagre soldier's pay in a coin ('stater') which bears his head, but 'clipped' off at the neck and hair, an indignity he accepts, knowing he must keep 'the finite course he has resolved on'.[36]

There were further deaths, too, in those four years, most notably that of George Mallory, who died during his third attempt to climb Mount Everest, only 800 feet (245 metres) from the summit, on either 8 or 9 June 1924. (Since his climbing partner, Andrew Irvine, died with him, it is not known whether they had reached their goal.) Graves had visited Mallory and his wife Ruth regularly since leaving Charterhouse and attended the last lecture Mallory gave at Oxford in January 1924, when John Graves entertained them both in his rooms at St John's.

Only a year after Mallory's death in June 1924, a much younger friend, 'Sam' Harries, who had been a scholar at Balliol and a frequent visitor at 'World's End', died suddenly in India. Robert and Nancy had known him since 1922 and were close enough to want to name their fourth child, born in January 1924, after him. Robert remembered Harries in *Good-bye to All That* as an odd combination of 'communist, atheist, keen footballer, and fan of experimental film', though 'most puritanical in matters of sex'.[37]

But the Graves's growing unhappiness at Islip had as much to do with Robert and Nancy themselves and the decisions they had made as with the outside world. The cottage in winter was no longer the idyllic country retreat it had seemed when they moved in, in midsummer; now the damp, the draughts and the lack of indoor sanitation made it far less attractive. Already by 15 October 1921, Graves was telling Barrett of the 'rough passage' he and his family were having and of 'an accumulation of unpaid bills'.[38] With Nancy in the later stages of pregnancy and suffering constant ill-health, he found himself burdened more than ever with domestic responsibilities and resorted to his wartime technique of 'getting through things somehow'.[39] When his mother came to stay on 21 November her initial concerns were with their 'bad' water supply and lack of money. But after a few days she was more worried by Nancy's 'low and restless' state, which all Robert's 'hard work' and 'unselfishness' seemed unable to relieve.[40] By the time she left ten days later she had had 'a very trying time indeed', yet was full of praise not only for Robert's unselfishness but also for Nancy's devotion to him and the children.[41] She believed that if their health allowed, they would get through it.

Only five days later, however, on 5 December, a telegram arrived at Erinfa from Robert, begging 'Claree' to come to help them, 'as the Doctor had forbidden Nancy to go on working'.[42] Neither parent wanted Clarissa to go, fearing another bad nervous breakdown like her most recent one in 1915, but eventually Clarissa was (to quote her father) 'sacrificed'. She spent the next few months at 'World's End', helping out, while Nancy left in early January 1922 to stay with her father and Edie near Brighton for the birth of her third child, Catherine, born after an anxious delay on 4 February.

Remarkably, despite his increased domestic responsibilities, Graves had another volume of poems, *Whipperginny*, more or less finished by the end of the year, when he sent it to Marsh. Since he planned to dedicate the volume to him, it was unfortunate that Marsh found the poems in it obscure, a modern trend he deplored; while acknowledging 'the passion and spirit' in the verse, he failed to 'catch the drift', especially in 'The Feather Bed', a long poem that would eventually be published in a separate volume.[43] Graves assured Marsh that he was *not* wasting his time on 'the unnecessary', reminding him: 'I am not a leisured scribbler; I do my fourteen hours [of housework] a day seven days of the week and hardly have time to touch pen and ink.'[44] When he offered to withdraw the dedication, however, Marsh insisted he keep it and included three of the collection's poems in *Georgian Poetry 1920–1922*.

It would be a long time before the publication of *Whipperginny* was settled with Heinemann in England and Knopf in America, and life continued to be difficult for Graves. Although Nancy had had an easy confinement, for once, and a break from her thyroid problem after the birth, she fell ill again in April 1922. And when, after her recovery, she insisted on one of her favoured 'bursts for freedom' – a trip by caravan to the West Country at the end of July – the holiday went disastrously wrong. Robert made the best of it in entertaining accounts to friends, explaining to Blunden for instance that their caravan was one 'by courtesy only, a very ancient baker's cart drawn by a horse (born (actually!) before the invention of motorcars)'.[45] Knowing very little about horses, they learned how to feed them 'from blokes by the way', he told another friend, and on their advice bought a whip, a 'skidpan' and nose bag.[46] They lost Nancy's poodle, Smuts, on the journey, fortunately returned to them in a taxi by William and Edie Nicholson with whom they had been staying at Rottingdean. Travelling at most ten miles a day, they failed to meet their two main targets, Thomas Hardy at Dorchester and Nancy's old nurse at Tiverton. And when they did succeed in getting to the farm of Sassoon's friend Frank Prewett, near Abingdon, they found him deeply depressed. Lytton Strachey was out when they called. Not surprisingly, Robert's plan to write his new book at night was equally a failure: he was simply too exhausted. But he was able, retrospectively, to make literary capital out of this unfortunate holiday in an entertaining account in *Good-bye to All That*.[47]

Exaggeration must always be allowed for in Graves's recollections and there were happier and more fulfilling interludes at Islip, especially when he had time to spend on his own work. His poetry, as always, came first and *Whipperginny* was ready for the agent he had acquired in 1919, J. B. Pinker.[48] The long poem of which Marsh had disapproved, 'The Feather Bed', was reserved for a small separate volume and, when eventually published, would not be a great critical success. But it would be the means of introducing Graves to the small but highly respected firm run by Leonard and Virginia Woolf, the Hogarth Press, who would go on to publish five more of his works.[49] Leonard Woolf would also agree to publish a collection of poetry recommended by Graves, John Crowe Ransom's *Grace After Meat*, and would invite Graves to write an introduction to it. He would also accept two other recommendations from Graves, Laura Riding's *The Close Chaplet* (1926) and *Voltaire: A Biographical Fantasy* (1927). And when Pinker was looking for a publisher for what would become *The Meaning of Dreams*, which Constable thought 'too dangerous' for them, Graves suggested offering it to the Hogarth Press: 'It is not a book that will sell by commercial advertising and, if at all, [will sell] on its own merits and among a highbrow public. So please try Woolf with it.'[50] Enclosing an essay on *Contemporary Techniques of Poetry* in another letter to his agent in 1925, he would observe: 'Hogarth Press is the only firm for a book of its kind.'[51] Blunden had alerted Graves to Leonard Woolf's admiration for his work just a few months before Graves advised Pinker to try him with *The Feather Bed*, though he was well aware of the Hogarth Press by then. And T. S. Eliot had almost certainly sent *The Feather Bed* poems to Leonard Woolf after rejecting them as unsuitable for the *Criterion*.

Graves did not visit the Hogarth Press in person until the end of April 1925, but told Sassoon (who had) that he 'very much want[ed]' to meet the Woolfs as early as February 1924.[52] When he did finally turn up unannounced at 52 Tavistock Square on 24 April 1925, Virginia feared at first that 'the bolt eyed blue shirted, shockheaded hatless man in a blue overcoat' standing 'goggling' on their doorstep was one of the 'genius[es]' who wrote for Leonard at the *Nation and Athenaeum*, anxious to 'unburden himself'.[53] Although Graves had come only from the nearby London Zoo, which he had been visiting with his children and Sassoon, he seemed to Virginia to have been 'rushing through the air at 60 miles an hour and to have alighted temporarily'.[54] Once Graves identified himself and had been offered tea, she had nearly three hours in which to observe him:

> The poor boy is all emphasis protestation and pose. He has a crude likeness to Shelley, save that his nose is a switchback and his lines blurred. But the consciousness of genius is bad for people. He stayed till 7.15 (we were going to 'Caesar and Cleopatra'...) and had at last to say so, for he was so thick in the delight of explaining his way of life to us that no bee stuck faster to honey. He cooks, his wife cleans; 4 children are brought up in the elementary school; the villagers give them vegetables; they were married in Church; his wife calls herself Nancy Nicolson [*sic*]; won't go to Garsington, said to him I must have a house for nothing; on a river; in a village with a square church tower; near but not on a railway – all of which, as she knows her mind, he procured. Calling herself Nicolson has sorted her friends into sheep and goats. All this to us sounded like the usual self-consciousness of young men, especially as he threw in, gratuitously, the information that he descends from dean rector, Bishop, Von Ranker [*sic*] etc. etc. etc.: only in order to say that he despises them. Still, still, he is a nice ingenuous rattle headed young man ... Then we were offered a ticket for the Cup tie, to see wh. Graves has come to London after 6 years; cant travel in a train without being sick; is rather proud of his sensibility.[55]

Allowing for a tendency to exaggerate not unlike Graves's own, Virginia's account of someone physically striking, possibly a genius but undoubtedly still very young and uncertain of himself, is a fair picture of Graves aged nearly 30.

An equally revealing reaction to Graves at this time comes from the poet who would be published by the Hogarth Press through Graves's efforts, John Crowe Ransom. Graves's first letter to Ransom, in mid-1922, went astray and it was only through a shared friend at Oxford, William ('Bill') Elliott, that Ransom learnt of it. His own first letter, of 11 July 1922, was full of praise for Graves's work, especially *The Pier-Glass*, which Bill Elliott had shown him. Ransom also included some of his own recent verse, which he was thinking of dedicating to Graves. This was followed up with the manuscript of *Grace After Meat*, which Graves had placed with the Hogarth Press. When it was published in October 1924 with its introduction by Graves, it also carried a dedication of the book to him from Ransom. Meantime, Graves would turn the lengthy preface of *The Feather Bed* (1923) into a verse-letter to Ransom.

Ransom himself would promote Graves's work in America, initially with a review of *On English Poetry* in the third number of the small but prestigious poetry magazine he ran from Vanderbilt University, with fellow poets Allen Tate, Donald Davidson and others. *The Fugitive*, as it was called, also requested two of Graves's poems for its next number.[56]

The relationship between Graves and Ransom would be confined to correspondence. But, coming as it does at a critical point in Graves's development, it adds useful insights into his poetry collections between 1922 and 1925. While Graves would be responsible for introducing an important American poet to the British public, via the Hogarth Press, Ransom would be directly responsible for altering the whole course of Graves's life in 1926 by introducing him to Laura Riding.

Graves started reading and admiring Laura's poems in the *Fugitive* in 1923 and was particularly impressed by 'The Quids', which had won the group's annual prize in 1924 and was brought to his notice by another admirer, Sam Harries, according to Nancy.[57] A teasing poem, which satirizes the literary world as Riding has experienced – or, as a woman, *not* experienced – it, it reveals a sophisticated and ingenious use of ideas and concepts (which Graves shared), centring around the Latin word 'quid', meaning 'something':

A quid here and there gyrated in place position,
While many essential quids turned inside-out
For the fun of it
And a few refused to be anything but
Simple, unpredicated copulatives.
Little by little, this commotion of quids,
By threes, by tens, by casual millions,
Squirming within the state of things,
The metaphysical acrobats,
The naked, immaterial quids,
Turned inside on themselves
And came out all dressed –

Each similar quid of the inward same,
Each similar quid dressed in a different way –
The quids' idea of a holiday.[58]

When Ransom told Laura of Graves's praise in 1925, she insisted that he send a collection of her poems to the Englishman who, as she knew, had already placed Ransom's poems with the Hogarth Press. Together with the poems, Ransom sent praise: 'She is a remarkable person ... and of tremendous promise.'[59] A kind man, he was evidently anxious to help someone who had made it clear how 'tired', 'strained' and frustrated she was at the failure to get her work recognized. Even after she had left Nashville to find work in New York, she continued to bombard Ransom with enquiries about Graves's progress in placing them, and by September 1925 Ransom's recommendation of her work to Graves is more qualified. But he clearly recognizes her as a force of nature and the word 'remarkable' is again to the fore:

> She is a brilliant young woman, much more so in her prose and conversation even than in her verse. She was recently divorced from her husband, a Louisville College professor. She has had a remarkable career – up from the slums, I think, much battered about as a kid, and foreign (perhaps Polish Jew?) by birth. English is not native to her, nor is the English tradition, greatly to her mortification. As a poet, she cannot to save her life as a general thing, achieve her customary distinction in the regular verse forms. And she tries perhaps to put more into poetry than it will bear. With these misgivings I will go as far as you or anybody in her praise ... She is very fine personally but very intense for company.[60]

Ransom's letter would have irritated Riding greatly had she seen it, but it clearly intrigued Graves, who, encouraged by her, applied shortly afterwards for a teaching post at her alma mater, Cornell University. Although nothing would come of the application, it led in 1926 to the beginning of a closer relationship with her that would change the course of Graves's life.

18

FROM PSYCHOLOGY TO PHILOSOPHY AND BEYOND

In India you, crossed-legged these long years waiting
Beneath your peepul tree, the spread of thought
That canopies your loneliness and mine ...

'To M[allik] in India'[1]

By the time Graves began to correspond with Ransom in the second half of 1922, he was already involved with the person who came to replace Rivers as his friend and guide, a 43-year-old Indian philosopher, Basanta Mallik. Mallik's influence is evident even before Rivers's death when Graves, in starting to plan his B.Litt. thesis, considered calling it *Poetry in Conflict and Reconstruction*: Mallik's main interest was conflict resolution.

Graves had first met Mallik at a reading that Graves gave to the Oxford Lotus Club, an undergraduate society of approximately 50 per cent Asian membership. The paper he read on that occasion was almost certainly an early draft of the first section of his B.Litt., which he had been invited to read to students at Leeds University in December 1922. He would call it 'What is Bad Poetry?', one of his central concerns in the book that eventually served as his thesis, *Poetic Unreason*.

It was an unlikely alliance, for, as Graves himself admitted, his education had given him 'a contempt against anyone of non-European race'.[2] (This included most Jews, he confessed, with the exception of Sassoon.) But he did not experience such prejudice with Mallik, who displayed none of the characteristics of a 'subject race', according to Graves.

Graves claimed to have 'loathed philosophy' until he met Mallik, just as Mallik claimed to have 'loathed poetry' until he met Graves.[3] Mallik's philosophy, as far as Graves understood it, was 'a development of formal metaphysics, but with a characteristically Indian insistence on ethics': 'He believed in no hierarchy of ultimate values or the possibility of any unifying religion or ideology.'[4] Mallik's relativistic theory would make its influence felt most strongly in *Poetic Unreason*, where the question of using terms like 'good' or 'bad' is discussed in literary, rather than ethical terms, Graves's conclusion being that he did 'not see the possibility of an absolute right or wrong, God against the Devil, so in an aesthetic sense I hold that the term Bad is in effect only relative'.[5]

Mallik visited 'World's End' frequently after their first meeting, bringing with him some of his loyal disciples, a few of whom like Sam Harries remained close friends of Graves after the philosopher left Oxford. Their long discussions together, often over a plate of 'wonderful vegetable stew' cooked by Mallik, made Graves realize that it was 'scholastic philosophy' he disliked, rather than the 'abstract ideas' they debated so enthusiastically.[6]

Another link with Mallik was anthropology, which Mallik had studied for two years before turning to philosophy. As a Bengali he was familiar with the supremacy of the Mother Goddess in some interpretations of Hinduism, in which, incidentally, there was a white goddess as well as a black one. This tied in with Rivers's studies of early matriarchal cultures and was almost certainly a factor in the development of Graves's theories about the White Goddess. Mallik and Graves both also had a shared belief in 'strict personal morality consistent with scepticisms of social morality'.[7] One of Mallik's disciples, Alan Collingridge, has left an engaging account of their discussions at Islip that emphasizes how intuitive Graves's thought processes were, 'like a flash of lightening', compared with Mallik's carefully constructed 'crown of jewels'.[8] However much Graves differed from Mallik, he admired him greatly as one of an elect group of three people who, he claimed, could truly 'think': the other two were T. E. Lawrence and Laura Riding.[9]

After Mallik returned to India in October 1923, his influence lived on for a time in Graves's work, poetry as well as prose. All five poetry collections published between 1923 and 1925 show signs of Mallik's philosophy; even *Whipperginny* (1923) and *The Feather Bed* (1923), written largely under Rivers's influence, were revised in the light of his new mentor's theories. 'The Lord Chamberlain Tells of a Famous Meeting', for instance, one of the few poems in *Whipperginny* to allude to war, in which two princes 'of East and West' meet 'over a ragged pack of cards' to resolve the danger of war between their respective nations, can be seen as a commentary on the relationship between Mallik and Graves, both greatly concerned with the question of conflict resolution.

Those collections written wholly under Mallik's sway – *Mock Beggar Hall* (1924), *Welchman's Hose* (1925) and *The Marmosite's Miscellany* (1925) – were largely undiluted by more accessible poems as *Whipperginny* had been. *Mock Beggar Hall*, as Graves points out, was 'almost wholly philosophical ... the result of my meeting with Basanta Mallik'. T. E. Lawrence's response when Graves sent it to him was that it was 'not the sort of book that one would put under one's pillow at night'.[10] It contained an entire play by Mallik, an actionless drama, *Interchange of Selves*, in which (in Graves's words) his 'Indian philosopher' presents 'a new philosophic system in brief through the persons of a practical man, a mystic and a man with your English genius for compromise'.[11] (It was written in such poor English that Graves felt it necessary to rewrite it before including it, initially, in *The Winter Owl* of 1923.)

John Crowe Ransom's response to *Mock Beggar Hall* pinpoints its shortcomings as a poetry collection; while praising the 'tremendous variety and contrariety of thoughts and images' it aroused in him, particularly 'Full Moon', he found it for the most part 'half discursive with reason and half focused into poetry' – and therefore 'too caviar to the general'.[12]

A year later Mallik's influence was still detectable in *Welchman's Hose* in poems such as 'Alice', where Alice speculates on the relationship between the world outside the looking glass and the one seen through it, asking herself in relation to the 'chessboard personages' she meets:

... 'Suppose I stood behind
And viewed the fireplace of Their drawing-room

From hearthrug level, why must I assume
That what I'd seen would need to correspond
With what I now see? And the rooms beyond?'[13]

An interesting question though it is for the philosopher, it is too cerebral
for the average reader, despite being leavened with Graves's usual wit. Even
the critics found this kind of poetry dull and were largely dismissive. The
main interest of *Welchman's Hose* lies in three poems that show Graves
returning yet again to the First World War, one of them a satire closer
to Sassoon's methods than his own, 'Sergeant-Major Money'. Based on
a real incident that Graves would also include in *Good-bye to All That*
(though with an added ironic twist), it tells of two Welsh coalminers
who are driven so hard by their sergeant major that they kill him. But its
concluding stanza points to the impossibility of applying the usual moral
standards in war:

Well, we couldn't blame the officers, they relied on Money;
    We couldn't blame the pitboys, their courage was grand;
Or, least of all blame Money, an old stiff surviving
    In a New (bloody) Army he couldn't understand.[14]

In 'A Letter from Wales', another verse-letter to Sassoon in effect, Graves
speculates further on the effect of the war not only on himself (named
Richard Rolls in the poem), but also on Sassoon (called Abel Wright), both
of whom he claims died in the war and have returned to life as different
people. It is a clever poem, as might be expected from Graves, and highly
philosophical:

Who are we?...
That is, again, of course, if I am I –
This isn't Descartes' philosophic doubt,
But, as I say, a question of identity.[15]

It is also a revealing poem, hinting at how deeply shaken Graves, and he
believes Sassoon, have been by their experiences in France. The clear
implication is that something was destroyed in both of them in the war
and that the two men who returned were not the same people after it. The
narrator's questions emerge as signs of this loss of certainty in a life shaken to

its core. This permanent uncertainty and the anxiety caused by it conclude
the poem with a question that is so difficult it cannot even be formulated:

> What I'm asking really isn't 'Who am I?'
> Or 'Who are you?' (you see my difficulty?)
> But a stage before that, '*How am I to put*
> *The question that I'm asking you to answer?*'[16]

The third 'war' poem in *Welchman's Hose*, 'At the Games', pursues similar
questions but more light-heartedly, as a Frenchman and an Englishman, who
have met and both been wounded in the First World War, embark on a long
philosophical debate based obliquely on the controversy over a boxing match
between a Frenchman and an Englishman in the Olympic Games of 1924.
(Graves was awarded a prize for his poem by the Olympic Games Committee.)
They discuss, among other things, what war is, the rights and wrongs of it,
Graves's own ambivalent attitude clearly reflected in the Englishman's position:

> Eng[lishman] ... You have in France
> > As many, I dare say, as we in England,
> > Enthusiasts who wish to end all War,
> > To wipe it from the world with 'never again'?
>
> Fr[enchman]
> > I have wished the same myself, in hospital
> > While waiting for my thirteenth operation.
>
> Eng.
> > So too have I, and in the trenches even,
> > When the barrage rolled forward, wreathed in gas.
> > But now, I am doubting whether War, as such,
> > War, even modern War, is man's worst fault.
>
> > Is conflict so much uglier seen in War
> > When patent, more dramatically staged,
> > Than seen in Commerce, Social life, the Arts,
> > Disguised in their official mask of Peace?

The most entertaining of the verse collections influenced by Mallik, *The
Marmosite's Miscellany*, originated, Sassoon believed, in that same trip to

London Zoo which led to a visit at the Woolfs at Tavistock Square, though Graves implies in his opening lines that it was at a 'World Exhibition' that he saw the marmosets.[17] After appearing in *Calendar* magazine in September 1925, the title poem would be published with the addition of a few other poems by the Hogarth Press in December 1925, nine years before Leonard Woolf by a neat quirk of fate acquired his own signature marmoset. A satirical poem of 421 lines, Graves felt it prudent to sign what he proudly attributed to Samuel Butler's influence with the pseudonym John Doyle. But his gentle digs at contemporaries such as Aldous Huxley, who 'juggled up a skull and a loofah', or John Masefield, 'astride on his notable nag, / Its name was Right Royalty, out of Grand Slam', do not call for such caution. Written in a week and 'patched up' in two,[18] 'The Marmosite's Miscellany' is also a light-hearted glance at religion and a quick look at his own 'principles', which coincide quite closely with Mallik's at this point:

> I have, but only one or two,
>> Firm enough foundation for a busy mind.
> First to reverence God, but not from any pew;
> No Frankenstein monster of a furious mind.
>
>> ...
>
> Next, to myself and my neighbours at once
>> I owe this respect without favour or fear...[19]

Speaking through the marmoset, the poet goes on to voice his respect for the apparently irrational 'maunderings of the maniac' and the moon as 'the mistress of escape and pity', two more hints at the White Goddess to come.

Graves dedicated *The Marmosite's Miscellany*, in verse, 'To M[allik] in India'.[20] Mallik had been back in India only two years at most when this poem was written; they had seemed 'long years' to Graves who, by the end of 1925, still counted Mallik among the 'few friends' of this Islip period. They had been years, he tells Mallik in terms which suggest that the war is never far from his mind, when:

> In England I
> Bruised, battered, crushed often in mind and spirit
> But soon revived again like the torn grass
> When, after battle, broken guns and caissons
> Are hauled off and the black swoln corpses burnt.[21]

One of the other few close friends made at Islip, also in mid-1922, who might have been expected to have a more positive effect on Graves's poetic development, was Edith Sitwell. Known, together with her younger brothers Osbert and Sacheverell, as one of the 'stormy petrels' of modern literature, she was also regarded in her own right as the High Priestess of Modernist Poetry. This was partly due to her editorship of the annual poetic anthology *Wheels*, which, though not aggressively avant-garde, was seen as a counter-balance to Marsh's more conventional *Georgian Poetry* anthology, which Graves himself was beginning to question. When she and Graves met in April 1922, Edith had just completed her highly experimental 'entertainment', *Façade*, in which her poetry was accompanied with music by William Walton. She would leave her mark on Graves's work, but more on his prose than his poetry. His admiration for T. S. Eliot, for instance, whose *The Waste Land* was published the year Graves and Sitwell met, owed much to her belief in Eliot, repeated in her many letters to Graves between 1922 and 1926. Graves would include a long, respectful passage on *The Waste Land* in *Poetic Unreason* in 1925.

Their correspondence had started on 5 April 1922, when Edith wrote to say how disappointed she had been to miss seeing him on her visit to Oxford to read her poetry. Her letter was accompanied by a copy of the poems from *Façade* and an invitation to London, to read his own work to the Anglo-French Poetry Society she ran with her ex-governess, Helen Rootham, and Arnold Bennett's French wife, Marguerite. Despite initial doubts over Nancy's health, Robert went on 29 April, taking with him a signed copy of a book that underlined how much they shared in content but how widely they differed in poetic technique, *Country Sentiment*. (In the event he forgot to present his book.)

His view of Edith's poetry at this point was decidedly patronizing: 'I find her very interesting as an extreme case of the romantic poet writing by free association and at any rate on the surface pleasant,' he explained to Sassoon, who was annoyed that Graves had become friends with Edith at a time when Sassoon was angry with Osbert Sitwell for his attack on Graves and Turner's appearance in *Georgian Poetry*.[22] A year later Graves would review her *Bucolic Comedies* kindly,[23] but as his numerous other comments on her poetry show, he was not entirely in sympathy with her technique. She was so hurt by his criticisms in *Poetic Unreason*, for instance, that she stopped writing to him for a time in 1925. He managed to repair matters with his Hogarth Press Essay, *Contemporary Techniques of Poetry: A Political Analogy* (1925), which he dedicated 'To Edith Sitwell in All Friendship'. 'A treatise on the various/rival techniques of modern poetry', according to Graves, in which Laura Riding's 'Quids' is singled out for praise long before he met her, Edith admired as an attempt to 'straighten out the muddle about modern poetry'.[24] She quoted from *Contemporary Techniques* in her own Hogarth essay 'Poetry and Criticism', attributing her concern with 'texture' in verse to him.

The relationship between these two unlikely friends was carried on mainly by letter, though Edith did pay one visit to 'World's End' a year after their introduction at the Anglo-French Society. She had been reading her poetry at Oxford University again and gone on to spend the weekend with the Graveses. The visit had had an unfortunate start when Graves cycled down to the station with an injured arm to meet her; unable to manage both his bicycle and her suitcase, he remarked as she struggled along with it herself that it was nice to see a fine strapping woman (she was strikingly tall) 'who could carry her own suitcase', not a remark she appreciated.[25] Once safely installed in 'World's End', however, Edith surprised Robert and Nancy by her gentle domesticity. Whereas her poetry had led them to expect something of the 'stormy petrel', she spent the time 'sitting on the sofa and hemming handkerchiefs'.[26] She also boasted of being 'a very good knitter'. And, unlike some of Robert's friends, she got on well with Nancy. This may have had something to do with another story she told of Robert warning her as they approached his cottage to 'leave Nancy alone and she'll leave you alone'; he had issued a similar warning, it transpired, to Nancy as he left for the station.

The friendship would continue for the next few years, despite differences of opinion on poetry, for they also shared some important values. They were both dedicated poets, both suffering financial hardships in the cause and writing prose only when absolutely necessary to earn money. Each was fascinated, at least for a time in Graves's case, with fairy tales and the world of childhood, Graves reviewing Sitwell's *Sleeping Beauty* in 1924.[27] They both believed in the supra-natural, Edith writing eagerly to Robert of her discovery of a rare book on witches and dedicating her 'ghost' poem to Robert and Nancy. (Having sent them the volume in which it appeared, *The Sleeping Beauty*, inscribed 'For Robert Graves and Nancy Nicholson in admiration from Edith Sitwell', she was very cross later to find that Robert had sold it when short of money.) Robert in turn, included his verse-letter to Edith, 'The College Debate: "That this House approves the Trend of Modern Poetry"' in *Welchman's Hose*. Both had a quick wit and well-developed sense of humour: when he sent her *Whipperginny* in 1923, for instance, besides praising certain poems in it, she could not resist adding a comment about one of the many poets of whom she disapproved: 'On Tuesday next, either I am going to kill Alfred Noyes, or he is going to kill me...'[28] Like Sassoon she took a particular dislike to the popular versifier Humbert Wolfe: '... such a tiresome little man ... such effeminate little whimperings ... sometimes he gets into my woodwork as Sachie [Sacheverell Sitwell] expresses it'.[29] Both were essentially kind and generous beneath a sometimes abrasive surface, however, especially to younger poets they thought promising: Peter Quennell, for instance, who had first visited the 'World's End' as a 16-year-old schoolboy in 1921, and Dylan Thomas, whom Edith would later take under her wing. Edith, eight years older than Graves and rather motherly towards him, showed something of this desire to encourage in her response to Graves's poetry: though she disliked the turn he had taken towards psychology and philosophy, her comments on both *Whipperginny* and *Welchman's Hose*, for example, are wholly positive. She simply picks out what she can honestly praise – ' "A Dewdrop" is a dream of a poem', she comments on *Whipperginny* – and ignores the rest. Fortunately, theirs was a relationship uncomplicated by any question of romance; beside the difference in age, Edith was more drawn to homosexual men, as her attraction to Sassoon and the Russian painter Pavel Tchelitchew showed.

When the friendship ended, it would have more to do with outside interference than any personal differences. Looking back on 1926 in *Goodbye to All That*, Graves wrote – undoubtedly under the influence of Laura Riding, who believed that, with her, time had stopped – that '1926 was yesterday when the autobiographical part of my life was fast approaching its end'.[30] With it ended many of his friendships, including that with Edith. It may be that Laura had sensed Edith's hostility towards her and her work, and had struck first. Perhaps she had sensed that Edith, in her words to T. S. Eliot, found Laura's poetry 'the biggest bore'.[31] The final break seems to have come when Edith read an article in *transitions* in 1927 in which Laura, then living with Robert, included her with Eliot and others as poets who felt the need to caricature a tainted ordinary language before they could communicate directly. She was persuaded not to pursue the matter further by Sassoon, who had become a valued friend by 1927, but made it clear that she was desisting, 'not out of consideration for Robert's feelings, (he should have kept her in her place)', but simply because Sassoon had requested it.[32] Further criticism of her work in the Graves/Riding collaboration, *A Survey of Modernist Poetry* (1927), would be the final straw. From having once thought of Graves as 'a tentative English nightengale [*sic*]', by 1927 Edith began to regard him as 'an American loon or screech owl'.[33]

Graves described the friendships that mattered most to him at 'World's End', including Edith's, in *Good-bye to All That*. He also referred to the many troubles that dogged him there, in particular the deaths and absences of a number of those friends and his struggle to find a way of continuing to write poetry while making enough money to support his family. But there is one problem he omits, perhaps not consciously: his relationship with Nancy during this period. There are general references to her ill-health and her two confinements. But apart from his hint in 'Houses in My Life' that it was 'domestic crises' at 'World's End' which brought about his eventual separation from Nancy, he says very little of their relationship. And in contemporary letters to friends he insists how happy they are despite their problems. At the beginning of 1924, for instance, he hotly denies the 'drudging domestic duties' Sassoon refers to, though he does confess to being 'absolutely broke' and happy to accept his offer of a loan.[34] At the same time he warns Sassoon that:

> friendship at 'World's End' implies friendships towards the whole damn lot of us, and until you realize that I am completely satisfied with this life, debts and all, and am not so far as I know Nancy's drudge or 'the Hen-Pecked Husband or Hammond's Depressed Villager or the Impoverished Genius with the Awful Wife and the Squalling Brats' ... you and I are at too great cross-purposes to be really friends again for a while...[35]

Nancy herself has left little on record, apart from conversations she is reputed to have had with a friend complaining of Robert's clumsiness in sexual matters and his excessive demands in that area. We do not even know whether she planned or welcomed her two further pregnancies at Islip, though there is no doubt of her devotion to Catherine and Sam after their arrival in 1922 and 1924 respectively. A visual rather than verbal person, she seems to have been even less ready than Robert to talk about their marriage.

Although Robert himself was prevented by a pronounced sense of loyalty to the women in his life from discussing their relationship in prose, however, his poems between 1921 and 1925 suggest that he could not keep his feelings out of his verse. This is especially true of the more personal ones in *Whipperginny*, written before Rivers's influence is fully felt. The title alone hints at disillusionment with women, since 'Whipperginny' is among other things an archaic term for a promiscuous woman. A failure to connect, even in the intimacy of the sexual act, is implied in both 'Children of Darkness' and 'Song of Contrariety', in which 'love shall come at your command / Yet will not stay'.[36] And in 'The Unicorn and the White Doe', the narrator describes the unicorn's fruitless pursuit of the white doe, asking despairingly: 'Where have you fled from me? / I pursue, you fade...'[37] The narrator of 'A Lover Since Childhood', 'dazed by the thought' of the beloved, is 'starved for a word or look' to renew his hope.[38] The poet's turbulent feelings of alternating reverence and scorn and his wildly mixed experience of love are spelled out in the ambivalent imagery of 'The Lands of Whipperginny':

> For stern proud psalms from the chapel on the moors
>> Waver in the night wind, their firm rhythm broken,
> Lugubriously twisted to a howling of whores
>> Or lent an airy glory too strange to be spoken.[39]

'Love in Barrenness' presents an even bleaker view of love in *Whipperginny*. Written in 1921, like 'The Unicorn and the White Doe' and 'A Lover Since Childhood',[40] it suggests that Robert's sense of frustration and disillusionment had begun even before the move to Islip. The woman in the poem, though still beautiful in her 'body's inward grace', seems to the poet 'no longer flesh and blood' but as unfeeling and 'set' as a marble statue, almost certainly that of Nike, the Greek goddess of victory. Whereas Nike is winged, however, the statue here is 'wingless', a paradox that draws attention to the barrenness of the situation. This sterility is reflected in the setting, where 'even the long dividing plain / Showed no wealth of sheep or grain'.[41] Patrick Quinn argues convincingly that the 'North Wind' of the final stanza is 'symbolic of the poet's passionate desire' as it 'rises and presses "with lusty force" against the woman's dress', but to no avail.[42]

Although a poem like 'Sullen Moods' in the same 1923 collection shows the narrator excusing his own occasional withdrawals ('Mere indignation at my own / Shortcomings, plagues, uncertainties'),[43] it is an exception and the lack of response is shown to come mainly from the woman, with the situation becoming progressively worse. By *Mock Beggar Hall* (1924) the increasing coldness between the lovers is set out in dramatic terms in 'Full Moon', which transports us to the nightmare landscape of Coleridge's 'The Ancient Mariner' again, and, with it, the sense of an unexpurgated sin:

> And now warm earth was Arctic sea,
>   Each breath came dagger-keen;
> Two bergs of glinting ice were we,
>   The broad moon sailed between;
> There swam the mermaid, tailed and finned,
> And love went by upon the wind. ...[44]

It seems significant that Mock Beggar Hall is the name of a former leper house that Graves dreamt was full of quarrelling ghosts.

The most convincing sign that Graves did not find his situation at Islip entirely satisfactory, however, is his decision to apply for two full-time jobs in 1925. His own explanation was that he needed the money badly, and that the doctor had advised a warmer climate for Nancy, whose health had broken down again badly after the news of Sam Harries's death from typhus in India in July that year. But he had lived with very little money since his marriage in 1918 without seeming to care too much. And he had applied for the first of these jobs at Cornell University *before* Nancy's breakdown and the doctor's recommendation of a warmer climate. In fact, since both jobs depended on his having a degree, Graves's decision must have been taken at least a year earlier when he made a serious effort to complete the B.Litt. thesis he had discussed with Raleigh as far back as 1921. When he started to write his thesis, however, he 'found it difficult to keep to the academic style'[45] and wrote it as a book instead. It was as a typescript of *Poetic Unreason* that he submitted it to Oxford University in December 1924. By the time the university accepted it as a thesis in June 1925, the book had been out three months. Graves's provocative views on such hallowed 'masters' as Milton had not pleased the critics, nor did they fully convince his examiners in the *viva voce* that followed later in June. Although he had 'not convinced his Examiners entirely', as his father recorded with some dismay on 9 June, he was awarded his degree, mainly, he believed, because of Alfred's 'persistence and assistance'.[46] Once his thesis had been submitted, 1925 became an enormously productive year, with seven books published, though none very successfully. Graves was especially dismissive of *John Kemp's Wager*, published by Blackwell's in May that year, 'a Ballad Opera' he had been trying to write under the title *The Hobby Horse* since 1921. Basically a 'play with folk-songs', Graves later described it as 'waste', which 'marked the end of what I might call the folk-song period of my life'.[47]

After Amy had paid the necessary fees to Oxford University Robert wrote at once to Cornell University enquiring about a teaching post. He then set about gathering the required recommendations and by early July, with his father's help again, was able to send off an impressive set of references from the Poet Laureate (Robert Bridges), the Vice-Chancellor of Oxford University (Joseph Wells, also, conveniently, Warden of Wadham College), John Buchan, and another Oxfordshire neighbour, Lord Oxford (Herbert Asquith). Rejected at the interview Cornell arranged for him that same July, it was his father, once again, who came to his rescue. He asked his son, Philip, Robert's elder brother, in Cairo to approach the High Commissioner there, George Lloyd, with a view to offering Robert the well-paid Professorship of English at the newly opened Royal Egyptian University. It was a Foreign Office appointment and both Philip Graves and T. E. Lawrence knew Lloyd well, a hopeful beginning. Alfred also prevailed on Sir Sidney Lee and Sir Israel Gollancz, who joined him in urging Graves to apply for the position in mid-October.

Graves did so immediately, forwarding in addition his Cornell references – 'heavy introductions from Pontine Bob [Bridges]; Colonel Sevenpenny [i.e. John] Buchan; the Vice-Chancellor of this University; and Old Old Squishy Oxford'.[48] T. E. Lawrence and E. M. Forster also agreed to use what influence they still had in Egypt. Even Arnold Bennett, whom Graves suspected of 'crabbing [his] chances',[49] wrote to reassure him that he had, in fact, recommended him for the post, an incident which drew a revealing admission from Graves to Sassoon: 'I have a very poor opinion of other people's opinion of me – though I am fairly happy in my own conceit – and always surprised to find that anyone likes my work or character.'[50] He was still a curious mixture of over-confidence and lack of it.

An official offer from Cairo was finally made in late November, by the same post as the offer of a job from the University of Liverpool, to which Graves had also applied. The Royal Egyptian University offered a reduced salary (of £900 rather than the original £1,500) in the yearly pay, only £75 towards the heavy travelling expenses, and demanded a commitment to serve for a minimum of three years. Graves, to his parents' dismay, turned it down. It may have been Lawrence's positive response to the Cairo proposal, as well as their revised offer of £1,120 per annum, that caused Graves to reverse his decision:

> Even if you hate it, there will be no harm done. The climate is good, the country beautiful, the things admirable, the beings curious: and you are stable enough not to be caught broadside by a mere dislike for your job. Execute it decently, so long as you draw the pay, and enjoy your free hours (plentiful in Egypt, God's laziest country) more fully. Roam about.[51]

Detailed suggestions followed, including books on the subject. In his next letter Lawrence showed an unexpectedly sybaritic side to his nature, telling Graves that 'the important thing is GROPPI's, the Tea-garden shop: and the drink is iced coffee. Straws the process. 2 piastres the means. The children will love Groppi's. Chocolates all right too: but not in summer.'[52]

In all the excitement and relief offered by the Egyptian trip, the publication of *The Marmosite's Miscellany* in December 1925 went virtually unnoticed. Graves was, in any case, thinking of his next book, which he planned to start writing in Cairo. Part of the attraction of the job was the lightness of his workload and he now wrote to remind T. S. Eliot of a proposal he had put to him, a critical survey of Modernist poetry on which he had suggested they collaborate, with Eliot responsible for the American aspect. He had first met Eliot in 1916, when he struck him as 'a startlingly good-looking Italianate young man, with a shy, hunted look',[53] but had not got to know him until the early 1920s, by which time Eliot was editor of the

Criterion.[54] Graves had also consulted him about Ransom's poetry. Eliot was sufficiently interested in the idea of a joint critical survey by 2 November 1925 to start suggesting names of the poets he thought should – or should *not* – be included; Robert Frost, for instance, was excluded by Eliot as 'not modern enough'.[55] He did also, however, warn Graves that he could not do anything 'for a full year'.[56] Writing to congratulate Graves on his Cairo appointment two months later, Eliot asked him to let him know how he got on with the project, provisionally entitled *Untraditional Elements in English Poetry*.

A passage was booked on the S.S. *Ranpura* for 8 January 1926 for Robert, Nancy, their four children and Doris Harrison, the Nicholsons' nanny for the daughter born to them in the early 1920s. William, with his usual generosity, had offered her help to look after Jenny, David, Catherine and Sam, all of whom were in various stages of mumps at this point. 'I suppose it would be hopeless to suggest you coming to Cairo with us ... as my assistant,' Robert wrote to Sassoon just before their departure.[57] Sassoon's polite refusal coincided with a letter from Ransom's protégée, Laura Riding, announcing that she was planning to visit the Graveses in England, as they had suggested, and she seemed a satisfactory substitute. Both he and Nancy appear to have reached a point in their marriage where they welcomed a third person in it. Nancy had never stimulated him much intellectually; once away from England and from friends like Sassoon, he may have feared a void. Laura, a poet he had come to admire greatly and clearly a person of powerful intellect and strong feminist opinions, of a similar age to Nancy, might be the ideal person to fill it.

Laura was, therefore, invited to join them in Egypt as Robert's secretary. She went, however, she told Harriet Monroe of *Poetry* magazine, as a member of Graves's family and imagined that they would soon be literary collaborators. As Laura's letters to her New York friend, Polly Antell, announcing her hasty departure show, she clearly anticipated a great deal from the relationship.[58] A woman of great determination, what Laura 'anticipated' she usually brought about.

19

INTO THE UNKNOWN: CAIRO AND LAURA
RIDING (JANUARY–JUNE 1926)

The trenches are filled in, the houseless dead
Disperse and on the rising murder-storm
Cast their weak limbs, are whirled up overhead
In clouds of fear...[1]

When Graves met Laura Riding off the boat-train from Portsmouth on 3 January 1926, he could not have known how central she was to become to his life. His first reaction, according to William Nicholson, who went with him to Paddington Station, was one of dismay: 'My God! what am I going to do?'[2] A slim woman within a fortnight of her 25th birthday, Laura was a little below medium height, with a reasonably pretty face, made striking by bright blue eyes and an intense, intelligent expression, her shortish hair caught back with a girlish ribbon. But it was her heavy make-up that had disturbed Graves, and also Nicholson apparently, neither of them used to seeing a respectable woman travelling alone wearing make-up. To most Englishmen of their class and time it suggested an attempt to attract men sexually.

Whether you believe this version, which Martin Seymour-Smith claimed was given to him by Graves himself, or Riding's own wholly positive report of the event – the welcome 'warm and courteous', prompt help with her luggage, 'witty pleasantries about her make-up bag'[3] and the smartness, but the modesty of her travelling outfit 'in unemphatic taste' – the different versions are, as Riding's first biographer claims, 'emblematic of the entire fourteen-year Graves-Riding relationship and the ... bickering that followed it'.[4]

They are also a reflection of how widely reactions to Riding differed, the only word usually agreed upon being 'remarkable'. Ransom, for instance, who had used the word in a wholly positive sense when first describing her to Graves, would later accuse her (to another *Fugitive* poet, Allen Tate) of being a 'deep and mischievous person'.[5] Graves's own assessment of her shortly after they parted in 1939 would be equally mixed:

> The Americans only knew her as 'the highest apple on the British intellectual tree'. In England she was assailed as a 'leg-puller', 'crossword puzzle setter', 'Futurist', 'tiresome intellectualist', and so on: none of her books sold more than a few dozen copies, nor did she ever ... consent to give the larger public what it really wanted. She was the one poet of the time who spun, like Arachne, from her own vitals without any discoverable philosophical or literary derivations: and the only one who achieved an unshakable synthesis. Unshakable, that is, if the premise of her unique personal authority were granted, and another more startling one – that historic Time had effectively come to an end.[6]

Nancy Cunard, the English poet and heiress of the shipping line, began by admiring Riding and her poems, publishing some of them at her Hours Press in 1930. But she broke with her not so long after, describing her as 'the so-superior Laura Riding', 'very tense, dominating and quietly American'.[7] 'Like a brooding sultry day,' she claimed, 'there was electricity around, if not visible; a sense of contained conflict.'[8]

It was undoubtedly what Cunard also called this 'other world' quality in Riding that drew people to her like a magnet, but could equally repel them. One critic compared Riding's psychic 'power' to Salvador Dali's, describing it as 'paranoiac delirium ... an active element determined to orient reality

... an assertive conquering force'.[9] Riding's powerful self-belief, he claimed, acted as a form of hypnosis.

The novelist Antonia White, who saw mirrored in herself Riding's vanity, lack of confidence (despite her assertions of uniqueness and superiority) and her sexual oddity – though not Riding's consistency and ruthlessness – pronounced her 'very dangerous but powerful in her personal relations', with a 'pronounced witch-like look'.[10] Allen Tate confirmed from personal experience that she was frighteningly intense.

There were wilder claims, of Riding being a 'megalomaniac', a 'shrill fickle presence' or 'explosively freakish'.[11] One critic referred to her 'baby-doll nastiness' and another former lover, the poet Hart Crane, playing on her married name of Laura Riding Gottschalk, christened her 'Rideschalk Gotting' or 'Laura Riding Roughshod'.[12]

For Graves, however, what emerged from her poetry, letters and their first meeting was what Allen Tate acknowledged, even after their brief affair was over, her 'pervasive ... intelligence'.[13] Graves called it her 'bladed mind' and continued to regard her as 'supreme' even after she had abandoned him.[14] Riding had grown up as the favoured daughter of a working-class Jewish intellectual and had been taught to think for herself from an early age, to debate and to challenge the establishment. She was ideally suited to Graves in this respect. It had been for her mind, for intellectual stimulus, that he had invited her to accompany them to Egypt, though possibly also as a buffer between himself and Nancy in a progressively unsatisfactory relationship.

Riding clearly had other ideas. She had left behind a series of unsuccessful relationships and disappointments in America, first in her student marriage to Louis Gottschalk, then in her dealings with the *Fugitive* poets in Nashville, and finally in New York where, despite what a later lover called her 'superhuman manipulativeness',[15] she had failed to win the recognition she believed her poetry merited. Whether you call it excessively go-getting, as Seymour-Smith did, or simply highly ambitious, she was determined to establish herself in the literary world and saw Graves as a means to that end. If in the process she fell in love with him, that had not been her original motive, though it would make her plan a great deal easier to execute.

Fall in love with him she did, and immediately, her letter to Polly Antell in New York implies. Being Riding, with a strong belief in her magical powers, she viewed this as a superhuman intervention, a concept Graves was more than ready to accept. As she and Graves travelled from Paddington to Oxford that first day through a stormy, flooded countryside, an intense illumination, 'brighter than light', she claimed, lit up their train compartment, leaving them both dazzled and speechless.[16] It was the first of many shared experiences in that 'other world' identified by Nancy Cunard, a world of magic and witches which would cast a spell over Robert, possibly the moment when he first came to believe that 'one lives on a great store of magical power when one *really* loves'.[17] He would hint at times that Laura herself was a witch, though a 'white' witch. Others would see her as a 'black' one. His friend Ken Barrett, after meeting her, called her a 'magician'.

Laura's own belief in her magical powers was a conviction that struck at least one of her biographers as verging on 'derangement'.[18] Rosaleen Graves, a qualified doctor by 1926, who had admired Laura at the start, would regard her by mid-1929 'more as a borderline mental case than anything else': such 'colossal egotism', she claimed, 'is not sane'.[19] Laura's first biographer relates that family and friends remembered her violent temper tantrums as a child, which sometimes ended in fainting fits. They hinted at mental instability in Laura's mother, Sadie, Nathan Reichenthal's second wife, and in a brilliant but damaged younger brother, Bobby, who had attempted suicide and been institutionalized on at least one occasion. Laura herself would come to believe that 'Bobby had inherited his madness ... from his mother', which, as Deborah Baker concludes, leaves open the question of what Laura's mother might have bequeathed to her.[20] Robert and his friends would witness her similar rages and fainting fits as an adult, when she failed to get her own way.

Allen Tate, for one, claimed that Riding was 'the maddest woman' he had ever met and, hearing of her joining Graves in England, 'feared disaster'.[21] 'If Graves isn't already mad – which I'm inclined to suspect from his issuance of a blind invitation to the lady read but unseen,' Tate wrote to Donald Davidson, 'he will be a maniac before a month.'[22] Graves was made of tougher stuff, however; despite his apparent subservience to the women in his life, he was able to look after himself, protected perhaps by his own needs as an artist.

But it is not clear whether he gained or lost more from the relationship. Riding's unshakable faith in her own rightness, for instance, came at a time when Graves was still looking for certainties in a life badly affected by the First World War. This searching had informed some interesting poetry between 1918 and 1925, however, as he had turned first to psychiatry then philosophy for help, and Riding's certainty was not necessarily what he needed as a poet in 1926. (He himself argued that 'tranquillity is of no poetic use'.)[23]

The claim that Riding cured Graves of his neurasthenia is debatable. Rivers had predicted that it would improve with time and by 1926 eight years had passed since the end of the war. And since her arrival coincided with a complete change in Graves's circumstances, relieving him of domestic drudgery and giving him far more time for his own work, his improvement in spirits could be explained by other factors. His temporary relief from money worries, for instance, almost certainly helped.

Riding's insistence on precision of technique has also been cited as a positive influence on Graves. While this would, ironically, lead to her own eventual silence as a poet, however, it did not basically change Graves's poetic practice. He had been drilled endlessly by his father and schoolmasters on the importance of precision in metre and verse forms, and had revised his own verse mercilessly long before Riding's advent – in the case of 'The Troll's Nosegay', for instance, 38 times. His readiness to correct the technique of fellow poets such as Sassoon, Nichols and Owen suggests that he had no need of Riding's insistence in this area.

Where Laura might be seen to have had a positive influence on his poetry was through the sexual relationship that began between them shortly after they met. Unhampered by his own lingering prudishness about sex, Laura would introduce him to a sensuous world that his earlier verse suggests had been closed to him. The love poetry that followed would be among the most lyrical of the twentieth century. And if there was something Graves had previously considered 'forbidden' in their sexual relationship, it undoubtedly added to the excitement for him. As Seymour-Smith noted, almost wistfully, after discussing the matter with Graves, Laura took him to areas of experience most people would never visit. She also provided him with the poetic Muse he sought, her god-like view of herself making her ideal for the role. Although she may not have been the only inspiration behind his creation of the White Goddess, she was without doubt one of the strongest influences on it.

One inadvertent benefit of being with Laura would be the prose books that resulted from his need to earn money to support both of them, as well as Nancy and the children. Not long after Laura's arrival he would write two of his most lucrative books, *Lawrence and the Arabs* (1927) and *Good-bye to All That* (1929), followed in the 1930s by his *Claudius* books, all of them more widely known to the public than either his poetry collections or his books of prose criticism. On the other hand, Laura would eventually alienate a number of Robert's friends and cause a rift lasting some years between him and his family.

Graves wrote nothing of his worship of Laura, starting in 1926, left no account, either, of that first meeting on 3 January or of their journey to Islip the same day, and made no direct reference to her in *Good-bye to All That*. But he did conclude the first edition of his autobiography with a 'Dedicatory Epistle to Laura Riding'. Written in portentous language more characteristic of Laura than himself and deliberately ambiguous, it nevertheless confirms Laura's contemporary account of the intense relationship that sprang up, not only between her and Robert, but also between Laura and Nancy:

> For how could the story of your coming be told [Graves wrote] between an Islip Parish Council Meeting and a conference of the professors of the Faculty of Letters at Cairo University? How she [Nancy] and I happening by seeming accident upon your teasing *Quids*, were drawn to write to you [Laura], who were in America, asking you to come to us. How, though you knew no more of us than we of you, and indeed less (for you knew me at a disadvantage, by my poems of the war), you forthwith came. And how there was thereupon a unity to which you and I pledged our faith and she [Nancy] her pleasure.

Nancy's own feminist principles demanded that she adopt an enlightened view of her husband's introduction of a second woman into their lives, but she also liked Laura, whose charm, when she chose to exercise it, was one quality most of her critics omit to mention, together with her sense of fun at times. Apart from Nancy's relief at finding that Laura really did share many of her views, she was admiring of her efficiency and zeal, her obsessive attention to detail, which was of great help in preparations for Egypt. While Nancy was apt to get distracted by such curious possibilities as the need for cotton wool in Cairo, Laura, more practically, would take notes from Philip Graves's wife, Millicent, about local customs, health concerns, servants and food. It would be Laura, not Nancy, who supervised the household's Sudanese servants and the preparation of meals when they got to Cairo. Nancy, meantime, was able to devote her energies to her poetry and to creating clothes for Laura as well as the children.

From Laura's point of view the situation was ideal. Nancy, abrupt to the point of brusqueness, made it clear from the start that there was no question of jealousy (though she would later change her mind). She may even have indicated that Laura was welcome to relieve her of having to satisfy what she saw as Robert's excessive sexual needs. Whatever the truth of the initial situation, as Laura stood at the window of her Islip bedroom on her first day in England, she felt 'the purest joy'.[24] The 'love' that had sprung up between the three of them immediately, she told Polly, was 'a divinely inspired love', their 'destiny'.[25] She loved Robert 'as Nancy loves him' and Robert loved her 'as he loves Nancy', while Nancy, apparently, loved Laura 'as much for [her] love of Robert as for [her] love of her':[26] 'it is a tremendous power,' she wrote, 'when a marriage of three occurs'.[27] It would not be long before they were referring to themselves, quite seriously, as 'the Trinity'. Robert himself confirmed that 'at first everything was wonderful'.[28]

**

After a day relishing all the quaintness of English cottage living – the tin bath by the fire with water brought in by Robert from the pump, supper cooked by Nancy on a Cotswold coal stove, and four children, whose chubbiness and clothes designed by Nancy made them look as though they had stepped out of a storybook – it was time for Robert and Laura to return to London, together with Nancy and the children. On 4 January 1926 the whole family, including the nanny, were at Apple Tree Yard for two days of last-minute preparations and goodbyes. William Nicholson was there to welcome them and on the evening of their arrival there was a dinner for Robert's parents, his sister Rosaleen and E. M. Forster, described in Alfred's diary as 'Robert's friend of Egyptian experience'.[29] Linked to Forster mainly through the friendship they both enjoyed with Sassoon and T. E. Lawrence, Graves had been corresponding with Forster since 1923 and had invited him to Islip on at least one occasion. Forster, who had served with the Red Cross in Alexandria from November 1915 to January 1919, had been glad to recommend him for the Cairo professorship and now gave him an introduction to a Greek poet living in Alexandria, Constantine Cavafy, whose importance would be recognized only after his death in 1933. Although Forster was an exciting glimpse of the English literary world for Laura, his advice on Egypt rather bored Robert, she suspected, and he spent the rest of the evening singing folk songs with Rosaleen. Rosaleen, still close to Robert, also helped him reassure their parents that taking Laura with him to Cairo was a perfectly respectable arrangement. One important aim of the dinner had been to introduce his 'lady secretary', 'Miss Gottschalk', as Laura called herself even after divorcing Mr Gottschalk.[30] She would later be described by Robert's anti-semitic half-brother Richard as a 'racial disease', but Alfred referred to her simply in his diary that evening as a 'German Jewess poet'.[31] His and Amy's trusting acceptance of the situation at this point was in sharp contrast to that of Edith Sitwell, who would write to T. S. Eliot shortly after the Graves's departure for Egypt:

> Robert has always been a bit of a Pilgrim Father – the only fault in an otherwise perfect character, – and his departure from England had rather too much of that kind of thing about it. For I understand that he took with him, not only Nancy and all the children, which of course was quite right, but also Miss Laura Gottschalk [Riding] – whose poems I think are the biggest bore, and I hope you agree; but Robert is encouraging her recklessly.[32]

Later she would refer less obliquely to Graves's 'harem'.[33]

In London in early 1926, however, the situation was still accepted as entirely proper: on 6 January both Nancy and Laura were taken to visit the Woolfs at the Hogarth Press, Nancy as wife and Laura as their future author. Fearing another prolonged visit from Robert, Virginia wrote to Vita Sackville-West on 5 January, begging her to come the next day 'as early as possible – I'm threatened with Robert Graves, Mrs R, and Nancy [*sic*] Gottschalk, so come early'.[34] Two other important introductions to the English literary scene followed for Laura, with a visit to Graves's agents, J.B. Pinker and Son, who agreed to take her on as a client, and a trip to the theatre with Siegfried Sassoon.

Sassoon was also at London Docks on 8 January to see the party off on the S.S. *Ranpura*, his parting gift a new car in the hold to replace the ancient one Nancy had driven at Islip. The ship, a P&O liner bound ultimately for Bombay, touched first at Gibraltar, where a tour of the town in an open carriage eating fresh figs made Robert feel what a 'fool' he had been to refuse a wartime posting there in preference to Rhyl. His request to be sent to Egypt had been turned down on that occasion and, as the ship sailed on to Port Said via Marseilles and Malta, he was excited at the prospect of seeing the country at last. But when, after 12 days at sea, the journey was finally over, his main sensation was one of relief; as his mother suspected, he was not a good sailor.

Once on land at Port Said, family connections came into play. A friend of Graves's half-sister Molly helped the party through customs and onto the train: 'And so to Cairo, looking out of the windows, delighted at the summer fields in January.'[35]

After a chaotic arrival and several weeks in temporary accommodation, the family moved from a dark, gloomy flat to a much lighter one with a garden. Not in the most exclusive residential suburb of Gizereh, favoured by Robert's half-brother Richard and other diplomats, it was situated in a less expensive area a few miles east of the city centre, Heliopolis. To Robert, who knew of the 'ancient dead Heliopolis', one of the oldest cities of ancient Egypt and cult centre of the gods Ra, Osiris and Horus, the name of their modern Cairo suburb of Heliopolis brought to mind a fabled land, very different from their 'brand-new dead town on the desert's edge, built by a Belgian company, complete with race course and Luna Park, where the R.A.F. planes flew low at night among the houses'.[36]

Their flat seemed pleasant enough, however, and life agreeable to begin with, the food good and the sun welcome. Although the cost of living was high, even with Graves's generous salary, the standard of living was also high compared with what he had been able to afford in England, with two excellent Sudanese servants to do the housework and cooking and Doris to nanny Jenny, David, Catherine and Sam. It seemed 'queer' to him to be no longer looking after the children or doing the housework, 'almost too good to be true to have as much time as [he] needed for [his] writing'.[37]

The choice of a garden flat had been made mainly with the children in mind, but by the time the move was arranged at the beginning of February all four children, from seven-year-old Jenny to two-year-old Sam, were in an isolation ward in hospital with measles. Sam had been the first to go down with the disease and would be the only one to suffer lasting consequences from it, when scarring from the repeated ear infections that followed caused permanent damage to his hearing. But the effect on Sam would not be realized for some time and Robert's impression of Cairo remained positive for a time. With the 'decent little garden flat' in view and no one pressing him to present himself at the university, there was leisure to 'settle down agreeably', he wrote to Sassoon on a postcard from the Mosque Madrassa of Sultan Hassan in the old city; Sassoon's car had already proved invaluable and Nancy frequently took them sightseeing.[38] While Nancy found the Pyramids 'boring', Robert was fascinated by the Great Sphinx of Giza, which was in the process of being unburied from centuries of sand, admiring its 'really beautiful face and a tail newly unearthed, coiled round its haunches like a kitten's' with 'a copybook between its paws'.[39] His favourite sight was 'the noble face of old King Seti the Good unwrapped of its mummy-clothes' in the Cairo Museum.[40]

Laura accompanied Robert and Nancy on all these sightseeing trips and Robert ended his first postcard to Sassoon in a way which suggests that Sassoon still had doubts about her inclusion in the venture: 'You need have no qualms about Laura G[ottschalk], who in every way confirms our happiest suspicions about her.'

Everything at this point seemed fine. But just under a fortnight later, having started work at the Royal Egyptian University, Graves was less certain. While he accepted that Cairo was 'not to be despised' as a tourist attraction, the university, he told Eliot, was 'a beautifully constructed farce in the best French style and dangerous if taken in the slightest degree seriously'.[41] He found it appropriate that its quarters, a former royal palace, had housed a harem. (Edith Sitwell would have found it even more so.) After four months there he would rate the university as 'nothing but elementary school, say 6th standard', and suggested to Eliot a poem on it could be the only possible sequel to 'The Hollow Men'.[42] Conscious of his high salary for what turned out to be no more than one lecture a week and the impossibility of getting any work done with the students, he was 'rather ashamed' of himself.[43] (Malcolm Muggeridge, who was there in 1927, said that the students were either stupefied with hashish, or on strike.) As Robert wrote to his father, the situation made his 'integrity hard to keep'.[44]

In a Faculty of Letters staffed mainly by French-speakers with very little English, lecturing to students who spoke even less French than they did English, Graves felt increasingly as though he were in the middle of a comic opera:

> I have never been so useless in my life before or with such pomp and circumstance [he told Sassoon after two months' teaching]. I had a lecture a week ago and have my next a week hence. 'Shakespeare was a great poet. He lived in London and wrote plays. London is in England. Plays are what you get at the theatre. A poet is a person who ... Oh yes, I'll spell the word on the blackboard. POET. No, Shakespeare is not another word for Byron.[45]

The essays of even the most competent students filled him with despair.

Despite Graves's jokiness on the matter to friends, it is clear that he was both disappointed and greatly depressed by his job. He had enjoyed lecturing in France, even on routine army matters, and was good at it. One of the few positive things to emerge from the situation was another contribution to the Hogarth Essays, *Impenetrability*, which would become his third in the series, following quickly on his attack on rhetorical poetry and the claims made for the scientific attitude in *Another Future of Poetry* (1926). *Impenetrability or the Proper Habit of English* was based on his course of public lectures at Cairo University – all of them quite beyond the understanding of his students with their limited English, he knew – questioning received truths about English. Some of them arose directly from his beleaguered position in a mainly French department, such as 'that English is an easier language to learn than French', or 'that French is a more exact, philosophic language than English'.[46] He used the chance to introduce a poem of Laura's to illustrate that English can achieve subtleties that French cannot. He also took the opportunity to criticize Joseph Conrad and Robert Bridges for their attempts to reform or purify English.

French was not the only language in evidence at the university. There were professors of every nation, Robert wrote despairingly to his father, and the staff fought the Conseil Général, which in turn fought the Ministry. Committee meetings in the Faculty of Letters were like a modern Tower of Babel, 'slapstick' events in which first 'Noisy' and 'Hasty', followed by 'Hearty', 'Ragman', 'Critic' and 'Synthesis' made their meaningless contributions to the rowdy debate:

> ... With cream-bun fallacies
> With semi-nudes of platitudes
> And testamentary feuds
> Rushed at a slap-stick rate
> To a jangling end.[47]

Not surprisingly, Graves spent as little time as possible with his fellow lecturers. Nor did he have any intention of 'mixing with the British official class, joining the golf-club or paying official calls'.[48] Laura was particularly scornful of Egyptian society in Cairo, dismissing Richard Graves as an upper-class bore, despite his evident wish to help Robert and his family. From her American and socialist perspective anyone other than the working classes, including Nancy and Robert himself, was seen as upper class and therefore suspect.

Robert's own reaction to class was equally decided. Urged by Richard, he finally called on the British High Commissioner, Lord Lloyd, one of the most powerful men in Cairo, at that time a British Protectorate. Since Lloyd had helped secure Graves his professorship, gratitude as well as etiquette and even self-interest dictated an early call, but Robert left his visit until just before the end of the academic year. And when Lloyd asked him, during the dinner at the Residency that followed, how he found Egypt, Robert replied rather grudgingly 'All right'.[49] 'He believed in his job rather more than I did in mine,' he explained.[50] He had less difficulty with the Egyptian upper classes, partly because in attending a levée at the Abdin Royal Palace he mistook the king – 'a quiet Turkish-looking gentleman of middle age' – for the Grand Chamberlain and found the occasion over before he knew it.[51] He also accepted an invitation to a royal soirée where he enjoyed the 'Arabian Night buffet' more than the variety show that preceded it.[52] His only comment on his visit to the national poet of Egypt, Chawki Bey, at his Moorish mansion by the Nile, was how like Thomas Hardy he seemed. It is evident from this list and from an entertaining account he gave of a trip to the Pyramids with one of his more intelligent students and tea afterwards with a Greek student and his 'three beautiful sisters', Pallas, Aphrodite and

Artemis, that his social life in Cairo was not quite so barren as he represented it in *Good-bye to All That*.

Most of Graves's working time was spent at home writing and editing. Among other things he was completing an entertaining little book, *Lars Porsena, or the Future of Swearing and Improper Language*.[53] As Graves explained in *Occupation: Writer*, when the weather grew hotter, his colleagues and students more difficult and his flat was invaded by 'swarms of offensively large and queer insects', his language 'soon recovered much of its war-time foulness' and for lack of anything better to do, he wrote 'a critical monograph on the subject of swearing'.[54] ('Isn't that what psychologists call sublimation?' he asks in the Preface to a new edition in 1936.) Full of references to favourite writers such as Butler, Sterne and Coleridge, it is enlivened by wonderfully absurd examples of genteel efforts to avoid true swearing: 'Few people enjoy being sworn at, but there are no forms of humour more boring than guaranteed non-alcoholic substitutes for the true wine of swearing. 'Great Jumping Beans!', 'Ye little fishes!', 'Snakes & Ladders!' and 'Mind your step, you irregular old Pentagon!'[55] Graves's own inventiveness makes him relish such ingenious curses as the one applied by a general to a contingent of the Royal Artillery: 'a pack of consumptive little Maltese monkeys'. Although 'a get-penny of no importance', *Lars Porsena* led to 'a queer correspondence from all quarters of this planet', he reported to an Oxford friend L. A. G. Strong in 1927.[56]

Graves also managed to complete *The English Ballad*, a 'short critical survey' that he had started with his father's help in 1925.[57] 'The Primitive Ballad' had become his self-chosen lecture course when he realized how his students were struggling with more sophisticated subjects and, as so often, he saw the chance of a book in it. Ernest Benn had published a sixpenny selection of his poems in 1925 in their *Augustan Books of Modern Poets* series, which had sold well enough for them to welcome another book by him. Benn would also ask him to edit a selection of Skelton in 1927.

It was almost certainly the choosing of his own poems for Benn's 1925 edition, with the opportunity to revise them as he did so, that prompted Graves to think of selecting a larger number for *Poems (1914–1926)*. The running head to the book published in June 1927, then a few months later and with nine poems added as *Poems (1914–1927)*, was 'Collected Poems of Robert Graves', and *Poems (1914–1927)* formed in effect the first of

Graves's many *Collected Poems*. But as Graves emphasized, it was 'selective rather than collective, intended as a disavowal of over half the poetry that I had so far printed'.[58] Out of nearly 300 poems published since 1911, only 134 would survive the culling. Both editions were dedicated 'To N. and L.' and Laura's influence in particular is clear. It was she who encouraged the inclusion of 'only real poems' in the book, Graves told Sassoon,[59] a policy he emphasizes in his prefatory note. (He does not, however, clarify what 'real' means.)

The most ruthless pruning took place in the early work, especially the war poetry. The 'War: 1915–19' section is by far the shortest, containing only 16 poems, two of which were written in 1925 and 1926 respectively. It was almost certainly Laura who had encouraged him to discard remarkable poems such as 'A Dead Boche', 'A Child's Nightmare', 'The Assault Heroic', 'To Lucasta Going to the Wars' and 'The Adventure'. All the pieces in the 'Retrospect' section of *Country Sentiment*, except 'The Leveller', were omitted and other later poems well worth preserving, such as 'Sergeant Major Money', from *Welchman's Hose*. The result was to downplay Graves as a war poet at a time when poets like Sassoon, Owen and even Rosenberg were being promoted as such.

Any negative effect Laura might have had, however, was balanced at the start by the wholly positive effect she had on his love poetry, which was transformed. 'Pure Death', written in 1926, makes it clear that he fell in love with her instantly – 'We looked, we loved', 'It happened soon, so wild of heart were we'[60] – and that it was a love which invited terror and wildness. Familiar from his wide reading with sexual orgasm being referred to as the 'little death' (*'petite mort'*), Graves's choice of 'Pure Death' for his title strengthens the impression that the relationship described is a fiercely sexual one and that there is nothing 'little' about the feelings experienced between the two lovers. The insistent linking of love and death, a 'gift' that the lovers exchange 'simultaneously', anticipates Graves's 'Dedicatory Epistle to Laura Riding' in *Good-bye to All That*, where he praises her 'true quality of one living invisibly against kind, as dead, beyond event'.[61]

When trying later to describe his initial, intense attraction to Laura, Robert would use imagery similar to her own in her account of their first meeting, that she 'glowed with a sort of light',[62] both of them implying that there was a supernatural element to their relationship. There were other, more obvious explanations for their attraction: the unsatisfactory state of his marriage by 1926, his need for a Muse, and Laura's magnetic personality and physicality. There is little doubt that Laura did what she could to excite Robert sexually, sharing with him, in the name of complete honesty between them, 'all the obscenities of my utterly vile mind'.[63] And since Nancy was included in this pact of entire openness between them, she seems to have given her blessing to their affair. Later on, presumably to spice up their sex life, Laura would invite another man into their bed, and her first biographer writes that she may have shared it also with Nancy in Egypt: 'with all three, enthralled and each allowed to test the limits of their intimacy, Laura went very far indeed'.[64]

It was not sex, however, that formed the basis of Robert's irresistible attraction towards her, though this was important to him. Even after she began to deny him sex in the early 1930s, he would still be drawn to her. For Laura believed, like him, that poetry was 'that sense of life so real that it became the sense of something more real than life' and that it was 'the meaning at work in what has no meaning'.[65] Working together closely as they did in Cairo on each other's poems almost certainly brought them together physically, too. While she helped him prepare *Poems (1914–1926)*, he was advising Laura on her first verse collection for the Hogarth Press, which she was revising heavily 'to depict more glamorously their love for one another', Nancy included.[66] Laura became, for Robert, the embodiment of his greatest love – poetry – transforming his life and bringing a sense of hope and renewal, expressed strongly but simply in 'A Love Story' as the arrival of spring in winter:

> Her image was my ensign: snows melted,
> Hedges sprouted, the moon tenderly shone,
> The owls trilled with tongues of nightingale.[67]

While there is no concrete evidence that the physical side of the relationship started in Cairo, and Doris Harrison said she saw no evidence of it, the poetry Robert wrote there points strongly to that conclusion. 'Pygmalion to Galatea', written by April 1926, for instance, opens with a recognizable tribute to Laura, laced with echoes of Charles Sorley's haunting refrain in 'All the Hills and Vales Along' ('So be merry, so be dead'):

> As you are woman, so be lovely:
> Fine hair afloat and eyes irradiate,
> Long crafty fingers, fearless carriage,
> And body lissom, neither short nor tall.
> So be lovely![68]

It is impossible not to see the Greek legend of a sculptor who breathed life into a beautiful statue he had created as a parallel for Graves's own longing for a closer physical relationship with the woman he had to some extent created. But it must be a relationship of equals: she must 'prize' her 'self-honour', leaving him with his.

His poem 'In Single Syllables' appears to describe the next stage of the relationship, when:

> ... love rose up in wrath to make us blind,
> And stripped from us all powers of heart and mind,
> So we were mad and had no pulse or thought
> But love, love, love in the one bale-fire caught.[69]

Apart from its two extra lines, this poem is true to the Petrarchan love sonnet in its passion for and worship of the 'lady' addressed (also called 'Laura') and the narrator's turbulent emotions, though more explicit than the model on which it is based:

> You pass, you smile: yet is that smile I see
> Of love, and of your all-night gift to me?
> Now I too smile, for doubt, and own the doubt,
> And wait in fear for night to root it out,
> And doubt the more; but take heart to be true,
> Each time of change, to a fresh hope of you,
> That love may prove his worth once more and be
> Fierce as the tides of Spring in you and me,
> And bear with us till dawn shall break, though soon
> With dreams of doubt to vex me at high noon.[70]

The poem that shows most clearly the electrifying effect Laura had on Robert and his poetry, however, is the highly sensuous 'The Nape of the Neck'. In it the poet creates an almost physical sensation of tracing his lover's spine down from the neck – where intellect and body join – to its base, with seductive effect:

> To speak of the hollow nape where the close chaplet
> Of thought is bound, the loose-ends lying neat
> In two strands downward, where the shoulders open
> Casual and strong below, waiting their burden,
> And the long spine begins its downward journey:
> The hair curtains this postern silkily,
> This secret stairway by which thought will come
> More personally, with a closer welcome,
> Than through the latticed eyes, or portalled ears;
> Where kisses and all unconsidered whispers
> Go smoother in than by the very lip,
> And more endeared because the head's asleep
> Or grieving, the face covered with the hands...[71]

The 'close chaplet' of the first line, from which Laura would take the title for her collection of poems, alludes both to the ribbon that usually circled Laura's hair and to a form of Christian prayer using a circle of beads to count the prayers said. The play between the two is maintained throughout, suggesting an inseparable link between the physical and the spiritual, between body and mind, between the lovers' flesh and their thoughts, the 'nape' of their relationship in which, for the first time in Robert's life, the body and mind seem truly linked.

The contrast between these joyful as well as sensuous and abandoned love poems and the mainly troubled ones that had followed Robert's marriage to Nancy makes clear the nature of the bond formed between Robert and Laura in 1926. She became in his mythopoeic mind a goddess, or character from Greek legend, addressed as 'Andromeda', 'mad Atalanta', 'Niobe', 'Helen' and, at least partially, the incarnation of the White Goddess. The voice of the mature Graves can finally be heard in his poetry, unfiltered by Rivers, Mallik or even Laura, powerful though her effect on him was. It would be the start of a body of love poetry among the greatest composed in the twentieth century.

By the end of March 1926, Graves was openly including Riding in his marriage, writing to a still-dubious Sassoon: 'It is extremely unlikely that Nancy, Laura and I will ever disband, now we've survived this odd meeting and continue to take everything for granted as before.'[72] He had already written to Eliot in February asking whether he had 'any objection' to Riding collaborating with him on what would become *A Survey of Modernist Poetry*, the project he had initially proposed to Eliot, and he made it clear to family and friends that she was a fixture in his life. Although he implied that Nancy shared his feelings, there is no evidence of how she felt. She left no account of her life in Cairo and Robert subsequently destroyed all her letters to him up to 1929. Laura's version of events in letters home to friends, in which she placed Nancy firmly in 'the Trinity', is hardly impartial. Her letters to Polly do, however, make clear her attachment to Robert, described by her as 'tall, well-read, clumsy, strong, clumsy sweet, eyes blue-gray, a voice for ballads, tender with everything'.[73]

One hint that Nancy may not have felt quite so accepting of the situation as Robert claimed publicly occurs in a curious short story he conceived in Egypt, as he 'walk[ed] in the desert near Heliopolis' and 'stopped to pick up a few misshapen pebbles' that seemed to have a story in them.[74] The first draft of this story, which became 'The Shout', was written in March 1926, constituting the nearest account we have of events as they unfolded.[75] A sinister tale of a three-sided relationship that ends with the death of one of them, 'The Shout' deals with the tensions introduced into the marriage of two of the main characters, Richard and Rachel, by a stranger they have jointly seen in dreams, Charles. The story takes a sinister turn when it becomes clear that Charles has magical powers, the ability to give a shout so terrifying that it can kill anyone who hears it. When Charles falls in love with Richard's wife, Rachel, Richard's equally supernatural solution is to smash the pebble in the nearby sandhills that he believes contains Charles's soul, and Charles duly dies. Graves, who considered himself incapable of constructing a good short story, explained that he had not set out to write 'The Shout', but that it had sprung unbidden from his unconscious. He came to view its 'macabre strangeness' as a prophecy of future events, after the addition of 'a most important character'.[76] The character with the 'devil' face in the story (Charles), he believed, was an anticipation of Geoffrey Phibbs, as Laura's lover, in their lives three years later.

Although 'The Shout' gives no reliable details of Nancy's state of mind in Cairo, it may indicate an unease on Robert's part with the triangular relationship there. It certainly gives more than a hint of his increasing sense of evil and death as the weeks passed. His initially agreeable impressions had quickly vanished, turning Egypt, he wrote, into 'the land where the dead parade the streets' and where the three of them 'met with demons' who 'drove [them] up and down the land'.[77] The words are from his 'Dedicatory Epistle to Laura Riding' and it was Laura who sensed the presence of the dead before he did, when she pronounced their first flat 'haunted'. By late March their Sudanese servants had become 'devils' in her eyes and Robert himself was seeing ghosts.[78] Robert's family would later claim that Laura had 'vampirized' him and T. E. Lawrence viewed him as 'bewitched and bitched' by her.[79]

Robert's subsequent reactions to Egypt strongly suggest that she had indeed influenced him. Outwardly attractive features of life in Cairo, such as his garden, filled with fruit trees and flowering shrubs, turned sinister, and he could see only 'lean and mangy cats dozing in the [flower] beds', with kites, 'their foul counterpart in the sky and in the palm-trees', even claiming to have encountered a 'fabulous cross-breed' between cat and kite, which woke him every morning with its 'strangled' cry.[80] The suggestion is of something sinister in its unnaturalness, Nature turning against itself as in *Macbeth* after Duncan is murdered.

By the time Robert's brother Charles arrived in pursuit of the woman he wanted to marry, he found Robert in a bad way. Did Laura, as Deborah Baker claims, transform Cairo for him into 'a city of unbridled sensuality, of bizarreries and grotesqueries, macabre and cruel happenings'?[81] And did she revive in his imagination 'the ancient land of the fatal Woman, of Cleopatra, Salomé, Nefertiti and Isis, a land obsessed by secret intrigue and the Occult'?[82] Living on the site of the ancient city of Heliopolis had probably already had that effect on Robert. And his interest in mythology may have alerted him to another deadly triangle linked to the city, that of the Nature goddess Isis, wife to her brother Osiris, who was killed by their brother Set in a jealous rage and became the god of the dead and ruler of the underworld, as well as the god of resurrection and fertility.

As the heat grew more intense, Graves's students and colleagues more difficult and the flat swarmed with insects, Egypt seemed more sinister than ever. An earthquake, the murder of an Englishwoman in a neighbouring street, added to the lurking stray cats in the garden, all were seen as further ominous signs. Laura now believed that the camels which filled the streets were evil spirits and on at least one occasion reported having been chased by ghosts, convictions that lie behind her poem 'Egypt':

> ... Egypt is then the devil's undisputed pit
> Which he, King of life before life was,
> Now populates with carcases,
> The souls of those who may not be
> Since the upper air is bespoken fairly
> And is not bottomless.[83]

Robert, passionately in love with Laura and highly suggestible, joined in at once and by early summer the atmosphere at 6 rue de Sabbagh, Heliopolis, was one of near-hysteria. The aim now was to get as far away from Egypt and its demons as possible. A tentative plan to spend the summer break in Cyprus was abandoned and by May he had 'practically decided' not to return to Cairo after the summer, however good the pay, but to look for lecturing work in America.[84] He gave his reasons as the thanklessness of the work and 'the beastly climate'; to other friends he blamed the children's health, which Nancy believed had suffered in Cairo. To yet another friend he would explain, no doubt with the ubiquitous camels in mind, that 'one can live off one's hump for only so long'.[85] Charles Graves had felt extreme disappointment at the Egypt he had dreamed of and the reality he had encountered:

> Tall houses, dusty streets, the broad and sluggish Nile, a lack of orchids, an abundance of beggars, rain which turned into mud on your hat, Cook's tourists and Cook's officials, conceited English cavalry officers, English girls rising thirty and making a last desperate effort to get married...[86]

But Robert's reaction went far deeper than that – 'I hate the East', he would write to Nancy Cunard eighteen years after leaving it[87] – and is more difficult to disentangle. It is unlikely that he would have sensed so much death and evil in Egypt, for instance, if he had gone there without Laura.

As it was he dated his stay in Cairo as the start of a 'disintegration' of self, a necessary process, he implied, in order to share Laura's 'true quality of one living invisibly, against kind, as dead, beyond event'.[88] Like the god Osiris, Robert's old self must die before he could be resurrected to live a new life with Laura, he believed.

Meantime the more practical business of arranging passage home had to be dealt with. Unplanned and unbudgeted for, this meant third-class tickets on an Italian cargo ship carrying onions to Venice. On 1 June 1926, Robert, Nancy, Laura, the four children and their nanny set sail for Europe, with 'the demons still treading behind', according to Robert, but escaping towards the familiar, with the inviting prospect before them of a more temperate summer in the gentle rural surroundings of Islip.[89]

20

THE WORLD WELL LOST (JUNE 1926–APRIL 1927)

... There's a cool web of language winds us in,
Retreat from too much joy or too much fear:
We grow sea-green at last and coldly die
In brininess and volubility.

But if we let our tongues lose self-possession,
Throwing off language and its watery clasp
Before our death, instead of when death comes,
Facing the wide glare of the children's day,
Facing the rose, the dark sky and the drums,
We shall go mad no doubt and die that way.[1]

Graves may not have had John Dryden's tragedy of the Egyptian lovers Antony and Cleopatra, *All for Love, or the World Well Lost*, in mind when he returned to England in June 1926, but he would demonstrate very clearly during the next three years that he considered the 'World Well Lost' for *his* Cleopatra. Under her tutelage and in her cause he would antagonize not just most of his family but some of his best friends. (Edward Marsh would later boast of being the only close friend to survive the general cull.)

The first people to be sacrificed would be Nancy and the children, though this was not immediately apparent. The 'Trinity' of Robert, Nancy and Laura appeared to have been consolidated by the stay in Egypt and to have survived the return to London in early June, then after a few days at Apple Tree Yard, to Islip. Once established in their own house at 'World's End', however, the situation grew more challenging. Here, finally, their changed relations to each other were brought into the open, with Robert and Laura sharing the large attic room and Nancy sleeping alone in the marital bedroom below. On the ground floor Doris looked after the children, all of whom except Sam now attended the village school. Nancy pursued her drawing, painting and fabric design in the big double-bedroom she had once shared with Robert, while he and Laura worked on *A Survey of Modernist Poetry*. While Robert devoted himself to Isaac Rosenberg, Laura, now officially responsible for American poets, tackled John Crowe Ransom and Marianne Moore. According to her, they were all 'ridiculously happy'.[2] Freed by the rigorous analysis and self-analysis of the Trinity from what she saw as her compulsive habits, her wickedness and her inbred neuroses, she felt herself to be a much nicer human being, a 'good' person.[3]

Robert, too, seemed 'very happy at Islip', his father reported.[4] By the middle of July he was expressing his satisfaction with the arrangement to Sassoon: he was starting to write again and had nearly completed editing what he still referred to as his 'Collected Poems'. But Sassoon would also receive a letter from Nancy which showed that at least one member of the trio did not find the situation ideal. Despite her feminist ideals she quickly became jealous of Laura in the new arrangement and could not hide it entirely. According to Amy who, faced with the greater threat of Laura, drew closer to her daughter-in-law, Nancy began suffering from 'sudden and very black moods of despair in which she even hated Robert'.[5] Nancy also begged Laura at one point to go back to America: Laura, predictably, refused to do so.

A difficult situation was made worse by Robert's need for money once again, despite T. E. Lawrence's further gift of a first edition of *Revolt in the Desert*, an abridged version of *Seven Pillars of Wisdom*, marked 'Sell when read'. The £300 it brought in could not last long in an extravagant household of eight people. Robert's only hope of earning a living was to write more, yet with the arrival of the school holidays at the end of July and the house filled with noisy children, he found it impossible to concentrate. So he was

25. RG and Nancy Nicholson at Maes-y-Neuadd, Wales in June 1918, five months after their wedding.

26. John Masefield in a photograph inscribed 'for Siegfried Sassoon from John Masefield. Nov. 9, 1918', two days before the Armistice.

27. RG with his first child, Jenny Nicholson.

28. RG, Nancy (holding Catherine), with David and Jenny at Islip.

29. 'The Hon. Mrs Michael Howard (left) with Miss Nancy Nicholson outside the shop' at Boars Hill, photograph from the *Daily Mirror*, 7 October 1920.

30. The site of the Boars Hill shop, with a glimpse of Masefield's house on the right.

POETS' SHOP.

SPELLS BEHIND THE COUNTER.

There is a little shop at Boar's Hill, near Oxford, where you can not only buy everything from a collar-stud to a saucepan, but —if you happen to be passing just at the right time—you may receive your purchase from the hands of a distinguished poet.

For this is the shop opened by the Hon. Mrs. Michael Howard and Miss Nancy Nicholson for the benefit of the colony of poets and scientists that has grown up at Boar's Hill, and the fashion seems to be to take turns behind the counter. Here is a list (without prejudice) of some of the people who live there:

Dr. Robert Bridges, the Poet Laureate.
Mr. John Masefield.
Mr. John Galsworthy.
Professor Gilbert Murray.
Sir Walter Raleigh, and
Miss Lillah McCarthy.

"You see we are nearly four miles from the nearest stores in Oxford," Mrs. Howard told a *Daily Mail* representative yesterday, "and poets as well as peasants want to buy candles and cheese, paraffin and sweets, at a handy place. Miss Nicholson and I conceived this idea together in my garden opposite, and in less than a month we got the ground, built the shop, and found out what to get and where to get it.

"Next week we shall send round from house to house to see if we can supply them with groceries. Several women have offered to come and take a hand in serving behind the counter."

31. Article from the *Daily Mail*, 8 October 1920.

BUSY DAYS IN
POETS' VILLAGE.
Famous Residents Go to a Pretty Wedding.
VISIT TO THE STORE.
Hon. Mrs. Howard and Charm of Commercial Travellers.

From Our Special Correspondent.

BOAR'S HILL, Thursday.

When you have been twenty-four hours in Poets' and Peasants' Land you begin to realise what an extraordinary "live" place it is for a baby village sitting atop a windblown Oxfordshire hill.

I discovered yesterday the quaintest allsort shop just opened by the Hon. Mrs. Michael Howard and Miss Nicholson, daughter of the well-known artist.

This morning a motor-car and a motor cyclist came into collision, and no one was hurt. This afternoon a fashionable wedding took place at Sunningwell, a couple of miles away.

PEASANT'S DILEMMA.

Nevertheless, I began to notice a certain emptiness about Boar's Hill at half-past one. Not a poet pricked in the lane, and the only peasant in the vicinity was in the Poets' and Peasants' shop wondering whether to buy a pennyworth of brandy balls or a ten-and-sixpenny patent clothes washer.

"I suppose you know that Charles Petrie and Ursula Dowdall are being married at Sunningwell this afternoon?" asked Mrs. Howard, wrapping up the sweets. "Everybody's going except poor shopkeepers like me.

"The bridegroom is the younger son of the late Sir Charles Petrie, and the bride the eldest daughter of the Hon. Mrs. Dowdall."

And at Sunningwell I saw the prettiest wedding taking place at a prettier church than ever was painted in a picture.

CONGREGATION OF GENIUS.

A bride in fawn charmeuse, trimmed with Limerick lace, crowned with a Gainsborough picture hat of fawn and gold, adorned with a sweeping plume, was attended by bridesmaids in tunic dresses of Chinese yellow silk, trimmed with fur, and hats of autumn leaves.

And at every pew and corner of the church a far-famed poet or a scientist whose learning has set the world agape!

Not being a guest, I returned with the peasants, and had a further conversation with Mrs. Howard and Miss Nicholson.

The Hon. Mrs. Howard believes that her little stove full of soap and cheese and kettles and saucepans and potato peelers and whatnots will one day grow into a great big store, full of carpets and mangles.

COMMERCIAL TRAVELLERS.

Some time or another, she observed, this part of the world might develop—into a garden suburb, perhaps. Then there would be telephones and electric light, and even a policeman!

"Then great poets will not sell your baking powder or buy your toffee!" I suggested.

"You leave the poets alone," cried Miss Nicholson. "A distinguished poet certainly bought some toffee here the other day, but we want to sell you about the commercial travellers.

"I'd never met one before I opened the shop," said Mrs. Howard, "and I had no idea they were so nice. Even when I criticised the stuff he brought, he was still nice."

"So we had to buy it," said Miss Nicholson.

"Of course," said I. "Such are commercial travellers."

32. Article from the *Daily Mirror*, 7 October 1920.

33. Edmund Blunden as RG first knew him.

34. T. E. Lawrence.

35. Thomas Hardy shortly before his death in 1928.

36. Cover of *The Owl* magazine (1919–1923), designed by William Nicholson and based on a 17th Century Staffordshire Slipware plate.

37. A drawing of RG at work by William Nicholson.

38. Dingle Cottage.

39. Geoffrey Phibbs by William Nicholson.

40. Laura Riding c.1928.

41. Nancy Nicholson on RG's barge with (from l. to r.) Catherine, Sam, Jenny and David.

42. Siegfried Sassoon's annotations to the frontispiece and title page of his personal copy of *Good-bye to All That*.

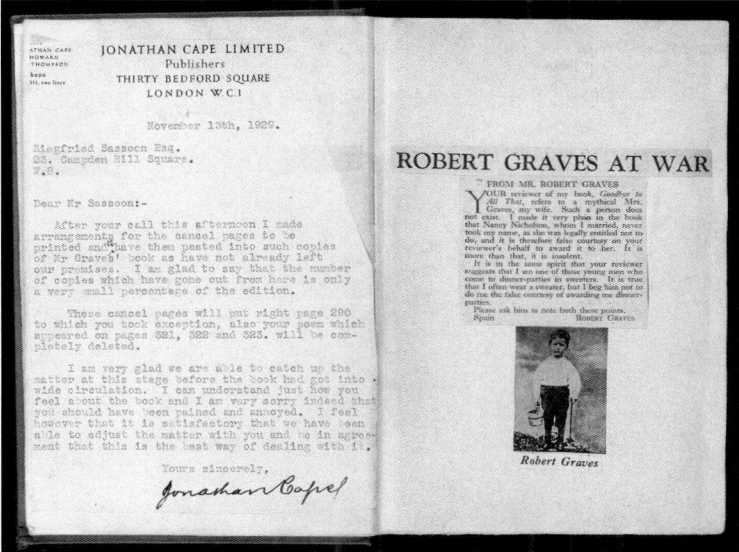

43. Jonathan Cape's letter agreeing to the cancellation of passages in *Good-bye to All That*, inserted in the prelim, together with other insertions by Siegfried Sassoon in his personal copy of the book.

44. Ca Sa Salerosa, the first house RG lived in when he arrived in Deia in October 1929, photographed by RG's son, William Graves.

more than ready to agree to Nancy's request to be left alone at 'World's End' with the children, and he and Laura departed for a month in London at the beginning of August. Although Rosaleen agreed to join them as a chaperone to lend an air of respectability to proceedings, Alfred and Amy still found it 'strange that Nancy should allow this', even though they had been assured that 'she prefer[red] running [the] house now herself' and that 'Miss Gottschalk is doing a book of poetry with Robert'.[6]

Robert's anxiety to maintain a veneer of respectability when he and Laura moved into a basement flat at 9 Ladbroke Square in west London meant that to begin with Laura had to take a room with the landlady until a separate one was ready for her in the flat and Rosaleen was free to join them. This was a less fashionable area in those days, the rent was cheap and the flat itself conveniently close to Kensington Gardens, several underground stations and Sassoon's apartment in Campden Hill Square – the main reason, Robert told him, for his choice. In the event, Sassoon was touring Europe with Ottoline Morrell and her family, but as Robert informed him, he and Laura had 'plenty of writing commissions to get on with'.[7]

The most pressing of these commissions was his collaboration with Laura on a critical analysis of modern poetry, which he had managed to place with Heinemann. Although he had assured Eliot that this was not the book resulting from his original proposal of a book on *Untraditional Elements in Poetry*, in which he would deal with modern British literature and Eliot with modern American literature, it clearly was. But Graves was careful to get Eliot on side: 'The only satisfaction we have with regard to you', he concluded his letter on the subject flatteringly, 'is that we are now permitted to discuss your poems: and without your work a discussion of modernist poetry is *Hamlet* without ... well ... at least ... the Gravediggers and the Ghost'.[8] It was not a development designed to make Eliot think well of Laura Riding, but he made no difficulties and he is one of a relatively small number of poets to emerge positively from what became *A Survey of Modernist Poetry*. Since, as Charles Mundye and Patrick McGuinness point out, Graves and Riding's 'neutral-seeming title mask[ed] a personal agenda ... like many poet-critics before them', their *Survey* became more of a personal manifesto, by which they judged their fellow poets. Few of them would escape unscathed.[9]

Survey is also a valuable guide to what Graves was reading and thinking of modern British poetry by 1926. Eight of its nine chapters cover topics such as 'The Plain Reader's Rights', 'The Problems of Form and Subject-Matter', 'The Unpopularity of Modernist Poetry with the Plain Reader', 'Dead Movements' in Modernist poetry, the way poems are made, the relation of Modernist poetry to 'civilization', its 'Variety' and the 'Humorous Element' in it. But its most significant and memorable chapter is a detailed analysis of the original punctuation and spelling of Shakespeare's 129th sonnet ('Th'expence of Spirit in a waste of shame'), the section William Empson claimed contributed to his own theory of 'close reading' in *Seven Types of Ambiguity*. Supporters of Graves saw this as proof that he was responsible for the most enduring insights in *Survey*, but Riding insisted that they originated with her. Even when Empson clarified his debt to Graves by pointing to the influence of his earlier books, written before he met Riding, *On English Poetry* and *Poetic Unreason*, she still argued that she was the originator and so a founding member of the 'New Criticism'.

The preponderance of English poets over American ones in *A Survey of Modernist Poetry* also suggests that Graves's contribution was significantly larger. There is no doubt that Riding would have insisted on a word-by-word analysis of the finished text, as she claimed, since she was obsessed by precision. But the majority of the ideas themselves can be seen to originate with Graves. The section on war poetry, for instance, clearly came from him. At Sassoon's prompting he had been re-reading Wilfred Owen and found it 'all real enough'.[10] His dislike of war poetry with a 'message' emerges in his statement that 'the poetry is not in the propaganda, but in spite of the propaganda'. Graves still got 'absolutely dithery thinking about the War so can't judge Owen fairly,' he told Sassoon, 'but I say he's all right and risk it'.[11] Praise for his favourites, Rosenberg, Hardy, Housman and less well-known poets like his friend Frank Prewett, together with scorn for Sitwell and Sassoon's *bête noir*, Humbert Wolfe, was also clearly written by him. His influence can be glimpsed even in the sections on American poets – praise of Robert Frost as a nature poet, for instance, or admiration for Eliot's mastery of form in a long poem such as *The Waste Land*. There is also evidence that Graves would contribute to the section on e. e. cummings. The organization of the book and the lucidity of its style are certainly his, since Laura's prose was ponderous and often very difficult to read, unlike the *Survey*.

The *Survey* was almost completed when Rosaleen left on holiday after three weeks of pretending to chaperone Robert and Laura at Ladbroke

Square. Still anxious to keep up appearances, they returned to Islip a week before their lease on the flat expired. With the children still on holiday, 'World's End' was as noisy and chaotic as when they had left. The family could not afford their usual summer visit to Harlech and, now that Laura was part of the household, Amy did not offer to pay their fares. Less than a month after returning from London, Robert announced that he was leaving with Laura for a year. Once again he claimed that this was Nancy's idea, writing to Sassoon on 18 September 1926:

> She finds that now she's well she can't bring herself to resume the responsibility of the house unless we aren't here to force it on her: and that she can't begin to draw again unless she is alone, and she is longing to draw. We find in our turn that we can't get on with our work unless we have her equally busy. So we are going to Vienna or somewhere near and be damned to scandal. At Christmas we'll try to come back for a visit. And in the Summer, Nance and the children will come to us there.[12]

Although Graves ended by assuring Sassoon that they were 'all very happy about it', there is no evidence that Nancy was. And despite him telling Sassoon that 'we'll miss each other very much, of course, and especially ... the children', his decision makes it plain that Laura was now his priority. It was, in effect, the end to his marriage and to any close relationship with his children. Graves's official explanation to his parents and more conventional friends was the need to leave the country to avoid paying income tax on his Egyptian salary. While perfectly valid, it did not explain the need to separate from his wife and children for a whole year. Life abroad was a great deal less expensive than in England in the 1920s and they could have afforded to live together there if he had really wanted to. His father, for one, was not reassured, referring to 'Robert's consternating letter' about 'going with Nancy's consent with Laura to Vienna'.[13] But neither his joint wire to Nancy with Amy and Clarissa, begging her to 'withdraw consent', nor Amy's letter to Nancy's stepmother on the subject, had any effect, except to provoke a 'very unreasonable unaddressed letter' from Robert.[14]

    Robert's omission of his address on his letter home was deliberate. (Sassoon would be the only person he trusted with it.) He did not want unannounced visitors turning up who might see that he and Laura shared a bed as well as a flat. Vienna was ideal in this respect. Neither he nor Laura had friends or family there and they talked to no one except shopkeepers, 'and then in German',[15] which Robert spoke fluently if ungrammatically. He felt, as an adult, that he knew German 'far better than French', having learnt it at an impressionable age and spoken it with his mother and her relations as he grew up.[16] Laura, who was returning to her father's Austro-Hungarian-Jewish roots, also spoke the language.

Renting a flat at Mühlgasse 9 in central Vienna, near Karlsplatz and the Belvedere Palace, Robert and Laura were for the first time truly alone. They found Vienna 'a lovely town' and went out occasionally to the cinema or concerts.[17] (Robert was particularly struck by the 'magnificence' of the African-American lyric tenor Roland Hayes singing spirituals.) But most importantly they worked together, spinning the 'cool web' of language that would bind them together throughout their thirteen-year relationship more closely than sex. His poem 'The Cool Web' may even have been written in Vienna, for though it clearly relates to Graves's wartime experience ('the tall soldiers drumming by', 'the soldiers and the fright'), it is also about a power over language absent in children, who are 'dumb' to express both the joys and terrors of life.[18] But the poem ends on a note of ambivalence about the value of language, which, the poet suggests, may allow us to 'retreat from too much joy or too much fear' instead of facing (as Graves the man is facing with Laura) the whole range of human experience – '... the rose, the dark sky and the drums' – bringing with it the inescapable risk of madness.[19]

In the meantime they continued to work on their *Survey of Modernist Poetry*. They also collaborated on a second book, *A Pamphlet Against Anthologies*, in which they argued that, with the exception of 'anthologies of fugitive verse', most anthologies 'did actual harm' to poetry.[20] Graves was particularly hard on 'false anthology pieces like Yeats's absurdly sloppy "Innisfree"'.[21] As with the *Survey*, the original idea for the book came from Graves, who had written to *The Times Literary Supplement* in 1921 to support Eliot's criticism of certain anthological practices, with Yeats's 'Innisfree' again coming in for attack, together with Walter de la Mare's 'Arabia'. Five years later, in *A Pamphlet Against Anthologies*, Ralph Hodgson, Robert Bridges, Rupert Brooke, John Masefield, even Wordsworth and Milton are found wanting by him in this respect, while Laura has fun mocking Edna St Vincent

Millay. It is a witty little book that nevertheless becomes slightly tedious in its repeated cleverness towards the end. Yet it is, as Helen Ramage (Goethals) has argued, closely linked to *A Survey of Modernist Poetry* and therefore 'central to any discussion of ... Graves's connection with Modernism'.[22] As she further points out, the *Pamphlet* was certainly 'the first, and has remained almost the only substantial, work of sustained thinking about the anthology as a significant form of marketing poetry'.[23]

Graves and Riding also worked separately, Riding completing *Contemporaries and Snobs*, described by Graves as her 'bombshell for the *Criterion, Dial, Calendar* and similar coteries'.[24] Consisting of essays written in America, Egypt, Islip and Vienna, all of which except 'A Prophecy or a Plea' had been rejected by the same magazines she was attacking, *Contemporaries and Snobs*, like much of her prose work, was an attempt to prove herself right and the rest of the literary world wrong. It would be published, mainly through Graves's influence, with Cape in February 1928, three months after the *Survey*. Arnold Bennett would head his *Evening Standard* review of the book, 'The Monstrous Conceit of Some Modernists'.[25] Further proof of Riding's disillusionment with the London literary establishment, in which Graves was making his name while she could not, would come in *Anarchism is Not Enough*, published also by Cape in May 1928. The most provocative of its highly provocative pieces is called 'Why Poe?', aimed at 'showing up the whole unwholesome Poe cult'.[26] Like Graves, she enjoyed ruffling feathers.

His own work, apart from editing *Poems (1914–1926)*, consisted of two essays, one on Wordsworth's letter to his great-uncle, the Rev. Robert Graves, written to make money, the other a labour of love. The well-known anthropologist Bronislav Malinowski, once a devoted student of Rivers's, had been attacking his former mentor's work in his recent books, and Graves's essay for the *Criterion* was an attempt to defend Rivers.[27] He also managed to write 'a few nice poems'.[28]

There is no evidence of which poems Graves wrote in Vienna, but one of the most likely candidates is the one he eventually entitled 'Sick Love'. First published in *Poems 1929* as 'Between Dark and Dark', it is one of the most striking love poems he ever wrote and is clearly based on his passion for Laura by the end of 1926. Read under the title 'Sick Love', its opening stanza suggests that it is addressed to the beloved, warning of the precariousness of human love:

> O Love be fed with apples while you may,
> And feel the sun and go in royal array,
> A smiling innocent on the heavenly causeway,[29]

But looked at under its revised title for *Poems 1926–1930*, 'O Love in Me', it becomes clear that the poet is addressing the personification of Love in himself, rather than the beloved, and therefore urging himself to savour the present, a variation on the *carpe diem* theme he knew so well from poems such as Herrick's 'Gather Ye Rosebuds' and Marvell's 'To his Coy Mistress':

> Take your delight in momentariness,
> Walk between dark and dark – a shining space
> With the grave's narrowness, though not its peace.[30]

Read in either light, such imagery as 'apples' and 'sun' can be seen as straightforward bucolic symbols of simple pleasures. But the qualification in stanza two, with its allusion to sexual frenzy, reminds the reader of another reality:

> Though in what listening horror for the cry
> That soars in outer blackness dismally
> The dumb blind beast, the paranoiac fury:[31]

This awareness of sin and death then makes those 'apples' of the first stanza more ambiguous, bringing to mind the forbidden fruit of the Tree of Knowledge, which Eve persuaded Adam to share with her in the Garden of Eden and in so doing introduced sin and death into the world. The 'smiling innocent on the heavenly causeway' of the opening lines becomes the creature of 'tainted blood' by stanza four, who is nevertheless instructed to 'enjoy ... the shivering glory not to be despised', the physical side of love. Such paradoxes were central to Graves's own ambivalent attitude towards sex. The stanza form – a tercet, or poetic triplet in which each line of each verse rhymes on the same rhyme – is unusual for Graves, though not unknown to him from his wide reading;[32] and his recent study of Wilfred Owen would have familiarized him with half-rhyme, which is the most experimental feature of the poem, helping him to convey a progressive sense of groping for meaning throughout the piece.

Neither feature proves Riding's influence on his technique, however, though her constant questioning and analysis almost certainly encouraged in him a sharpening of thought and greater willingness to depart from his usual practices. In telling Sassoon how 'sweet' she had been to him in Vienna, he claimed that she was 'gradually ... teaching [him] to ratiocinate'.[33] Occasionally in poems like 'Guessing Black or White' there are greater signs of her influence – her playing with logic and word order, her intellectuality. Reading Thomas Moult's review of Graves's *Poems (1914–1926)* and *A Survey of Modernist Poetry* in *The Observer*, Alfred Graves shared Moult's regret at 'the intellectual line' his son had pursued, 'hoping that he could find "heart" again in his verse'.[34] Ironically, since it was not top of Riding's own list of priorities, it was she who had helped to restore the singing quality to Graves's verse and would continue to do so. He had found the Muse he needed, but according to him not one who influenced his style in any meaningful way: 'I never wrote anything in Laura Riding's style as far as I know,' he told Peter Buckman and William Fifield.[35] As he went on to point out, he 'learnt from her a general attitude to things, rather than verse-craft'.

Other poems written at this time, such as 'A Former Attachment', reflect Graves's sense of excitement at this new start with a new love, in imagery taken from his recent voyage to Egypt:

> ... a calm delight
> When the port's cleared and the coast out of sight
> And ships are few, each on its proper course,
> With no occasion for approach or discourse.[36]

The joy of Laura's presence, it seems, was increased by their isolation. So it is puzzling to find Robert accepting his parents' invitation to visit them in the Austrian health spa of Bad Hofstein. The most likely explanation is that Robert was still anxious to gain his parents' approval of the new arrangement: his acceptance was accompanied, Alfred noted, by 'a really wonderful letter ... about the strange Trinity of friendship and love between him, Nancy and Laura'.[37] If so, Robert succeeded, Amy replying at once to say that they 'quite accepted the situation'. Two days later Robert and Laura travelled the 170 miles from Vienna to visit them on tickets paid for by Amy.

But what 'situation' did Alfred and Amy accept? Rosaleen, anxious to protect both sides, had told her parents that Robert and Laura were 'still quite innocent' and their son did nothing to destroy this illusion. As Laura reported to Polly, Mr and Mrs Graves understood the Trinity only in 'idealized and Platonic terms'.[38] Her own insistence on truthfulness and outspokenness in all matters seems to have been rationalized in exchange for four pleasant days of walking, picnics and conversation. For Robert's parents to learn that she and their son shared a bed, she concluded, would have caused them too much pain.[39] And in any case, though sex was certainly a significant aspect of the Trinity, the way in which Laura described it played down its significance. At Bad Hofstein she was her most charming and docile self, delighting Amy with her firm but affectionate way with Robert and the enthusiasm with which she discussed their work together. Amy believed Laura to be:

> ... very unselfish and she is more brain than body and has Robert well in hand. They are like a very intimate brother and sister together. She tells him plainly when he is at fault or she does not agree with him. She wears a picture of Nancy hanging round her neck and falling to her chest and speaks of her just as naturally as a sister might.[40]

Laura was truly appreciative of Amy's financial help with the Islip home and support of the children, but however genuinely she and Robert wanted to spare his parents pain by concealing their sexual relationship, they made the situation for them much worse in the long run; when Amy and Alfred finally learnt the true nature of the relationship, they felt deceived as well as shocked. Amy, predictably, would react more strongly than her softer-hearted husband, refusing ultimately to have tea with Robert and his children if Laura was present.

Robert and Laura returned to Vienna on Sunday, 17 October 1926. England still seemed far away to them. While Robert wrote dutifully to Nancy and Laura sent postcards to each of his children, their world was now narrowed down almost solely to each other and their work. Laura's

The Close Chaplet had been published by the Hogarth Press, a copy sent as a 'thank-you' present to Robert's parents (who found it 'difficult'),[41] and Robert was expecting proofs of his *Poems (1914–1926)* from Heinemann. (Laura, he told his father, had been a 'severe critic' of them.)[42] He also read proofs of his survey of *The English Ballad*, which he sent on to Alfred, who added a few corrections on the Irish ballads included under his guidance and returned it to the publisher, Ernest Benn.

By December they had done such a 'hell of a lot of work', Graves told Sassoon, that they were returning to England.[43] But just why, when their plan to work together had succeeded so well, they needed to return home nine months earlier than originally planned is not satisfactorily explained. They may simply have lacked the money to pay the rent. A more likely explanation, however, lay in Laura's need for a high level of emotional stimulus, friendly or otherwise. In fact, as Deborah Baker notes, after one of Laura's many feuds, 'to excite "loathing interest" from others was to create an intimacy more wild and powerful than the rhetoric of romantic love, physical passion, or emotional or intellectual intimacies would allow'.[44] Once she had experienced the latter with Robert and the excitement of being truly alone with him had worn off, she may have become bored. Frances Wilson argues that 'three people were needed to play Laura's game',[45] and this certainly seems to have been the case up to the time she met Robert. Once in England she had had that third person in Nancy. Whether Nancy had sent her off with her blessing to Vienna, with a 'trousseau' made specially for the event, and contraceptives supplied as one version has it, or in a more hostile spirit as Amy implied, Nancy may have been necessary to Laura for a satisfactory relationship with Robert. Whatever her feelings, Nancy was there to meet Robert and Laura at Apple Tree Yard when they arrived back in London. And though this initial friendliness quickly wore off once back at 'World's End', Laura was back in her element, in a world of violent emotions.

Nancy's family was not at all happy at Laura's return; her normally tolerant father, William, who had reduced his daughter's allowance when Laura joined the household, now stopped it completely. Their financial situation, made worse by Robert's renting of a nearby cottage for him and Laura to work in, lurched once more into crisis. Tired of writing books for money unsuccessfully, Robert applied for a regular, paid job with the Extra-Mural Department of Oxford University, but without success. Apart from a small fee earned from a lecture at Cambridge, no money came in. It was exactly what Alfred and Amy had feared would happen when they discovered in late summer that their son had resigned from the first well-paid job of his life, in Cairo. Nevertheless Amy came to their rescue, as usual, and sent £20 to 'tide them thro' till April'.[46] Even Robert's journalist uncle, Charles, highly critical of his nephew's unconventional domestic arrangements, tried to find him work.

Just when it seemed that the situation could not get worse, at the end of February, after a particularly wet winter in a cold and draughty house, the whole family came down with flu. Whether to escape it, or in an effort to convince William Nicholson to resume Nancy's allowance, Laura fled the sick household to stay with friends in Norfolk. Left in sole charge of six invalids, the nanny Doris Harrison's own health broke down and she was ordered complete rest by her doctor. As so often, it was Robert who had to take over. Nancy's flu had been followed by jaundice and she had another of her nervous breakdowns, fleeing herself on 11 March to stay with her brother Ben and his wife Winifred Roberts in Cumberland. (It was an act she later came to regret since it left her open to the charge of desertion of the children.) Robert survived, he told his parents, on Easton's Syrup, a fearful-sounding tonic of quinine and strychnine. And the moment Nancy left for Cumberland, he contacted Laura and begged her to return, which she did immediately, ostensibly to help Robert with the children. Nancy, clearly unhappy with this arrangement, found work and accommodation near her brother and sent for the children, leaving Robert and Laura alone at 'World's End'.

Realizing how compromising the situation now looked, Laura once more set about reassuring Robert's mother with half-truths; that Robert was weak and ill and needed help was true, but that she was 'not staying on but only to see Robert over the worst' was once again a deliberate deception.[47] Doris's unexpectedly early return in April to 'World's End', where she found Robert and Laura still living on their own, may have reminded them of how the small community at Islip was likely to view their unconventional arrangements; by the end of the month they had left together for the more impersonal surroundings of London.

21

'FREE LOVE CORNER'[1] (MAY 1927– OCTOBER 1928)

> I forced this quarrel; it was not
>   So much disgust with all you did
> As sudden doubt of whom and what
>   My easy friendship hid...
> I carefully offended.
>   Accept this antic kick from one
>   Who used to be his father's son
>   Discreet in blind devotion.
>
> *'Dismissal'*[2]

By the end of May 1927 Laura had, with characteristic efficiency, found herself and Robert somewhere to live in London. A maisonette at 35A St Peter's Square, Hammersmith, it lay between King Street and the Thames, only a short walk away. An attractive development of Georgian paired villas in classical style, with stuccoed fronts and Ionic porches grouped around a communal garden, 35A and the surrounding houses had seen better days and were now mainly divided up into flats and rooms. As a result rents were reasonably cheap. Robert's landlord, Mr Dawson, who owned most of the houses on their west side of the square and lived only a few doors away, made no trouble about their unmarried status, though he may not have known of it. It was, in any case, a bohemian area favoured by painters and writers, 'thought in other circles', as Naomi Mitchison (who lived there at this time) recalled, 'very *avant-garde*'.[3]

In deference to Laura's views Robert had put the flat in her name, though he was registered as the sole occupier and, as usual, provided the money for the rent. Having let 'World's End' for £109 for the year, he could now afford to repay his mother, who charged him only about half of that, with a little left over. The maisonette at 35A occupied the top two floors of the four-storey house and, apart from the usual living room, kitchen and bathroom, it allowed separate studies for Robert and Laura, a large joint bedroom and a spare room, theoretically for Nancy and the children when they visited, but let out to a female barrister when money was even scarcer than usual. Both studies overlooked a neglected basement yard and garden at the back. It was a pleasant flat, made even more attractive by Laura's skilful interior design. But Robert hated renting, finding 'enforced tenancy ... like having to borrow a pair of old shoes: though the size may be correct, the creases in the uppers have been made by another foot, and though he may wear his own socks, and buy his own shoelaces, they remain loyal to their owner'.[4]

This particular tenancy would end with an attempted suicide and accusations of murder, but it started peacefully enough, perhaps too peacefully, since Graves, for one, began to feel paranoid about their lack of visitors. Still not quite free of his parents' bourgeois values, he worried about what his friends might think of his irregular situation, writing to Sassoon in an unusually conciliatory, almost pleading tone:

> Dearest Siegfried
>
> Laura and I are sharing a flat and would like you to come and see us when you can face it. We have rather sore heads at the moment because of the breakdown of a number of friends who have not been able to stand the embarrassment of this move; and we are apt to anticipate insults never intended. But I know that your nerves are as bad as ours and that your heart is true; so shall draw no wrong inferences whatever you do about us.
>
> Nancy will stay here when she comes up to London but is, like us, trying to settle herself more composedly. How are you?
>
> Affectionately,
> Robert[5]

If the reference here had been to the older members of his family rather than to 'friends ... unable to stand the embarrassment' of the move, Graves's fears might be understandable. As soon as his parents realized that Robert and Laura were living together, Amy refused to visit while Laura was present. And Robert's half-brother, Richard, continued to regard her as a bad influence on Robert. But the younger members of the family made every effort to remain in touch, with the exception of brother Charles, whose relationship with Robert had not improved over the years. Rosaleen still visited when she was in London, and John, though he had not initially taken to Laura, made a point of going to their flat, as did Clarissa. When Clarissa and John stopped visiting, it would not be because they disapproved of the relationship, but in reaction to Laura's scolding. John was told off on one occasion, for instance, when he referred in all innocence to 'Robert's study':

> *Sensation.* It was an insult. The room was their common work room and I could swallow that if I liked [John wrote in his journal]. She soon followed me up and continued the squabble ... She spoke of the insult to Nancy at Islip and to her in London when people came to see Robert and not her (Ha Ha!) and what an insult to be called or thought of as Robert's mistress, when they merely kept house together.[6]

When Clarissa, after a reprimand from Laura, eventually called at St Peter's Square, she was initially greatly impressed by Laura. But when she wrote a friendly letter, telling Laura how much she admired her and had enjoyed the evening, Laura reacted violently, with a long letter of reproof. Clarissa, for all her apparent frailty, was able to stand up to the bullying, signing her reply 'Yours, with some desire to laugh – Clarissa Graves'; but it was the end of any meaningful relationship between them.[7]

Since Laura behaved in a similarly high-handed way with Robert's friends, it is not surprising that a number of them chose to stay away. Sassoon, despite his recent differences with Graves, tried hard to retain their friendship. Ironically, it was just as Sassoon was becoming reconciled to Nancy that Laura had taken her place in Graves's life. In spite of repeated efforts to like the American poet – he invited her to dinner with Graves and visited them several times in 1927 – Sassoon was 'finally driven away by her intense egotism and eccentricity'.[8] He also felt threatened by her confrontational Modernist views and their possible effect on Graves, which made him feel like a lumbering 'intellectual Pickford [removal] van'.[9]

Peter Quennell, a frequent visitor at Islip in the early 1920s, who regarded Graves as his 'trusted literary mentor', remembered Riding as Graves's 'belligerent transatlantic muse', who 'hastened to make a clean sweep of most of his previous acquaintances', including himself.[10] Tom Driberg, another friend from Oxford, was told off sharply when he called at 35A and asked whether he could call Laura 'Mrs Graves' now that she was living with Robert. That was the end of his friendship, leaving him only with memories of the man he described as 'tall and burly, with a heavy, gypsy-like face that looked, in repose, sulky, and a sensual mouth'.[11] L. A. G. Strong, who had also known Robert since Oxford days, felt less than welcome when in reply to his suggestion of a meeting he received the offhand answer:

> Thanks for the post-card but I never move out of Hammersmith and people who want to see me vigorously enough sometimes come here. But not often, for I have lost all my small talk. This flat is principally Laura Riding's (Gottschalk), a Cumberland cottage principally Nancy Nicholson's, and a barge on the river principally mine: but we shift about...[12]

Strong does not appear to have written again for seven years.

Even first-time visitors who knew little of the situation were put off by Riding. Jack Lindsay, for example, a young Australian writer who started his own publishing house, the Fanfrolico Press, in 1927 and came to ask Graves to contribute an essay on the ballad for one of his publications, was antagonized by her. While he took to Graves – 'a tall rawboned slightly gaunt fellow, with a touch of the wilderness about him, like a mountain-dog trying to keep his tail up among the city tykes' – and 'liked him at once', Laura struck him as 'a disagreeably self-centred person with a hard discontented face'.[13] Lindsay also noted that Graves treated Riding 'with the utmost respect and tenderness' and turned his own crusade 'for truth and independence' into 'a crusade for Laura'.[14] Since few of his friends liked her for long, not many of them survived. Under Laura's guidance, Graves began to scorn many of his earlier friendships, as his poem 'Dismissal' shows. Family, too, was sacrificed in the process.

The effects would not be apparent immediately, however, and in any case by June 1927 Graves was so busy with a commission from Cape that he had no time to brood on it. T. E. Lawrence, who would be one of those eventually distanced from Graves because of Riding, was initially anxious to help them as they faced yet another financial crisis. Although Robert had assured his father that he and Laura had found work in London and were busily engaged on a Children's Dictionary, he was very short of money again. Knowing this, Lawrence had nominated Graves as the most suitable person to write a short book on Lawrence that Cape was planning. Coincidentally, Graves had given a radio broadcast on *Revolt in the Desert*, Lawrence's abridged version of *Seven Pillars*, a few months previously,[15] and Cape (and their American counterpart, Doubleday, Doran), who had been delighted by the sales of this more accessible version of Lawrence's Arabian adventures, now wanted a *Lawrence's Adventures* for boys. 'The terms were generous,' Graves recalled, 'and I replied that I would undertake the job.'[16] Unaware that Lawrence himself had recommended him for the job, he added the proviso, 'if Lawrence g[i]ve[s] his consent',[17] which of course he did, with the single word 'Yes' wired from Karachi where he was now stationed with the RAF.

Since Cape wanted *Lawrence's Adventures* published as a Christmas book, they gave Graves only six weeks in which to write it. A demanding job was made much more so when Lowell Thomas, the American journalist who had brought Lawrence to public attention originally, issued his 1924 book along similar lines in an English edition. Graves's book, Cape now decided, had to be three times the agreed length and directed at adults rather than boys. But the advance would be £500, an enormous sum to Graves, and royalties on sales likely to be very good indeed; Graves could not afford to refuse. Although he was allowed a few more weeks for the extra material needed, it meant working at least 12 hours a day for about 12 weeks. Both he and Lawrence afterwards agreed that he had worked 'too quickly', but there seemed little choice at the time.[18]

Given the circumstances, *Lawrence and the Arabs* (as it was now called) is surprisingly well done. It is both readable and reasonably accurate, considering Lawrence's famed secrecy about certain areas of his life, his sexuality in particular, and incidents such as the flogging at Dera'a. Graves sent long letters full of queries to India as he wrote it and Lawrence responded with detailed replies and suggestions. Graves had not been Cape's first choice, nor had Lawrence's motives in recommending him been entirely altruistic, as his confession to his All Souls friend Lionel Curtis shows:

> Robert Graves is writing a life of me for [Doubleday] Doran, who ramped about England asking many of the worst people to do it! ... On the whole better Robert Graves than another. He is a decent fellow, does not know too much about me: will think out some psychologically plausible explanation of my spiritual divigations: and will therefore help to lay at rest the uneasy ghost which seems to have stayed in England when I went abroad.[19]

Graves was determined to do as thorough a job as possible. He did a great deal of research, though whatever he checked in Lawrence's stories 'always proved true or understated'.[20] He went to see General Allenby, Lawrence's commander in the Middle East; his brother Philip Graves, who had access to the files at the Arab Bureau in Cairo; Lawrence's friends such as Robin Buxton, who had been in the Imperial Camel Corps; his fellow archaeologist D. G. Hogarth; his Oxford friend Vyvyan Richards; his brother Arnold; his mother (who refused to help); George Lloyd, with whom Graves had dined when he was High Commissioner in Cairo; his fellow aircraftsman Sergeant Pugh; 'and a dozen more'.[21] He tried to talk to anyone who had known Lawrence, including his own friends such as Sassoon, Forster and Hardy's wife Florence. He even wrote to Buckingham Palace 'to get the truth of T.E.'s famous interview with George V' and was delighted when the reply from the king actually 'improved on the story T.E.' had told him, about refusing the medals offered.[22] Although Graves never caught Lawrence out in a lie, he realized that he had evaded questions, such as exactly what had happened to him at Dera'a, an incident which Graves passes over in eight and a half lines.

Apart from one or two 'tiny spots' in it, Lawrence pronounced *Lawrence and the Arabs* a 'good book', proof of Graves's conscientious research and of how carefully he had followed *Seven Pillars of Wisdom* (his copy borrowed from the artist Eric Kennington).[23] Lawrence's approval may also have resulted from Graves's treatment of his homosexuality. Graves found any suggestion that Lawrence was a homosexual 'absurd and indecent'; he believed that the flogging at Dera'a had rendered him impotent and 'unable to consummate his heterosexual love for a mysterious woman, identified only as "S.A."[24] Wisely, however, since there is no firm proof of this and some evidence to the contrary, that 'S.A.' was male, Graves did not make it a focal point of his account.

Graves's first-hand knowledge of fighting in the First World War, though in a different theatre, enabled him to enter convincingly into Lawrence's adventures in Arabia. Revisiting that global conflict, so soon after his apparent rejection of it in the 1926 edition of his poems, evidently made him rethink his attitude towards war generally as he attempted to analyse Lawrence's attitude towards it:

> ... he has no stronger objection to war, as war, than to the human race as the human race; but he does not like wars in which the individual is swallowed up in the mass. He commented to me once on the anti-war poetry of Siegfried Sassoon, who had the misfortune to serve, on the Western Front, in divisions that were accustomed to lose the equivalent of their full strength every four or five months, that had Sassoon been serving with him in Arabia he would have written in a completely different vein. That is very likely true. On the other hand, Lawrence's revolt in the desert was a form of fighting so unlike 'civilized' war, and so romantically appealing, that it is perhaps fortunate that Siegfried Sassoon, Wilfred Owen, Edmund Blunden, and the other poets who got badly involved in the war were all infantrymen in France.[25]

Another interest of the book is Graves's analysis of what he calls Lawrence's 'exasperatingly complex personality'.[26] Although anxious to avoid any suggestion of a hagiography, he found himself 'inclined to accept ... the popular verdict that [Lawrence] is the most remarkable living Englishman'.[27] While making it clear that he was not attempting to give 'a general review of the Arab freedom movement and the part played by England and France',[28] he is careful to place events in their geographical and historical context. But he does not hesitate to liven his text up with some personal references, such as Lawrence's financial help to 'a poet who had lost money, in an attempt to start a grocery-shop'.[29]

And when asked the usual question by his publisher about 'new material', Graves was also able to boast that his book included a hitherto unknown long letter from Lawrence to Vyvyan Richards, from July 1918, 'a most magnificently illuminating one'; fresh material from Lawrence's archaeological dig at Carcemish between 1912 and 1914; 'a summary of what happened to the other Arab characters in the story...'; a lot of 'University period stuff'; and fresh information about Lawrence's years in the Tank Corps between 1923 and 1925.

Altogether, it was a book guaranteed to appeal to popular taste, 'a journalistic job, done quickly', but, he hoped, 'inoffensively', with the writing 'as subdued and matter of fact' as he could make it.[30] Advance sales were impressive, the reviews mainly positive. Graves, more like his father than he wished to acknowledge, had tried to 'fix' one or two of these in advance, writing for instance both to Gosse and to Blunden, who had just returned from three years at the University of Tokyo. When Gosse complained to Sassoon about this, Sassoon wrote indignantly to Graves, who denied ever having tried to 'arrange a review' of one of his own books.[31] His excuse was that he did not regard it as his 'own book' at all, but 'merely a collation of Lawrence material supplied from various sources and commissioned by Cape and (accidentally) edited by [him]self as a sort of joke; so unauthorial indeed that I can even act as a tout for it'.[32] As an example of Graves's special pleading it was a good letter, but understandably Sassoon was not convinced and wrote to Riding complaining of such behaviour. At this point Graves apologized, or came as near as he ever did to it, though only because he was worried about Laura's opinion: 'If you can honestly say [to her] that you regard Robert as thoughtless, but no longer blame him for suggesting to Gosse that he might like to notice the Lawrence book, it will put things fairly right again.'[33] He ended on an even more conciliatory note, reminding his friend: 'Siegfried, we're all fools and blockheads. And you and I have forgiven each other a lot in the last eleven years or so.'[34] The quarrel was duly made up, but the end of Graves's friendship with Sassoon was one step nearer.

When *Lawrence and the Arabs* was published in November 1927, it was evident that it had no need of Gosse's support, selling initially at the rate of 10,000 copies a week. By the end of the month it had gone into a fourth impression, the sales helped by the addition of seven striking illustrations of the Arab leaders by Eric Kennington before publication. The resulting royalties were by far the highest Graves had so far earned from his writing. Equally importantly, it established him as someone who could sell books and from this point on he could be certain of getting commissions and commanding high advances. *Lawrence and the Arabs* would be the first in a series of 'best-sellers', books written in an easy, readable style around good, racy stories, including in the next few years *Good-bye to All That*, *I, Claudius* and *Claudius the God*. There were other benefits, which almost certainly helped Laura to overcome her jealousy of his success. In signing Cape's contract, Graves had stipulated that the firm must undertake to publish not only his second collaboration with Riding, *Pamphlet Against Anthologies*, but also Riding's two collections of essays, *Contemporaries and Snobs* and *Anarchism is Not Enough*. While she worked to complete *Anarchism* in London, he recovered from weeks of unremitting work with Nancy and the children. Nancy, now settled in a cottage near Brampton, a small village about eight miles to the north-east of Carlisle, claimed to have found there 'the true sense of absolute rural quiescence' she said she needed,[35] but she left to stay with Laura in London during Robert's visit to Cumberland. Laura was now 'a member of our household', Robert felt it necessary to warn Edward Marsh.[36]

Graves's anxiety to promote Riding – 'she can write like hell', he told Marsh[37] – is a marked feature of their relationship and as he became more successful, his efforts increased. Ironically, now that he was finding it easier than ever to place his own poetry, articles and reviews in magazines, he almost stopped trying to do so, for fear of highlighting Riding's continued rejections.[38] When, in August 1927, *Criterion* published a damning review of Laura's first publication for the Hogarth Press, *The Close Chaplet*, together with a favourable one of Graves's *Poems (1914–1926)*, he wrote angrily to the magazine's publisher, T. S. Eliot, demanding that his letter be published. The reviewer, John Gould Fletcher, had accused Riding of being derivative, claiming that 'her poems of detached and exhaustive comment ... owe nearly everything to Miss Marianne Moore; her more serious poems come from Mr Ransom or Mr Graves; and her more lyrical outbursts recall just as persistently Miss Gertrude Stein.'[39] Two months later John Crowe Ransom, who had first noted her in his *Fugitive* magazine in 1923 for her 'quality of originality', would describe her to fellow *Fugitive* poet Allen Tate as a 'borrower, or anything but *sui generis*'.[40] Nothing could be more calculated to infuriate Riding, who prided herself above all on her uniqueness. To be seen to be influenced by Graves, in particular when she saw her role as influencing *him*, was insufferable. Graves's furious denial on her behalf was so forceful that Eliot, who still considered himself his friend, asked him whether he was sure he wanted the letter printed. In response an even angrier letter followed from Graves, together with blistering criticism of the *Criterion*'s low literary standards. He also spurned Eliot's invitation to submit some of his own poems to the magazine, offered no doubt as an olive branch. There would be no more letters between the two men for nearly 20 years. In the course of this row, Graves had informed Eliot, in an echo of Riding, that he had now arrived at the point 'of always saying exactly what [he] mean[t] in matters concerning poetry', and that when this led, as it must, to the loss of all his literary friends, there would be 'a natural and graceful end' to his writing career.[41] Eliot had been the first of these 'friends' to be so sacrificed.

It was partly in an effort to be independent of editors and the publishing world generally, partly to bolster Laura yet further, that Robert now spent a sizeable part of his earnings from Cape on a printing press. He would appoint her 'Chief Manager', himself merely 'partner', and register the press in her name, though he paid for its running. He had discussed the idea with Lawrence, who thought 'owning a private press [was] one of the richest things a man can do'.[42] Lawrence had wanted to own one with Vyvyan Richards since their pre-war time together at Oxford, but his subsequent travels had made this impossible. Richards, however, had gone on to own a private press and was ready to advise Robert and Laura about purchasing their own. He found them a Crown Albion of 1872, similar to the one William Morris had used at the Kelmscott Press. A large machine that printed eight octavo pages at a time, it weighed 17 hundredweight, close to a tonne, but nonetheless was hauled up to their maisonette where it was installed in its own room in pristine splendour. Nancy Cunard, who would start her own small publishing house, the Hours Press, this same year, noted the 'terrific, clinical tidiness of everything' when she visited, remembering the Crown Albion in particular 'with its accessories about it in a way no printer would take time off to keep so clean, almost as if in a museum'.[43] Laura's obsessive tidiness and perfectionism would make hand-printing even more stressful for her than for Robert, who could happily wear mismatched socks, for instance, without even noticing.

The somewhat recherché name of the press, 'Seizin', an arcane legal term meaning 'possession of land by freehold', was almost certainly chosen to signify possession of the means of production. According to Laura, 'One may, hence, read back into the launching of the Press with "Seizin" for its name a spirit of moral resolve to use it well.'[44] As their first prospectus made clear, by 'use it well' Laura did not mean as a generator of 'fine' printing on beautiful hand-made paper, such as the recently founded Nonesuch and Gregynog Presses produced: it was content that mattered. 'Our editions', the prospectus read, 'are decidedly not addressed to collectors but to those interested in work rather than printing – of a certain quality.'[45] 'Miss Riding and I publish no books except those we consider necessary and which we commission from necessary people,' Robert wrote self-importantly to their hapless agent, J. B. Pinker, who had asked in all innocence whether Robert was interested in a book for publication at their press: 'In other words we are not "looking for" books.'[46] Robert's father, foolhardy enough to suggest an anthology of family writings, was rebuffed with equal firmness.

Both Robert and Laura had found a home for their less 'popular' work at the Hogarth Press, which had undoubtedly influenced their own decision to start a private press, and the nature of it when they did so. Deborah Baker argues that the founding of the Seizin Press was also an 'answer to Bloomsbury and its Hogarth Press'.[47] Like Leonard and Virginia Woolf, however, Robert and Laura did not find printing easy, despite Vyvyan Richards's patient help and encouragement. Laying the type was both complicated and demanding, preparing and dampening the pages for printing even more so, especially for a perfectionist like Laura. But the printing of their prospectus was fairly straightforward compared with that of their first book, Riding's *Love as Love, Death as Death*, one of seven books published at the press between 1928 and 1934. A far more ambitious and extensive project than a one-page prospectus, it also involved the more specialized task of setting poetry. (They had intended to publish a *Children's Dictionary* as their first publication, but it never materialized.) It took them a year to produce 175 copes of *Love as Love, Death as Death* and by the time it was ready Laura had already got Gertrude Stein to agree that she would submit something to the press. When Stein's *An Acquaintance with Description* arrived, it would threaten to be even more challenging, since they could not decide whether it was poetry or prose.

The Seizin Press would prepare one more work for publication in England, Graves's *Poems 1929*, then four more in Majorca, before becoming the outlet for Riding's ambitious hard-bound magazine, *Epilogue*, which would run between 1935 and 1938. After their first struggles to set her poems, they would farm out their typesetting and the press would become less time-consuming, though still an important part of their identity, particularly for Riding. For her to be able to commission books from someone of Stein's stature, or suggest that T. E. Lawrence write them a book on speed, for instance, gave her the literary credentials and confidence that Graves was determined she should have.

The writing of *Lawrence and the Arabs* had kept Graves away from his poetry from June to August, as did the setting up of the Seizin Press in September and October. But he seemed in no hurry to return to it and in December 1927 started converting a barge bought with his royalties, the *Ringrose*, for Nancy and the children to live on during trips to London.[48] Apart from a trip to Cumberland for Christmas with them, he continued the hard manual work involved well into January. Presumably, since royalties were still very healthy, he chose to do this rather than delegating the work and focusing on poetry, which raises the question of Riding's overall effect on his poetry in the late 1920s. He was to write less verse between late 1926 and mid-1929 than he had, for instance, during his most stressful time with Nancy, between 1923 and 1925. Several men would complain of Riding rendering them physically impotent, but in Graves's case she seems to have inhibited him mentally in an area he claimed to care most about, perhaps as a result of her unrelenting close dissection of his efforts.

Work on the *Ringrose*, moored on a nearby stretch of the Thames, was finished towards the end of January, when Jenny, now nine, David, seven, Catherine, five and Sam, three years old, moved in with their nanny, Doris. But it was midwinter, the boat damp and inadequately heated, and there was no Nancy to supervise them. Both boys became ill, David with a severe cold and Sam, more seriously, with bronchitis. Rosaleen was alarmed by Sam's high temperature and wanted him in hospital, but was overruled by Laura and Robert. It was not until his bronchitis turned to pneumonia that he was taken to hospital by Nancy, who had been wired for. (A diphtheria scare would follow for the children in April.) Laura and Robert blamed the nanny, whom they sacked instantly, but their own self-absorption was clearly to blame. According to Doris, neither of them was willing to take responsibility for the children. Although Robert saw the children fairly regularly, either in Cumberland or London, his central concern remained Laura. And though she was punctilious in her attentions to his children, she was inexperienced and had other more pressing interests.

As another incident at this time suggests, it was not callousness so much as unawareness that dictated Graves's treatment of his children. When Thomas Hardy died on 11 January 1928, Graves was sad but not devastated. Sassoon, who had known Hardy much better and loved him almost as a father, felt it very badly indeed. He could hardly bear to attend the funeral at Westminster Abbey on 18 January. Surrounded by publicity, controversy and outright wrangling, it seemed to him a disgrace. Like Hardy and Florence themselves, he believed Hardy's body should be laid to rest in the family plot in Stinsford churchyard, near to their Dorset home, and was enraged by Sir Sidney Cockerell's insistence, as co-executor, that it should be buried in Poet's Corner. ('Efficient but devoid of all feeling,' Sassoon commented of Cockerell on this occasion.) The gruesome compromise eventually reached, that Hardy's heart should go to Stinsford, his ashes to the Abbey, seemed to Sassoon to lack any kind of dignity or appropriateness and depressed him even further. He was equally disgusted by Graves's 'presumptuous' article on Hardy in the *Sphere*, 'a vulgar and hasty exploitation', he felt, of the fact that Graves had stayed one night at Max Gate in 1920. The whole affair, Sassoon told Ottoline, 'drove [him] distracted' for several weeks and made him 'hate' the world. It was in this context that Graves wrote tactlessly to Sassoon, telling him that he had turned down two requests from publishers to write a short biography of Hardy, but that he had suggested to one of them, Cape, that Sassoon should write it instead. Sassoon was appalled by what seemed to him another exploitation of Hardy and did not write to Graves again for another two years.

Two months after this break T. E. Lawrence, who had felt increasingly alienated by Graves's growing harshness of judgement, wrote to him: 'We must be travelling different ways. You are getting exasperated, hating the dullness and stupidity of mankind. I'm losing my cutting edge, and therefore understand better, sympathise with people like W[ells] and Bennett and the rest, who slide down the easy slope into fatuity. Only I'll slide down silently.' What he does not say, though evidently suspects, is that Riding was largely responsible for Graves's growing intolerance. He would make it clear, in a tactful letter to Graves just before Lawrence's death in May 1935, that it was Laura who had come between them: 'Laura saw me too late, after I had changed direction. She is, was, absolutely right to avoid communication with me. There are no faults on either side, but common sense, the recognition of a difficulty too arduous to be worth the effort of surmounting.'[49]

But if old friends were lost, new ones were made. Not long after the Hardy incident, for example, Graves got to know a much younger poet, Norman Cameron. He and Riding had first met Cameron briefly at Oxford in 1927, when he had invited them to speak at the English Club. A Scot, born in 1901 the same year as Riding, Cameron had been educated at Fettes College in Edinburgh before going on to read English at Oriel College, Oxford. His closest friend at the university was John Aldridge of Corpus Christi, who would become a painter of some repute. Despite his different college, Cameron had become part of a group known as the Corpus Aesthetes. 'A strange tall man with an uncombed mop of hair', according to one friend, he had 'a kind of breezy, serious gusto' that drew people to him.[50]

After completing his degree Cameron moved to London and was living in the same bohemian area of Hammersmith as Graves and Riding by mid-1928, sharing a studio near St Peter's Square with Aldridge. Graves, who would remain good friends with Cameron (unlike Riding) until his death in 1953 aged only 47, thought highly of his slim output of poetry and would agree to write an Introduction to Cameron's *Collected Poems* a few years later. In it he remembered the poet with evident respect and affection as 'tall, pale, never very strong, with a stutter in his voice, gentle, witty, clumsy, shrewd, over-generous and utterly reliable'.[51] When asked who was 'any good' as a poet in later life, Graves would cite Cameron. He particularly admired 'Forgive Me, Sire' for its manly resolve, expressed so wittily and sparingly:

> Forgive me, Sire, for cheating your intent,
> That I, who should command a regiment,
> Do amble amiably here, O God,
> One of the neat ones in your awkward squad.

Although there is no evidence that Graves influenced the younger man, they had fairly similar poetic tastes. Like Graves (and as Graves points out), 'Modernist fashions in metres, diction and theme scarcely interested him, though he admired well-considered writing in experimental form and had a particular liking for e. e. cummings', as did Graves himself.[52] Dylan Thomas, who became a close friend towards the end of Cameron's short life, would christen him 'Normal' Cameron.

Yet as Graves rightly detected, there were two very distinct sides to Cameron – 'alternately a Presbyterian precisian [*sic*] [like his clergyman father] and a pagan poet and boon-companion'.[53] The latter was well to the fore in 1928, as Graves witnessed for himself at Cameron's wild parties in his nearby studio. There were even rumours of visits he had made with Aldridge to the infamous drug dens of Ham Common, though no suggestion that Graves accompanied them. Graves's experiments with drugs would come later. But in 1928 Cameron and his friends were an introduction of sorts to a more hedonistic lifestyle for Graves and he seems to have shed his inhibitions willingly. Taught by Laura to dance, he abandoned himself to it enthusiastically and joined in with other, more esoteric rituals that apparently involved a lot of shrieking and lying on the floor.[54]

One of the most unconventional people at these parties, who accounted for much of their zaniness, was Len Lye, like Cameron the same age as Laura and therefore six years younger than Robert. An aspiring filmmaker who saw greater chances of success in Europe than in his native New Zealand, he had worked his passage to England as a stoker in 1927, at the age of 26. He was living on A. P. Herbert's barge, the *Avoca*, next to the *Ringrose* when Robert bought it at the end of 1927. An early innovator in animated films, Lye was doing what Walt Disney did before Disney and doing it better, according to some of his admirers. Penniless on arrival in England, he had been taken in by Eric Kennington, who had arranged for him to live on Herbert's *Avoca*. And it was almost certainly Kennington who introduced the ebullient New Zealander to Graves. Lye formed a close relationship with both Graves and Riding: 'If they were going up town to get a good steak or something, or going up to Maidenhead to have a swim, or to Oxford,' he recalled, 'they would be sure I came along.'[55] Alastair Reid, a poet who became friends with Graves, claimed that:

> Robert treasured Len as someone who seemed as though he had come from a different planet. Len always left the same residual impression in everybody – whenever you mentioned Len, they always lit up and immediately you would hear stories that had some smack of eccentricity.

He created such an amazing visual environment. When he set the table it would have some little extra layout to it that no one would have thought of but him. On a winter's night when Len would light a fire it would be like a huge celebration, it would be like the first fire anybody had ever lit, and we just had to watch it. He really sparked things all the time.[56]

Lye's biographer, Roger Horrocks, believes that Lye's company 'could bring out the joyful side of the sometimes melancholy poet' and that 'Graves was still struggling to free himself from some aspects of his upbringing'.[57] Riding, too, valued Lye as a fellow Modernist who was, if anything, more extreme in his experiments than she was herself. She relished in particular his totally unconventional, extremely lively letters that she helped him edit for their Seizin Press, though the two would eventually fall out, as Riding did with so many of her friends. Graves, together with Kennington and Cameron, would subsidise Lye for some years to come, starting with his avant-garde animated film *Tusalava*. Lye, in turn, would design striking Modernist book covers for the Seizin Press and silkscreens and batiks for Graves and Riding's walls. He would infect them all with his enormous enthusiasm and complete disregard for convention and would, like Cameron, remain a lifelong friend. Graves was especially interested in Lye's six-month stay in Samoa before coming to England, since it linked up with Rivers's study of mother rights there. So firmly did he and Riding believe in Lye's genius that they would plan to build him a film studio when they moved to Majorca.

One of the most exciting new friends made during this period, however, did not live anywhere near St Peter's Square: Gertrude Stein. Graves had started reading her work before he met Riding, possibly in response to Edith Sitwell's question: 'Do you know the work of that extraordinary, gifted, mad woman Gertrude Stein?'[58] But Stein's startling experiments with language were much more to Riding's taste than to his own and it was at her suggestion that Stein was invited to contribute her work to the Seizin Press. It was also at her instigation that she and Graves visited Stein at 26 rue de Fleurus in Paris to discuss her proposed contribution, *An Acquaintance with Description*, which would be their second publication. So, in the summer of 1928, after three weeks spent at Hyères in Provence with Riding's friend Polly, they travelled back to London via Paris to visit Stein and her lover, Alice B. Toklas.

Whilst Riding had been enraged at Fletcher's suggestion that her work had been influenced by Stein, she had written most admiringly of the much older American writer in 'The New Barbarism and Gertrude Stein', published in the experimental Modernist magazine *transition*. It was this essay that, with some revisions by both Graves and Riding, had concluded their *Survey of Modernist Poetry* in 1927:

> Nothing that we have said here should be understood as disrespectful to Gertrude Stein. She has had courage, clarity, sincerity, simplicity. She has created a human mean in language, a mathematical equation of ordinariness which leaves one with a tender respect for that changing and unchanging slowness that is humanity and Gertrude Stein.[59]

Riding's essay had been revised yet again to make up, in an expanded form, the second part of her *Contemporaries and Snobs*, in which she argued that Stein had supplied a much-needed 'new sense of time' that she herself hoped to develop. She also claimed in her second series of essays, *Anarchism is Not Enough* (1928), that Stein had freed language from its inhibiting historical and mythological associations, using words as if they had no 'experience'.[60] Riding described Stein's experiments as writing 'allowed to become disorganized until so loose grammatically that it could be reorganized as if afresh, without regard to how words and their combinations had been sympathetically affected by usage',[61] a point illustrated effectively from her own work, despite her denial of Stein's influence, in such poems as 'Elegy in a Spider's Web':

> What to say when the spider
> Say when the spider what
> When the spider the spider the spider what
> The spider does what
> Does does dies does it not
> Not live and then not...[62]

Other essays by Riding had been published in *transition* apart from that on Stein as well as some of her poems and stories, and Riding was anxious to meet the magazine's editor, Eugène Jolas, during her trip to Paris in the summer of 1928. But she was so contentious when she met Jolas and his wife Marie at a lunch also attended by Graves that she was not asked to contribute to *transition* again. Another of the magazine's contributors, Kay Boyle, who was at the same lunch, found both Riding and Graves so overbearing that she left the restaurant in disgust. The meeting with Stein was more successful, resulting in the establishment of a warm friendship and an invitation to visit Stein and Toklas at their country house, Bilignin, at Belley in the south-east of France.

When Robert and Laura arrived back in Hammersmith at the end of June it was to an equally satisfactory situation. He had found better moorings for his barge and the children returned there with their new nanny, Miss Millard, for a much happier second visit. He also made sure to set aside time to see the children daily and to take them for walks along the Thames. In addition he started to help Sam with speech difficulties brought on by his deafness. When Nancy came down from Cumberland to visit in the autumn, she decided to rejoin the Trinity, though choosing to live on the barge with the children this time. Meantime the rest of Robert and Laura's summer had been spent working mainly on their first Seizin Press book, *Love as Love, Death as Death*. (Alfred was grateful for his son Philip's attempts to explain what he called 'the Triangle',[63] but was also puzzled by the 'queer specimen' from the press that Robert had sent him, 'one of Laura's last poems'.)[64]

These were the good times with Laura, when Robert was forming new friendships to compensate for those he had lost through his relationship with her. But the war was still with him intermittently; Laura's most rigorous purgings of his past could not rid him of it altogether. Cape had asked him to write an Introduction to *The Enormous Room*, e. e. cummings's account of his experience as an American prisoner of war in France, which they published for the first time in July 1928: cummings's book had been brought to Graves's attention by one of its great admirers, T. E. Lawrence, who had read it in the American edition of 1922. Reading it carefully again before writing his Introduction had brought back his own still-vivid memories of the war for Graves, who would include two of them in his piece. At the same time he was reading Sassoon's more similar experiences to his own in *Memoirs of a Fox-Hunting Man* and Blunden's *Undertones of War*, part of a spate of war memoirs flooding the market by 1928. At this point Graves had no intention of adding his own contribution to the flood, but when he did so it would be much nearer in style and approach to cummings's directness and lack of reverence for authority than to Sassoon's and Blunden's heavily nostalgic, highly poetical, gently humorous and deliberately understated treatments.

When Graves did sit down to write his own account, *Good-bye to All That*, nearly a year later, it would be as a result of a dramatic incident already taking shape imperceptibly by the end of October 1928, when Riding dispatched him to Ireland to 'inspect' an admirer of her work and potential new disciple, Geoffrey Phibbs.

22

'LIKE THE PLOT OF A RUSSIAN NOVEL'[1] (FEBRUARY–APRIL 1929)

If strange things happen where she is,
So that men say that graves open
And the dead walk, or that futurity
Becomes a womb and the unborn are shed,
Such portents are not to be wondered at,
Being tourbillions[2] in Time made
By the strong pulling of her bladed mind
Through that ever-reluctant element.

'On Portents'[3]

'Such colossal egotism is not sane,' wrote Rosaleen Graves, less than two months after she had helped save Laura's life – and mobility – following her leap from a fourth-storey window on 27 April 1929.[4] Nor is 'such colossal egotism' usual, which is one reason why the events of that day strike most people as completely bizarre and almost unbelievable.

Laura's plunge was the culmination of events that had begun in earnest nearly three months earlier in February 1929, when she had summoned her Irish admirer, Geoffrey Phibbs, to London. Vetted by Graves in Ireland in late October 1928, Phibbs had apparently passed muster and by February 1929 Laura needed a fresh diversion. She had been with Robert nearly as long as she had lived with her ex-husband, Louis Gottschalk, and was evidently becoming bored. Although what she called the 'Holy Trinity' of herself, Robert and Nancy had recently been revived by Nancy's move back from Cumberland to the Thames barge, the threesome had lost its early excitement. Laura almost certainly hoped to restore it by adding Phibbs to the mix. The Trinity, she decreed, would become 'the Four', or 'the Holy Family'.

The most interesting of the many questions surrounding the events precipitated by Phibbs's arrival is how such an intelligent, normally rational man like Graves could have allowed himself to become so entangled in the situation that he himself would jump from a third-storey window after Laura. As Martin Seymour-Smith, who discussed the affair with Graves at some length, testified, after carrying out Riding's instructions to vet Phibbs, Graves had felt obliged to conceal his contempt for both the man and his poetry and 'indulged in his best hopes and wishes, as unfortunately he always did'.[5] Seymour-Smith argued that 'if Phibbs came into the picture, then Graves should have refused to stay in it'.[6] But as he also pointed out, it was not easy for Graves: 'He loved Laura, and did not yet realize that she was looking for adulation from a new quarter.'[7]

Another problem in interpreting the mixture of high farce and very real tragedy that followed Phibbs's entry into the 'Holy Circle' is distinguishing actual facts from the many fictions subsequently invented to soothe bruised egos, extreme jealousy, intense guilt, or due simply to the vagaries of memory. Graves, Riding and Phibbs each left several different accounts of what happened and why, parts of which contradict each other completely.

Who first contacted whom in 1928, for instance, is not clear, though it is evident from Phibbs's letter to Graves the day after the latter's October visit to him that the Irishman had been reading Riding's 'Jocasta' essay in *Anarchism is Not Enough* and had found it, together with her other work studied over the previous six months, 'more important' than anything else in his life.[8] It had changed his view of his own poetry, published by the Hogarth Press in two volumes, completely.[9] They now struck him as 'witty and cynical in an undergraduate mode, their symbolism perverse and their technique licentious'.[10] According to Riding, he had contacted her first to convey his admiration for her work, though according to Phibbs, it was Riding who had written first, praising a poem of his in the *New Statesman*. Whatever the sequence, it is clear that during Graves's 1928 visit Phibbs had begged him to let him know of any jobs available in England: 'I'm tired of dissembling in Ireland.'[11] Riding's subsequent summons to him to come to work for her and Graves in London seemed to him 'like an invitation from one of the Muses to sport on Mount Helicon'.[12] Riding may sometimes have regarded herself as divine, but on this occasion her motives were more human: both she and Graves needed help with the Seizin Press and she herself wanted a fresh collaborator for her latest ambitious project, a philosophical work dealing with the knowledge of good and evil, to be followed by a dictionary of sorts. And once the young poet known as the 'Irish Adonis'[13] appeared in person at 35A St Peter's Square on 7 February 1929, she also felt that he would make a stimulating addition to the huge bed she shared with Graves, over which hung her sky-blue banner announcing: 'GOD IS A WOMAN'.

The object of Laura's interest, Geoffrey Phibbs, came from the Anglo-Irish landed gentry and to his friend, the working-class writer Frank O'Connor, seemed a creature from a more privileged world, with 'all the grace of a thoroughbred'.[14] It was a quality that Riding, who had come from equally humble beginnings, appreciated. Born in England in 1900, the year before Riding, he was taken as a small child to Ireland and brought up there, and later sent back for the requisite English education. When he returned in 1918 it was to serve briefly in the Royal Irish Rifles, then, when the war ended, to enter Trinity College, Dublin's Protestant University, where Robert's own father and uncles had studied in the late nineteenth century. Failing to complete his zoology degree (just as Laura had failed to complete her own degree in English at Cornell), Geoffrey next took a job as a scientific demonstrator at Dublin's Royal College of Science. He eventually took up work as assistant organizer of the new libraries being set up in Ireland by the American philanthropist Andrew Carnegie.

It was while working as a librarian in Wicklow that Phibbs had met O'Connor, who remembered him as 'tall and thin and dark, with a long lock of black hair that fell over one eye, a stiff, abrupt manner, a curt high-pitched voice and a rather insolent air',[15] and that he had the thick 'sensual lips of the poet', reminding him of Proust's Baron de Charlus.[16] O'Connor also noted that he possessed 'a sort of animal beauty' and, O'Connor suspected, 'a touch of animal cruelty'.[17] Riding, who left her own account of Phibbs in her autobiographical novel, *14A*, found something 'very black-looking' and 'burning' about him, with a face that seemed always 'dark and hot'.[18] Although his eyes were deep blue, these too seemed to her 'dark' and her first words to him, she claimed, were 'You are the Devil!'[19] O'Connor's landlady had also called Phibbs 'the Devil' and refused to have him in her house, unlike Riding, who was thrilled by the comparison. Like Phibbs, she dabbled in the 'black arts', flirting with magic and the occult, as Graves's friend Lord Tredegar had done at Oxford and one of Phibbs's Dublin friends, W. B. Yeats, had done in joining the theosophical (Hermetic) Order of the Golden Dawn. Aleister Crowley and his followers were still making such practices fashionable in England. Phibbs entered willingly into Riding's cabbalistic practices, though neither of them knew much of the ancient Jewish esoteric mystical tradition of Cabbala. (Riding's rituals were at times more akin to voodoo.) He rather enjoyed having his horoscope drawn up for him, for instance, and approved of the resulting description of himself as 'fiery, energetic and somewhat restless ... impulsive, enthusiastic, courageous, frank and enterprising ... [but] sometimes quarrelsome and petulant'.[20] Graves appears to have stood a little apart from these practices. Asked by Ken Barrett, who was more deeply involved in the subject, whether Graves knew that Riding was a 'magician', Riding answered that Robert, out of self-protection, did not let himself know more than he needed to know, but that he was the only person to whom she revealed exactly who she was.[21]

Like Riding, too, Phibbs believed that marriage was an outdated institution, despite his own marriage at the age of 24 to a talented artist eight years his senior, Norah McGuinness. He was a great admirer of Havelock Ellis's *Psychology of Sex*, which replaced for him the Bible he had rejected during his Protestant upbringing. He also 'really enjoyed pornography', according to the more puritanical Catholic O'Connor, who nevertheless quoted one of Phibbs's bawdier verses in his account, with relish. At the same time it was clear to O'Connor that Phibbs 'really loved poetry as no one else [he had] ever known loved it',[22] Shelley in particular. Phibbs was determined to follow Shelley's revolutionary ideas on free love in his own marriage, though when his wife started an affair with the writer David Garnett (a notable member of the Bloomsbury Group), he found it hard to live up to these ideals. But when introduced to Graves and Riding's so-called

'Free Love Corner', he cooperated readily enough at first, taking his turn with Riding in her triple bed, while Graves looked on. (As Graves recalled it later to Seymour-Smith, Phibbs was given more than his fair share of the action initially.)

But before any of this could take place, Riding believed it necessary to purify or purge Phibbs of his previous life. When Graves had warned him of the amount of intellectual baggage he would have to 'shed ... before one reaches her [i.e. Laura's] entire position',[23] Phibbs had not realized that he would have to 'shed' most of his clothes too, that is after 'shedding' his wife Norah, who had accompanied him to London. Understandably suspicious of her husband's summons to London by an unknown younger woman, Norah had insisted on accompanying Geoffrey, which was not at all what Laura had in mind. While Geoffrey was received 'with open arms', Norah remembered, 'I was unimportant and must be got rid of':[24]

> Laura, as cold as the cheap, sparkling trinkets with which she was covered, accompanied Geoffrey and they brought me to the Regent Palace Hotel – thrust a bottle of brandy into my hand and said 'Drink this and forget your tears'. Then they left me in the desolate bedroom.[25]

After three miserable days alone in her hotel room with the brandy bottle, Norah finally managed to contact a female friend who took her off to Chelsea. Returning briefly to Ireland to supervise the transfer of her husband's large library of books to London, she set off to Paris for a course of painting in André Lhote's studio.

Geoffrey's precious collection of books, too, would be purged of anything Laura disapproved of, but first came the ritual burning of his clothes. Apart from £6 borrowed from his parents and a knapsack, they were all that he possessed. Laura insisted, however, that they must all – save, curiously, his trousers – be destroyed, and Robert was instructed, as her careful inventory notes, to 'lend' him '7 shirts, 2 jerseys, a brown coat, a silk dressing-gown, underclothes' (including two pairs of silk underpants which would cause trouble later on), 'socks and four or five neckerchiefs – value £7'.[26] For her part Laura insisted on lending him 'an 18th century blue tie pin value £1, a batik silk scarf, value £2, and two other silk scarves value £1'.[27] This obsessive concern for the financial as well as the aesthetic aspects of the case points to a conflict in Laura herself, who was quick to look after her own material interests, usually at Robert's expense. At the same time, it was crucial to her to have everything of the finest, including her acolytes' clothing. To this end, according to Geoffrey's subsequent report to David Garnett, Laura 'drove him all the way from Hammersmith to the Burlington Arcade in a taxi where she bought him an immensely expensive pair of black silk pyjamas for him to wear in bed with her. She had the bill sent to Robert ... explaining that [T. E.] Lawrence would provide the money.'[28] Phibbs also told Garnett that Laura believed that 'he had been sent providentially to help in the great work' and 'had everything planned out. And her plan was to shake the Universe itself.'[29] It was this messianic side to Laura, which Robert accepted unquestioningly, that terrified Geoffrey and would finally drive him away. Before long she had told him 'as a great secret, that she was going to stop TIME, and that his help was necessary for this operation'.[30] Whether she told him, or merely indicated that 'stopping time was carried out in bed', Garnett does not specify, but she evidently believed that with what Garnett calls 'the assistance of this vigorous new young lover' she was going to 'break the frame of the universe'.[31] As Henri Bergson and others had shown, concepts of time were changing radically by the 1920s, but Laura's claim to be able to arrive at ' "finality", end of history, end of the tyranny of time, annihilation of matter' seemed to Geoffrey to go too far.[32] Her claim to be more than human seemed to him unbalanced, at the very least.

There were other factors involved. Geoffrey had survived the culling of the fine library he had so lovingly put together in Ireland, managing to save a few of the valuable books being claimed as Seizin Press property. He was also ready to join in Laura's esoteric rites: 'She required her poets in their pagan priestly role to do the housework, which involved laying the table [for meals] as if it were an altar,' he told another writer friend, Richard Murphy.[33] He remembered how her 'sloppy habit of leaning her elbows on the table had been sublimated into a ritual. Mats of different colours had to be placed where each of her elbows could lean during moments of meditation between dainty mouthfuls of herbal food.' If Geoffrey reversed the colours, either through carelessness or frivolity, then 'Laura would throw a divine tantrum and demand to be appeased'.[34] Geoffrey's apprenticeship with the Seizin Press was more to his taste and one of the early brochures lists a projected work by him. He also dutifully made a few notes towards his collaboration with Laura on the knowledge of good and evil. There were plans too for the four of them to go on a walking tour together in Germany.

All appeared to be going well at the start. But after seven weeks Geoffrey had had enough and it was Robert who almost certainly provided the excuse for his sudden departure. For the sake of appearances Geoffrey was said to be living on the *Avoca*, the smaller of the two barges Robert now owned, with Nancy and the children alongside on the *Ringrose*. And although he was in fact sleeping, as Robert was, in Laura's bed at 35A St Peter's Square, he spent some of his time on the barge, getting to know Nancy and the children in the process. It would be Nancy to whom he turned when the situation among the four adults reached the inevitable crisis point.

Despite this pretence over sleeping arrangements, however, Robert no longer cared much what his friends and family thought. He may even have relished the fact, when he knew of it, that his father had just been involved in a literary dispute with 'that blighter Phibbs' in the pages of the *Irish Statesman*.[35] Alfred himself was appalled to learn that his son had 'chummed' with him.[36] Amy, as always, was most concerned for the children and when the consequences of the split in the 'Holy Family' became evident, would make their welfare her priority.[37] Robert's half-sister Susan Macaulay was the most forthright and perhaps the most clear-sighted of the family when she wrote to John Graves only four days before the crisis erupted at the beginning of April:

> Robert is writing dreadful stuff in the *Evening Standard* and *Express* so this talk about 'Laura' being his inspiration seems nonsense. I'm afraid you know, John, from what I hear, that Robert and Nancy are fools and that Laura is just a bad woman. Perhaps it's a good thing tho', as if she is, when she's exploited them long enough she'll be up and off with another![38]

Although it would take ten years, these prophetic words would be realized.

Other members of the Graves family had different views. Rosaleen was still too admiring of Laura at this point to question the situation, and John appeared to be trying for neutrality. But Clarissa, a person of great emotional intelligence despite her mental frailty at times, began to feel sorry for Geoffrey, suspecting rightly that he was finding the four-sided relationship a great strain. Laura continued to feel threatened by Geoffrey's wife Norah, for instance, and had 'locked herself in the lavatory for eight hours', according to Norah, 'because Geoffrey said I [Norah] was taller than she was (as I was). She only came out when Geoffrey lied ... and said I was much smaller.'[39] Scenes like this were not uncommon and hugely draining for Geoffrey. Laura's demands, both in bed and out of it, had, he claimed 'impaired his virility', and he was becoming impotent in all senses of the word.[40]

Geoffrey was also disturbed by letters and a visit from Frank O'Connor, who claimed that in this state of what he considered 'temporary insanity', Geoffrey had 'sacrificed the finest woman in Ireland', Norah, and would soon be the 'most miserable man' in that country.[41] Norah, he warned, was now on the verge of a nervous breakdown. O'Connor had been increasingly alarmed by the change in Geoffrey's letters which, from being characteristically 'explosive and malicious', under Laura's influence now 'took on a tone of unction more suitable to a hysterical ecclesiastical student. They were sprinkled with words like "right" and "wrong", but the moral context was missing.'[42] When O'Connor visited Geoffrey on Good Friday on his way to see Norah in Paris, he failed to persuade him to accompany him. But the seed was planted and by Easter Sunday, 31 March, Geoffrey was ready to flee. According to Laura, he begged her to run away with him that same day,[43] arguing that Robert and his family occupied too much of her time and attention. In her version of events, she tried to calm him with a long, random journey by bus and taxi round London. His own explanation for going to her was that he wanted to leave with her blessing; he still revered her as a great thinker and hoped for her approval. When she felt unable to give it, he saw no alternative but to leave unannounced, a decision clinched, he claimed, by a conversation with Robert the following morning. Whether Robert found the date, the first of the new month and April Fool's Day, significant, it must certainly have seemed appropriate to Laura, who thought Geoffrey very foolish indeed to leave her and was furious with Robert.

During the seven weeks of Geoffrey's stay with them, Robert had made the best of the situation, trying to persuade himself that the handsome, younger Irishman was crucial to Laura's overall plan to 'stop TIME'. He and Geoffrey had something in common in terms of background, education and literary interests, and in other circumstances might have been good friends, but he would have been less than human not to feel jealous at having to share Laura, not just in bed but in her various projects. So that while Laura was talking to Nancy on one barge that Easter Monday morning, on the other Geoffrey was hinting to Robert about his plans to escape; and Robert could no longer suppress his feelings. 'He told me what I already knew,' Geoffrey wrote to Laura less than a week later, 'that the only life he could have with you was when I was away.'[44] Anxious not to get Robert into trouble, Geoffrey added that Robert 'would never have agreed to my going away even for some time'.[45] This did not stop Laura from blaming Robert entirely for Geoffrey's escape. But it is clear from a letter Geoffrey wrote to an Irish friend on Sunday 31 March, in which he referred to Robert and Nancy as 'victims' and Laura as a 'virago', that he had already made up his mind to leave before his conversation with Robert.[46] Using dinner with his aunt as an excuse to get out of 35A St Peter's Square on 1 April, he discussed the problem with her, his resolution strengthened by her report that Norah really was ill and unhappy. Borrowing money from his aunt, he left to join Norah in Paris that same evening.

From Paris, Geoffrey and Norah travelled on to Rouen for a second honeymoon of sorts. But Geoffrey's letter of explanation to Laura indicated his whereabouts and she was determined to pursue him. Although the letter itself contained no address, that was tricked out of Geoffrey's aunt by a wily Len Lye, who with Norman Cameron had been summoned to help. Before Geoffrey's whereabouts were known, however, Robert was obliged to join in with the hunt for a man he was delighted to see gone. Alarmed by Laura's hysterical reaction to Geoffrey's departure, he began to feel guilty for his part in it. Ordered to Ireland, where Laura reasoned Geoffrey had fled, he left the next day, 2 April, for the crossing from Fishguard to Rosslare, a journey he found full of bad omens that forced him to 'relive' memories of the First World War and 'the changes of many past years':[47]

> And through a port-hole of the Fishguard boat,
> That was the hospital-boat of twelve years back,
> Passengered as before with doubt and dying,
> I saw the moon through glass, but a waning moon –
> Bad luck, self-doubtful, so once more I slept...[48]

As superstitious as Laura, Robert began to fear disaster. Everything now struck him as ominous, 'the hard cackling laughter of the men / And the false whinnying laughter of the girls'.[49] All that would once have seemed charming and characteristic now appeared threatening. At Limerick, for instance, he claimed 'to have met Old Ireland herself, sitting black-shawled and mourning on the station bench and telling of the Fall',[50] words written after Laura's actual fall from the window, which Graves believed also marked her metaphorical 'fall' from grace as a poet. Even the 'beautiful city of Sligo celebrated in song by [his] father' seemed sinister and refused to yield any hope – 'the place near Sligo, not the place' – and Geoffrey's whereabouts 'unknown to his parents'.[51] Taking another tiring overnight journey back, 'this time by the Wales of the Royal Welch Fusiliers'[52] (Dun Laoghaire to Holyhead), Robert was off again the next day, Friday 5 April, on yet another overnight boat trip, this time to Dieppe – his third in four days. But Robert's welfare seemed of little concern to Laura, who was relentless in her pursuit of Geoffrey and entirely absorbed in what Robert thought of with religious awe as her 'parable'.[53] To someone less in love with her, Laura's action might more accurately have been described as crazed, as well as selfish, but Robert was still firmly under her spell.

When Robert, Laura and Nancy arrived at Rouen in the early morning of 6 April, off the train from Dieppe, Geoffrey and Norah's two days of peace and reconciliation were brought to an abrupt end, Norah recalled, by a message from a waiter: 'Three people wanted to see [them] – they had a most important statement to make.'[54] Norah was so astonished that she 'could only suggest breakfast'.[55] She was even more startled to learn during this meal that 'they' (really Laura, she believed) 'must have made a mistake in shutting me out of the Holy Circle ... and that their mission was now to gather me in'.[56] Norah, a perceptive observer of human nature who had already deplored Laura's taste for flashy jewellery, noted that on this occasion she 'had every Woolworth ornament on her, even sparkling buckles on her shoes ... I expect to fascinate Geoff'.[57] Of the five of them, Norah was the only one exempt from Laura's mesmeric powers. Unimpressed by 'a long morning in the hotel ... [spent] mostly in symbolic language and signs', made in an effort to lure her in, she left the four of them there to take a walk in Rouen by herself.

Meantime Robert had arranged for them to lunch at a hotel that stood on a hilltop near the site of his Rouen hospital of 13 years previously, a place he maintained had witnessed his resurrection from the dead. It would, he hoped superstitiously, host a similar miracle in restoring Geoffrey to Laura. Although undoubtedly jealous of the Irishman, he was desperate for Laura's forgiveness, which now seemed dependent on Geoffrey's return to the 'Holy Family'. After a very good lunch, Geoffrey and Norah were sent off into the nearby woods to make their decision. Geoffrey was clearly torn, but promised his wife that if she did not want to join them, he would not:

> However, I said *I* wanted to keep sane [Norah wrote], and nothing, not even losing Geoff, would induce me to go to what I thought was the mad house of Hammersmith. Even though I had been told Geoff and I would have our own flat – all physical contact would cease between Laura and Geoff (?) and that they would meet only to continue the great work – a dictionary.[58]

So Norah just said 'No' and provoked a reaction from Laura that Norah described with scorn and extreme distaste, noting 'how "God" in the Public Lounge threw herself on the floor, had hysterics, threw her legs in the air and screamed. The Manager got two waiters to remove this spectacle from the alarmed eyes of the wealthy French onlookers.'[59]

Robert, who as Laura had observed was good at blinding himself to what he did not want to see, was appalled at this challenge to her authority and wholly sympathetic. Rather than the spectacle of a thwarted woman throwing a childish tantrum, he saw her divinity threatened, describing the event in quasi-religious terms – 'the hill-top where you seemed to die'[60] and linking it with his own near-death experience and 'resurrection' of 13 years previously. Rather than helping him to forget his wartime traumas, Laura was again unwittingly bringing them back to him.

But Laura, 'superhumanly manipulative' according to Geoffrey,[61] was determined to keep the Irishman under her spell and wrote to him from Rouen Station on her journey back to England a letter of such reasonableness that he began to waver. He hardly spoke to Norah on their own return journey to Ireland, and her dream of a second honeymoon 'became a nightmare', her 'ardour for him start[ing] to cool from that point'.[62] Like the leader of a cult, however, who fears the departure of even one of her disciples, Laura would not or could not let go. Strange objects started to arrive by post at Geoffrey's parents' house where he was staying – bus tickets, bits of twisted wire, coins and coloured ribbons accompanied by symbolic signs Norah could not understand. She was disturbed to see that beside being annoyed, Geoffrey was also 'proud to feel important again'.[63]

Laura's voodoo magic failed to bring Geoffrey back, however, and she next took the more practical step of sending Nancy to do so, knowing how fond she and Geoffrey had become of each other. Geoffrey was in bed with asthma when Nancy arrived and his mother refused to allow her to talk to him, or even enter the house. But Norah wanted the situation clarified and insisted he be shown Nancy's telegram announcing her arrival. While he and Nancy were discussing the matter in the avenue at the back of the parental house, they were interrupted by Geoffrey's furious father, Mr Phibbs, who, pointing at Nancy, shouted: 'Get out of my grounds, you scarlet woman!'[64] Geoffrey, who hated his 'conventional Anglo-Irish fishing and shooting family',[65] and got on particularly badly with his father, described him as looking at that moment like 'a raging bull'.[66] Not intimidated in the least, and more than a little in love with Nancy, Geoffrey replied that he was so ashamed of his father's remark that he was changing his name from Phibbs to his mother's maiden name of Taylor.

Geoffrey also promised Nancy that he would return to London as soon as possible. He stayed in Ireland another week to be with Norah, but she did not want his divided loyalties and decided to return to Paris on her own. Leaving Lisheen together, they shared the journey as far as London, when Norah left for Paris. Still tormented by indecision, instead of returning to Hammersmith, Geoffrey then caught a train to Huntingdon on 26 April, to visit his wife's ex-lover, the more worldly-wise David Garnett, for advice. According to Garnett, Phibbs had:

> ... decided that on no account would he go back to live with Laura. It was not that he was afraid she would prove right [re. stopping TIME] and that he would suddenly find himself an Immortal ... suspended in a timeless universe. No. It was not the *consequences* that scared him, but the *process* designed to bring it about. He could not and would not face it any longer...[67]

Wisely or not, Geoffrey had sent a telegram to St Peter's Square announcing his decision: 'Will never return to Laura.'[68] Instantly, a reply came from

Robert: 'Laura cannot live without you.'[69] Encouraged by Garnett, Geoffrey dared to reply: 'Absolutely refuse to return to Laura.'[70] But it was a useless protest in the face of Laura's implacable will and Robert's next telegram announced: 'Am coming to fetch you. Matter of life and death.'[71] Norah later learned from Garnett that before setting out to 'fetch' Geoffrey, a distraught Robert had telephoned to threaten that he would 'kill Geoffrey if he wouldn't return to Laura'.[72]

By this time it was late in the day and there were no regular trains running; Robert might have hoped for a short reprieve, but Laura could not wait, ordering him to take a 'special' train to Huntington and bring Geoffrey back that same evening.[73] Laura had once again unwittingly forced memories of the war on Robert, for it was at Garnett's home, 'Hilton Hall', on the farm there, that Robert had begun courting Nancy in late 1917. This may help to explain his subsequent reversion to a soldierly style when he arrived at 'Hilton Hall', 'burst[ing] in upon – as it happened – David Garnett ... gulping his vintage port and scandalising him with [my] soldiers' oaths', and denying him 'a speaking part' in what Robert still insisted on seeing as Laura's 'parable'.[74] Although he had never met Garnett in person, he had enjoyed friendly relations with him up to that point, inviting him to contribute to the *Winter Owl* in 1923, for instance, and describing him affectionately as 'little David Garnett, a cage-mate of mine' (with reference to Garnett's *Man in the Zoo*) in *The Marmosite's Miscellany*. Robert had also contributed a poem to Garnett and Francis Birrell's Nonesuch Press anthology, *The Weekend Book*.[75] Now, suddenly, at 'Hilton Hall', harbouring the hapless Phibbs, Garnett had become the enemy.

By the time Robert and Geoffrey arrived back at 35A St Peter's Square, late on the evening of 26 April, Laura had already devoted four weeks to the pursuit of the man she had decreed would help her with her great work. What followed next, when he continued to resist her, would delay her work of any kind for at least another three months, an irony that escaped her. It would also result indirectly in one of Graves's best-known works, *Good-bye to All That*.

23

'A DOOM-ECHOING SHOUT'[1] (26 APRIL–JUNE 1929)

We love, and utterly,
Unnaturally:
From nature lately
By death you freed me,
Yourself free already ...

'Survival of Love'[2]

When Robert and Geoffrey rejoined Laura and Nancy in the late evening of 26 April 1929 they were all exhausted, all in a state of near-hysteria, which accounts to some extent for the bizarre and dramatic events of the next morning. But the motives for Laura and Robert's extreme reactions were not at all straightforward and differed in each case.

For Laura there seems to have been a mixture of frustration and pique at not getting her own way, as well as a terrifying attempt to save face once it became clear that her emotional blackmailing of Geoffrey had failed. Convinced that back in her presence Geoffrey would capitulate, she was astounded to find him obdurate. After several hours of intense, hysterical argument and a few more of snatched sleep in the early hours of Saturday 27 April, the debate continued in Laura's room overlooking the garden behind the house, when she finally realized that she could not force Geoffrey to do her will. Still dressed in the Donegal tweeds in which he had travelled from Ireland, he continued to repeat that he was '*not* ... going to live with or near Laura',[3] even after she threatened suicide.

Laura, still in her nightdress and looking particularly vulnerable, finally left the room, announcing on her return that she had taken Lysol, the poisonous household cleaner with which the poet Charlotte Mew had killed herself a few months previously in a well-publicized case. Geoffrey believed she was bluffing; no one had witnessed her swallowing the Lysol and there were no apparent effects from it. He remained adamant, convinced by now that Laura was insane, a condition brought on, he argued, by venereal disease. He had written to Nancy from Ireland to say so, intending to include an entry torn from his family's encyclopaedia on general paralysis of the insane. But another apparently reasonable letter from Laura had intervened and the letter to Nancy was never sent, so whether Nancy agreed with him is not known. She did, however, share his belief that Laura was bluffing, since when Laura moved towards her large sash window, open to the new day, and Robert tried to stop her, Nancy restrained him.[4] According to Geoffrey, Laura, now sitting on the windowsill, threatened three times to jump, confirmation in his eyes that she was indeed bluffing, still hoping to blackmail him into agreement. To everyone's horror and disbelief, however, she finally said 'Good-bye, chaps' and jumped from her fourth-storey window onto the stone area forty or fifty feet below.

Laura's extraordinary act was not unpremeditated. There is evidence that she had contemplated suicide several times before April 1929. Only two years previously, in her poem '1927', for instance, she had described looking down from the front of 35A St Peter's Square on Robert in the square below, feeling furious and unhappy about their relationship; she had 'debat[ed] if the window / Is worth leaping out of and by whom'.[5] More recently, and far more disturbingly, she had suggested, in Robert's absence, that his seven-year-old daughter, Catherine, whom she had invited to sit with her on the windowsill in her room, should make the experiment[6] (with or without Laura, Catherine did not say). Looking down into the garden and 'patting Catherine's hand', Laura 'told her a wonderful story of a tree which grew outside the window. Its leaves were magical. Behind each leaf, just visible in the movement of light and wind in the branches, was a delicious sweet'.[7] Catherine's only thought was to get hold of the tempting sweets and Laura told her that if she stepped out of the window, a magic staircase would rise from the ground to catch her feet.

Fortunately, Catherine, though severely tempted by the thought of sweets, was not convinced by the magic staircase and ran back to the barge without waiting for her father's return. Terrified by Laura's warning of a policeman coming to punish her if she ever repeated the story, she told no one at the time. Laura was to repeat her warning about punishment by a policeman a year later in a small book published by Nancy Cunard's Hours Press, *Four Unposted Letters to Catherine*, which she sent to the barge in 1930. Catherine kept her secret until 1993.

If any further evidence were needed of Laura's unbalanced state of mind by 1929, this surely is it. She was fond of Catherine and it is scarcely credible that she truly wanted to kill her, which suggests that she actually believed her own story about a magic staircase appearing to lead the child to safety. Convinced of her own magical powers, she almost certainly believed something similar when she herself jumped from the same window shortly afterwards. Why else would she have written to a friend, Merrill Moore, to insist that she had not been attempting to commit suicide, merely to jump out of a window?[8]

Laura had shown signs of megalomania before, believing, for example, that each friend who turned the exotic silks and velvets she sent them into squares for the beautiful patchwork rug which covered the floor of her room 'became my subjects. And so I became Queen.'[9] And in her fictionalized and rationalized account of events at 35A St Peter's Square, as Deborah Baker shows, a thinly disguised Laura describes herself quite seriously as a kind of moral stimulant who, 'in sufficient dosages … might cause the people around her to become either very, very good (like herself) or absolutely horrid'.[10] (This novel, *14A*, was quickly withdrawn when Norah threatened libel proceedings.) Laura herself had underlined the words 'pure madness is the finest sense' in her copy of Emily Dickinson's poems.

Robert knew little of Laura's thoughts as she jumped. His only concern was to join her, wherever she had gone, in that 'new region', that 'strange region' which he had heard her enter with 'a doom-echoing shout'.[11] Desperate to reach her, either alive or dead, after a panicked rush down the first half-flight of stairs, and no other exit to the back of the building available to him, he jumped out of a window himself on the third storey, landing near Laura on the stone area.

Miraculously, both were still alive on landing and Nancy phoned at once for an ambulance, then for Robert's doctor-sister Rosaleen. By the time the ambulance arrived, Robert had picked himself up, shaken and bruised but basically unhurt. His escape was in some ways even more miraculous than Laura's survival from only one storey higher, which would involve nearly three months in hospital and a long, painful convalescence. By the time the ambulance arrived to take Laura to Charing Cross Hospital, Robert was sufficiently recovered to help carry her stretcher up from the basement area.

By this time Rosaleen had arrived and administered morphine to Laura, who was not expected to live. As far as the medics could establish, she had cracked her skull and sustained multiple fractures of the pelvis and spine, and, if she did survive, was expected to be paralysed for life. Robert regarded Laura's recovery largely as proof of her extraordinary force of will and her supernatural powers, but it seems to have been more a matter of luck; though she had broken her spine, she had not ruptured the spinal cord.

Rosaleen, who greatly admired Laura's 'courage' in such pain and discomfort in hospital,[12] nevertheless believed more realistically that she owed her full recovery not simply to determination and stoicism, but to the surgeon Mr Lake, a leading expert in spinal surgery. Just back from research in America, he had agreed to operate on Laura once the inflammation in her spine had subsided. He did so on 16 May, rising to the challenge of Laura's severe injuries with some relish: 'It is rarely that one sees the spinal-cord exposed to view especially at right-angles to itself,' he remarked calmly as he removed a shattered piece of bone from the spine and replaced it with a piece taken from Laura's shin bone.[13]

Rosaleen, who had done part of her training at the hospital and had pulled strings to have Mr Lake operate, was present at the operation and watched in awe as Laura's spinal cord slipped back into position. Laura would have to lie on her front for three weeks to allow the extensive wound to heal, but there was every hope she would walk again. When Rosaleen praised Mr Lake's skill to Laura, however, she was shocked by Laura's mixture of ingratitude and megalomania: 'How do you know I didn't invent Mr Lake?'[14] Rosaleen was even more disillusioned by Laura's response when she sympathized with the pain Laura must be in to scream out loud in a ward full of suffering patients, only to learn that it was not pain that had caused the screams, but boredom, 'just to have something to do'.[15] Having been 'overwhelmingly sorry' for Laura at the time of her accident, it was at this point that Rosaleen began to view her as a 'borderline mental case'.[16] Laura's subsequent behaviour did nothing to dispel these suspicions.

Drugged heavily with morphine directly after her fall, once Laura began to recover she quickly regained control. Robert spent all the time he could at her bedside, or carrying out her requests. But there were numerous practical matters to be dealt with. Friends needed to be informed and one of his first acts on the day of the accident had been to send a telegram to Gertrude Stein, begging her to come to see Laura, who had had a vision of Stein, under morphine, dressed improbably in Highland costume. Although Stein was prevented by 'family complications' from doing so, she sent a letter praising Laura – 'so poignant and upright' – and arguing that there was a 'dualism' in Geoffrey Phibbs which had prevented him from reaching her high standards. She was convinced that this apparent disaster would 'make Laura a very wonderful person, in a strange way a destruction and recreation of her, purification', words which pleased Laura so much that she had Robert copy them out from Stein's scrawl in his more legible handwriting.[17]

Robert also contacted T. E. Lawrence, now stationed with the RAF near Plymouth, learning about speedboat engines. (After his visit to her in hospital, Lawrence wrote to his friend Charlotte, wife of George Bernard Shaw, with little apparent sympathy for Laura but a great deal for Robert, 'a most excellent and truthful person, drowning in a quagmire'.)[18]

Two of the few other friends who 'counted' to Robert and Laura at this time were Len Lye and Norman Cameron, who still lived nearby. Robert's first telephone call had been to Lye, who went at once to the hospital. He and his partner, later wife, Jane Thompson, would prove to be a great support, visiting Laura in hospital regularly and helping Robert prepare for her eventual return home. Cameron, on the point of leaving for a government post in Africa, sent a generous cheque for £100 from a small legacy he had received, to help with what he always referred to as 'the window event'.[19]

There were further letters to be written to other friends and acquaintances, Wyndham Lewis and Herbert Palmer among them. One of Robert's most important letters was to his parents, from whom once more he needed to borrow money. Laura had spared no expense in her pursuit of Geoffrey; the hire of a 'Special' train, for instance, may not have been dear by modern standards, but it was far more than the ordinary fare Robert would have paid if Laura had allowed him to wait and catch a scheduled train the next day. Royalties from *Lawrence and the Arabs* had been high, but so had his spending since then and he was now faced, in a country not yet blessed with a National Health Service, with large hospital bills. He also had to provide somehow for Nancy and the children.

It took Robert three days to write to his parents with what Alfred called 'the shocking news that Laura had thrown herself out of a fourth floor [*sic*] window on to the concrete'.[20] Alfred sent money at once, emphasizing that he would put no pressure on Robert to repay it. But Robert, worn out and over-sensitive from the physical and emotional trauma of the past month, took offence at his letter and returned the £40. Amy, as usual, smoothed things over; the money was sent again and this time Robert accepted it.

It was a generous amount, but not nearly enough to solve Robert's problem; he needed a speedy source of income that his parents could not be expected to supply. *Lawrence and the Arabs* had shown that he could earn a great deal of money with his prose, and Cape was anxious to follow up on his success. Although he had abandoned his own attempt to write about the war in 1916, he realized how popular the subject had become by 1929. One of the first of the war memoirs had been written by his fellow officer and friend in the Royal Welch Fusiliers, Bernard Adams, whose *Nothing of Importance* had been published in 1917, shortly after his death on the Western Front. It was the start of a flood of prose war books that continued throughout the 1920s and reached its high point in 1928 with the publication of *All Quiet on the Western Front* by Erich Maria Remarque, Sassoon's *Memoirs of a Fox-Hunting Man* and Blunden's *Undertones of War*. Writing an introduction to yet another war memoir, e. e. cummings's *The Enormous Room,* in 1928 evidently encouraged Graves to consider adding his own version of events, though he had sworn not to. Conscious of how well Sassoon's and Blunden's books had sold by 1929, he started negotiations with Cape for a book of his own on the war. It seemed his best chance of making money quickly.

By this time he himself was in hospital with violent stomach pains and a suspected ulcer. Deeply sympathetic though Graves was to Laura, he complained both to his parents and to Rosaleen that no one seemed to care what effect the crisis might have had on *his* health.[21] Physically he had escaped unhurt, but the anxiety and strain he faced daily were taking their toll. His mother was upset by his 'unhingedness' and Clarissa described him by early May as 'long-haired and overwrought'.[22] Five days after 'the Fall' (as he always subsequently called it), he had temporarily given up the struggle and sought medical help.

While Robert lay in a ward of the Royal Homeopathic Hospital in Great Ormond Street waiting for the results of tests and trying to get a little rest at last, more problems arose. By 3 May, when Nancy visited him in the hospital, she made it clear that she now intended to live with Geoffrey, whom she had brought with her. Although her story of bumping into him by accident in the foyer of a local cinema just after the accident did not convince Robert, who had witnessed their growing closeness, he might have been expected to see a more intimate relationship between them as a solution to the quadrilateral problem, as Laura initially did. Instead, he was furious; though he had shown beyond doubt that his loyalty was to Laura, he was consumed with a jealousy he fought hard to overcome.

Writing to Nancy two days after her visit a rambling letter that reads as if written by Laura – '[Geoffrey's] good is different from Laura's good', for example – he now admitted that he had been 'wrong [another favourite word of Laura's] in trying to insist that the old association between us should continue sentimentally'.[23] Rosaleen counted 21 instances of 'good' in one letter alone of Laura's.[24] However convoluted Robert's language, comically so at times, it is clear that he was making a genuine effort to be completely honest with Nancy and not to deny his past with her: 'dearest Nancy, I love you greatly and deny nothing of how good we were together once and see the necessity of it'.[25]

But while Robert refers to their children, 'to prove it was good', in the same letter he also seems ready to relinquish them without much struggle: 'The children are yours, you are their mother. I am their father, but they are not my charges, I feel, only my friends. I hate being away from them but I do not feel anxious about them in a paternal way.'[26] This willingness to give up his children, from a father who had looked after them for long stretches of time through Nancy's illnesses and been very close to them, is almost certainly another sign of the spell Laura had cast on him.

In case there was still any doubt in Nancy's mind, Robert told her that he had burnt all her old love letters to him – 'I must not be sentimental about you again' – and made his loyalty to Laura completely clear:

I love Laura beyond anything thinkable and that has always been so. Our love has always been strong, human, unquestioned; in spite of my muddling I do not fear her or worship her or desire to possess her or anything that should not be.[27]

Robert's guilt at encouraging Geoffrey to leave Laura on 1 April – what he calls his 'muddling' – may lie behind such protestations of great love for her after the accident.

A second, calmer letter to Nancy followed the next day, in which he made the extraordinary claim that Laura's jump had been 'a great good'.[28] It had given him 'a sense of complete freedom and sureness' in himself, and had 'finished the old Laura-Geoffrey combination', which 'wasn't just a rather messy bit of drama. It was the end. She found herself.'[29] The letter concludes with Robert insisting that he 'must see' either Nancy or Geoffrey the next day, 6 May, the date, he claimed in *Good-bye to All That*, that 'Nancy and I suddenly parted company'.[30] It is not difficult to imagine how Nancy had reacted to his rather pompous, slightly mad letter of 5 May, with its list of demands at the end: for clothes ('including shoes and an umbrella'), apples, his post, 'the Dostoievsky I was reading', 'Richmond Gems' (i.e. cigarettes) and 'also money'.

Nancy's reaction alone may not have caused the break that followed. According to Laura's biographer, it was the sight of Nancy and Geoffrey together on their first joint visit to see her in hospital that brought about an end to any possibility of the quadrilateral arrangement surviving, even in a different form. The sight of them together, bearing a propitiatory offering, a small bust of Nefertiti – cheap plastic, Laura noted – was more than she could stomach: 'The point of this presentation,' Laura recalled in her furious response to Martin Seymour-Smith's 1982 biography of her, 'was explained as a homage to [her] beauty.'[31] Once Robert was out of hospital, she ordered him to talk to Nancy and Geoffrey again and make a full report of the discussion for her.[32] When he did so, meeting Nancy and Geoffrey on the barge they now lived on together – *his* barge – the 'Holy Family' came to a stormy end; Geoffrey swore at one point, for example, that if he thought that Laura was in any way to alter his feelings for Nancy in the slightest degree he would pitch her out of the window and break her neck.

After much debate it was decided that Nancy should keep the use of the larger barge, the *Ringrose*, together with that of the smaller one, the *Avoca*, and receive an allowance from Robert for the children. It was a sad end to a relationship that had started with such goodwill and had helped Robert get through the last years of the war. It had resulted in four children, of whom they were both proud. The older, more aware children would find it hard to forgive their father for his apparent abandonment of them.[33]

All this would take time to unfold. A more immediate problem for Robert was dealing with the police, who were investigating the circumstances around his threats to Geoffrey and Laura's jump from the window. They had interviewed Geoffrey first, who gave them full details of the event, as Robert complained to Edward Marsh, to whom he turned for help:

> God knows what [Geoffrey] didn't say. He dragged in the whole sex-complication quite gratuitously and vulgarly [another of Laura's favourite words]. I had merely emphasised L's distress at his going off and leaving their joint work in the air. Made it literary, merely. (And the sex side *was* unimportant to L. and me at least.) The police thought L. a sort of vampire, as G.P. put it.[34]

However outrageous Robert considered Geoffrey's statement, the police believed it, describing him as 'a sound young man' to Laura's stepsister Isabel, who had come all the way from California to help look after her. (Laura was not grateful.) After hearing Geoffrey's account of how Robert had threatened to kill him on 26 April if he refused to return to Laura, the police began to suspect Robert of insane jealousy and of having pushed Laura out of the window when she begged Geoffrey to stay. Fortunately, Nancy, who was interviewed with Robert, swore that he was out of the room searching for an emetic for the Lysol when Laura jumped, a lie Robert instantly confirmed.

The possible charge of attempted murder was dropped, but only to concentrate on Laura, now open to that of attempted suicide, a crime punishable by deportation for foreigners in 1929. Although safely on the road to recovery by mid-June when the charge was made, she was faced with losing everything she and Robert lived for. It was at this point that Robert turned to Marsh, emphasizing that Laura was a formal business partner with him in the Seizin Press, was self-supporting and had been 'under doctors for general run-down-ness before the Geoffrey Phibbs thing started', and that they intended in any case to leave England when Laura was fit enough to travel. He had also obtained Lawrence's promise to stand 'surety' for Laura and give a 'testimonial' to her 'as a person to be treated with every possible consideration'.[35] It is a revealing letter, showing how ready Robert still was to 'pull strings' and how scornful he was of the police, who were in his opinion 'tak[ing] an old-fashioned moral view and ... behaving in the usual bullying way'.[36] He believed (rightly) that they would not be the only ones, however, to 'blame it all on Laura and think that G[eoffrey] was the innocent hero decoyed into a den of perverts'.[37] Fortunately for Robert and Laura, this appeal to Marsh for 'action from above' was heard: Marsh took it to a friend in the Home Office and all charges were dropped.[38]

Freed at last from the fear of deportation and well on the way to a full physical recovery, Laura began to create the first of her many versions of an event that by now was the talk of literary London. Edith Sitwell, for instance, wrote gleefully to Sassoon three weeks after the jump, adding some intriguing details to the story that may or may not have been true:

> Then there is the Mormon Father of Islip, or who used to be of Islip. The most terrific gossip is going on ... Everybody is saying that the Concubine [i.e. Riding] is dead, having thrown herself out of a window, and I hear that some months ago she imported a very bad Irish poet and married man to live with her and the Mormon Father, because she said he (the I.P.) was the most beautiful person she'd ever seen. But after a few months he escaped, first to his Aunt, then to France and his wife, because A he was not allowed enough to eat, B he was made to scrub out the bath, and it took him three hours every day, and C the Concubine wouldn't allow him to wear any underclothes, even in the depths of this awful winter, because she said they would spoil his figure.[39]

Sassoon himself did not agree with his friend, Nellie Burton, who thought Laura's rumoured death 'good riddens [*sic*]'; he wished Graves no ill and might even have tried to help, but was nursing his lover, Stephen Tennant, in Bavaria and was therefore too far away to be of any practical use.

Laura's response to such gossip would be enigmatic, appearing both to confirm and to contradict the interpretation of her as an all-too-human figure:

> Rejoice, the witch of truth has perished
> Of her own will –
> Falling to earth humanly
> And rising in petty pain.
>
> It was the last grandeur,
> When the witch crashed
> And had a mortal laming...[40]

In one of her first prose works on the subject, 'Obsession', the precursor of a book on suicide she was planning to write in hospital, Laura cast Geoffrey, as she had done from the start, 'as of old the Devil', who was incapable of seeing Laura as anything other than a witch – a claim she repeated *ad nauseam* in her first collection of poems to follow 'the Fall', *Poems: a Joking Word* – in thinly veiled allegorical terms in which Nancy is cast first as the Virgin Mary, then as the Greek sorceress and murderer Medea:

> Once upon a time I was standing in a room with the Virgin Mary who was also Medea and so on, and the Devil who was also a Judas and so on ... And the Devil and so on, though pretending to be with doom ... He was only the Devil and so on. And he knew it ... And as he was the Devil and so on and therefore could behave only underhandedly ... The Devil and so on might be called a poet against poems. But standing in that room the quick result was that he was only the Devil and so on.[41]

By the time Laura's fictionalized version of events was published four years afterwards in *14A*, Geoffrey's diabolical role had been so laboured and exaggerated that his wife Norah had no difficulty in having the book suppressed as libellous.

Later, after Riding had left Graves, she would cast him as the villain in one of her many rewritings of her life, arguing that he had deliberately failed to restrain her when she threatened to jump. She also claimed that he had reached her in the basement by a fire escape rather than a window, though there was no fire escape at 35A St Peter's Square in 1929.[42] Her own motives are made out to be noble and idealistic: faced by 'a plainly-spelt-out-to-me impasse of general human futurelessness', she had merely sought a 'means of bodily departure'.[43]

In mid-1929, however, Laura's miraculous recovery seemed sufficient answer to any criticism or ridicule of her. It gave her a renewed self-belief and, as Deborah Baker notes, she 'appeared to gain in vitality, incorporating her fall into her sense of herself as endowed with uncommon and transcendent purpose, entering a period of intense and remarkable activity'.[44] It seemed to Graves at the time that, in Phibbs's words, 'Laura's claim to represent the goddess' was 'vindicated by the [relative] lightness of her injuries and the [relative] speed of her recovery'.[45]

For Graves, too, Riding's survival resulted in a period of intense literary activity. Yet there is no more than a passing reference to her 'surviv[ing] [her] dying, lucid interval' and the surgeon's reaction to her bent spine in the book written as she lay recovering in hospital, *Good-bye to All That*.[46] Apart from his account to Marsh in response to police threats and his frank letters to Gertrude Stein, he gave few specific details to friends, perhaps still fearing police interest. His letter to Ken Barrett, for instance, with whom he was usually so frank, was a rewriting of events after the facts, both highly ingenuous and evasive:

> What happened was that Nancy decided to live with the one man in the world that made it impossible for me to live with her thereafter; and not wishing to remain in the same country ... (particularly as the children have been misinformed as to the facts of the situation) I was luckily free to go anywhere I liked. Not alone, either, but with Laura Riding... [who] owed a broken back and pelvis to the same situation which made my break with Nancy.[47]

It is in Graves's poetry that his feelings emerge more truly, without rationalization or an attempt to justify himself. In his 'Dedicatory Epistle' to Laura in *Good-bye to All That* he celebrated her 'true quality of one living invisibly against kind',[48] using the word 'kind' in its archaic sense of 'Nature in general', also as it is used in 'humankind' and possibly with a wordplay on 'kind' as conveying a gentle or benevolent nature, which Riding never claimed to possess. In a poem that follows, 'Against Kind', he appears to celebrate her defiance of death, which places her in a category beyond ordinary mortals, one of the many hints at her superhuman status:

> Become invisible by elimination
> > Of kind in her, she none the less persisted
> > Among kind with no need to find excuses
> For choosing this and not some alien region.[49]

Her failure to die and her apparent independence of ordinary human needs – 'laundry, light or fuel', 'drink or food' – are seen too as reasons for her fellow creatures' violent reaction to her. Like disciples in a religious cult, 'they waited for a sign, but none was given', because she was yet 'discrete', separated from them by her divinity, which they finally acknowledge, but too late: she must 'stay discrete', or apart, and they 'stay blind'.[50]

'Survival of Love', also written after the event and an even greater testimony to Graves's reverence for Riding at this period, gives a startling account of the effect her survival has had upon him. Three five-line stanzas, each rhymed on one rhyme or half-rhyme only, it shows him experimenting with his technique, 'freed' by her (to use the poem's word) in more senses than one, as he claims in the first stanza. All the pain and punishment of the past few months are rationalized in a celebration of the 'unnatural' and paradoxical:

> And indeed merriest when
> The gasp and strain
> Will twitch like pain,
> Clouding the former brain
> Of us, the man and woman.[51]

The woman of 'poetic genius' and 'learning, beauty and loneliness', based undoubtedly on Laura, would be described by Graves in his prose piece, 'Juana Inés de la Cruz'. The poet 'loves [her] in a more than human sense'; she may 'reject and deceive him', but he can 'vent his disillusion in a memorable poem', as Catullus did when he parted from Clodia. 'The case for the woman poet, however, is a thousand times worse,' the narrator argues:

> ... since she is herself the Muse, the Goddess without an external power to guide or comfort her, if she strays even a finger's breadth from [the] path of divine instinct she must take violent self-vengeance.[52]

Laura Riding, it seems, was still leading Graves painfully but wonderfully towards his cruel Muse, the White Goddess, and for the sake of his poetry he would willingly endure another ten years of her guidance, her divinity proved beyond doubt for him by her resurrection from the dead. She had created 'new legends' out of the ancient Greek ones, he claimed in his poem of that name, combining in her one person the several extraordinary qualities of some of the women of Greek legend and history:

> Content in you,
> Andromeda serene,
> Mistress of air and ocean
> And every fiery dragon,
> Chained to no cliff,
> Asking no rescue of me.
>
> Content in you,
> Mad Atalanta,
> Stooping unpausing,
> Ever ahead,
> Acquitting me of rivalry.
>
> Content in you
> Who made King Proteus marvel,
> Showing him singleness
> Past all variety.
>
> Content in you,
> Niobe of no children,
> Of no calamity.

Content in you,
Helen, foiler of beauty.

Another technically highly skilled experiment of stanzas of decreasing length, held together by the repetition of their opening line, 'Content in you', the greatest interest of 'New Legends' remains its message of strengthened commitment to a woman who Graves claims 'ask[s] no rescue' of him, 'acquit[s] [him] of rivalry' and involves him in 'no calamity', words which by 1929 might already have struck an outsider as deeply ironic.

24

GOOD-BYE TO ALL THAT
(JUNE–NOVEMBER 1929)

> After which.
> After which, even anecdotes fail. No more anecdotes. And,
> of course, no more politics, religion, conversations, literature,
> arguments, dances, drunks, time, crowds, games, fun, unhappiness.
> I no longer repeat to myself: 'He who shall endure to the end, shall
> be saved.' It is enough now to say that I have endured. My lung,
> barometric of foul weather, speaks of endurance, as your spine,
> barometric of fair weather, speaks of salvation.[1]

By 17 June 1929, a month after her operation, Laura was considered sufficiently recovered to be released from Charing Cross Hospital. Before returning home, however, she insisted on four weeks in a private ward at the Royal Homeopathic Hospital, which cost six guineas a week, excluding massage. 'But who's to find the money?' Alfred Graves asked, conscious of Amy's recent further loan to Robert and probably anxious in case his wife would be expected to do so. He need not have worried; Robert, confident now of his own earning power, had already started work on his autobiography for Cape, *Good-bye to All That*.

Anticipating another best-seller, Cape had agreed generous terms, but they also insisted on a very tight deadline in order to catch the Christmas sales. So once again Graves was working against the clock, committed to completing a book of 448 pages in only 11 weeks. (He claimed to have worked 18 hours a day for the whole summer.) Normally he worked well under pressure, as his book on T. E. Lawrence had shown, and Jane Thompson volunteered to type up notes for him from his dictation, but there were other factors involved now. Between four and five hours of his day were taken up with visits to Laura in hospital, and even before he started work on 23 May further problems had arisen with Phibbs.

Reassured by Graves's agreement at their meeting on 12 May to return his manuscripts to him, Phibbs called at 35A St Peter's Square to collect them three days later. Meantime Riding, fearing that some of her own writing might have become mixed up with his and that it might be used against her, ordered Graves to refuse him the papers. When Phibbs turned up at 35A on 15 May and was informed of this, he was furious and the situation deteriorated badly. Still irrationally jealous of Phibbs living with the wife he had left for Riding, Graves seized every opportunity to thwart even Phibbs's most reasonable suggestions; when Phibbs offered in early June, for instance, to buy back a hundred books from what had in fact been his own library, the idea was dismissed out of hand. Graves's response had been to threaten a libel action against Phibbs for hinting that Riding was suffering from general paralysis of the insane, brought on by venereal disease.

Graves also demanded the return of the clothes Riding had insisted on lending or buying Phibbs after burning his own, including the contentious two pairs of silk underpants. Such pettiness put Graves in the wrong, even if it was a result of his overwhelming desire to protect Riding as well as his barely suppressed jealousy. Of the jealousy there was no doubt; normally so generous with money when he had it, once he realized that Phibbs was still with Nancy on the barge he began to question every item of her modest expenditure, even threatening to withhold money for the children altogether if Phibbs continued to live with her. While his violent reaction to Phibbs on 15 May, the day before Riding's operation, could possibly be blamed on his anxiety and worry over her, by 18 June he had no such excuse. She was 'quickly recovering the use of her legs', he reported to Gertrude Stein,[2] and by 12 July she was back at 35A St Peter's Square. By the beginning of September she was walking down the several flights of stairs to the street, with his support.

Graves's writing was also going well; by 24 July 1929, his 34th birthday, he had completed a draft of *Good-bye to All That*. But none of this changed his and Riding's implacable hostility towards Phibbs. Rosaleen, despite Riding's behaviour in hospital, which had 'sickened' the staff and made Rosaleen's name 'mud' there, was still trying to help resolve the situation. But when she attempted to introduce reason into the affair, dismissing the argument over books and clothes as 'sordid', 'Laura blazed out at her'.[3] Rosaleen had continued to visit Nancy, Phibbs and the children throughout and was eventually informed by Robert that if she went on doing so, she must forfeit his and Laura's friendship. Her brother, she reported to their parents, was 'now completely under Laura'.[4] Robert's half-sister Susan, who had been inclined to blame Nancy to an extent for the split from Robert, now 'exonerated' her completely, ready to believe Nancy's explanation that Laura had '"vampired" Robert from the week she met him'.[5]

Despairing of any informal agreement, and after seeing some of his own books for sale in a local bookshop, Phibbs finally consulted a firm of lawyers, who issued a writ against Riding on 25 July for the return of no fewer than 300 of his books. ('He's better than a novel!' Graves wrote to Marsh.)[6] Arriving as it did the day after his birthday and the completion of a draft of *Good-bye to All That*, the writ was not taken seriously by Graves or Riding, who authorized the return of only 16 books, with 17 more promised in late August if Phibbs came to collect them. When he did so, however, Graves became violent and Phibbs, finally, had had enough. On 12 September, more than three months after his first mild request for the return of his manuscripts and books, he took out a summons against Riding at the county court, demanding the return of 80 books within the fortnight. When a policeman turned up at St Peter's Square, Riding pleaded ill-health as her reason for not attending court and the policeman next visited Phibbs, who agreed to drop the case if the books were returned. To save face, presumably, Riding returned only 50 of the 80 books to him. But when Phibbs wrote again the next day demanding 17 more, she sent them, refusing however to sign the apology Phibbs had drafted. One reason for leaving England, she told Stein, was to escape further questioning by the police and to 'live untroubled'.[7]

Riding had now spent eight months obsessed by Phibbs in one way or another. So, too, had Graves, who was more than ready to leave England. By the end of August he had finished revising *Good-bye to All That* and by the beginning of October Riding, though still walking with a stick, was fit enough to travel. Graves believed that a warmer climate would help her recovery and they had decided on Spain, agreeing to visit Stein on the way. One of Graves's last acts before leaving, fuelled by his venom towards Phibbs, was to write a 'hateful' letter to Rosaleen about her refusal to give up her friendship with Phibbs and Nancy.[8] Three days later, on 4 October 1929, he 'vanished',[9] leaving his youngest son, Sam, desolate: 'Father gone, Laura gone – all gone,' he told his mother.[10]

That same day Graves and Riding crossed to France, accompanied by Riding's own private masseuse, another sign of how freely Graves spent money in the normal course of events. From the very first day of her accident, when Riding had seen Stein in a morphine-induced vision, she had thought of her as an answer to her needs. As with Phibbs and many others in her life, however, she became quickly disappointed and the visit to Stein's summer house, Bilignin, at Belley, near Aix-les-Bains in the Haute Savoie, lasted less than two weeks. Staying in a small *pension* in the town and still unable to walk far, she relied more than usually on conversation: Stein's, she complained, was surprisingly mundane, taken up mainly with the weather. Quite apart from possible considerations, such as Stein's needing a break from the highly intellectual demands of her difficult writing, or her concern that her guests should enjoy fine weather, Riding was unfair to accuse Stein of talking only of the weather. She also asked about Riding's progress on her work on suicide ('Obsession') and, knowing of their intention to live in Spain, tried to advise Graves and Riding on this. She and Toklas had stayed there during the opening year of the First World War and Stein, at least, was enthusiastic about it.

It was a discussion that was to change the course of Graves's life. For Stein made Majorca, the largest of the Balearic Islands in the Mediterranean, sound so attractive that before leaving her, he and Riding had abandoned his original idea of settling in the Basque provinces in favour of Majorca. The cost of living in either place, Stein confirmed, would be about a quarter of that in England, but Majorca would be both quieter and warmer. It also had an appealingly exotic history of successive settlement by Phoenicians, Romans, Vandals and Moors, among others, leaving it with a rich cultural heritage. Graves and Riding left Belley fully intending to try living on the island.

Riding would later claim that Majorca had been her idea alone and showed no gratitude towards Stein. On the contrary, only a year later she would quarrel with her badly, terminating their relationship abruptly. It began when Stein asked, quite reasonably, whether she was due any royalties on *An Acquaintance with Description*, published by the Seizin Press in 1929 and eagerly solicited by Riding. Riding's evasiveness and delay in sending a cheque brought Stein's letters and the relationship to an end. To Stein, who was herself Jewish, it exposed Riding as 'the worst kind of Jew', who camouflaged her 'materialism' under a pretence of 'intellectualism'.[11] Graves, who believed the break was caused merely by 'a fit of spleen' on Riding's part, regretted it greatly: Stein had become 'very close to his heart', he told her fifteen years after that visit.[12] Her response would be instant and equally warm, though she was only months away from her death when she wrote it: 'I was awfully pleased to hear from you, I always had considerable tenderness for you, a very special tenderness indeed.'[13]

Graves had also enjoyed Belley more than Riding, especially the view of Mont Blanc in the distance. But their next port of call, Freiburg, just across the border in Germany, did not excite them, and it seemed no more than a convenient resting place on their way to Spain. He had left his revised manuscript of *Good-bye to All That* with Cape, which was now hurrying it through the press. As he noted somewhat cynically, the book contained all the ingredients of a best-seller, included, he implies, deliberately. By 6 November, just over a month after he left England, Cape was able to send out advance copies, in search of endorsements and reviews. Sassoon, Blunden and Marsh all received one and all three reacted strongly to the book, much to Cape's dismay. Publication had been set for 13 November, only a week later, but Marsh was insisting on a significant correction and Sassoon was threatening an injunction.

The objections were not entirely unexpected, for it is clear from Graves's opening paragraph that *Good-bye to All That* will be both forthright and unsentimental, possibly rather shocking: there is a defiant note to it that distinguishes it sharply from Sassoon's *Fox-Hunting Man* and Blunden's *Undertones of War*. It is nearer in tone not only to e. e. cummings's *The Enormous Room* but also to another book about the war published in 1929, Richard Aldington's *Death of a Hero*:

The objects of this autobiography, [Graves warns his reader] written at the age of thirty-three, are simple enough: an opportunity for a formal good-bye to you and to you and to you and to me and to all that; forgetfulness, because once all this has been settled in my mind and written down and published it need never be thought about again; money.[14]

Of the three reasons given here for writing his book, the first is the most intriguing, especially its last phrase – 'an opportunity for a formal good-bye to you and to you and to you and to me and to all that'. At its most obvious level, 'all that' probably refers to the problems Graves has encountered in England, especially since living with Riding. But he is also thinking in broader terms of his whole life up to 1929 and his first five chapters are devoted to his childhood in Wimbledon, Bavaria and Harlech, together with his years at various prep schools, some of it recalled with not a little nostalgia, his 'good-bye' not quite as resolute as perhaps he had intended.

The same might be said of his next three chapters, devoted to what he insists were five unhappy years at Charterhouse, though the picture he paints is by no means one of unrelieved misery. But Graves himself believed that his comments were 'quite ruthless', albeit written 'without indignation', he told Stein.[15] No wonder that his parents, knowing that Riding disapproved of them and what seemed to her their bourgeois ways, were worried about what their son might write about them. They were understandably relieved when Charles, who in his capacity as a journalist got hold of an advance copy, reported the book to be fairly harmless.

Nevertheless Graves's father leapt at the idea put to him by Jonathan Cape, the publisher of both father and son, of adding a chapter to the memoirs he was writing for Cape, correcting some of his son's more offensive inaccuracies and misrepresentations, and to call his own autobiography *To Return to All That* (1930). In response to his son's charge that his father 'never once tried to teach me how to write, or showed any understanding of my serious work', for instance, Alfred Graves responded sorrowfully:

He gives me no credit for the interest I always felt and showed in his poetry. During the war I offered poem after poem of his to editor after editor, and even arranged with Harold Monro of the *Poetry Bookshop*, to whom I introduced Robert, for the publication of [his first book] *Over the Brazier*.[16]

All of which is true. But the 'truth' to Graves, as *Good-bye to All That* would make plain, was not factual so much as emotional, that is, how it felt to Graves himself, or rather how he remembered it by 1929. It was not just Blunden who felt that Graves was behaving like a 'Bull in a China Shop'.[17]

And although Graves's next chapter, an account of climbing trips with George Mallory, offended nobody, this idyllic interlude prefaces a long section which infuriated many of Graves's readers, that is his description of his four years in the British Army, relating his participation in two of the bloodiest battles of the First World War, Loos and the Somme, his severe wounding and near death, and his return to serve on until the end of the war.

Finally, after describing his early marriage and bringing up four children with Nancy, Graves's story comes to an abrupt end. He makes no attempt to relate the last few years of his life, perhaps understandably, but it is a rare lapse of candour in a book characterized by honesty. Miranda Seymour argues that 'the candour which gives the book its enduring vitality was fuelled by Graves's sense that [Riding] had liberated him from the shackles of duty and obligation'.[18] If so, it seems ironic that this candour did not extend as far as describing the two years they lived together in London.

But it was evidently the war period to which Graves felt the strongest need to say 'good-bye'. If the 16 chapters devoted to it, that is over half the book, are any indication, the 'all that' of the title includes the First World War as the most important element. He had already used the phrase 'all that' to refer specifically to the war in his Introduction to cummings's book in 1928 and had also defined it as 'the god-awful' in another book the same year, *Mrs Fisher*.

It was Graves's cavalier attitude towards the 'facts' in this wartime section that enraged Sassoon and Blunden and added to their already existing animosity against him. Graves had antagonized Blunden earlier by implying that he had alcoholic tendencies, by his typically clumsy attempts to resolve Blunden's marital problems and by an unsympathetic review of *Undertones of War* in December 1928. (Blunden would retaliate with a damning review of *Good-bye to All That* in *Time and Tide* a year later.) Sassoon's grievances against Graves were even stronger. Quite apart from his keen dislike of Laura Riding, he felt that Graves had behaved badly towards his old friends, Edmund Gosse and Thomas Hardy. In addition, he had a particular dislike of factually vague war books, as his dismissal of *All Quiet on the Western Front* had shown. Partly because he and Graves had been such close friends during the war, when he had visited the Graves family in Wales and Robert had returned with him to the Sassoon family home in Kent, he now reacted violently to what he saw as Graves's betrayal of trust in describing this Kent visit in *Good-bye to All That* and Graves's reference to Mrs Sassoon's desperate attempts to contact her son through spiritualism in his book. Although Graves did not name Mrs Sassoon or the fellow officer with whom he had been staying, Siegfried was appalled at his tactlessness.

He also objected strongly to Graves's entirely unauthorized inclusion of a long, disturbed verse-letter Sassoon had sent him from hospital in July 1918 while recovering from a head wound. *Good-bye to All That*, he told Graves, could not have appeared at a worse moment, as he struggled 'to recover the essentials of [his] war experience' in *Memoirs of an Infantry Officer*; the book 'landed on [his] little edifice like a Zeppelin bomb'. Elsewhere he noted that he felt as if Graves had 'rushed into the room and kicked [his] writing table over, thrown open all the windows, let in a big draught'. It seemed to him that Graves had 'blurted out [his] hasty version' like a hack journalist with scant regard for accuracy, the 'antithesis' of his own method. He was particularly critical of Graves's account of his (Sassoon's) protest, which fell a long way short, he believed, of the 'impartial exactitude required for such a sensitive topic'. 'He exhibits me as a sort of half-witted idealist,' he complained to Louis Untermeyer and his wife, 'with a bomb in one hand and a *Daily Herald* in the other.'

So Sassoon readily agreed to Blunden's suggestion that they should do a 'demolition job' on the book and place it in the British Museum, 'to preserve the correct version of what happened in France'.[19] More than half the annotations were made by Blunden, who began by noting on the first page that Graves's specified 'objects' in writing were 'all selfish'. This still left Sassoon ample room to add his own comments, but it was clearly not enough to satisfy him, obsessional as he had become on the subject. He remained sufficiently aggrieved to make copious comments on a further eighty-five pages of his own personal copy, continuing to correct the factual errors that had so enraged him when he first read Blunden's copy.[20] Some of the corrections Sassoon made are significant. When, in chapter 15, for example, Graves claims that a colonel with 'a slight wound' on his hand 'joined the stream of wounded and was carried to the base with it', Sassoon appears fully justified in commenting: 'a libel, he was hit on the head as well'. But on the whole the effect of this constant factual correction is to make Sassoon seem pedantic. Are most readers really going to care if Graves dates his Quartermaster Joe Cottrill's award of the DSO to 1916 rather than 1917, or if there are slight inaccuracies of transcription in an extract from the poet John Skelton?

If Sassoon had limited himself to correcting Graves's 'facts', this second copy would add little to what we learn from Blunden's. But in his own private copy Sassoon reveals far more of his changed feelings towards his former friend, and more freely. Some annotations consist simply of a scornful, single word, such as 'rot', 'fiction', 'faked' or 'skite'. Others are more discursive. When Graves notes on page 440 that Bernard Shaw had 'mistaken me for my *Daily Mail* brother' (Charles Graves wrote a column for that popular newspaper), Sassoon observes 'a pardonable error'. And when Graves tells his reader on the next page: 'My critical writings I did not tidy up; but let them go out of print', Sassoon adds, with what sounds like professional jealousy: 'they were mostly remaindered, and no new editions could possibly have been called for'. What Sassoon had once found forgivable, even endearing faults in Graves – 'his tactlessness, his intelligence, and dirty habits' – now irritated him greatly. So that, when Graves writes that the Prince of Wales was 'a familiar figure in Béthune. I only spoke to him once; it was in the public bath, where he and I were the only bathers one morning', Sassoon cannot resist underlining 'the public bath', with the gloss 'rarely visited by the author'. The effect again is to make Sassoon seem petty.

The real interest of this second annotated copy, and its main difference from Blunden's, lies in the 40 pages of press cuttings Sassoon has added, most pasted down, a few inserted loosely into the text. Not only do these give further insights into Sassoon's character, particularly his often whimsical sense of humour, and allow us a late glimpse of the satirist who had dominated his war poetry and verse collections of the 1920s, but they also turn his effort into a minor work of art. (He was to do something similar with Edith Sitwell's *Aspects of Modern Poetry*, 1933, once their friendship had cooled.) Coming from a family of painters and sculptors on his mother's side, Sassoon had a strong visual sense and has embellished his copy of *Good-bye to All That* with evident relish. Every available space on the 16 leaves of endpapers and prelims is crammed with cuttings, and at all angles. Any subsequent blank pages, or parts of pages, such as ends of chapters, are similarly utilized. There are numerous reviews of *Good-bye to All That*, both good and bad, the latter including Blunden's damning indictment. When a positive review is by someone Sassoon had thought his friend, such as the poet Robert Nichols, he has pasted beneath it a cut-out headline, printed in red, 'Special Mate Article'. In the case of a glowing unsigned review in the *TLS*, having failed to find a suitably dismissive caption, he merely adds his own comment: 'This review caused Max Beerbohm to give up taking the *Times Literary Supplement*.' He includes, presumably with tongue in cheek, a newspaper 'puff' for *Good-bye to All That*, together with snippets from the gossip columns on the high value of those copies that include the subsequently suppressed passages. Articles and letters to newspapers about the book's inaccuracies are cut out and inserted at the relevant point, such as an angry rebuttal by 'Black Watch' of Graves's charge that the Scots were cowards at the Somme and ran away.

The most notable letter, however, is not cut from a newspaper but the original itself, a response from Cape to Sassoon's visit of 13 November 1929 with his threat of an injunction: 'After your call this afternoon I made arrangements for the cancel pages to be printed and to have them pasted into such copies ... as have not already left our premises...' Sassoon cannot resist showcasing his triumph and this letter is pasted prominently on the verso of the title page. Since Blunden and Sassoon had finished annotating Blunden's copy on 7 November, almost a week before Sassoon's visit to Cape, it seems that it was the annotating of this second copy which provoked Sassoon to make his demands of Cape, and finally bring his friendship with Graves to an end.

Sassoon's copy of *Good-bye to All That* makes it clear how much his opinion of Graves had changed after the advent of Laura. The most entertaining of the insertions are the selection of commercial illustrations, photographs and drawings that poke fun at the two of them. A perfectly innocuous frontispiece photograph of Graves is rendered absurd by the cut-out caption 'LITTLE JACK RABBIT' pasted beneath it. And Eric Kennington's fine pastel drawing of Graves is accompanied by an even more ridiculous caption from a newspaper: 'Breeding will tell / Just why this should be is difficult to say; for, as previously stated, there were no exceptional gadgets on the model.' At the end of a chapter on Oxford, Sassoon conveys his opinion that Graves can be something of a stuffed shirt simply by including a cut-out advertisement for a white shirt-front. If he thinks Graves is talking nonsense, he merely inserts an incomprehensible extract in Chinese, Swedish or Dutch.

Sassoon's allusions to Laura are aimed at achieving a similarly absurd effect; there is an advertisement for 'The Central Cycle *Riding* School [my italics]' and a picture of two ladies on bicycles in Edwardian costume, captioned: 'Spinning down the road from Calais to St Omer'. But the references to Laura also reveal the depth of his dislike of her; one illustration, for example, shows a man and a woman struggling together, with the caption, 'You shall not die! You shall not die!', an unmistakable and highly unsympathetic allusion to her suicide attempt earlier in the year. Best of all perhaps is Sassoon's replacement of Graves's subtitle, 'An Autobiography', with the cut-out title of a popular children's book by 'Marion', illustrated by Jessie M. King, *MUMMY'S BEDTIME STORY BOOK*. It is all sheer make-believe, he is implying.

Although Graves never saw Sassoon's and Blunden's annotations, Sassoon had made his objections clear to him. But Graves refused to apologize for any inaccuracies in his book, arguing that there are two kinds of reality. One is what actually happened, which is the realm of the historian, or chronicler of Regimental Histories: the other is what it was like, what happened to the person who was there, which belongs to the individual. While Sassoon and Blunden strove conscientiously for strict factual accuracy – and may even have lessened the immediacy of their accounts by doing so – Graves had no time to try for it. Nor would he have done so had he been able, he claimed. For, as he explained in his 'PS to *Good-bye to All That*' (published in *But It Still Goes On*, 1930), factual accuracy did not seem to him the prime aim in the personal memoir:

> It was practically impossible (as well as forbidden) to keep a diary in any active trench-sector, or to send letters home which would be of any great post-War documentary value; and the more efficient the soldier the less time, of course, he took from his job to write about it. Great latitude should therefore be allowed to a soldier who has since got his facts or dates mixed. I would even paradoxically say that the memoirs of a man

who went through some of the worst experiences of trench warfare are not truthful if they do not contain a high proportion of falsities. High-explosive barrages will make a temporary liar or visionary of anyone; the old trench-mind is at work in all over-estimation of casualties, 'unnecessary' dwelling on horrors, mixing of dates and confusion between trench rumours and scenes actually witnessed.[21]

Paul Fussell goes so far as to argue that 'if *Good-bye to All That* were a documentary transcription of the actual it would be worth very little, and would surely not be, as it is, infinitely re-readable'.[22] It is ironic that the main reason Sassoon and Blunden objected to *Good-bye to All That* – its factual inaccuracy – might be part of the reason why it appealed to so many readers. Written in great haste, over only 11 weeks, it is undeniably careless in a number of ways and, as Martin Seymour-Smith, Graves's first serious biographer and friend, argued, was not meant to be a work of art. But, he claimed, it has something the other two more 'composed' works by Graves's best-known critics do not have, that is, it sums up the fears and hopes of the generation who experienced the war with a pertinence that could hardly admit of a strictly literary treatment. The point of Blunden's and Sassoon's non-journalistic memoirs was that they had not rejected the past, even though they had lost it. Graves, on the other hand, was a rebel, not against the kind of tradition that Blunden and Sassoon loved, and for which their nostalgia is so compelling, but against the present. Fussell argues, convincingly, that we need all three viewpoints, Graves's as much as his more conscientious rivals, that together, they have 'effectively memorialized the Great War as a historical experience': they are all three 'the classic memoirists' of the period, the more self-consciously literary works of Sassoon and Blunden balancing Graves's more spontaneous account. Although *Good-bye to All That*, unlike *Fox-Hunting Man*, did not win any literary prizes, it sold very well indeed. Within a month sales had reached 30,000, easily exceeding Sassoon's impressive sales of 15,000 in just under three months. Since Graves's most compelling reason for writing his memoirs was, as he candidly admitted in its opening paragraph, 'money', his aim had been achieved.

As for Sassoon, a poem written shortly after the publication of *Good-bye to All That* but never published in his lifetime suggests that the chance to vent his spleen in his own copy had had a cathartic effect:

> Should one assume a mild magnanimous look
> When effigied and blurtingly displayed
> In a – presumably – profit-seeking book
> By someone scribbling on the downward grade?
> Resentment asks permission to protest
> Silence replies that silence answers best...[23]

For Graves, too, his detailed account of the wartime experiences that had haunted him for over a decade seems to have had a cathartic effect, helping him to overcome his neurasthenia more effectively than either his poetry or Rivers or Riding had managed to do.

***

By the time *Good-bye to All That* was published, cancelled pages and all, on 18 November, Graves had said an even more obvious 'good-bye' to his life in England. For by that date he had been in Spain for approximately three weeks and had no intention of returning to the scene of the many painful experiences he now believed he had finally put behind him. In addition, his and Riding's choice of Majorca was living up to Stein's description of it to them as 'paradise if you can stand it'.[24] Although Riding had 'detested' the idea of Spain in advance, she quickly found the village and small stone cottage they settled in 'exactly right'.[25]

Arriving first at Majorca's capital, Palma, at dawn on the overnight crossing from Barcelona, they had been impressed by the soaring Gothic cathedral that dominated the skyline. They loved its sense of history, those traces of an ancient, turbulent past, and its air of culture, much of it showing the influence of the Italian Renaissance. Graves in particular loved Palma's many antique shops, in which he searched daily for bargains.

The city, however, was not quite what either of them wanted. They were hoping to find somewhere in the country, where rents would be cheaper and land available to grow some of their own vegetables and fruit. Using the Grand Hotel in Palma as their base, they began to explore the possibilities, led on by their dream of a completely new start. It was quite by chance that they found the village that would become Graves's home until his death, apart from a period of exile during the Spanish Civil War and the Second World War. Talking to a disabled German café artist they had befriended when he asked to sketch Graves,[26] they were directed to Deià, a small fishing and farming village beyond the Tramuntana mountains on the north-west coast of the island.

A Palma letting-agent, Mr Short, found a simple stone cottage for them, well within their price range, and situated just outside the village itself, as they had requested. At the southernmost edge of Deià on the Valldemossa side of the circular valley in which it was set, Ca Sa Salerosa, as it was called, faced north, the lack of sun being one reason they would move to the opposite side of the valley later, to a plot of land directly facing them. But they were happy to move into Ca Sa Salerosa in late October 1929. Set back from the road up a dozen steep steps, it had spectacular views of the wide, terraced valley and offered a glimpse of the sea from its small front terrace, with two downstairs rooms for working in, two bedrooms upstairs, and a small outbuilding where the Seizin Press was installed. Built into the rock face, Ca Sa Salerosa had no room for a garden at the back, but there was a reasonable patch at the side of the house in which Graves could grow vegetables.

Ca Sa Salerosa seemed to suit both Graves's and Riding's needs in November 1929. Writing to her friend Polly that month, Riding waxed lyrical about 'the olive harvest ... the trees ... purple with fruit', and the rows of women in headscarves and straw hats filling small rush baskets with olives as they sang traditional harvest songs.[27] In the evening on saints' days candle-lit processions descended the nearby hill on which the village church perched. (Graves himself would be buried in the neighbouring churchyard over 55 years later.)

Graves's own first impressions were equally favourable. 'It is very good to be here,' he wrote to Marsh a fortnight after their arrival, 'and we intend to stay a long time. Sun. Olives, figs, oranges, fish, quiet. [Laura] is much better and can limp two or three miles at a go now'.[28] Six months later, he wrote to Ken Barrett:

These are the Classical Hesperides where it never freezes and never gets too hot and where it costs nothing to live if one is content to go native, and where the population is the most hospitable, quiet, sensible and native, and well-being that you can imagine. We are near the sea and Palma a big town is within reach for any European necessities ... And I am feeling good again after 1929 which was Hellish and that's all the news.[29]

He also focused on the strangeness and unfamiliarity of his new home, hemmed in by the Teix mountain that loomed over the valley and rose sheer behind Ca Sa Salerosa, cutting off both sun and sky and turning his known world upside down, as Riding had done. Addressed to Laura, 'The Terraced Valley' celebrates his new start alone with her after her 'doom-echoing shout' as she fell had signalled the end of his old life:

> In a deep thought of you and concentration
> I came by hazard to a new region:
> The unnecessary sun was not there,
> The necessary earth lay without care –
> For more than sunshine warmed the skin
> Of the round world that was turned outside-in.
>
> Calm sea beyond the terraced valley
> Without horizon easily was spread,
> As it were overhead,
> Washing the mountain-spurs behind me:
> The unnecessary sky was not there,
> Therefore no heights, no deeps, no birds of the air...[30]

Deià would seal what Graves had begun in *Good-bye to All That*, his final farewell to his life in England and all it had led to. He believed that once his wartime experience had been settled in his mind it need never be thought of again and he had suppressed many of his war poems to that end. Although he would not reinstate those poems after *Good-bye to All That*, however, he would return to the subject of war in the future. But with this difference, that he would be able to view that war more objectively and see it from a greater distance, not quite 'recollected in tranquillity', but in a far calmer, less tortured state of mind:

> ... What, then, was war? No mere discord of flags
> But an infection of the common sky
> That sagged ominously upon the earth...
> Fear made fine bed-fellows. Sick with delight
> At life's discovered transitoriness,
> Our youth became all flesh and waived the mind.
> Never was such antiqueness of romance,
> Such tasty honey oozing from the heart.

And old importances came swimming back –
Wine, meat, log-fires, a roof over the head,
A weapon at the thigh, surgeons at call.
Even there was a use again for God –
A word of rage in lack of meat, wine, fire,
In ache of wounds beyond all surgeoning.

War was return of earth to ugly earth,
War was foundering of sublimities,
Extinction of each happy art and faith
By which the world had still kept head in air,
Protesting logic or protesting love,
Until the unendurable moment struck –
The inward scream, the duty to run mad...[31]

***

Robert Graves and Laura Riding would remain together for the next ten years, the first six of these in Majorca. With the outbreak of the Spanish Civil War in 1936, they would be forced to leave the island, living first in England, then France and finally America, where Riding would leave Graves for Schuyler Jackson in circumstances almost as dramatic as her jump from the window in 1929. I look forward to continuing the story.

ABBREVIATIONS

Note: **Throughout this book ampersands (&) have been replaced with the word 'and'.**

MAIN CORRESPONDENTS

AG	Amy Graves (RG's mother)
APG	Alfred Perceval Graves (RG's father)
BG	Beryl Graves
BLH	Basil Liddell Hart
CG	Charles Graves (RG's brother)
Clarissa	Clarissa Graves (RG's sister)
CLG	Charles Larcom Graves (RG's uncle)
CSM	Charles Scott Moncrieff
EAC	Esther Antell Cohen ('Polly')
EB	Edmund Blunden
EG	Edmund Gosse
EM	Edward Marsh
ES	Edith Sitwell
GP	Geoffrey Phibbs
GS	Gertrude Stein
JCR	John Crowe Ransom
JG	John Graves (RG's brother)
KB	Kenyon Barrett
LL	Len Lye
LOM	Lady Ottoline Morrell
LR	Laura Riding (née Reichenthal, later Jackson)
NC	Norman Cameron
NM	Norah McGuinness
NN	Nancy Nicholson
RC	Rosaleen Cooper (née Graves, RG's sister)
RG	Robert von Ranke Graves
RN	Robert Nichols
RR	Robert ('Robbie') Ross
SS	Siegfried Sassoon
TEL	T. E. Lawrence
TSE	T. S. Eliot

TSM	Thomas S. Matthews
WHRR	Dr William Halse Rivers Rivers
WO	Wilfred Owen

ARCHIVES

Beinecke	Beinecke Library, Yale University
Berg	Berg Collection, New York Public Library
BL	British Library, London
Brotherton	Brotherton Collection, University of Leeds
Buffalo	Library of the State University of New York at Buffalo
CUL	Cambridge University Library
HRC	Harry Ransom Humanities Research Center, University of Texas at Austin
IWM	Imperial War Museum, London
Lilly	Lilly Library, Indiana University, Bloomington
NLS	National Library of Scotland
Princeton	Princeton University Library
SIU	Morris Library, Southern Illinois University at Carbondale
SJCO	St John's College Oxford Library
Tate	Tate Archives, London
Tulsa	Tulsa University Library
Wrexham	Royal Welch Fusiliers' Archives at Wrexham

ROBERT GRAVES'S WORKS (MAINLY UP TO 1930)
(Place of publication London, unless otherwise stated)

AFP	*Another Future of Poetry*, Hogarth Press, 1926
BISGO	*But It Still Goes On: An Accumulation*, Cape, 1930
CS	*Country Sentiment*, Secker, 1920; Knopf, New York, 1920
CTP	*Contemporary Techniques of Poetry: A Political Analogy*, Hogarth Press, 1925
EB	*The English Ballad: A Short Critical Survey*, Benn, 1927
FB	*The Feather Bed*, Hogarth Press, 1923
FF	*Fairies and Fusiliers*, Heinemann, 1917; Knopf, New York, 1918
GD	*Goliath and David*, Chiswick Press, 1917
GTAT	*Good-bye to All That: an Autobiography*, Cape, 1929; Cape and Smith, New York, 1930
I	*Impenetrability or The Proper Habit of English*, Hogarth Press, 1927
JKW	*John Kemp's Wager: A Ballad Opera*, Blackwell, Oxford, 1925; T. R. Edwards, New York, 1925
LA	*Lawrence and the Arabs*, Cape, 1927; pub. as *Lawrence and the Arabian Adventure*, Doubleday, New York, 1928
LP	*Lars Porsena or the Future of Swearing and Improper Language*, Kegan Paul, Trench, Trubner, 1927; Dutton, New York, 1927
MBH	*Mock Beggar Hall*, Hogarth Press, 1925
MD	*The Meaning of Dreams*, Cecil Palmer, 1924; Greenberg, New York, 1925
MF	*Mrs Fisher or The Future of Humour*, Kegan Paul, Trench, Trubner, 1928

MHMH	*My Head! My Head!*, Secker, 1925; Knopf, 1925
MM	*The Marmosite's Miscellany* (pseud. John Doyle), Hogarth Press, 1925
OB	*Over the Brazier*, The Poetry Bookshop, 1916; St Martin's Press, New York, 1975
OEP	*On English Poetry*, Knopf, New York, 1922; Heinemann, 1922
PA	*A Pamphlet Against Anthologies* (co-author Laura Riding), Cape, 1928; pub. *Against Anthologies*, Doubleday, New York, 1928
P-G	*The Pier-Glass*, Secker, 1921; Knopf, New York, 1921
Poems [1925]	*Poems*, Benn, 1925
Poems (1914–1926)	*Poems (1914–1926)*, Heinemann, 1927; Doubleday, New York, 1929
Poems (1914–1927)	*Poems (1914–1927)*, Heinemann, 1927 *Poems 1926–1930*, Heinemann, 1931
Poems 1929	*Poems 1929*, Seizin Press, 1929
PU	*Poetic Unreason and Other Studies*, Cecil Palmer, 1925
SMP	*A Survey of Modernist Poetry* (co-author Laura Riding), Heinemann, 1927; Doubleday, New York, 1928
TB	*Treasure Box*, Chiswick Press, 1919
TELTHB	*T. E. Lawrence to His Biographer, Robert Graves*, Doubleday, New York, 1938; Faber, 1939
TPM	*Ten Poems More*, Hours Press, Paris, 1930
W	*Whipperginny*, Heinemann, 1923; Knopf, New York, 1923
WH	*Welchman's Hose*, The Fleuron, 1925

OTHER ABBREVIATIONS

AB	*Among the Bohemians*, Virginia Nicholson, Viking, 2002
BOD	*The Bad Old Days*, Charles Graves, Faber, 1951
CMWP	*Robert Graves: War Poems*, ed. Charles Mundye, Seren Press, Bridgend, 2016
CP	*The Complete Poems*, Robert Graves, ed. B. Graves and D. Ward, Penguin, 2003
CP38	*Collected Poems*, Robert Graves, Cassell, 1938
CSS	*Complete Short Stories*, Robert Graves, ed. Lucia Graves, Penguin, 2008
EF	*A Mannered Grace: The Life of Laura (Riding) Jackson*, Elizabeth Friedmann, Persea Books, New York, 2005
EPRG	*The Early Poetry of Robert Graves*, Frank Kersnowski, University of Texas Press, Austin, 2002
GEC	*Games of an Edwardian Childhood*, Rosaleen Cooper, David and Charles, 1982
GWMM	*The Great War and the Missing Muse*, Patrick Quinn, Susquehanna University Press, 1994
IE	*In Extremis: The Life of Laura Riding*, Deborah Baker, Hamish Hamilton, 1993
Kirkham	*The Poetry of Robert Graves*, Michael Kirkham, Athlone Press
MBL	'Miss Briton's Lady-Companion', *Complete Short Stories*, Penguin, 2008
MS	*Robert Graves: Life on the Edge*, Miranda Seymour, Doubleday, 1995
MS-S	*Robert Graves: His Life and Works*, Martin Seymour-Smith, Bloomsbury, 1995
RPG1	*Robert Graves: The Assault Heroic*, Richard Perceval Graves, Weidenfeld & Nicolson, 1986
RPG2	*Robert Graves: The Years with Laura*, Richard Perceval Graves, Papermac, 1990
TLS	*Times Literary Supplement*
TRAT	*To Return to All That*, A. P. Graves, Cape, 1930

NOTES

Introduction

1 'Peace', *CP*, p. 741.
2 RC to BG, 12 November 1980, SJCO.
3 The manuscript, which lay buried in the Berg, has recently been published in full in Charles Mundye's edition of Graves's *War Poems* (Seren, 2016).
4 'War Poetry in This War', *The Listener* 26 (23 October 1940), reprinted in *The Common Asphodel*.
5 Ibid.
6 *CP*, p. 27.
7 *CP*, p. 32.
8 *CP*, p. 15.
9 *CP*, p. 51.
10 D. N. G. Carter, *Robert Graves: The Lasting Poetic Achievement*, Macmillan, 1989, p. 118.
11 Patrick Quinn, *The Great War and the Missing Muse*, Associated University Presses, 1994, p. 13.
12 Michael Longley, *Robert Graves: Selected Poems*, Faber & Faber, 2013, p. XX.
13 EB to RG, 20 February 1966, SJCO.
14 Review of RG's *Selected Poems*, ed. Michael Longley, *The Guardian*, 8 November 2013.
15 *CP*, p. 31.
16 *BISGO*, diary entry for 22 September 1929.
17 See 'Foreword', *Collected Poems (1955)*, p. XI.
18 *OEP*, p. 37.
19 Peter Parker, *The Old Lie*, Constable, 1987, p. 191.
20 'The Art of Poetry No. 11', *The Paris Review*, no. 47 (Summer 1969), interviewers Peter Buckman and William Fifield.
21 D. Baker, *In Extremis: The Life of Laura Riding*, Hamish Hamilton, 1993, p. 205.
22 See www.bbc.uk/archive/writers/12243.shtml
23 RG to EB, n.d. [1922?], HRC.
24 RC to RG [1967], SJCO.
25 MS-S, p. 23.

26   RG to BLH, 25 April 1954, HRC.
27   T. Graves, *Tuning Up at Dawn*, Harper Collins, 2004, p. 27.
28   See 'The Necessity of Arrogance', *OEP*, pp. 134–6.
29   *Collected Poems*, 323.
30   RG to William Merwin, 6 April 1960, Reese collection, Beinecke Library.
31   *CP38*, pp. xxiii–iv.
32   MS, p. xvi. Miranda Seymour was able to interview a number of RG's surviving friends in the 1990s.
33   So-called diary entry for 3 September [1929] in 'A Journal of Curiosities', *BISGO*, p. 131.
34   F. Wilson, *Literary Seductions*, Faber & Faber, 1999.

Chapter 1 'A Mixed Litter'

1   *BOD*, p. 12.
2   *OEP*, p. 33.
3   *GTAT*, p. 276.
4   'A Child's Nightmare', *CP*, p. 3.
5   MS-S, p. 9.
6   'Miss Briton's Lady-Companion', *Complete Short Storie*s, Penguin, 2008, p. 314 [MBL].
7   MS-S, p. 422. Jack the Ripper was an unidentified serial killer who operated in Whitechapel between 1888 and 1891; Paul Kruger was President of South Africa during the Boer War; Og was an Amorite king, killed with his whole army by Moses.
8   MBL, p. 315.
9   RG's brother, John Graves, believed that the Tiarks were originally from Norway.
10   *GTAT*, p. 18.
11   Ibid.
12   *GTAT*, pp. 17–18.
13   *My Early Life*, now at SJCO, dated 1936–7.
14   Ibid., p. 50.
15   First published in *The Crane Bag*, Cassell, 1969.
16   For Malcolm Muggeridge TV interview see: www.bbc.uk/archive/writers/12243.shtml
17   Clarissa to RG, 1 September 1945, SJCO.
18   MBL, p. 319.
19   *GTAT*, p. 51.
20   MBL, p. 320.
21   Ibid., p. 315.
22   *GTAT*, p. 52.
23   MBL, p. 35.
24   *GTAT*, p. 55.
25   Ibid.
26   *GEC*, p. 82.
27   MBL, p. 320.
28   Ibid.
29   *GTAT*, p. 25.
30   MBL, p. 320.
31   Paul Marston, 'Poet in the Family', *Advertiser* (Friday 4 November 1977).
32   Ibid.
33   MBL, p. 314.
34   MBL, p. 322.

35 *GTAT*, p. 22.
36 *GTAT*, p. 20.
37 See Alfred Perceval Graves's *'TRAT*, p. 324, and his reservations.
38 Stefan Collini, *Arnold: Culture and Anarchy and Other Writings*, Oxford University Press, 1988, p. 21.
39 'Five Score and Six Years Ago', *The Crane Bag*, Cassell, 1969, p. 141.
40 *GTAT*, p. 23.
41 Published by Maunsel & Co, Dublin, 1908.
42 Ibid., p. vi.
43 Ibid., pp. v–vi.
44 *GTAT*, p. 27.
45 *GTAT*, p. 24.
46 *GTAT*, p. 23.
47 *GTAT*, p. 55.
48 *GTAT*, p. 25.
49 *GTAT*, pp. 23–4.
50 RG to Gina Lollobrigida, 'A Red Book Dialogue' [September 1963], in Robert Graves, *Conversations with Robert Graves* (ed. F. Kersnowski), University Press of Mississippi, 1989, p. 61.
51 *CP*, p. 3.
52 RG's personal copy of OB now at SJCO.
53 *OEP*, p. 123.

Chapter 2 Victorian Beginnings and an Edwardian Education (1895–1909)

1   RG interview with Peter Buckman and William Fifield, *The Paris Review,* no. 47 (1969), pp. 119–45.
2   'The Tenement', *CSS*, p. 279.
3   *TRTAT*, p. 272.
4   *TRTAT*, p. 273.
5   *CP*, p. 3.
6   RC to RG, 9 February 1956, SJCO.
7   Clarissa to RG, 17 September 1953.
8   *GTAT*, p. 28.
9   In *GTAT*, RG uses it to describe the immediate rapport he had with Nancy Nicholson: 'My child-sentiment and hers – had a happy childhood to look back on – answered each other.'
10 'Down', *The Pier-Glass, CP*, p. 112.
11 *BOD*, p. 17.
12 *GTAT*, p. 28.
13 *BOD*, p. 9.
14 Ibid.
15 *BOD*, pp. 16–17.
16 *GTAT*, p. 27.
17 *Seven Days and Other Poems,* Methuen, 1927.
18 *BOD*, p. 10.
19 Clarissa to RG, 20 September 1945.

20 *GTAT*, p. 57.
21 'Richard Perceval Graves's obituary of Rosaleen in 1989.
22 RC to Max Arthur, in his recording of First World War voices.
23 This was called 'Why Jigsaws Went out of Fashion'.
24 RC to RG, 19 December 1973, SJCO.
25 RC to BG, 14 February 1985, SJCO.
26 'The Poetic State', *CP*, p. 240.
27 See 'Babylon', *CP*, p. 25, and *GTAT*, p. 53.
28 See RG's prose piece on the subject, written on 10 June 1915 and sent in a letter of 11 June to Edward Marsh.
29 RG to BG, 21 March 1987, SJCO. Favourites were 'Go to bed sweet muse, take thy rest' and 'Flow not so fast sad fountains'.
30 RC to RG, n.d., SJCO.
31 RC to BG, 11 February 1984, SJCO.
32 'My Best Christmas', *CSS*, p. 307.
33 JG's draft biography, 'My Brother Robert', Berg.
34 *GTAT*, p. 28.
35 RC to RG, 6 February 1970.
36 'Harold Vesey at the Gates of Hell', *CSS*, pp. 169–70.
37 'Houses in My Life', ts at SJCO. Now listed as a Grade 2 building, no. 1 Lauriston Road, as it became, is virtually unchanged today with the pub and livery stables still opposite the house, though the stables are under threat.
38 *TRTAT*, p. 271.
39 Ibid.
40 'Houses in My Life', SJCO.
41 'My Best Christmas', *CSS*.
42 *GEC*, p. 12.
43 'Houses in My Life', SJCO.
44 Ibid.
45 *BOD*, p. 16.
46 *CP*, p. 45.
47 Amy to her father, Heinrich von Ranke, 2 June 1905, RPG1, p. 53.
48 *GTAT*, p. 32.
49 Ibid.
50 *GEC*, p. 11.
51 'Houses in My Life', SJCO.
52 *BOD*, p. 22.
53 The origin of 'Laufzorn' appears to be from the settlement of AD 800, originally named 'Laufzoro', i.e. 'a clearing for the collection of dead game animals'. The house still stands today.
54 *GTAT*, pp. 44 and 47.
55 See MS-S, p. 124.
56 *GTAT*, p. 44.
57 Ibid.
58 *GTAT*, p. 46.
59 'The Whitaker Negroes', *CSS*, pp. 132–3.
60 RC in interview with Paul Marston, 'Poet in the Family', *Advertiser*, 4 November 1977.
61 *GTAT*, p. 48.
62 *GTAT*, pp. 49–50.

63   *GTAT*, p. 50.
64   *GTAT*, p. 58.
65   *GTAT*, p. 51.
66   *BOD*, p. 12.
67   Ibid.
68   *GTAT*, p. 24.
69   *GTAT*, p. 58.
70   Ibid.
71   'Rocky Acres', *CP*, p. 71.
72   'My Early Life', SJCO.
73   RC to RG, 19 December 1973, SJCO.
74   *GEC*, p. 11.
75   *GEC*, p. 12.
76   Ibid.
77   See RG to RC, 24 February 1918, private owner.
78   *GEC*, p. 12.
79   'Houses in My Life'.
80   *GTAT*, pp. 57–8.
81   *CP*, p. 71.
82   *GTAT*, p. 55.
83   'Houses in My Life', SJCO.
84   *GEC*, p. 12.
85   *BOD*, p. 55.
86   *GTAT*, p. 14.
87   RC to RG, 12 April 1981, SJCO.
88   RG to RC, [23 November] 1917, private owner.
89   'My Best Christmas', *CSS*, p. 307.
90   Ibid.
91   *GTAT*, p. 289.
92   *GTAT*, p. 38.
93   Ibid.
94   Founded in 1877 at 47 Woodhayes Road, Wimbledon, Rokeby had moved in 1879 to larger premises at 17 The Downs. Threatened with closure in 1965, Rokeby moved again to its present site in George Road, Kingston.
95   *GTAT*, p. 38.
96   Ibid.
97   *GTAT*, p. 39.
98   Ibid.
99   *GTAT*, pp. 39–40.
100 *GTAT*, p. 40.
101 Ibid.
102 Ibid.
103 *GTAT*, pp. 40–1.
104 *The English Ballad: A Short Critical Survey* (1927) and *English and Scottish Ballads* (1957).
105 *GTAT*, p. 41.
106 *Forever England*, Biteback Publishing, 1997, p. 4.
107 *GTAT*, p. 41.
108 Ibid.

109 This and the following reminiscences by Duncan Grant were taken from *With Duncan Grant in Southern Turkey*, Honeyglen Publishers, 1982.
110 *GTAT*, p. 41.
111 *BOD*, p. 319.
112 *GTAT*, p. 42.
113 *TRTAT*, p. 319.
114 *GTAT*, p. 43.
115 *TRTAT*, p. 319.
116 *GTAT*, p. 43.
117 *TRTAT*, p. 319.

Chapter 3 Charterhouse: 'the Public School Spirit' (1909–12)

1 *GTAT*, p. 61.
2 *GTAT*, pp. 50–1.
3 *GTAT*, p. 63.
4 *GTAT*, p. 410.
5 See RG's review of *Floreat Charterhouse: an Open Examination written by the Boys*, ed. Kenneth Mason, 1964, at SJCO.
6 Ibid.
7 Ibid.
8 Ibid.
9 *BOD*, p. 27.
10 *GTAT*, p. 66.
11 *GTAT*, pp. 64 and 66.
12 Frank Fletcher, *After Many Days*, Robert Hale, 1937, p. 138.
13 Ibid., p. 148.
14 *GTAT*, p. 63.
15 In 1911.
16 Fletcher, *After Many Days*, p. 162.
17 Ibid.
18 *GTAT*, p. 64.
19 i.e. 'My New-Bug's Exam', *Green Chartreuse*, July 1913.
20 *GTAT*, p. 63.
21 G. D. Martineau, in W. G. Holmes, *The Charterhouse We Knew,* British Technical and General Press, 1950, pp. 53–62.
22 H. L. Gandell to John Graves, 4 February 1974, Berg.
23 Ibid.
24 *GTAT*, pp. 64–5.
25 *GTAT*, p. 67.
26 *BOD*, p. 27.
27 *GTAT*, p. 67.
28 *GTAT*, p. 86.
29 *GTAT*, p. 67.
30 *GTAT*, p. 68.
31 Ibid.
32 *The White Goddess*, 1961 edn, p. 17.
33 *GTAT*, p. 84.

34   Raymond Juzio Paul Rodakowski was born on 15 May 1895, but Graves wrongly notes a larger age difference between them, perhaps because Rodakowski was a year ahead of him in school.

35   *GTAT*, p. 84.

36   *GTAT*, p. 69.

37   D. Robertson, *George Mallory*, Faber & Faber, 1969/1999, p. 120.

38   Ibid.

39   *GTAT*, p. 70.

40   Ibid.

41   APG, 21 June 1911.

42   APG, 1 August 1911.

43   *GTAT*, p. 74.

44   *GTAT*, p. 76.

45   *GTAT*, p. 75.

46   Martineau, *The Charterhouse We Knew*, p. 59.

47   Fletcher, *After Many Days*, pp. 138–40.

48   Ibid., p. 162.

49   APG, 23 July 1913.

50   RG to CG, 23 May 1917, HRC.

51   Fletcher, *After Many Days*, p. 150.

52   APG's account of RG's letter to him, Diary, 10 October 1911.

53   Martineau, *The Charterhouse We Knew*, p. 60.

54   APG, Diary, 26 June 1911.

55   George Mallory to Lytton Strachey, 27 September 1911, Bonham's Auction Catalogue, lot 179, June 2015.

56   *GTAT*, p. 80.

57   Cottie Sanders, quoted in Robertson, *George Mallory*, 1999, p. 80.

58   *GTAT*, p. 80.

59   JG's draft biography, 'My Brother Robert', Berg.

60   RG to JG, n.d. [1919?], Berg.

61   Ibid.

62   RG to Cyril Hartmann, January [1918], RWF Archives, Wrexham.

63   M. Holroyd, *Lytton Strachey*, Penguin, 1994, p. 2,056.

64   Francis Spalding, *Duncan Grant*, Chatto and Windus, 1997, p. 16.

65   *GTAT*, p. 91.

66   *GTAT*, p. 95.

67   Ibid.

68   See 'Broken Neck', CP, p. 55.

69   A technical term at Charterhouse that meant being cheeky to one's seniors.

70   RG explained that 'this was a reference to one of the "Clerihews" we used to sing to a mournful Gregorian hymn tune:

Archbishop Odo
Was just in the middle of "Dodo", [a popular novel by E. F. Benson]
When he remembered that it was Sunday.
"Sic transit gloria mundi".

RG to George Mallory [late April 1913], quoted in Robertson, *George Mallory*, p. 84.

71   George Mallory to Lytton Strachey, 17 May 1914, Bonhams Auction Catalogue, lot 179, June 1915.

Chapter 4 Charterhouse: Of Cherry-Whisky and Other Matters (1912–14)

1   'Is My Team Ploughing...?', unsigned article, *The Carthusian*, October 1915.
2   April 1913 number, pp. 86–8.
3   *CP*, p. 7.
4   'My Brother Robert', Berg.
5   'The Lake of Garda' would win the Newdigate Prize in 1920.
6   *GTAT*, p. 76.
7   Ibid.
8   The 1st Baron Derwent was created in 1881 for George Johnstone's grandfather, Sir Harcourt Vanden-Bempde-Johnstone. George's older brother was next in line; since he died in the First World War, George became 3rd Baron Derwent in 1929.
9   Quoted in Andrew Rose, *The Prince, The Princess and the Perfect Murder*, Coronet, 2014, fn 228.
10 *BOD*, p. 41.
11 *BOD*, p. 25 – 'Brussels where a very pretty girl fell in love with Robert to his immense embarrassment'.
12 RG to Edward Carpenter, 30 May 1914, Sheffield City Libraries.
13 Ibid. Richard Middleton, 1882–1911, a British poet and prose writer, who committed suicide; now remembered if at all for his ghost stories.
14 Ibid.
15 Final verse of Middleton's 'Hylas'.
16 October 1913, 'Jolly Yellow Moon'.
    do.   'Rondeau: The Clouds' (*CP*, 726)
    Nov. 1913   'Love & Black Magic' (*CP*, 49)
    do.   'Am and Advance: A Cockney Study' (*CP*, 727)
    Dec. 1913   'Ballad of the White Monster' (*CP*, 728)
    do.   'Alcaics addressed to My Study Fauna' (*CP*, 730)
    do.   'The Future' (*CP*, 729)
    do.   'Pan Set at Nought' (?)
    do.   'The Cyclone' (*CP*, 731)
17 *CP*, p. 49.
18 Frank Fletcher, *After Many Days,* Robert Hale, 1937, p. 163.
19 *GTAT*, 1957, p. 38.
20 *CP*, pp. 20 and 806.
21 *GTAT*, p. 77.
22 APG, 22 June 1913.
23 *GTAT*, p. 77.
24 APG, 22 June 1913.
25 RG's annotated copy of the *Green Chartreuse*, now at Charterhouse, identifies each contribution with initials.
26 Christopher Hassall, *Edward Marsh, Patron of the Arts*, Longmans, Green & Co., 1959.
27 APG, 28 February 1914.
28 *GTAT*, p. 88.
29 *Carthusian*, vol. XI, no. 372 (December 1913), p. 220.
30 Ibid., no. 373 (February 1914), p. 225.
31 APG, 4 May 1914.
32 CG to Amy, n.d., Berg.
33 *GTAT*, p. 79.

34   G. D. Martineau, in W. G. Holmes, *The Charterhouse We Knew,* British Technical and General Press, 1950, p. 6.
35   'The Tyranny of Books', *Carthusian*, vol. XI (July 1914), p. 311; *CP*, p. 737.
36   My italics: APG, 22 June 1913.
37   See *CP*, pp. 731–7.
38   *CP*, p. 8.
39   Richard Barham Middleton (1882–1911): the first publication of his work was *Poems and Songs* (1913).
40   RG to JG, 6 July 1914, Berg.
41   *GTAT*, p. 85.
42   *GTAT*, p. 87.
43   Ibid.
44   APG, 20 July 1914.
45   Ibid.
46   Ibid.
47   *GTAT*, p. 88.
48   *GTAT*, p. 62.
49   RG to JG, 6 July 1914, Berg.
50   Martineau, *The Charterhouse We Knew*, p. 64.
51   Quoted in Max Beerbohm, *Mainly on the Air,* Heinemann, 1946, p. 93.
52   RG to Cyril Hartmann, 25 October 1914, IWM.
53   Ibid.

Chapter 5 'On Finding Myself a Soldier' (August 1914–May 1915)

1   *CP*, p. 12.
2   'On Finding Myself a Soldier', *CP*, p. 12.
3   APG, 30 July 1914.
4   A French socialist politician and advocate of international peace.
5   *TRTAT*, p. 326.
6   *The Collected Letters of Charles Hamilton Sorley*, ed. Jean Moorcroft Wilson, Cecil Woolf Publishers, 1990, p. 209.
7   *GTAT*, p. 62.
8   *GTAT*, p. 61.
9   RG to JG, 11 September 1935, Berg.
10   *GTAT*, p. 99.
11   Ibid.
12   Ibid.
13   RG to Cyril Hartmann, 25 October 1914, IWM.
14   Charles Hamilton Sorley to Arthur Watts, 16 June 1915, *The Collected Letters of Charles Hamilton Sorley*, p. 228.
15   RG to Cyril Hartmann, 25 October 1914, IWM.
16   Ibid.
17   *PU*, p. 146.
18   *GTAT*, p. 100.
19   *GTAT*, p. 101.
20   APG, 12 August 1914. 'Dick Poore' was Admiral Sir Richard Poore, husband of Alfred's sister Ida and Commander in Chief on the East Coast.

21 APG, 12 August 1914.
22 *Punch*, 7 June 1916.
23 *GTAT*, p. 117.
24 *GTAT*, pp. 118–19.
25 *GTAT*, p. 118.
26 *Sergeant Lamb of the Ninth* (1940) and *Proceed Sergeant Lamb* (1941) were printed as two separate volumes because of wartime restrictions on paper.
27 RG to David Graves, 13 November 1939, Lilly.
28 *GTAT*, p. 121.
29 *CP*, p. 10.
30 Ibid.
31 *GTAT*, p. 33.
32 RG to CSM [20 August 1917?], NLS.
33 'Robert Graves', *Today*, no. 24, vol. 4 (February 1916), p. 213.
34 *GTAT*, p. 33.
35 See RPG1, p. 117.
36 Quoted by MS-S, p. 382.
37 Ibid.
38 MS, p. 40.
39 *CP*, p. 9.
40 *GTAT*, p. 102.
41 Ibid.
42 *GTAT*, p. 104.
43 RG to JG, n.d. [September 1914], Berg.
44 Ibid.
45 *GTAT*, p. 104.
46 *The Enormous Room*, Cape, 1928, p. 11.
47 Ibid.
48 *CP*, p. 11.
49 *GTAT*, p. 107.
50 *GTAT*, pp. 105–6.
51 Ibid.
52 *GTAT*, p. 99.
53 5–12 September 1914.
54 19–27 November 1914.
55 26–30 August 1914.
56 RG to Cyril Hartmann, 25 October 1914, IWM.
57 *CP*, p. 12. RG has noted on his own copy at SJCO that this poem was written at Le Havre, which would date it mid-May 1915, though by then he had been a 'soldier' for nine months.
58 *CP*, p. 13.
59 *GTAT*, p. 108.
60 APG, 20 August 1914.
61 *GTAT*, p. 107.
62 APG, 7 December 1914.
63 Ibid.
64 The house was at 18 Bina Gardens, South Kensington.
65 RG to EM, 15 November 1915, Berg, and RG to Cyril Hartmann, 15 June 1918, IWM.
66 RG to EM, 26 December 1914, Berg.

67   APG, 28 December 1914.

68   APG, 2 January 1915.

69   APG, 5 January 1915.

70   APG, 4 January 1915.

71   RG to EM, 22 January 1915, Berg.

72   *The Weald of Youth*, Faber & Faber, p. 139.

73   RG to EM, 3 February 1915, Berg. RG exaggerates characteristically; APG never met Wordsworth and met Tennyson only once.

74   Ibid.

75   See introduction to *My Head! My Head!* (1925), pp. 24–5.

76   *BISGO*, p. 155.

77   Ibid.

78   APG mentions one in his diary for 3 May 1915 called 'Old and Young Poet', which was subsequently dropped because of RG's uncle Charles's dismissal of it.

79   APG, 1 May 1915.

80   Johnny Basham (1890–1947), a Welshman, had been with the RWF at Wrexham since 1912 when RG met him. He was the first welterweight to win the Lonsdale Belt outright and would go on to become both British and European welterweight and middleweight champion.

Chapter 6 'These Soul-Deadening Trenches' (May–July 1915)

1   'Return', *CP*, p. 808.

2   *The Collected Letters of Charles Hamilton Sorley*, ed. Jean Moorcroft Wilson, Cecil Woolf Publishers, 1990, p. 228.

3   'The Poets of World War II', *The Common Asphodel: Collected Essays on Poetry, 1922–1949*, Hamish Hamilton, 1949, p. 308.

4   RG to EM, 22 May 1915, Berg.

5   'It's a Queer Time', *CP*, p. 19.

6   RG to EM, 22 May 1915, Berg.

7   'This incident was at Harlech in 1899 at the end of the sandy road crossing the golf links', RG notes in his personal copy of *Over the Brazier*, SJCO.

8   *CP*, p. 15.

9   *The Spectator*, 11 September 1915, p. 330.

10   *Rupert Brooke: The Poetical Works*, ed. Geoffrey Keynes, Faber & Faber, 1960, p. 17.

11   RG to EM, 22 May 1915, Berg.

12   APG, 15–17 May 1915.

13   APG, 7 June 1915. These letters would be published in *The Spectator* on 11 September 1915 and differ slightly from those quoted by APG in *To Return to All That*. There are some significant differences in them from RG's account in *GTAT*.

14   RG to EM, 22 May 1915, Berg.

15   *The Spectator*, 11 September 1915.

16   *GTAT*, p. 134. Captain Dunn of the 2nd Welsh was different from Captain/Dr J. C. Dunn of the 2nd RWF, whom RG would meet later.

17   *GTAT*, p. 143.

18   *The Spectator*, 11 September 1915, p. 330.

19   Robert told his parents to whom he wrote at least once a week.

20   *The Spectator*, 11 September 1915, p. 330.

21 Ibid.
22 *GTAT*, p. 154.
23 Ibid.
24 *GTAT*, p. 151.
25 *GTAT*, p. 143.
26 *The Spectator*, 11 September 1915, p. 330.
27 RG to EM, 28 November 1918, Berg.
28 Ibid.
29 APG, 24 May 1915.
30 *GTAT*, pp. 141–2.
31 *GTAT*, p. 152.
32 Ibid.
33 *GTAT*, p. 182.
34 Ibid.
35 *GTAT*, p. 153.
36 Ibid: This incident would contribute to his poem 'The Gnat' later on.
37 *GTAT*, p. 153.
38 *GTAT*, p. 154.
39 *GTAT*, p. 155.
40 *The Spectator*, 11 September 1915, p. 330.
41 APG, 4 June 1915.
42 APG, 2 June 1915.
43 *GTAT*, p. 154.
44 *GTAT*, p. 161.
45 *The Carthusian*, October 1915, repub. *Gravesiania*, vol. III, with an illuminating commentary by Dr Eric Webb.
46 *GTAT*, p. 155.
47 *Over the Brazier*, 1916 edition.
48 *Diaries 1915–18*, Faber & Faber, 1983, p. 21.
49 SS to Nellie Gosse, 6 January 1916, BL.
50 *GTAT*, p. 155.
51 *The Spectator*, 11 September 1915, p. 330.
52 Ibid.
53 'Through the Periscope', *CP*, p. 805.
54 *The Spectator*, 11 September 1915, p. 30.
55 RG to his family, 2 July 1915, Berg.
56 SJCO.
57 APG, 13 July 1915, Berg.
58 *CP*, p. 11.
59 Ibid.
60 This was Mr Kelly of *The British Review*.
61 RG to Cyril Hartmann, 2 January [1918], IWM.
62 *CMWP*, p. 19.
63 Copy of *Over the Brazier* at SJCO.
64 *CP*, p. 14.
65 RG to RC, 24 February 1918.
66 *CP*, p. 13.
67 'The Last Drop' is annotated 'Le Havre, 1915'. See *CP*, p. 804.
68 2nd RWF, 1st Scottish Rifles, 1st Middlesex, 2nd Argyll and Sutherland Highlanders, 5th Scottish Rifles.

Chapter 7 The Battle of Loos (August–October 1915)

1   *CP*, p. 806.
2   *GTAT*, p. 164.
3   *GTAT*, p. 172.
4   *GTAT*, p. 182.
5   APG, 31 August 1915.
6   *CP*, p. 17.
7   *GTAT*, p. 167.
8   *TRTAT*, pp. 330–1.
9   APG, 26 August 1915.
10 *GTAT*, p. 182.
11 *GTAT*, p. 187.
12 Ibid.
13 *CP*, p. 20.
14 *GTAT*, p. 188.
15 APG, 9 September 1915.
16 APG, 11 September 1915.
17 APG, 14 September 1915.
18 *GTAT*, p. 163.
19 Ibid.
20 *GTAT*, p. 164, and RG to G. Johnstone, 5 August 1915, SJCO.
21 *CP*, p. 20. First published in the *Westminster Gazette,* 2 March 1916.
22 *CP*, p. 806.
23 APG, 20 September 1915.
24 *GTAT*, p. 196.
25 Ibid.
26 *GTAT*, p. 197.
27 *First World War*, Weidenfeld & Nicolson, 1994, p. 199.
28 *CP*, p. 806: see opening quote to chapter.
29 See *GTAT*, pp. 201–3.
30 *CP*, p. 18: see also *GTAT*, pp. 205–6, for RG's prose account.
31 *EPRG*, p. 11.
32 *CP*, p. 18. These words were added in RG's copy of 1920 edn of *OB*.
33 *GTAT*, p. 205.
34 Ibid.
35 *GTAT*, p. 205.
36 *GTAT*, p. 211.
37 Helen McPhail and Philip Guest argue, in *Graves and Sassoon*, Leo Cooper, 2001, p. 51, that the attack was not simply 'diversionary', but a 'main attack' with 'limited objectives', i.e. 'an anticipated advance of almost two miles, bearing to the left, designed to give protected cover on the northern flank for those in action further south'.
38 APG, 27 September 1915.
39 APG, 2 October 1915.
40 APG, 4 October 1915.
41 APG, 6 October 1915.
42 *GTAT*, p. 217.
43 HRC.

Chapter 8 Siegfried Sassoon and a Recipe for Rum Punch (October 1915–March 1916)

1   TS of a poem unpublished until 2016, Buffalo.
2   RG to EM, October 1915, Berg.
3   Ibid.
4   Hill visited RG's parents on his next leave in January 1916. APG, 17 January 1916.
5   'Through the Periscope', 'Limbo', 'The Adventure' and 'The First Funeral'.
6   RG to EM, October 1915, Berg.
7   APG, 26 October 1915.
8   MS at Wrexham.
9   APG, 8 November 1915.
10 RG to EM, October 1915, Berg.
11 Ibid.
12 *CP*, p. 98.
13 APG, 15 November 1915.
14 APG, 18 November 1915.
15 *GTAT*, p. 219.
16 *GTAT*, p. 213.
17 J. C. Dunn, *The War the Infantry Knew*, P. S. King, 1938, p. 166.
18 Edmund Dadd's brother, Julian, would become a close friend of Sassoon. They were nephews of the eccentric painter Richard Dadd, one of whose pictures Sassoon would donate to the National Gallery.
19 RG to EM, 10 December 1915.
20 Ibid., Berg.
21 This copy, quite different from the copy SS annotated jointly with Edmund Blunden and Dr Dunn, which is in the Berg collection at New York Public Library, is now at the Beinecke Library, Yale University.
22 Diary 1, entry for 28 November 1915, p. 21.
23 C. Hassall, *Edward Marsh: Patron of the Arts*, Longmans, Green & Co., 1959, p. 79.
24 Siegfried Sassoon, *Memoirs of an Infantry Officer*, Faber & Faber, 1930 (Faber & Faber 1985 edition used), p. 108.
25 Orig. Gen. C. I. Stockwell to SS, copied in SS's hand in a letter to Julian Dadd, 3 March 1931, IWM.
26 SS to RR, 18 March 1917, Lilly.
27 Sassoon, *Memoirs of an Infantry Officer*, p. 108.
28 Ibid.
29 *GTAT*, p. 224.
30 RG to EM, 15 March 1916, Berg.
31 *GTAT*, p. 225.
32 *GTAT*, p. 227.
33 APG, 5 December 1915.
34 'Night March', *CP*, p. 811.
35 Another reason was that it had been included in *The Patchwork Flag*, a collection RG subsequently abandoned.
36 SS to EM, 22 December 1917, Berg.
37 *GTAT*, p. 228.
38 Ibid.
39 Beinecke.

40 There is a puzzle about RG's annotation to '1915', 'written at Havre in the winter of 1915', since RG arrived there in May and stayed only a few days. He did not return to Le Havre until January 1916, by which time his first collection had been sent to Monro, including '1915'.

41 APG, 2 December 1915.

42 Note to volume 3 of the hardback ed. of *CP* (1999), p. 546.

43 RG to EM, 9 February 1916.

44 Ibid.

45 RG to EM, 24 February 1916.

46 Ibid.

47 RG to EM, 10 December 1915.

48 RG to EM, New Year's Day 1916, and RG to SS, [? May 1916], Berg.

49 RG to EM, New Year's Day 1916, Berg.

50 *GTAT*, p. 228.

51 *GTAT*, p. 229.

52 RG to EM, 10 December 1915, Berg.

53 *GTAT*, p. 229.

54 S. Sassoon, *Memoirs of a Fox-Hunting Man,* Faber & Faber, 1928, p. 256.

55 Dunn, *The War the Infantry Knew*, p. 287.

56 RG to EM, New Year's Day 1916, Berg.

57 Ibid.

58 *GTAT*, p. 231.

59 *GTAT*, p. 232.

60 RG to EM, 9 February 1916, Berg.

61 RG to EM, 9 February 1916.

62 Ibid.

63 *CP*, p. 806.

64 Ibid.

65 APG, 16 February 1916.

66 RG to EM, 24 February 1916, Berg.

67 Ibid.

68 See 'Rooks' and 'Rooks II', *Collected Poems of Charles Hamilton Sorley*, ed. Jean Moorcroft Wilson, Cecil Woolf Publishers, 1985, pp. 42–3.

69 RG to Edmund Gosse, 24 October 1917, Brotherton.

70 *Collected Poems of Charles Hamilton Sorley*, p. 88.

71 RG to Prof. William Sorley, 5 March 1917, HRC.

72 RG to SS, n.d. [early May 1916], Berg.

73 APG, 8 March 1916.

Chapter 9 The Road to High Wood (March–July 1916)

1 *CP*, p. 36. RG dates this 'July 13th, 1916'.

2 RG to Amy, 12 March 1916, SJCO.

3 *The Regimental Record of the Royal Welch Fusiliers*, compiled by C. H. Dudley Ward, Forster Groom, 1928, vol. 3, p. 186.

4 RG to his parents, 17 March 1916, IWM.

5 RG to Amy, 19 March 1916, IWM.

6 Ibid., and *GTAT*, p. 249.

7   EB to RG, 11 September 1919, SIU.

8   *GWMM*, p. 42.

9   RG to Amy, 19 March 1916, IWM.

10 'Lesboeufs and Morval', *The New Witness*, 12 April 1917, quoted by Jean Findlay in *Chasing Lost Time: The Life of C. K. Scott Moncrieff*, Vintage, 2015, p. 126.

11 'Robert Graves', *Today*, vol. 4, no. 24, February 1919, p. 211.

12 A note beside these subsequently deleted lines refers to 'my bitterness of rage and fire/ God's a liar'.

13 *CP*, p. 24.

14 *GTAT*, p. 288.

15 *London Review of Books*, 7 May 2015.

16 *CP*, p. 24.

17 *GTAT*, pp. 288–9.

18 The original for this poem was Private Challoner, RG said: *GTAT*, p. 161.

19 Rebecca West thought that RG's account in *GTAT*, p. 161, conveyed the 'weird atmosphere of devastated France' very well indeed.

20 RG to Amy, 19 March 1916, IWM.

21 RG to SS, 2 May 1916, Berg.

22 RG to EM, 4 April 1916, from Millbank Hospital.

23 RG to EM, 4 August 1916, Berg.

24 RG to EM, 13 April 1916.

25 P. Fussell, *The Great War and Modern Memory*, Oxford University Press, 1975, p. 39.

26 *GTAT*, p. 253.

27 RG to SS, 2 May 1916. The four poems are 'Over the Brazier', 'A Cottage', 'Familiar Letter to Siegfried Sassoon' and 'Sorley's Weather'.

28 *CP*, p. 39.

29 RG to SS, n.d. [early May 1916?], Berg.

30 *CP*, p. 24.

31 RG to EM, 4 April 1916.

32 APG, 20 May 1916.

33 *The Spectator*, 17 June 1916, p. 752.

34 *TLS*, 20–27 May 1916.

35 RG to SS, 27 May 1916, Berg.

36 RG to LOM, 'New Year' 1917, BL.

37 RG to LOM, 28 November 1916, BL.

38 RG to Amy, 1 June [1916], IWM.

39 *GTAT*, p. 254.

40 RG to SS, 7 May 1916.

41 RG to SS, 23 June 1916, Berg.

42 Siegfried Sassoon, *Memoirs of an Infantry Officer*, Faber & Faber, 1930 (Faber & Faber 1973 edition used), pp. 78–9.

43 I am indebted to Dr Eric Webb for this information. There is a ms draft of the poem at Buffalo.

44 i.e. the feminine form of 'Pierre', or 'Peter' in English.

45 *CP*, p. 48.

46 RG to SS, 23 June 1916, Berg.

47 Ibid.

48 RG to SS, 27 May 1916, Berg.

49 *CP*, p. 27.

50 *CP*, p. 25.
51 See MS-S, p. 45.
52 RG to Amy, 4 July 1916, SJCO.
53 Col. Crawshay to SS, n.d., CUL.
54 RG to Major Peter Kirkby, 6 June 1970, Wrexham.
55 RG to Amy, 7 July 1916, IWM.
56 *GTAT*, p. 261.
57 S. Sassoon, *Diaries 1915–1918* (ed. R. Hart Davis), Faber & Faber, 1983, p. 94.
58 'Familiar Letter to Siegfried Sassoon' (from Bivouacs at Mametz Wood, 13 July 1916), *CP*, p. 39. RG did not meet SS until 14 July 1916, so RG has the date wrong.
59 RG to his family, 17 July 1916, IWM.
60 *CP*, p. 27.
61 *GTAT*, p. 264.
62 RG to his family, 17 July 1916, IWM.
63 Ibid.
64 *GTAT*, p. 273.
65 J. C. Dunn, *The War the Infantry Knew*, P. S. King, 1938, p. 231.
66 J. C. Dunn to RG, 8 October 1925, Wrexham.
67 *GTAT*, pp. 273–4.

Chapter 10 The Survivor (July 1916–February 1917)

1   'The Survivor', *CP*, p. 439.
2   Although parts of APG's account do not tally with RG's in *GTAT*, his is the more factually reliable since, as he pointed out, he had transcribed his account from the diary he kept daily during the War.
3   *TRTAT*, p. 331.
4   RG to Amy, 24 July 1916, IWM.
5   IWM.
6   MBL, p. 321.
7   RG to family, 29 July 1916, IWM.
8   APG, 31 July 1916, and *TRTAT*, p. 332.
9   *TRTAT*, p. 332.
10 *GTAT*, p. 281.
11 APG, 3 August 1916.
12 RG to EM, 7 August 1916, Berg.
13 *GTAT*, p. 281.
14 J. C. Dunn, *The War the Infantry Knew*, P. S. King, 1938, p. 246.
15 The in-joke about the all-too-familiar Tickler's army jam was changed in the final version of the poem, 'Escape', to 'ration' jam.
16 RG to EM, 7 August 1916, Berg.
17 *CP*, p. 28.
18 *CP*, p. 27.
19 F. L. Kersnowski, *The Early Poetry of Robert Graves: The Goddess Beckons*, University of Texas Press, Austin, 2002, pp. 42–3.
20 RG to EM, 14 August 1916, Berg.
21 *CP*, p. 28.
22 MS-S, p. 49.

23 This is now at the Beinecke Library.

24 SS to Edward Dent, 29 July 1916, CUL.

25 SS to Dent, 4 August 1916, CUL.

26 RG to SS, 7 August 1916.

27 'The Survivor', *CP*, p. 439.

28 *GTAT*, p. 56.

29 These words were written in ink on the pencil ms of 'The Survivor Comes Home', at Buffalo.

30 SS's ms comment on the ts version of RG's intended collection, *The Patchwork Flag*, now at the Berg.

31 MS version, Buffalo.

32 APG, 29 August 1916.

33 *CP*, p. 22.

34 Foreword to *Collected Poems*, Cassell, 1937, p. xviii.

35 *GTAT*, p. 288.

36 *GTAT*, p. 289.

37 'Familiar Letter to Siegfried Sassoon', *CP*, p. 39.

38 RG to RR, 16 September 1916, IWM.

39 RG to RR, 16 September 1916, IWM.

40 RG to SS, 31 May 1922, Berg.

41 M. Holroyd, *Lytton Strachey*, Penguin, 1994, p. 692.

42 Ibid.

43 RG to SS, 21 April 1917, Berg.

44 RG to EB, 25 September, n.d. [1921?], HRC.

45 Ms note of EB and SS's annotated copy of *GTAT* at Berg.

46 RG to RR, 22 October 1916, IWM.

47 RG to RR, 16 September 1916, IWM.

48 RG to EM, 18 October 1916, Berg.

49 RG to RR, 12 October 1916, IWM.

50 Ibid.

51 Cf. *GTAT*, pp. 203–4, and the ms page of the novel in the RWF Archives at Wrexham.

52 RG to RR, 24 November 1916, Lilly.

53 RG to RR, 24 November 1916, Lilly, and RR to RG, 26 November 1916, Wrexham.

54 RG to RR, 12 November 1916.

55 *GTAT*, p. 290.

56 RG to RR, 24 November 1916.

57 APG, 5 December 1916.

58 RG to RR, 24 November 1916, IWM.

59 RG to SS, 30 November 1916, Berg.

60 RG to RR, 24 November 1916, Lilly.

61 RG to SS, 30 November 1916, Berg.

62 Ibid.

63 Ibid.

64 Ibid.

65 Charles Hamilton Sorley to the headmaster of Marlborough College, *Collected Letters*, 5 October 1915, p. 258.

66 *CP*, pp. 30–1.

67 *CP*, p. 31.

68 *GTAT*, p. 291.

69   *CP*, p. 38, quotes ll. 1–18 of 'The Legion' in the 'Foreword', preceded by this comment.
70   *CP*, p. 30.
71   *CP*, p. 31.
72   Wilfred Owen to SS, 27 November 1917, in Wilfred Owen, *Collected Letters* (eds H. Owen and J. Bell), Oxford University Press, 1967, p. 511.
73   F. E. Whitton, *History of the 40th Division*, Gales & Polden, 1926, p. 42.
74   Dunn, *The War the Infantry Knew*, p. 288.
75   *GTAT*, p. 296.
76   Ibid.
77   *GTAT*, p. 297.
78   *GTAT*, p. 300.
79   In the event, the section would be dedicated to someone else.
80   RG to SS, 25 January 1917, Berg.
81   RG to RN, 2 February 1917, Berg.
82   Ibid.
83   Ibid.
84   RG to LOM, 2 March 1917, BL.

Chapter 11 A Change of Direction (March–June 1917)

1   *CP*, p. 31.
2   *GTAT*, pp. 251–2.
3   RG to KB, 27 January 1921.
4   *GTAT*, p. 330.
5   Ibid.
6   Diary (copy), 26 March 1935, SJCO.
7   *CP*, p. 814.
8   *GTAT*, p. 354.
9   RG to CSM, 11 February 1918, NLS.
10   In the government's *Report of the War Office Committee of Enquiry into 'Shell-Shock'* of 1922, it was agreed that 'some 60–80% of shell-shock cases displayed acute neurasthenia'.
11   RG to EM, n.d., Berg.
12   *GTAT*, pp. 402–3.
13   RG to EG, 24 October 1917, Brotherton.
14   Ibid.
15   *CP*, p. 54.
16   Ibid.
17   *CP*, p. 55.
18   RG to EG, 25 March 1917. See RG's *The Less Familiar Nursery Rhymes*, produced by the same publisher, Benn, and in the same year, 1927, as his edition of *John Skelton (Laureate)*.
19   e.g. 'Double Red Daisies', 'A Child's Nightmare', 'I'd Love to Be a Fairy Child', 'A Boy in Church', 'Mr. Philosopher', 'I Wonder What It Feels Like to Be Drowned', 'The Cruel Moon'.
20   e.g. 'Dead Cow Farm', 'The Caterpillar', 'The Next War', 'Love and Black Magic'.
21   *CP*, p. 29.
22   *Robert Graves: War Poems*, ed. Charles Mundye, Seren, 2016, p. 19.
23   *CP*, p. 39.

24 'Bazentin 1916' was included in RG's *The Patchwork Flag*, unpublished in his lifetime; 'A Letter from Wales' appeared in *Welchman's Hose* (1925).

25 RG to SS, 26 March 1917, Berg.

26 RG to KB, 29 August 1933, Berg.

27 RG to RR, 13 March 1917, IWM.

28 RG to EM, 31 March 1917, Berg.

29 *GTAT*, p. 304.

30 RG to SS, 26 March 1917, Berg.

31 Ibid.

32 RG to LOM, 26 March 1917, BL.

33 RG to SS, 26 March 1917, Berg.

34 'John Skelton', *CP*, p. 44.

35 APG; 10 April 1917.

36 RG to RR, 18 April 1917, Berg.

37 APG to SS, 22 April 1917, CUL.

38 RG to SS, 27 April 1917, Berg.

39 L. B. Pearson, *Mike: The Memoirs of the Rt. Hon. Lester B. Pearson, vol. 1: 1897–1948*, University of Toronto Press, 2015, p. 32.

40 *GTAT*, p. 305.

41 Pearson, *Mike*, p. 32.

42 *GTAT*, p. 305.

43 *GTAT*, pp. 304–5.

44 RG to KB, 19 May 1917, Berg.

45 RG to EM, [summer] solstice [i.e. 21 June] 1917, Berg.

46 e.g. RG to RR, 20 June 1917, IWM.

47 RG to CSM, n.d. [20 August 1917], NLS.

48 RG to RN [November 1917], Berg.

49 RG to KB, 13 October 1919, Berg.

50 Caroline Gascoigne, 'Letters Unlock War Poet's Love Secret', *The Times*, 23 July 1995.

51 *GTAT*, p. 307.

52 RG to KB, 5 August 1917, Berg.

53 Ibid.

54 RG to KB, 5 August 1917, Berg.

55 RG to KB, 22 December 1917, Berg.

56 RG to KB, 13 October 1919, Berg.

Chapter 12 A Protest, Craiglockhart and 'A Capable Farmer's Boy' (June–July 1917)

1 One wing of Osborne Palace had been converted into a military hospital for officers.

2 *GTAT*, p. 310.

3 *GTAT*, p. 312.

4 RG to RN, n.d. [c. late June/early July 1917], Berg.

5 *GTAT*, p. 312.

6 *GTAT*, p. 314.

7 RG to SS, 3 July 1917, Berg.

8   Marsh eventually chose six instead of eight poems: 'It's a Queer Time', 'Star Talk' and 'In the Wilderness' from *Over the Brazier*, 'The Lady Visitor' and 'Not Dead' from *Goliath and David*, and 'A Boy in Church' from *Fairies and Fusiliers*.
9   RG to RR, 9 July 1917, IWM.
10 Ibid.
11 Ibid.
12 Ibid.
13 *GTAT*, p. 322.
14 Siegfried Sassoon, *Memoirs of an Infantry Officer*, Faber & Faber 1930 (Faber & Faber 1985 edition used), p. 235.
15 *GTAT*, p. 325.
16 See APG, 4 April 1921, i.e. after RG had told his parents on 5 March 1921 that he 'had a touch of shell-shock'; Dr Rivers had referred him to McDowall.
17 RG to RR, 19 July 1917, IWM.
18 Julian Dadd to SS, 1 January 1929 [1930?], IWM.
19 SS to EM, 26 July 1917, Berg.
20 *GTAT*, pp. 325–6.
21 RG to EB, [March 1921], HRC.
22 *GTAT*, p. 326.
23 See Peter Haworth's review of *Robert Graves: Selected Poems*, ed. Michael Longley, Faber & Faber, 2013, in the *London Review of Books*, 7 May 2015.
24 Ibid.
25 MS, p. 106.
26 RG to SS, 9 August 1917, Berg.
27 RG to SS, 9 September 1917, Berg.
28 APG, 6 August 1917.
29 *GTAT*, p. 330.
30 RG to SS, 31 July 1917, Berg.
31 *GTAT*, p. 333.
32 RG to RR, n.d. [but pre-9 August 1917], Berg.
33 RG to SS, 25 August 1917, Berg.
34 RG to EM, 25 August 1917, Berg.
35 SS to RG, 27 February 1917, SIU.
36 *GTAT*, p. 331.
37 *GTAT*, p. 332.
38 Ibid.
39 Ibid.
40 RG to KB, 7 July 1918, Berg.
41 *GTAT*, p. 332.
42 RG to SS, n.d. [25 November 1917?], Berg.
43 RG to SS, 20 November 1917, Berg.
44 Quoted in Frances Wilson, *Literary Seductions*, Faber & Faber, 1999, 'p. 99.
45 RG to SS, 20 November 1917, Berg.
46 *GTAT*, p. 332.
47 RG to RC, 7 March 1918, SJCO.
48 NN sadly destroyed all RG's letters to her before 1929.
49 RG to Alec Waugh, 4 February 1918, Sherborne School Archives.
50 Clarissa to JG, 31 January 1931, SJCO.
51 Author's note to *Whipperginny* (1923).

Chapter 13 The Fairy and the Fusilier (October 1917–January 1918)

1   *CP*, p. 810.

2   Author's note to *Whipperginny* (1923).

3   WO to Susan Owen, 5 November 1917, *Collected Letters of Wilfred Owen*, Oxford University Press, 1967, p. 505.

4   For a fuller account see Jean Moorcroft Wilson, *Siegfried Sassoon: The Making of a War Poet*, Duckworth, 1998, pp. 399–409.

5   WO to Susan Owen,? October 1917, *Collected Letters of Wilfred Owen*.

6   S. Sassoon, *Siegfried's Journey*, Faber & Faber, 1945, p. 58.

7   *GTAT*, p. 326.

8   Ibid. The Owen family certainly reacted to Graves's reference to the cowardice story and he inserted 'unjustly' before 'accused' in the revised English edition of 1957. In the American edition later in 1957, he replaced the whole statement with the comment that Owen had been an 'idealistic homosexual', a charge that Wilfred's brother Harold, who denied Wilfred's homosexuality, would not allow in the English edition.

9   SS to RG, 21 November 1917, Berg.

10 See Peter Parker, *The Old Lie*, Constable, 1987, p. 191.

11 *GTAT*, p. 26.

12 RG to WO, n.d. [October/November 1917], English Faculty Library, Oxford.

13 WO to Susan Owen, *Collected Letters of Wilfred Owen*, p. 280.

14 RG to EM, 29 December 1917, Berg.

15 RG to EM, n.d. [late December 1917/early January 1918], Berg and *GTAT*, p. 217.

16 WO to Leslie Gunston, 8 January 1918, *Collected Letters of Wilfred Owen*, p. 526.

17 WO to Susan Owen, 25 May 1918, *Collected Letters of Wilfred Owen*, p. 553.

18 SS to RG, 19 October 1917, SIU.

19 Ibid.

20 RG to SS, 27 October 1917, Berg.

21 RG to SS, 13 September 1917, Berg.

22 RG to KB, 19 September 1917, Berg.

23 *GTAT*, p. 396.

24 RG to KB, 13 October 1919, Berg.

25 *The Great War and Modern Memory*, p. 82. Fussell points to a similar dichotomy in the title of one of the most popular poetry books of the war, Nichols's *Ardours and Endurances*, and also in Ivor Gurney's *Severn and Somme*.

26 *CP*, 1938, p. xvii.

27 'Haunted', *CP*, p. 92: first intended for *The Patchwork Flag* in 1919.

28 APG, 22 November 1917.

29 RG to RC, n.d. [? 23 November 1917?], private owner.

30 Ibid.

31 Ibid.

32 NN's woodcut of a little girl looking into the treasure box, on the title page of the privately printed *The Treasure Box* (Chiswick Press, 1919), was the only illustration of NN's for RG's books ever published. *Country Sentiment* (1920) and *The Pier-Glass* (1921) were dedicated to NN, but there were none of her illustrations in either. NN refused to let RG use any other of her drawings. Their planned collaboration, *The Penny Whistle*, was not published until 1960. NN also illustrated some of the eight poems, plus the title page of an unpublished book of 1919, *Fourteen New Rhymes for children*.

33 RG to CSM, 'New Year' 1918, NLS.

34 *CMWP*, p. 169.

35 Ibid.

36 *GTAT*, p. 332.

37 RG to KB, 19 September 1917, Berg.

38 RG to SS, 20 November 1917, Berg.

39 RG to RN [c. 11–13 November 1917], Berg.

40 *CP*, p. 810.

41 Berg.

42 *CMWP*, p. 40.

43 *CP*, p. 810.

44 *CP*, p. 809, Charles Mundye gives this last line as a variant on RG's original words, 'Blame these black times: their fault not ours'. *CMWP*, p. 146.

45 *GTAT*, p. 335.

46 Mabel Nicholson to Ben Nicholson, 17 December 1917, Tate, and William Nicholson to Ben Nicholson, 20 December 1917, Tate.

47 William Nicholson to Ben Nicholson, 20 December 1917, Tate.

48 Ibid.

49 Mabel Nicholson to Ben Nicholson, 5 February 1918, Tate.

50 William Nicholson to Ben Nicholson, 24 January 1918.

51 APG, 18 December 1917.

52 Ibid.

53 NN loved the story of the ring's exotic provenance – 'cut in Alexandria 300BC & [was] given to Graves's great uncle by the lady who wrote "The Boy Stood on the Burning Deck" [Felicia Hemans]' (NN to Ben Nicholson, 30 December 1917).

54 William Nicholson to Ben Nicholson, 24 January 1918, Tate.

55 William Nicholson to Ben Nicholson, 31 December 1917, Tate.

56 Ibid.

57 *GTAT*, p. 337.

58 *GTAT*, p. 335.

59 William Nicholson to Ben Nicholson, 24 January 1918, Tate.

60 William Nicholson to Ben Nicholson, 24 January 1918, Tate.

61 *GTAT*, p. 335.

62 Ibid.

63 William Nicholson to Ben Nicholson, 24 January 1918, Tate.

64 *GTAT*, p. 335.

65 Ibid.

66 NN to Ben Nicholson, 31 January 1918, Tate.

67 Ibid.

68 Ibid.

69 NN to Ben Nicholson, 30 December 1917, Tate.

Chapter 14 Babes in the Wood (January 1918–January 1919)

1 *CP*, p. 811.

2 RG to RN, 16 February 1918, Berg.

3 NN to Ben Nicholson, 31 January 1918, Tate.

4 RG to SS, 28 January 1918, Berg.

5 Amy to JG, 15 February 1918, RPG1, p. 193.

6   These were 'Loving Henry', 'Neglectful Edward', 'True Johnny', 'The Cupboard', 'Careless Lady', 'Vain Man' and 'Betsy'.
7   RG to SS, 23 May 1918, Berg.
8   RG to CSM, 24 March 1918, NLS.
9   RG to SS, n.d. [January 1918?], Berg.
10 RG to C. Hartmann, 19 March 1918, IWM.
11 RG to CG, 14 August 1918, HRC.
12 See the series of letters from Eric and Celandine Kennington to RG at SIU, lavishly illustrated but mostly undated.
13 RG to SS, 9 July 1918.
14 RG to SS, 23 May 1918, Berg.
15 RG to SS, [before 9 July] 1918, Berg.
16 *GTAT*, pp. 340–1.
17 *GTAT*, p. 341.
18 RG to Cyril Hartmann, 15 June [1918], IWM.
19 RG to SS, [July 1918] and 9 July 1918, Berg, respectively.
20 RG to SS, [July 1918], Berg.
21 RG to SS, 9 July 1918, Berg.
22 RG to SS, 26 August 1918, Berg.
23 RG to SS, 16 July 1918, Berg.
24 Ibid.
25 *CP*, p. 97.
26 Graves included a version of this stanza in subsequent printings of the poem, as CM notes in *CMWP*, p. 310.
27 RG to SS, 26 August 1918, Berg.
28 Rose Cottage, Rhuddlan.
29 RG to RN, [mid-November 1918?], Berg.
30 RG to SS, 12 October 1918.
31 Ibid.
32 S. Sassoon, *Siegfried's Journey*, Faber & Faber, 1945, p. 6.
33 *GTAT*, p. 344.
34 RG to EM, 28 November 1918, Berg.
35 'Foreword' to RG's *Beyond Giving* (1969), p. vii.
36 *CP*, p. 633.
37 RG to EM, 28 July 1918, Berg.
38 RG to RN, [c. December 1918], Berg.
39 Ibid.
40 *GTAT*, p. 344.
41 Ibid.
42 RG to KB, 13 October 1919, Berg.
43 *William Nicholson, Painter: Paintings, Woodcuts, Writings, Photographs* ed. Andrew Nicholson, Giles de la Mare, 1996, pp. 174–5.
44 RG to SS, 18 November 1918, Berg.
45 RG to W. J. Turner, 29 May 1919, Gleeson Library, University of San Francisco.
46 RG to EB, [c. 1923], HRC.
47 RG to EB, [September 1922], HRC.
48 *CP*, p. 84.
49 *CP*, p. 61.
50 RG to SS, 7 January 1919, Berg.

51 e.g. 'Baloo Loo for Jenny' and 'A Song for Two Children', which was originally about 'Jenny and Nancy' and written a month after her birth: it was later emended to include RG's second child, (John) David.

52 RG to NN, 4 May 1929, Lilly.

Chapter 15 A Poet on Parnassus (January–October 1919)

1   *CP*, p. 71.

2   See *Poetic Unreason* (1925), pp. 114–16, for the evolution of this poem to include RG's second child, David, in 1920, when it became 'Song for Two Children', *CP*, p. 62.

3   RG to RC, 27 January 1919, private owner.

4   APG, 27 January 1919, Berg.

5   RG to SS, 22 November 1918, Berg. RG includes 'poet' in this category.

6   *GTAT*, p. 349.

7   *GTAT*, p. 351.

8   *GTAT*, p. 352.

9   APG, 6 March 1919, Berg.

10 *CP*, p. 236. RG figures as 'Richard Rolls' in the poem, SS as 'Captain Abel Wright'.

11 *The Poet's Choice*, ed. Paul Engle and Joseph Langland, The Dial Press, New York, 1962, p. 29.

12 *CP*, p. 102.

13 *GTAT*, p. 355.

14 *CP*, p. 71.

15 *GTAT*, p. 347.

16 SS to RG, 9 January 1919, SIU.

17 SS to RG, 13 January 1919, SIU.

18 *GTAT*, p. 355.

19 Printed by Chiswick Press, December 1919.

20 Two of the 24 poems from *The Penny Fiddle: Poems for Children*, Cassell, 1960, and Doubleday, 1961, namely 'Careless Lady' and 'Vain Man', would be combined into 'Vain and Careless'. Three more of PF's poems would be included in other collections in his lifetime: 'The Dream' (expanded as 'What Did I Dream') in *Treasure Box*, 'Betsy' in *Whipperginny* (1923) and 'The King's Story-Teller' (as 'Jock O'Binnorie') in *The Penny Fiddle* (1960).

21 RG to SS, 7 January 1919, and *GTAT*, p. 344.

22 *CP*, p. 74.

23 For a more detailed analysis of 'Allie', to which I am greatly indebted, see 'Allie and the Lost War', *The Lion and the Unicorn*, vol. 41, no. 2, April 2017, pp. 250–68.

24 *EPRG*, p. 61.

25 *CP*, p. 77.

26 *CP*, p. 82.

27 *CP*, p. 67.

28 *CP38*, Introduction.

29 *CP*, p. 92.

30 *CP*, p. 93.

31 *CP*, p. 79.

32 *CP*, p. 99.

33 *CP*, p. 100.

34 Ibid.
35 *Review of English Studies*, vol. 41, New Series no. 164, November 1990, p. 527.
36 *CP*, p. 70.
37 *CP38*, Introduction.
38 *CP*, p. 71.
39 APG, 4 April 1919, Berg.
40 APG, 29 April 1919, Berg.
41 APG, 17 June 1919.
42 Ibid.
43 RG to EB, 14 August 1919, HRC.
44 APG, 15 September 1919.
45 APG, 25 September 1919.
46 *GTAT*, p. 359.
47 *GTAT*, p. 364.
48 RG to KB, 13 October 1919.
49 RG's address at Masefield's memorial service, 20 June 1967, BL.
50 Ibid.
51 See MS-*S* for this quotation from Masefield's letter of 7 April 1920 to an unidentified American woman.
52 Constance Masefield's diary, quoted by MS-S, p. 77.
53 Ibid.
54 *GTAT*, p. 366. The quoted phrase is from a review by Edmund Gosse.
55 *CP*, p. 117.
56 EB to RG, 21 January 1927, SIU.
57 RG to JG, [1919], BL.
58 RG contributed a letter to the section 'On Hyphens, & Shall & Will' in 1915.
59 *Pamphlet Against Anthologies*, pp. 145–6.

Chapter 16 Oxford and 'Pier-Glass Hauntings'
(October 1919–March 1921)

 1 *GTAT*, p. 383.
 2 *GTAT*, pp. 362–3.
 3 *BOD*, p. 52.
 4 *GTAT*, p. 374.
 5 APG, 5 June 1921.
 6 *GTAT*, pp. 62–3.
 7 Ibid., p. 63.
 8 RG to EB, n.d., HRC.
 9 *GTAT*, p. 401.
10 Sir Walter Raleigh to RG, 12 June and 19 December 1921, SIU.
11 Ibid., 23 December 1921, SIU.
12 See MS-S, p. 77, for the critic F. W. Bateson's memories of 'sitting at the feet of Robert Graves' in 1920.
13 *TRTAT*, p. 129.
14 MS-S, p. 79.
15 RG to JG, 20 October 1920, BL.
16 Ibid.

17 *TELTHB*, p. 186.
18 Ibid.
19 Ibid.
20 Quoted in MS-S, p. 101.
21 RG to BLH, n.d. [1954?], HRC.
22 RG to BLH, 29 June 1954, HRC.
23 Ibid.
24 *TELTHB*, pp. 186–7.
25 TEL to Charlotte Shaw, 22 May 1929.
26 RG to TEL, 3–5 February 1922, BL.
27 *CP*, p. 125.
28 *GTAT*, p. 373.
29 My italics.
30 The term used for schizophrenia in 1920.
31 RG to EB, 10 March 1921, HRC.
32 Ibid.
33 *CP*, p. 103.
34 *CP*, p. 102.
35 'This myrrour that I tote in, *quasi diaphanum/Vel quasi speculum in aenigmate...*' (from Skelton's 'Speke Parrot').
36 *GTAT*, p. 340.
37 *GTAT*, p. 153.
38 *CP*, p. 108.
39 *OEP*, p. 164.
40 Ibid.
41 *CP*, p. 109.
42 *CP*, p. 110.
43 *GTAT*, p. 364.
44 APG, 10 December 1919.
45 EM insisted that RG should add an erratum slip to *GTAT* in 1929 about a reference on p. 398: '... there's not really any "Rupert Brooke Fund" administered by Mr Marsh. I much regret this error', etc.
46 'Intimations – A Question of Influence', BBC2, 16 November 1965.
47 *GTAT*, pp. 390–1.
48 *GTAT*, p. 375.
49 Ibid.
50 *GTAT*, p. 376.
51 *GTAT*, pp. 377–8.
52 *GTAT*, p. 379.
53 RG to EM, 7 October 1920, Berg.
54 Ibid.
55 Philip Stewart believes that the shop signboard was one discovered nearby – 'The wandering scholar' – and was 'almost certainly painted by Nancy Nicholson' [*Gravesiana*, vol. iii, no. ii], but RG makes no mention of such a distinctive sign and a contemporary newspaper report (*Daily Mirror*, 7 October 1920) says that the lettered 'BOARS HILL SHOP' sign 'was painted by Mr Nicholson'.
56 *GTAT*, p. 380.
57 Ibid.
58 RG to KB, [late 1920s], Berg.

59 RG to EB, 10 March 1921, HRC.
60 *GTAT*, p. 381.
61 *GTAT*, p. 382.
62 *GTAT*, p. 381.
63 *GTAT*, p. 382.
64 Ibid.
65 *GTAT*, p. 383.
66 RG to EM, 13 April 1921, Berg.
67 William Nicholson to RG, 'Whitmonday' [16 May] 1921, SIU.
68 RG to EB, 10 March 1921, HRC.
69 TEL withdrew one of the four chapters but the remaining three were sold successfully.
70 RG to EM, 13 April 1921, Berg.
71 *GTAT*, p. 383.
72 Ibid.

Chapter 17 'Roots Down into a Cabbage Patch' (1921–5)

1 RG to KB, 29 March 1921, Berg.
2 Ibid.
3 *GTAT*, p. 386.
4 Ibid.
5 RG to KB, 15 October 1921, Berg.
6 APG, 15 May 1921.
7 RG's contributions were 'Lost Love', 'Morning Phoenix', 'A Lover since Childhood', 'Sullen Moods', 'The Pier-Glass', 'The Troll's Nosegay', 'Fox's Dingle', 'The General Elliott' and 'The Patchwork Bonnet', six of which had already been published in *The Pier-Glass* by the time *Georgian Poetry 1920–1922* was published.
8 *GTAT*, p. 389.
9 *GTAT*, p. 390.
10 RG to EB, 12 July 1921, HRC. The last sentence is a reference to Tennyson's *The Princess*:

    The moan of doves in immemorial elms
    And murmuring of innumerable bees.

11 'To M. in India', *The Marmosite's Miscellany*, *CP*, p. 251.
12 'Houses in My Life', pp. 2–3, SJCO.
13 Ibid.
14 RG to EB, 12 July 1921, HRC.
15 Ibid.
16 Ibid.
17 *OEP*, p. vii.
18 WHRR to RG, 31 March 1921.
19 Ibid.
20 WHRR's *Conflict and Dream* would be published posthumously as a book in 1923.
21 WHRR to RG, 26 October 1921, SIU.
22 WHRR to RG, 1 November 1921, SIU.
23 WHRR to RG, 9 March 1922, SIU.
24 *GTAT*, p. 402.
25 EB to SS, 31 October [1921?], HRC.

26 Ibid.
27 EB to RG, 29 October 1922, HRC.
28 *OEP*, p. 37.
29 RG to MS-S, 25 July 1946, quoted at MS-S, p. 90.
30 See MS-S, p. 89.
31 Preface to the second edition of *Seven Types of Ambiguity*, quoted in the third edition (Hogarth Press, 1984), p. xiv: 'Mr Robert Graves ... is, as far as I know, the inventor of the method I was using here'.
32 Raleigh was researching the second volume of his *War in the Air* when he contracted the disease on a trip to the Near East.
33 Author's Note, *PU*.
34 *GTAT*, p. 407.
35 *Welchman's Hose*, *CP*, pp. 238–9.
36 *CP*, p. 240.
37 *GTAT*, p. 406.
38 RG to KB, 15 October 1921, Berg.
39 *GTAT*, p. 407.
40 APG, 30 November 1921.
41 Ibid.
42 APG, 5 December 1921.
43 RG to EM, 17 December 1921, Berg.
44 Ibid.
45 RG to EB, [? August 1922?], HRC.
46 RG to Mrs Hilda Harrison, 25 July 1922, Beinecke.
47 *GTAT*, pp. 391–2.
48 J. B. Pinker would die unexpectedly this year and be replaced by his sons James and Eric, who handled Graves's rights until the firm went out of business.
49 *Mock Beggar Hall* (1924), *Contemporary Techniques of Poetry: A Political Analogy* (1925), *The Marmosite's Miscellany* (1925), *Another Future of Poetry* (1926) and *Impenetrability, or the Proper Habit of English* (1927).
50 RG to Pinker, 1 November 1923, Tulsa.
51 RG to Pinker, 25 March 1925, BL.
52 RG to SS, 19 February 1924, Berg.
53 *The Diary of Virginia Woolf, vol. 3*, ed. A. O. Bell, Penguin, 1987, p. 13.
54 Ibid.
55 Ibid.
56 JCR's review of *On English Poetry* appeared in *The Fugitive*, October 1922, and the two poems published were 'The Poet's Birth' and 'Valentine', both of which were also published in *Whipperginny*.
57 See *The Person I Am*, vol. 2, Nottingham Trent University, 2011, p. 121.
58 *The Poems of Laura Riding*, Carcanet, Manchester, 1980, p. 41.
59 JCR to RG, 12 June 1925, Tulsa.
60 JCR to RG, 23 September 1925, Tulsa.

Chapter 18 From Psychology to Philosophy and Beyond

1 'On Preserving a Poetical Formula', *CP*, p. 138.
2 *GTAT*, p. 404.

3 RG to SS, [1923?], Berg.

4 *GTAT*, p. 405. See Madhuri Sondhi and Mary Walker, 'Basanta Kumar Mallik and Robert Graves: Personal Encounters and Processes in Socio-Cultural Thought', *Gravesiana*, vol. 1, issue 2 (1996), p. 113.

5 *Poetic Unreason*, p. 22.

6 RG to SS, n.d. [1923?], Berg.

7 *GTAT*, pp. 405–6.

8 Sondhi and Walker, 'Basanta Kumar Mallik and Robert Graves', p. 112, quoting an account by Collingridge intended for a tribute to Mallik, which arrived too late for publication.

9 RG to BHL, 15 January 1936, in Paul O'Prey, ed., *In Broken Images: Selected Letters of Robert Graves 1914–1946,* Hutchinson, 1982, pp. 263–4.

10 *GTAT*, p. 404.

11 RG to EB, [1923?], HRC.

12 JCR to RG, 4 July 1924, Tulsa.

13 *CP*, p. 217.

14 *CP*, p. 232.

15 Ibid.

16 *CP*, pp. 236–7.

17 This may be a reference to the British Empire Exhibition of 1924 to 1925 at Wembley.

18 SS to EB, 25 July 1925, HRC.

19 *CP*, pp. 257–8.

20 See chapter opening, *CP*, p. 251.

21 *CP*, p. 251.

22 Osbert Sitwell's satire appeared in *Wheels*, sixth cycle, 1921, pp. 57–8.

23 See *Nation and Athenaeum*, vol. 33 (26 May 1923), pp. 272–3.

24 ES to RG, [c. November 1925], SIU.

25 Richard Greene, *Edith Sitwell*, Virago, 2011, p. 165.

26 *GTAT*, p. 406.

27 *Nation and Athenaeum*, vol. 33, no. 88 (19 April 1924).

28 ES to RG, 2 May 1923, SIU.

29 Ibid., [1924?], SIU.

30 *GTAT*, p. 406.

31 ES to TSE, 14 January 1926, *The Letters of T. S. Eliot*, vol. 3, Faber & Faber, 2012, p. 15 n.

32 Greene, *Edith Sitwell*, p. 194.

33 Ibid.

34 RG to SS, n.d. [February 1924?], Berg.

35 Ibid.

36 *CP*, p. 122.

37 *CP*, p. 124.

38 *CP*, p. 121.

39 *CP*, p. 127.

40 'Love in Barrenness' was published in *Oxford Poetry* as 'On the Ridge', also in the *Nation* on 23 July 1921.

41 *CP*, p. 122.

42 *GWMM*, p. 97.

43 *CP*, p. 124.

44 'Full Moon' first appeared in the *Winter Owl* in December 1923, before appearing in *Mock Beggar Hall* (1924). *CP*, p. 179.

45 *GTAT*, p. 403.
46 APG, 9 and 21 June 1925. APG notes, for instance, on 11 June that his 'friend', the ex-Bishop of Birmingham, may be able to 'wangle' two sympathetic examiners for the *viva voce*.
47 *GTAT*, p. 409.
48 RG to SS [Oxford 1925], Berg.
49 Ibid.
50 RG to SS, n.d. [1925?], Berg.
51 TEL to RG, 21 October 1925 (*TELTHB*, pp. 35–6).
52 *TELTHB*, p. 37.
53 O'Prey, ed., *In Broken Images*, p. 161.
54 A literary magazine published from 1922 to 1939, mainly issued quarterly, founded by Eliot.
55 TSE to RG, 2 November 1925, *Letters of T. S. Eliot*, vol. 2, Faber & Faber, 2009, p. 768.
56 Ibid.
57 RG to SS, [? December?], Berg.
58 See Deborah Baker's helpful analysis in *In Extremis*, Hamish Hamilton, 1993, p. 86.

Chapter 19 Into the Unknown: Cairo and Laura Riding (January–June 1926)

1   'An Occasion', *CP*, p. 268.
2   MS-S, p. 114.
3   *IE*, p. 114.
4   Ibid.
5   JCR to Allen Tate, 18 June 1926.
6   *The Long Weekend* (with Alan Hodge), Faber & Faber, 1940, p. 189.
7   N. Cunard, *These Were the Hours*, Southern Illinois University Press, 1969, p. 104.
8   Ibid.
9   'Pure Mind', a review of Richard Perceval Graves's *The Years with Laura*, in *The New York Times* (11 November 1990).
10 MS, p. 132.
11 MS-S, p. 123.
12 *IE*, p. 79.
13 Allen Tate to Donald Davidson, 21 February 1924, quoted at MS-S, p. 119.
14 RG to Nancy Cunard, 15 December 1943, HRC.
15 Richard Murphy, *The Kick*, Granta, 2003, p. 168, in an account of Geoffrey Phibbs/Taylor's relationship with LR.
16 LR to Esther Antell Cohen (Polly), 26 March 1926, Berg.
17 RG to Donald Cooper, 6 October 1969, SIU.
18 MS, p. 132.
19 RPG2, p. 107.
20 *IE*, p. 42.
21 Allen Tate to Donald Davidson, 3 January 1926, *The Literary Correspondence of Donald Davidson and Allen Tate*, eds John Tyree and Thomas David Young, University of Georgia Press, 1974.
22 Ibid.
23 Interview by Peter Buckman and William Fifield in *The Paris Review*, no. 11, issue 47 (Summer 1969).

24 LR to EAC, 26 March 1926, Berg.

25 Ibid.

26 Ibid.

27 Ibid.

28 MS-S, p. 122.

29 APG, 5 January 1926.

30 Amy to JG, 8 January 1926, BL.

31 APG, 5 January 1926.

32 ES to TSE, 14 January 1926, *Letters of T. S. Eliot*, vol. 3, Faber & Faber, 2009, p. 15 n.

33 ES to SS, 14 May 1927, Pullman.

34 *Letters of Virginia Woolf, vol. 3*, pp. 225–6.

35 *GTAT*, p. 412.

36 *GTAT*, p. 437.

37 *GTAT*, p. 413.

38 RG to SS, p.c. [postmarked 3 February 1926], Berg.

39 RG to SS, [postmarked 31 March 1926], Berg.

40 Ibid. King Seti was pharaoh of the Near Kingdom, 19th Dynasty, and father of
    Rameses II.

41 RG to TSE, 16 February 1926, in T. S. Eliot, *The Letters of T. S. Eliot, vol. 3* (eds V. Eliot
    and J. Haffenden), Faber & Faber, 2012, p. 92 n.

42 RG to TSE, 24 June 1926, in Paul O'Prey, ed., *In Broken Images: Selected Letters of Robert
    Graves 1914–1946,* Hutchinson, 1982, 'p. 167.

43 Ibid., 16 February 1926.

44 APG, 12 April 1926.

45 RG to SS [postmarked 31 March 1926], Berg.

46 *Impenetrability*, p. 7.

47 *CP*, p. 273.

48 *GTAT*, p. 431.

49 Ibid.

50 *GTAT*, p. 432.

51 *GTAT*, p. 433.

52 *GTAT*, p. 434.

53 *Lars Porsena* would be published in 1927 by Kegan Paul, Trench, Truber & Co. and E. P.
    Dutton in New York. A revised and enlarged edition would appear in 1936.

54 R. Graves: *Occupation: Writer,* Creative Age Press, 1950, and Cassell, 1951, p. ix.

55 *Lars Porsena* (1936), p. 14.

56 RG to L. A. G. Strong, [1927?], HRC.

57 Published by Ernest Benn in 1927, then revised in 1957 and published as *English and
    Scottish Ballads* by Heinemann.

58 *GTAT*, p. 441.

59 RG to SS, 13 July 1926, Berg.

60 *CP*, p. 282.

61 *GTAT*, p. 445.

62 MS-S, p. 139.

63 LR to EAC, 26 March 1926, Berg.

64 *IE*, p. 128.

65 *Contemporaries and Snobs*, Jonathan Cape, 1927, p. 9.

66 *IE*, p. 127.

67 *CP*, p. 387.

68   *CP*, p. 272. The 'fine hair afloat' rules out NN, who by 1927 had become almost bald through ringworm; in addition she was definitely 'tall', unlike the woman in the poem.

69   *CP*, p. 276.

70   Ibid.

71   *CP*, p. 280.

72   RG to SS, 31 March 1926, Berg.

73   LR to EAC, 26 March 1926, Berg.

74   'The Shout', first published in 1929 by Matthews and Marron, then in *But It Still Goes On*, Jonathan Cape, 1930, pp. 79–104. Quote taken from *BISGO*, p. 79.

75   Note written on RG's copy of the 1929 publication.

76   *BISGO*, p. 79.

77   *GTAT*, p. 446.

78   APG, 2 April 1926, and LR to EAC, 26 March 1916, Berg.

79   MS-S, pp. 132–3.

80   *GTAT*, p. 437.

81   *IE*, pp. 125–6.

82   Ibid.

83   'Egypt', *Twenty Poems Less*, quoted in *These Were the Hours* by Nancy Cunard, Southern Illinois University Press, 1969, p. 105.

84   RG to Pinker, [? May 1926?], HRC.

85   Quoted by NC in a letter to RG of 8 July 1944, SJCO.

86   *BOD*, p. 109.

87   RG to NC, 2 May 1944, HRC.

88   *GTAT*, pp. 439 and 445.

89   *GTAT*, p. 446.

Chapter 20   The World Well Lost (June 1926–April 1927)

1   *CP*, p. 283.

2   LG to EAC, n.d., Berg.

3   *IE*, p. 136, based on LR's undated letter to EAC.

4   APG, 1 July 1926.

5   Amy to JG, 17 October 1926, quoted in RPG2, p. 35.

6   APG, 3 August 1926.

7   RG to SS, [early August 1926?], Berg.

8   RG to TSE, 18 September 1926, in Paul O'Prey, ed., *In Broken Images: Selected Letters of Robert Graves 1914–1946,* Hutchinson, 1982,' p. 169.

9   'Revisiting a Collaboration', *PN Review* (Manchester), July–August 2002, p. 46.

10   RG to SS, [1926], Berg.

11   Ibid.

12   RG to SS, 18 September 1926, Berg.

13   APG, 21 September 1926.

14   APG, 30 September 1926, Berg.

15   RG to SS, [1926], Berg.

16   *GTAT*, p. 51.

17   RG to SS, [1926], Berg.

18   See Carol Rumens, *The Guardian* (18 December 2017).

19   'The Cool Web', *CP*, p. 283.

20   RG to SS, [1926], Berg.

21   Ibid.

22   Helen Goethals, ' "A Militant Disdain": Modernism and *A Pamphlet Against Anthologies*', http://www.robertgraves.org/issues/45/8817_article_632.pdf.

23   Ibid.

24   RG to SS, [1926], Berg.

25   *IE*, p. 161.

26   RG to SS, [1926], Berg.

27   RG's review of Malinowski's *Crime and Custom in Savage Society* and his *Myth in Primitive Psychology* and Rivers's *Ethnology* was published in the *Criterion*, vol. 5 (May 1927), pp. 247–52.

28   RG to SS, [1926], Berg.

29   *CP*, p. 295.

30   Ibid.

31   Ibid.

32   e.g. Herrick uses it in 'Upon Julia's Clothes'.

33   RG to SS, [1926], Berg.

34   APG, 1 January 1928.

35   *The Paris Review*, vol. 47 (1969).

36   *CP*, p. 310.

37   APG, 10 October 1926.

38   *IE*, p. 150.

39   Ibid.

40   RPG2, p. 40.

41   APG, 23 October 1926.

42   APG, 30 October 1926.

43   RG to SS, [December 1926], Berg.

44   *IE*, p. 160.

45   F. Wilson, *Literary Seductions*, Faber & Faber, 1999, p. 111.

46   APG, 9 February 1927.

47   Amy to APG, 12 March 1927, SJCO.

Chapter 21 'Free Love Corner' (May 1927–October 1928)

1   RG to Alec Guinness, [late 1950s], MS-S, p. 155.

2   *CP*, p. 298.

3   *You May Well Ask: A Memoir 1920–1940*, Victor Gollancz, 1977, p. 80.

4   'Houses in My Life', pp. 3–4, SJCO.

5   RG to SS, 30 May 1927, Berg.

6   Extract from JG's journal for 6 January 1928, quoted in RPG2, p. 59.

7   See RPG2, p. 104.

8   *Letters to a Critic*, ed. Michael Thorpe, privately printed, 1976, p. 21.

9   Ibid.

10   P. Quennell, *The Marble Foot*, Collins, 1976, p. 167.

11   T. Driberg, *Ruling Passions*, Cape, 1977, p. 63.

12   RG to Strong, [1927], HRC.

13   Quoted MS-S, p. 153.

14   Ibid.

15 i.e. 4 April 1927.
16 *TELTHB*, p. 44.
17 Ibid.
18 TEL to Edward Garnett, 1 August 1927, in *The Letters of T. E. Lawrence*, ed. David Garnett, Cape, 1938, p. 533.
19 TEL to Lionel Curtis, 14 July 1927, ibid., p. 530.
20 RG to BLH, 19 February 1954, HRC.
21 Ibid.
22 Ibid.
23 TEL to Dick Knowles, 7 December 1927, in *The Letters of T. E. Lawrence*, p. 555.
24 RG to BLH, 19 February 1954, HRC.
25 *LA*, p. 417.
26 *LA*, p. 6.
27 Ibid.
28 Ibid.
29 *LA*, p. 153.
30 *TELTHB*, p. 47.
31 RG to SS, 31 October 1927, Berg.
32 Ibid.
33 RG to SS, 4 November 1927, Berg.
34 Ibid.
35 RG to EM, [October 1927], Berg.
36 Ibid.
37 Ibid.
38 In 1928 RG had no poems published in magazines, in contrast with at least 14 published in 1925, the year before he met LR.
39 *Criterion* (August 1927).
40 JCR to Allen Tate, 25 October 1927.
41 RG to TSE, n.d., in Paul O'Prey, ed., *In Broken Images: Selected Letters of Robert Graves 1914–1946,* Hutchinson, 1982, p. 177.
42 TEL to Ralph Isham, 22 November 1927, *The Letters of T. E. Lawrence*, p. 546.
43 Nancy Cunard, *These Were the Hours*, Southern Illinois University Press, Carbondale, 1969, p. 104.
44 MS-S, p. 148.
45 Quoted at *IE*, p. 181.
46 RG to J. B. Pinker, 22 August [1928?].
47 *IE*, p. 181.
48 There is some confusion about the two barges owned by RG, the *Ringrose* and the *Avoca*, namely which one came first. Len Lye's biography seems to prove that RG bought the *Ringrose* first, since Lye was still living next to it, on the *Avoca*, in 1927. See Roger Horrocks, *Len Lye*, Auckland University Press, 2001.
49 TEL to RG, 4 February 1935, *TELTHB*, p. 183.
50 William Samson, 'Coming to London (XI)', *London Magazine*, vol. 3, no. 12 (1956), p. 32.
51 *Collected Poems*, Hogarth Press, 1937, p. 9.
52 Ibid.
53 Ibid., p. 22.
54 Letter from the daughter of RG's landlord, Mary Dawson, quoted at MS, p. 158.
55 Interview with Allen Curnow, in R. Horrocks, *Len Lye*, Auckland University Press, 2001, p. 82.

56   Interview with Alastair Read, 1980, by Horrocks, *Len Lye*, p. 107.
57   *Ibid.*
58   ES to RG, [1925], SIU.
59   *SMP*, p. 287.
60   I am greatly indebted to Deborah Baker's analysis of Riding's works and ideas, here and elsewhere.
61   See *IE*, p. 184.
62   *The Poems of Laura Riding*, Carcanet, 1980, p. 91.
63   APG, 26 September 1928.
64   APG, 30 August 1928.

Chapter 22 'Like the Plot of a Russian Novel' (February–April 1929)

1   APG, 7 May 1929.
2   i.e. a kind of firework spinning in the air so as to look like a scroll or spiral column of fire; cf. the French 'tourbillon' or 'whirlwind'.
3   *CP*, p. 336.
4   RC to JG, 19 June 1929, quoted in RPG2, p. 107.
5   MS-S, p. 157. RPG disputes this, claiming that RG and GP 'liked each other at once' (RPG2, p. 74), basing his evidence on the account given to him by GP's second wife, Mary Taylor.
6   MS-S, p. 157.
7   MS-S, p. 158.
8   GP to RG, 28 October 1928, SJCO.
9   *The Withering of the Fig Leaf* (1927) and, under the pen name 'R. Fitzurse', *It Was Not Jones* (1928).
10   Quoted in RPG2, p. 342, for the source of this quote from Terence Brown's *Geoffrey Taylor [i.e. Phibbs]: A Portrait 1900–1956,* unpublished monograph.
11   GP to RG, 28 October 1928, SJCO.
12   R. Murphy, *The Kick*, in *Granta*, 2003, p. 97.
13   It was Wyndham Lewis who referred to Phibbs in this way in his account of 'Free Love Corner' in *The New Yorker.*
14   Frank O'Connor, *My Father's Son*, 'Macmillan, 1968, p. 24. 'Frank O'Connor' was the pen name of Michael Francis O'Donovan.
15   Ibid., p. 21.
16   Ibid., p. 24.
17   Ibid.
18   Laura Riding and George Ellidge, *14A*, Arthur Barker, 1934, p. 10.
19   *The Person I Am*, vol. II, Nottingham Trent University, 2011, p. 131.
20   GP to RG, 20 May 1929, SJCO.
21   *IE*, p. 244, based on LR's letter to KB, 21 September 1933.
22   O'Connor, *My Father's Son*, p. 25.
23   GP to RG, 28 October 1928, SJCO.
24   NM to TSM, 6 March 1978, Thomas S. Matthews Papers, Princeton University.
25   Ibid.
26   See MS-S, p. 158.
27   MS-S, pp. 158–9.

28 David Garnett's paper to the Memoir Club, quoted by Virginia Nicholson in *Among the Bohemians*, Viking, 2002, p. 43.
29 Ibid.
30 Ibid.
31 Ibid.
32 MS-S, p. 159.
33 Murphy, *The Kick*, p. 168.
34 Ibid.
35 APG, 26 March 1929.
36 APG, 22 March 1929.
37 For example, Amy would pay for both David's and Catherine's education after Robert refused to do so.
38 Susan Macaulay to JG, 28 March 1929, quoted in RPG2, p. 71.
39 NM to TSM, 6 March 1978, Thomas S. Matthews Papers, Princeton University.
40 Murphy, *The Kick,* p. 178.
41 Frank O'Connor to GP, n.d., Buffalo.
42 O'Connor, *My Father's Son*, p. 69.
43 See *IE*, 103–4, and MS, p. 168, quoting respectively from *14A* and 'Opportunities Rampant'.
44 MS-S, p. 160.
45 Ibid.
46 GP to Tom MacGreevy, MacGreevy Papers, Trinity College Dublin.
47 *GTAT*, p. 446.
48 'Return Fare', *CP*, p. 310.
49 Ibid.
50 *GTAT*, p. 446.
51 'Return Fare', *CP*, p. 310.
52 *GTAT*, pp. 446–7.
53 *GTAT*, p. 446.
54 NM to TSM, 6 March 1978, Princeton.
55 Ibid.
56 Ibid.
57 Ibid.
58 Ibid.
59 Ibid.
60 *GTAT*, p. 447.
61 Murphy, *The Kick*, p. 168.
62 NM to TSM, 6 March 1978, Princeton.
63 Ibid.
64 Ibid.
65 *AB*, p. 43, related by David Garnett to the Memoir Club.
66 NM to TSM, 6 March 1978, Princeton.
67 *AB*, p. 43.
68 Ibid.
69 Ibid.
70 Ibid.
71 Ibid., p. 44.
72 NM to TSM, 6 March 1978, Princeton.

73 'Specials', as they are known, are ordered privately from the train company. They were more common and less expensive to hire in the 1920s, when SS's aunt, Rachel Beer, for instance, often ordered one to take her to visit the Sassoon family in Kent.
74 *GTAT*, p. 447.
75 RG contributed 'A Lost Love'.

Chapter 23 'A Doom-Echoing Shout' (26 April–June 1929)

1   'The Terraced Valley', *CP*, p. 320.
2   *CP*, p. 316.
3   NM to TSM, 6 March 1978, Princeton.
4   See *IE*, p. 94.
5   *The Poems of Laura Riding*, Carcanet, 1980, p. 121.
6   This incident is based on MS's interview with Catherine Dalton in August 1993. See MS, pp. 170–1.
7   MS, p. 170.
8   LR to Merrill Moore, n.d., Library of Congress.
9   *Anarchism is Not Enough*, Jonathan Cape, 1928, p. 222.
10 *IE*, p. 104.
11 'The Terraced Valley', *CP*, p. 320.
12 RC to LR, 1 March 1932, SJCO.
13 *GTAT*, p. 447.
14 RPG in conversation with RC in 1982.
15 RC to JG, 19 June 1929: RPG2, p. 107.
16 Ibid.
17 GS to RG, n.d., in Paul O'Prey, ed., *In Broken Images: Selected Letters of Robert Graves 1914–1946,* Hutchinson, 1982, p. 191.
18 TEL to Charlotte Shaw, 22 May 1929, *The Letters of T. E. Lawrence*, ed. by M. Brown, Oxford University Press, 1991, p. 421.
19 NC to RG, 23 February 1948, SJCO.
20 APG, 1 May 1929.
21 See APG, 2 July 1929.
22 APG, 3 and 7 May 1929 respectively.
23 RG to NN, [4 May 1929], Lilly.
24 RC to LR, 1 March 1932, SJCO.
25 RG to NN, [4 May 1929], SJCO.
26 Ibid.
27 Ibid.
28 RG to NN, [5 May 1929], Lilly.
29 Ibid.
30 *GTAT*, p. 441.
31 *IE*, p. 208, quoting 'Opportunism Rampant'.
32 This has survived as 'Report', SJCO.
33 MS, p. 238.
34 RG to EM, 16 June 1929, Berg.
35 Ibid.
36 Ibid.
37 Ibid.

38   Ibid.
39   ES to SS, 18 May 1929, University of Washington at Pullman.
40   Laura Riding, 'Rejoice, Liars', *A Selection of the Poems of Laura Riding*, Carcanet Press, 1994, p. 102.
41   *Poems: A Joking Word*, Cape, 1930, pp. 15–18.
42   See these charges repeated in her autobiographical essays, *The Person I Am*, vol. II, Trent Editions, 2011, pp. 125–9.
43   Ibid., p. 147.
44   *IE*, p. 229.
45   Richard Murphy's report of what Phibbs told him, in *The Kick*, p. 170.
46   *GTAT*, p. 447.
47   RG to KB, 20 May 1930, Berg.
48   *GTAT*, p. 445.
49   *CP*, p. 300.
50   Ibid.
51   *CP*, p. 316.
52   Published in *Encounter 1*, no. 3 (December 1953), pp. 5–13.

Chapter 24 Good-bye to All That (June–November 1929)

1   *GTAT*, pp. 447–8.
2   RG to GS, 18 June 1929, in Paul O'Prey, ed., *In Broken Images: Selected Letters of Robert Graves 1914–1946*, Hutchinson, 1982, p. 191.
3   APG, 29 August 1929.
4   Ibid.
5   APG, 7 October 1929.
6   RG to EM, 29 July 1929, Berg.
7   LR to GS, n.d., Beinecke.
8   APG, 1 October 1929.
9   APG, 4 October 1929.
10   Amy to JG, 5 October 1929, quoted in RPG2, p. 120.
11   GS to RG, 4 February 1946, Beinecke.
12   RG to GS, 28 January 1946, in O'Prey, ed., *In Broken Images*, 'p. 137.
13   GS to RG, 4 February 1946, Beinecke.
14   *GTAT*, p. 13.
15   RG to GS, 18 June 1929, in O'Prey, ed., *In Broken Images*, 'p. 191.
16   *TRAT*, p. 333.
17   EB's annotation in his copy of *GTAT*, Berg.
18   MS, p. 180.
19   The result is extraordinary: 5,631 words of annotation in ink, on 250 of *GTAT*'s 448 pages, by EB, SS, Dr Dunn [? illegible?] and the poet Ralph Hodgson, a close friend of SS by 1929.
20   It had been sent to Sassoon by the book's unwitting publisher, Jonathan Cape, in the hope of advance publicity. Far from the glowing endorsement Cape hoped for from Graves's well-known friend, Sassoon's response was to threaten an injunction only six days before publication, unless two significant passages were removed (they were replaced by asterisks). At the same time, Sassoon annotated his copy independently and, if possible, even more scathingly than he had Blunden's. It lay buried in his library until 2007, when it was sold to

a private collector. But it was not until it was sold again last year to the Beinecke Library at Yale that it became possible to view it.

21   *BISGO*, pp. 41–2.

22   P. Fussell, *The Great War and Modern Memory*, Oxford University Press, 1975, p. 207.

23   Written in a ms notebook, now with the proofs of SS's *Memoir of an Infantry Officer*.

24   Cited in Deborah Baker, *In Extremis: The Life of Laura Riding*, Hamish Hamilton, 1993, p. 220. Stein's words were taken from one of her favourite popular songs, 'The Trail of the Lonesome Pine', based on a 1913 novel of that name by Manuel Romain.

25   LR to EAC, n.d., Berg, and LR to Hart Crane, n.d., Columbia.

26   RG did not like the sketch, which he threw away.

27   LR to EAC, n.d., Berg.

28   RG to EM, 12 November 1929, Berg.

29   RG to KB, 20 May 1930, Berg.

30   'The Terraced Valley', *CP*, p. 319.

31   Originally entitled 'Remembering War' in 1935 but published as 'Recalling War' in *CP38*. Written in 1935, *CP*, p. 358

SELECT BIBLIOGRAPHY
(Place of publication London, unless otherwise stated)

Baker, D., *In Extremis: The Life of Laura Riding*, Hamish Hamilton, 1993

Brown, M. (ed.), *The Letters of T. E. Lawrence*, Oxford University Press, 1991

Carter, D. N. G., *Robert Graves*, Macmillan, 1989

Collini, S., *Arnold: Culture and Anarchy and Other Writings*, Oxford University Press, 1988

Cooper, Rosaleen, *Games of an Edwardian Childhood*, David & Charles, 1982

cummings, e. e., *The Enormous Room*, Cape, 1928

Cunard, N., *These Were the Hours*, Southern Illinois University Press, Carbondale, 1969

Driberg, T., *Ruling Passions*, Cape, 1977

Dudley Ward, C. H., *The Regimental Record of the Royal Welch Fusiliers, vol. 3*, Forster Groom, 1928

Dunn, J. C., *The War the Infantry Knew*, P. S. King, 1938

Eliot, T. S., *The Letters of T. S. Eliot, vols 2 and 3* (eds V. Eliot & J. Haffenden), Faber and Faber, 2009 and 2012

Empson, W., *Seven Types of Ambiguity* (3rd edn), Hogarth Press, 1984

Engle, P. and Langland, J., *Poet's Choice*, Dial Press, New York, 1962

Findlay, J., *Chasing Lost Time: The Life of C. K. Scott Moncrieff*, Vintage, 2015

Fletcher, F., *After Many Days*, Robert Hale, 1937

Friedmann, E., *A Mannered Grace: The Life of Laura (Riding) Jackson*, Persea Books, New York, 2005

Fussell, P., *The Great War and Modern Memory*, Oxford University Press, 1975

Gilbert, M., *First World War*, Weidenfeld & Nicolson, 1994

Graves, A. P., *To Return to All That*, Cape, 1930

Graves, Charles, *The Bad Old Days*, Faber & Faber, 1950

Graves, Clarissa, *Seven Days and Other Poems*, Methuen, 1927

Graves, L., *A Woman Unknown*, Counterpoint, 1999

Graves, Robert, *Conversations with Robert Graves* (ed. F. Kersnowski), University Press of Mississippi, 1989

— *Poems About War* (ed. W. Graves), Moyer Bell, 1988

— *Robert Graves: War Poems* (ed. C. Mundye), Seren, Bridgend, 2016

Graves, R. P., *Robert Graves: The Assault Heroic*, Weidenfeld & Nicolson, 1986

— *Robert Graves: The Years with Laura*, Papermac, 1990

— *Robert Graves and the White Goddess (1940–1985)*, Weidenfeld & Nicolson, 1995

Graves, T., *Tuning Up At Dawn*, Harper Collins, 2004

Graves, W., *Wild Olives: Life in Majorca with Robert Graves*, Hutchinson, 1995

— *Poems About War (Robert Graves)*, Moyer Bell, 1988

Greene, R., *Edith Sitwell*, Virago, 2011

Hassall, C., *Edward Marsh, Patron of the Arts*, Longmans, Green & Co., 1959

Holden, W. H., *The Charterhouse We Knew*, British Technical & General Press, 1950

Holroyd, M., *Lytton Strachey*, Penguin, 1994

Horrocks, R., *Len Lye*, Auckland University Press, Auckland, 2001

Kirkham, M., *The Poetry of Robert Graves*, Athlone Press, 1969

Lawrence, T. E., *The Letters of T. E. Lawrence,* (ed. M. Brown), Oxford University Press, 1991

— *The Letters of T. E. Lawrence* (ed. D. Garnett), Cape, 1938

Lindsay, J., *Fanfrolico and After*, Bodley Head, 1962

Matthews, T., *Under the Influence*, Cassell, 1979

McPhaill, H. & Guest, P., *Graves and Sassoon*, Leo Cooper, 2001

Mitchison, N., *You May Well Ask: A Memoir 1920–1940*, Victor Gollancz, 1977

Murphy, R., *The Kick*, Granta, 2003

Nicholson, A., *William Nicholson Painter*, Giles de la Mare, 1996

Nicholson, V., *Among the Bohemians*, Viking, 2002

O'Connor, F., *My Father's Son*, Macmillan, 1968

O'Prey, Paul, ed., *In Broken Images: Selected Letters of Robert Graves 1914–1946*, Hutchinson, 1982

Owen, Wilfred, *Collected Letters* (eds H. Owen and J. Bell), Oxford University Press, 1967

Parker, P., *The Old Lie*, Constable, 1987

Pearson, L. B., *Mike: The Memoirs of the Rt. Hon. Lester B. Pearson, vol. 1: 1897–1948*, University of Toronto Press, 2015

Quennell, P., *The Marble Foot*, Collins, 1976

Quinn, P., *The Great War and the Missing Muse*, Susquehanna University Press, 1994

Riding, L., *Anarchism Is Not Enough*, Cape, 1928

— *Contemporaries and Snobs*, Cape, 1928

— *Four Unposted Letters to Catherine*, Hours Press, Paris, 1930

— *The Person I Am*, Nottingham Trent University, 2011

— *Poems: A Joking Word*, Cape, 1930

— *The Poems of Laura Riding*, Carcanet, Manchester, 1980

— and Ellidge, G., *14A*, Arthur Baker, 1934

Robertson, D., *George Mallory*, Faber & Faber, 1999

Roche, P., *With Duncan Grant in Southern Turkey*, Honeyglen Publishers, 1962

Rose, A., *The Prince, the Princess and the Perfect Murder*, Coronet, 2014

Sassoon, S., *Diaries 1915–1918* (ed. R. Hart Davis), Faber & Faber, 1983

— *Letters to a Critic* (ed. M. Thorpe), Kent editions, 1976

— *Memoirs of an Infantry Officer*, Faber & Faber, 1930 (1985 edition used)

— *Siegfried's Journey*, Faber & Faber, 1945

— *The Weald of Youth*, Faber & Faber, 1942

Schwarz, S., *William Nicholson*, Yale University Press, 2004

Seymour, M., *Robert Graves: Life on the Edge*, Transworld, 1995

Seymour-Smith, M., *Robert Graves: His Life and Work*, Bloomsbury, 1995

Sorley, C. H., *The Collected Letters of Charles Hamilton Sorley* (ed. J. M. Wilson), Cecil Woolf, 1990

Spalding, F., *Duncan Grant*, Chatto & Windus, 1997

Stevenson, D., *1914–1918: The History of the First World War*, Penguin, 2012
Strachey, J., *Forever England*, Biteback Publishing, 1997
Wilson, F. *Literary Seductions*, Faber & Faber, 1999
Wilson, J. M., *Siegfried Sassoon: The Making of a War Poet*, Duckworth, 1998
Woolf, V., *The Diary of Virginia Woolf, vol. 3* (ed. A. O. Bell), Penguin, 1987

ACKNOWLEDGEMENTS

My first thanks must go to the Robert Graves Estate and to William Graves, who has encouraged this project from the start. He has authorized access to unpublished and copyright material and his help and support has been invaluable in every way. His 1988 edition of the war poems and his online edition of his father's letters between 1914 and 1918 were of particular help to me. In addition, his hospitality on Majorca, together with that of his wife Elena, was unstinted.

I am also indebted to members of the Robert Graves Society for their help, in particular, to Lucia Graves Charles Mundye, Patrick Villa, Dunstan Ward, Paul O'Prey, Helen Ramage, Patrick Quinn, Michael Joseph and Carl Hahn, who resolved all my bibliographic problems the moment I put them to him. The Society's magazine, *Gravesiana*, has been very useful at many points. So, too, has the tireless research of Frances Twinn, whose findings have enriched this book.

I have, in addition, been grateful to all previous biographers for information about and insights into Graves and his work, especially to Miranda Seymour's *Robert Graves: Life on the Edge*, Martin Seymour-Smith's *Robert Graves: His Life and Work* and Richard Perceval Graves's monumental three-volume life. I am likewise indebted to Dunstan Ward and Beryl Graves's three-volume edition of Graves's *Complete Poems*, which I have consulted throughout and Paul O'Prey's *Selected Letters of Robert Graves 1914–1946* and Charles Mundye's edition of *Robert Graves: War Poems*.

Warmest thanks are due, too, to the following individuals who have helped in a variety of ways: Tim d'Arch-Smith, Lesley Arthur, Sebastian Barfield, Stephen Barkway, Veronica Cecil, Guy Cuthbertson, Jean Findlay, John Gillam, Jane Goldman, Nigel Jones, Pat Laurence, Stuart Laurence, Gus McLean, Myfanwi Meyrick, Vara Neverow, Jorge Ortega, William Reese, Michael Schmidt, Philip Stewart and David Turk.

Thanks are also due to the following institutions, librarians and archivists throughout Britain and North America: Kevin Repp at the Beinecke Library, Yale University; Isaac Gewirtz and Joshua McKeon at the Henry W. and Albert A. Berg Collection, New York Public Library; the staff of the Manuscript Collections at the British Library, London; the staff of the Brotherton Library, University of Leeds; the staff of the Library of the State University of New York at Buffalo; the archivist at Copthorne School; Catherine Smith for access to the archives at Charterhouse School; the staff of the University of Cambridge Library; Richard Watson and Pat Fox at the Harry Ransom Humanities Research Centre, University of Texas at Austin; the staff of the Imperial War Museum, London; the staff of the Lilly Library at Indiana University, Bloomington; the staff at the National Library of Scotland; the staff of Princeton University Library; Aaron Lisec at the Morris Library, Southern Illinois University, Carbondale; Stewart Tiley and Ruth Ogden at St John's College, Oxford Library; the staff at the Tate Archives, London; the staff at Tulsa University Library; and Karen Murdoch for help in viewing the archives of the Royal Welch Fusiliers at Wrexham County and Borough Museum.

My warm thanks also must go to Robin Baird-Smith and Jamie Birkett at Bloomsbury Publishing, Robin for commissioning this project in the first place and Jamie for his help and direction throughout. I am also grateful to my copy-editor, Richard Mason, for the care and attention he devoted to the text.

I could not have completed my book, however, without the support of my family, their patience and forbearance. I am especially grateful to my husband, Cecil Woolf, who has guided me at every point, and to our son, Philip Woolf, and grandson, Leonard Woolf, who transferred my manuscript so skilfully to the computer.

Jean Moorcroft Wilson, London, 2018

INDEX

Note to index: Chapter names and pages appear in bold

Note on Author

Jean Moorcroft Wilson is a celebrated biographer and leading expert on the First World War poets. Shortlisted for the Duff Cooper biography prize for her *Isaac Rosenberg*, she has also written biographies of Siegfried Sassoon, Charles Hamilton Sorley and Edward Thomas. She lectured for many years at the University of London, as well as in the United States and South Africa. She was married to the nephew of Leonard and Virginia Woolf, on whom she has also written a widely-praised biography of place.